# Thinking in Childhood and Adolescence

A volume in
*Lifespan Learning*
Paris S. Strom and Robert D. Strom, *Series Editors*

# Lifespan Learning

Paris S. Strom and Robert D. Strom, *Series Editors*

# Thinking in Childhood and Adolescence

**Paris S. Strom**
*Auburn University*

**Robert D. Strom**
*Arizona State University*

INFORMATION AGE PUBLISHING, INC.
Charlotte, NC • www.infoagepub.com

**Library of Congress Cataloging-in-Publication Data**

A CIP record for this book is available from the Library of Congress
http://www.loc.gov

ISBN:  978-1-62396-433-7 (Paperback)
       978-1-62396-434-4 (Hardcover)
       978-1-62396-435-1 (ebook)

Printed in the United States of America

# Contents

# PART II

## *Scope of Achievement*

## PART III

# *Planning and Direction*

# PART I

# Adjustment to Change

# 1

## *Thinking and Attention*

The communications revolution is providing unprecedented access to information and external stimulation. In this new enriched environment selective attention is essential so that concentration focuses on relevant information while less pertinent data is screened out. Concerns over the deterioration of selective attention relate to a rise in multitasking. Students believe they can do homework while texting friends, reading documents on the Internet, and downloading music. People of all age groups perform poorly as they try to manage simultaneous tasks, tend to overestimate how many things they are able to do well at one time, and admit to being distracted while following links and losing touch with the reference goals needed to guide their online activity. The prevalence of these problems is motivating research about ways to help students anchor their attention and sustain concentration. The goals of this chapter are to discuss evidence on multitasking, consider how screen skimming effects comprehension, describe methods to increase the attention span of students and minimize distraction, examine the merits of support for a dual emphasis on

*Thinking in Childhood and Adolescence,* pages 3–24
Copyright © 2013 by Information Age Publishing
All rights of reproduction in any form reserved.

linear and nonlinear modes of thinking, and recognize the importance of the visual domain to focus attention.

## Multitasking and Comprehension

### *Neuroscience and Public Opinion*

One of the challenges of being able to pay attention relates to the popular belief that multitasking improves productivity despite information processing experiments by neuroscientists that reach opposite conclusions. More serious is that multitasking boosts the level of stress-related hormones such as cortisol and adrenaline that can wear down adaptive systems through biological friction (Medina, 2009). The adolescents growing up now have always had access to the Internet, are habituated to split-screen presentations, texting, cell phones, and are comfortable in experiencing frequent interruptions. For them it is acceptable to move from doing one thing to another, to shift focus of attention back and forth. Nevertheless, effective thinking requires selective attention and concentration.

Concern about the documented decline of ability to give full attention to anything centers on multitasking. As early as middle school, students send their friends messages while they watch television or surf the web as well as perform schoolwork assignments. Consider David, an eighth grader at the desk in the bedroom. Within the span of a few minutes, David switches from Facebook to iTunes to texting. His parents are impressed with how he is able to balance multiple activities at the same time but they also worry that this pattern of thinking could interfere with development of other important skills. His mother explains, "I want David to be able to concentrate, to focus long enough so reflective thinking can be applied to solving problems." High tech jugglers like David are everywhere, and most are convinced that multitasking makes them more productive. Let's examine research findings to determine whether this common perception is accurate.

### *Mental Abilities and Multitasking*

Professors Ophir, Nass, and Wagner (2009) at Stanford University administered three tests to 100 adolescents to identify mental abilities in which multitaskers are more competent. *Multitasking* is defined as receiving and using multiple streams of unrelated information simultaneously. The students completed a questionnaire on linking different media. One question involved how often they were involved with more than one media category and asked the estimated amount of time. The students were put in two groups; those who do a lot of media multitasking and those who do little media multitasking.

In the first test, both groups saw two red rectangles sometimes surrounded by two, four, or six blue rectangles. The configurations were flashed twice before students were asked to tell whether two red rectangles in the second frame were in a different position than in the first frame. Directions stated that the blue rectangles should be ignored. The low multitaskers performed well but high multitaskers were continually distracted by blue rectangles so they performed poorly.

Because high multitaskers had been less able to ignore distractions, maybe they possessed better memories and would be more able to store and organize data. To find out, a second test presented sequences of alphabetical letters with the students asked to recall when any letter made a repeat appearance. Again, the low multitaskers performed well while heavy multitaskers did poorly. If the heavy multitaskers were less able to filter irrelevant information and less able to organize memories, perhaps they would excel at switching from one thing to another more quickly and efficiently. In a third test, students were shown images of letters and numbers at the same time and told what they should focus on. When directed to pay attention to the numbers, they had to determine whether digits were odd or even. When concentrating on the letters, they had to indicate if these were vowels or consonants. Again, heavy multitaskers performed poorly and light multitaskers performed well.

In review, the three abilities of filtering, working memory management, and task switching were assessed. *Filtering* involves the ability to ignore irrelevant data while focusing on relevant information. High multitaskers were captivated by distractions and irrelevant data. The more irrelevant information they saw, the more they appeared attracted to it. The second ability, *working memory management*, relates to possessing organized mental filing cabinets where data are carefully stored so that whenever information is needed we know immediately where the cabinet is to locate it. Again, the high multitaskers showed themselves much poorer at this task. The greatest surprise was the third mental ability of *task switching*, going from one task to another. It was assumed that the high multitaskers would be superior in this context but their performance was actually much slower and worse. The researchers concluded that heavy multitaskers draw on all of the information in front of them. They cannot seem to keep things separate in their mind, are unable to filter out the irrelevant, or pay attention to what matters most. By doing less, they could accomplish more (Ophir, Nass, & Wagner, 2009).

### Brain Task Switching and Memory

The brain slows down when a person has to juggle tasks. A group of 18 to 32 year olds was presented with two sets of images, colored crosses and geometric shapes like triangles. When the participants looked at colored crosses and shapes at the same time, they required a full second of reaction time to press a button. Even then, they made frequent errors. In contrast, when asked to identify images one at a time, crosses first and then shapes, the process took half as much time (Hallinan, 2010).

Switching back and forth from one task to another can produce other problems. You may forget what you were just doing or planning to do. The to-do list in the brain, called *working memory*, keeps track of the short-term things that should be remembered such as an email address that was just received. However, content of working memory vanishes fast, as quickly as two seconds. Within 15 seconds of considering some new problem, we may forget the task we were working on. In some cases the forgetting rate rises to 40%. Workplace studies have found that it takes about 15 minutes to regain concentration after experiencing some distraction. When the work habits of Microsoft employees were examined it took them, on average, 15 minutes to get back to serious mental tasks like writing computer codes or reports after having responded to incoming e-mails. The delay is usually attributed to straying away to answer email messages or to browse the Web (Mark, Voida & Cardello, 2012).

Other neuroscientists have discovered that multitasking jeopardizes the capacity for deep sustained attention while stunting ability to detect and comprehend lessons that are most relevant (Posner, 2012). Each time that attention shifts, the brain has to slow down to reorient. This means that the demands of multitasking on sustained attention reduce the ability to learn. Constant shifting of attention while online might create a greater readiness for multitasking but improving the ability to multitask actually hampers the ability to think deeply and creatively and degrades performance. Evidence suggests that the more someone multitasks, the less deliberative they become, the less able they are to reflect and to concentrate on problem solutions. In addition, recovery time is needed by the brain to consolidate memories and thoughts. If, instead, every quiet moment is taken by another phone call, text, or interruption related to electronic stimulation, the needed reprieve from external stimulation cannot occur (Jackson, 2009). Two thousand years ago, the Roman philosopher Seneca expressed an insight that seems to apply now. He said that to be everywhere is to be nowhere. The current problem, summarized by Clive Thompson (2008), is that information is no longer a scarce resource, attention is.

Parents often remind children to pay attention because this is an essential aspect of learning. However, the example adults provide is sometimes forgotten or overlooked when they multitask while interacting with children. This common mistake is illustrated by a father's observation of his 3-year-old daughter: "When she is vying for my attention and wants me to look at something she has created, finds interesting, or has questions about, I (particularly when focusing on some other matter) make confirmation statements like, 'uh huh,' 'oh, yeah,' or 'that's neat,' without turning my head to see. In these moments, her tone becomes insistent as she says, 'Daddy, look at me with your eyes.' It sounds so basic, but this is her method of getting my undivided attention in the only way that she knows to confirm it—when I look directly at her."

### *Screen Skimming and Reading*

Ziming Liu (2008) is professor of Library and Information Science at San Jose State University in California. His studies have determined that screen skimming the Internet has become the preferred mode of reading, replacing the reading of books that many people claim takes too long and requires greater patience than they can muster. Instead of skimming as a preliminary way to judge the relevance of material as people have done during the past, skimming is the method most often preferred to quickly sample data from many sources and try to make sense of the collective messages. Liu surveyed 30-to-45-year old professionals in engineering, teaching, business, industry, health sciences, and technology to assess how their reading habits had changed over the past 10 years. Over 80% reported they mostly engage in nonlinear reading of documents viewed on the Internet. About 45% acknowledged their linear in-depth type reading had declined. Only 16% reported devoting more sustained attention to reading books than in the past. According to Liu, the digital environment encourages exploration of numerous topics but often at a superficial level and hyperlinks further distract from careful reading and deep thinking. People spend more time reading today than the past but reliance on screen skimming differs significantly from concentrated reading that requires sustained focus of selective attention and reflection (Liu, 2008). We are also beginning to realize that the new world of the screen is a very different place from the world of the page.

Adolescents engage in multitasking and screen reading more than adults do. A national survey by the Kaiser Foundation found that over half of teenagers participate in some other media form while watching television. They multitask while on the computer or cell phone (Rideout, Foehr, & Roberts, 2010). Such behavior implicates preservation of creativity. Being able to concentrate, to value reflective thinking, and to pay attention for lengthy periods of time characterizes highly creative persons. The lesson for parents is to ensure that adolescents have a schedule of nonelectronic uninterrupted time for linear reading, family conversation, and opportunity for solitary reflection. This strategy can be difficult to implement but children will benefit from a merger of their favorite mode of learning with traditional methods of linear thought that are needed by every generation (Konnikova, 2012).

## Motivation for Attention and Distraction

### *Importance of Selective Attention*

William James wrote the first text in the field of psychology. In his *Principles of Psychology*, James (1890/2013) described attention as the mind taking possession of one out of several simultaneously possible objects or trains of thought. To be attentive to something calls for withdrawal from active consideration of other stimuli. James' conclusion was that being wise is knowing what to overlook. He referred to attention as the conductor that leads the orchestration of the mind. Shifting to the current setting it seems people's lives are increasingly shaped more by distraction than by attention.

The science of interruption was introduced a century ago with studies of telegraph operators. They had the first high stress, time-sensitive technology jobs. Psychologists found that, when anyone spoke to a telegraph operator who was in the process of keying a message, the number of errors significantly increased because cognition was scrambled by mentally having to switch channels. Later, it was determined that, for people in any job that requires careful data monitoring, presentation is extremely important. Given this knowledge, the airplane cockpit of fighter pilots was reconfigured so each meter and dial could be read quickly at a glance (Posner, 2012).

During the 1920s, Russian experiments revealed intriguing aspects of interruption. Bluma Zeigarnik (2007) instructed subjects to complete jigsaw puzzles and then interrupted them at various stages of their task. She discovered that persons least likely to complete a task were those who were interrupted near the beginning. Since they did not have enough time to become mentally invested in a task, they had more difficulty recovering from distraction. Subjects interrupted toward the end of assembling a puzzle more often were able to stay on track.

### *Attention and Academic Success*

Teachers of all grades have reported to parents that their child's lack of attention in class is seen as a cause for low levels of achievement. The origins of this problem may begin earlier than when children first begin to attend school. A research team from Oregon State University conducted an investigation with the National Institute of Child Health and Human Development (McClelland, Acock, Piccinin, Rhea, & Stallings, 2013). The purpose was to track 430 boys and girls from age 4 until age 25 to identify factors that would seem to have the most influence on completing a college degree. During early childhood, parents were asked to rate their daughter or son on items such as "s/he plays with a single toy for a long period of time" or "my child gives up easily if faced with difficulties." Reading and mathematics were assessed at age 7 using standardized tests and again at age 21. Contrary to expectation, the reading and mathematics scores did not significantly predict whether young children would eventually be able to finish college. Instead, those children rated one standard deviation higher on attention span-persistence by their parents at age 4 had nearly 50% greater odds of earning a bachelor's degree by age 25. Attention and persistence skills are malleable and ought to be taught.

Similar concerns about student attention were raised by a Kaiser Family Foundation national survey of 2,000 students from grades 3–12 (Rideout, Foehr & Roberts, 2010). Findings showed that these students, ages 8 to 18, spent an average of 7 hours and 38 minutes a day involved with e-media. The context that defined e-media included social networking such as Facebook and Twitter, video games, video websites like YouTube, music from iTunes, and television viewing. Texting was not counted as part of e-media but is an additional way students in grades 7–12 spend much time, an average of 1 hour and 37 minutes a day sending and receiving messages. Other disturbing results of the survey were that Black and Hispanic youth spend almost four more hours a day engaged with media than White children do. Time spent reading books was 25 minutes a day. Only 30% said their parents have rules about how much time they are allowed to engage e-media. Drew Altman, President of the Kaiser Foundation, observed that the amount of time young people spend with media has grown to where it is more than a full-time work week. When children spend this much time doing anything, we need to understand how it is affecting them.

Mark Bauerlein, professor of English at Emory University, has initiated a debate about attention and achievement of college students. In his book *The Dumbest Generation,* Bauerlein (2010) contends that, although adolescents have unprecedented access to a world of knowledge at their fingertips, many of them remain less informed and less literate than previous generations. Technology and its digital culture do not appear to be broadening the horizons of youth but narrowing them to a self-absorbed social universe that frequently blocks out almost everything else. The immediacy and intimacy appeal of social networking means that adolescents rely less on the Internet for learning than for communication with friends through texting, instant messaging, e-mail, ichat, and blogs. The language used in Internet communication with its peculiar spelling, grammar, and disregard for punctuation encourages illiteracy by endorsing writing errors as a socially acceptable practice.

Young people say they want to strike a better balance between work and leisure for themselves than was achieved by their parents. However, it seems that many of them fail to recognize that spending excessive time communicating with friends undermines productivity in schoolwork. Researchers from Louisiana Technical University explored how 654 college students use their cell phones (Buboltz, 2012). On average, 5 hours a day was devoted to interaction on the phone. Of the total 5 hours, over 3 hours was taken up talking on the phone. Students sent and received 12 voice calls a day for an average duration of 25 minutes a call. They sent 100 text messages and received 120 each day averaging 30 seconds each. In effect, one hour a day was spent sending and receiving about 220 text messages. Another 30 minutes involved watching videos with YouTube as the most popular site. Finally, males spent 30 minutes playing video games while girls played 5 to 10 minutes. Local, national, and world news were generally ignored by most of the students.

Bauerlein (2010) contends that many adults, expected to help shape the character and perspective of children, have abdicated their responsibility. Some parents find that it is easier to cave, to let adolescents retreat to their bedroom for hours surrounded by the cell phone, computer, audio equipment, and preoccupation with peer communication. A related downside is widespread failure of parents to engage their children in conversation on serious topics that should be examined to motivate the growth of every generation. Society should challenge the growing dependence of youth on technology for purposes of peer communication in favor of more time spent in family interaction and learning.

### *Family Communication Concerns*

Concerns about family communication with adolescents are illustrated by results from annual surveys carried out by the Annenberg Center for the Digital Future at the University of Southern California. Parents report a worrisome trend that is reflected by a drop of one-third in family face-to-face communication time (from 26 to 18 hours per week) in Internet households since 2007. A growing proportion of parents also report that Internet access at home is reducing the in-person time their children are with friends (Center for Digital Future, 2013).

Because of the explosion of sophisticated cell phone technology and social network websites like Facebook and Twitter, many people have concluded human relationships are blossoming as never before. Sherry Turkle at the Massachusetts Institute of Technology challenges this assumption in *Alone Together: Why We Expect More From Technology and Less From Each Other* (2011). She suggests that people appear determined to attribute human qualities to objects while being content to treat one another as things. Based on surveys of adolescent text messages, Turkle presents a sobering portrait of human disconnectedness in the face of expanding virtual connections in cell-phone, intelligent machine, and Internet use. She describes the anxiety of some adolescents when they do not receive an immediate reply to a text message. One girl pointed out that she needed to have her cell phone for "emergencies"; it turns out that what she meant by an "emergency" was having a feeling without being able to share it. Turkle offers the following observations: the identities of many teenagers are being shaped not by self-exploration but by how they are perceived by their online collective; mothers feel texting makes communicating with their children more frequent but less substantive; Facebook users who focus on shallow status updates devalue the true intimacies of friendships. Turkle makes a strong case that what was meant to be a mechanism to facilitate communication has pushed people closer to their machines and further away from each other in countless and disappointing ways.

This conclusion is corroborated by outcomes of a Pew Research Center (2010) survey of adolescents, describing them as history's first always-connected generation. More than 8 in 10 teenagers told researchers they sleep with their mobile phone next to their bed. Three quarters have created their profile on a social networking site and are more likely than adults to believe technology makes life easier and brings family and friends closer together. In contrast, business leaders warn that working in a collaborative setting requires being able to connect with others in the well tried and tested art of face-to-face communication (Tapscott & Williams, 2010b).

## Sleep Deprivation and Attention

In 1997 the Edina and Minneapolis, Minnesota boards of education changed the start time for students attending secondary schools from 7:30 am to 8:40 am. This decision was based on medical research indicating that teenagers differ from young children and adults in their sleeping and waking cycle. No matter where they live in the world adolescents have a natural pattern that causes a late-to-bed and late-to-rise cycle. From the onset of puberty, usually around age 13 until age 19, the brain chemical *melatonin* which is responsible for sleepiness is secreted from about 11 p.m. until 8 a.m. Typically, teenagers find it difficult to fall asleep before 11 p.m. and their brains stay in the sleep mode until 8 a.m. in the morning regardless of the time they went to bed. This means that when students have to get up early for school many are sleepy during the first two hours of their class and often seem unable able to pay attention.

Kyla Wahlstrom (2013) is director of the Center for Applied Research and Educational Improvement at the University of Minnesota. She and her colleagues have studied the work, sleep, and school habits of 7,000 students. Educators in Minneapolis and Edina reported that this is a different bunch of kids now with their later school start. They are awake and learning. School principals observed fewer disruptions during passing times in the hallways and the lunchroom. Counselors observed a decline in peer relationship problems. Most (92%) parents said they preferred the late start time because it had become easier to get along with their child who previously had to be reminded again and again to get up in the morning. Students said they had less difficulty learning, thinking, making decisions, using good judgment, and solving problems. Five years after Minneapolis changed the start time there was a statistically significant increase in the graduation rate. More students ate breakfast regularly, caught their bus on time, arrived when the first period began and had a better record of attendance. The students were seen by teachers as more alert, visited the school nurse fewer times, and presented less behavior problems.

Even a short delay in start time appears to be associated with improvement of adolescent alertness, mood, and mental health. Judith Owens and colleagues at Hasbro Children's Hospital in Providence Rhode Island studied 200 teenagers attending an independent high school. For purposes of the investigation, the start time for school was delayed 30 minutes, moving from the customary 8 a.m. until 8:30 a.m. instead. All students completed a retrospective sleep habits survey before and after the change in start time. Following the schedule shift, the mean amount of sleep duration on school nights increased by 45 minutes. The percentage of students who got less than 7 hours sleep decreased by 79%, and those reporting at least 8 hours of sleep increased from 16% to 55%. Students reported significantly greater satisfaction with their sleep and improved motivation. Daytime sleepiness, fatigue, and depressed mood were reduced (Owens, Belon, & Moss, 2010). Several hundred school districts have revised policies for school start time to allow adolescents the sleep they need to perform well (Wahlstrom, 2013).

### Maximize Student Attention

Students are exposed to many distractions that undermine concentration and reduce attention for thinking. Teachers, parents, administrators, and students should find more effective ways to minimize factors that interfere with learning and instruction. The suggestions provided in Table 1.1 could be posted on campus billboards and the school website for everyone to read and make an effort to assume their share of accountability.

## Need for Dual Modes of Thinking

### Influence of Media on Thinking

Marshall McLuhan at the University of Toronto was an instant celebrity with his publication in 1967 of *The Medium is the Massage*. He predicted the electric media, which at that time included phones, radio, television, and movies, would replace text as the main influence on human thoughts and senses. The premise was that content of media matters less than the medium itself in having an impact on the way that people think and act. McLuhan observed that it is common to assure ourselves that technology is just a tool and the way we use tools is what really matters. The comforting implication of this view is that people are in control (McLuhan & Fiore, 1967).

On the contrary, McLuhan suggested that every new medium has altered thinking processes for mankind. Adults do not think in the same way they did prior to the Internet. One strongly felt difference involves reading. A generation ago people found it appealing to become immersed in reading books so libraries were usually quiet places. That ability has become uncommon. Instead, most people admit their concentration starts to drift after they read only a page or two, feelings of uneasiness take over, there is an inclination to look for something else to do while also feeling we have to drag our attention back to the reading. The deep reading that once came naturally to people has become a struggle (McLuhan & Fiore, 1967).

### Mental and Cultural Consequences

McLuhan seems to have been correct in suggesting that influences of the media go beyond just providing additional sources of information. They do supply the essence of thought but also impact processes used for thinking (McLuhan & Fiore, 1967). Nicholas Carr (2010) has documented the mental and cultural consequences of how electronic media, cell phones, texting, and television change the way people think while diminishing the capacity for concentration and contemplation. For example, the more people use the web, the greater the difficulty they report in staying focused

---

**TABLE 1.1   Ways for Educators to Maximize Student Attention**

| Teacher Actions | Rationale for Implementation |
|---|---|
| Encourage Goal Setting | This strategy respects motivation of students and makes teachers initially aware about the goals individuals want to accomplish. Such knowledge can provide feedback on progress and achievement. |
| Invite Collaboration | The way a student feels about instruction can influence amount of attention to learning. Inviting teams to help determine individual and group assignments recognizes them as capable partners. |
| Pause After Questions | Calling on the first students to raise hands can cause other students to prematurely end their information retrieval process. Retrieval should include reflection and relating instruction to situations. |
| Differentiate Instruction | Direct instruction is common but when used exclusively produces the least retention. Differentiated instruction gives priority to individualized assignments and collaboration for group and personal accountability. |
| Provide an Agenda Guide | Teachers can provide outline notes so a planned sequence of issues is known, interaction triggers improvisation, and a synthesis of lesson content is provided without extending time for direct instruction. |
| Schedule Reflection | Educators can maximize student concentration by scheduling time in class for solitary deliberation on topics and tasks. Thereafter, team members can benefit from sharing implications of independent and collective thought. |
| Avoid Disruptive Announcements | Principals can reduce distraction from instruction by restricting school-wide intercom announcements to a specific time each day. The office should contact students and faculty without interrupting everyone else. |
| Respect Attention Span | Schedule 10–20 minute periods for direct instruction, alternate intervals that focus on teamwork, discussion, deliberation, group reporting, and interaction about questions, planning, interpretation, and application. |
| Assess Prior Knowledge | Teachers are more helpful when student skills are recognized. Everyone does not have the same knowledge base. Consulting portfolios is helpful if they can be accessed from other courses. |
| Take Renewal Breaks | Maintain a schedule with periodic 10–15 minute breaks. This practice allows students to step back from class demands, stretch, walk around, go to the restroom, snack, and have conversations. |

---

*Source: Learning Throughout Life: An Intergenerational Perspective,* by Robert Strom and Paris Strom, 2012, p. 131. Information Age Publishing Inc., Charlotte, NC.

when confronted by complex narrative text. Even adults who, at an earlier age, read and enjoyed lengthy pieces of literature admit that they can no longer do so. Coping with social network postings that extend beyond a few paragraphs can seem almost too much to absorb. Instead, the dominant preference is to rapidly skim and scroll.

For some people reading an entire book is considered a waste of time, a quaint way to gain information that could be quickly found by Google or another search engine. Tapscott (2009) described a year-long series of discussions about the Internet with 300 users from 4 to 20 years of age. Their digital immersion was found to have influenced how the group absorbed information. They did not necessarily read a page from left to right or top to bottom. The preference was rapid skimming to find pertinent data. They blogged, tagged, texted, and twittered but were not interested in reading books.

High school students who jump from link to link, are easily distracted, feel that being interrupted is ok, and participate in multitasking have difficulty when faced with the reading tasks required in most college courses. Based on placement test scores, 42% of students entering community colleges, and 30% of freshmen attending universities are involuntarily assigned to remedial reading classes they take without credit. According to American College Testing (2006), the primary cause of remediation for these students is their "inability to grasp complex texts." Unwillingness to participate in slow reading is implicated. The most powerful predictor that a college student will drop out is the need for remedial reading. A majority (58%) of students not assigned to remedial instruction earn a bachelors degree within 8 years but only 17% of remedial readers get a degree in the same amount of time (Vandal, 2010).

### Choices About Modes of Thinking

We seem to have arrived, as McLuhan forecasted, at an unprecedented stage in intellectual and cultural history, a time of transition between two very different modes of thinking. What we could be trading in return for the wealth of what is provided by the Internet is our competence with linear thought processes. Calm, focused, undistracted, the linear mind is gradually being set aside by the new mindset that prefers to take in and express information in short, disjointed bursts, the faster the better. Since the printing press made the reading of books possible 500 years ago, the linear mind has been at the forefront of art, science, and society. Gradually the linear mind is being shoved aside. Computers exert a subtle influence that impacts how we work and think. At some point many people discover it is no longer possible to edit on paper because they can only do it online. They feel lost without a scroll bar, cut and paste functions, a delete key. Some are mindful of their vanishing ability to pay attention to any one thing for more than a couple minutes.

To read a book silently requires the ability to concentrate for a lengthy period, to "lose oneself " in the pages. Developing such mental discipline takes time and can be difficult. The natural state of the brain reflects distraction. The predisposition is to shift attention from one object to another, to be aware of as much of what is going on around us as possible. Neuroscientists have located primitive mechanisms in the brain that respond rapidly to sensory input and shift attention involuntarily to visual features of potential importance. What draws our attention most is any changes in surroundings. When something alters, we take notice because it could present danger or opportunity. This fast reflexive shift in focus was once needed for survival to reduce the prospects that a predator would surprise people or overlook a food source. The usual path for most of human thought was anything but linear (Carr, 2010).

## Attention and the Visual Domain

Howard Gardner (2011), professor of education at Harvard University, proposed a theory of multiple intelligences that consists of eight separate types of ability. One of the domains is visual intelligence, reflecting visual-spatial abilities that allow people to create views of the world and think in pictures. Schools ignored this ability except for a small minority of students identified as gifted or talented in the visual arts. However, we live in an increasingly image-driven environment with media effects involving communication, awareness, and decisions as mediated by visuals provided by computers, digital cameras, cell phones, and television. The observation that "a picture is worth a thousand words" is generally accepted. Instruction that includes digital images is retained to a far greater degree than those acquired only by reading or listening (Williams & Newton, 2006).

Much of what students learn outside school attributes to visual images presented on the Internet, video gaming devices, and television. George Lucas, creator of *Star Wars* and other classic films, recommends that communication in all its forms be taught instead of written and spoken words only. Lucas (2005) maintains, "Everyone should understand the importance of graphics, music, and cinema that can be just as powerful and, in some ways, appears more deeply linked with the culture of young people. When people talk to me about the digital divide, I think of it not so much about who has access to technology as who knows how to create and express themselves in the new language of the screen. If students are not taught the language of sounds and images, shouldn't they be considered as illiterate as if they had quit college without becoming able to read or write?"

## *Memory for Visual Information*

Many educators do not know that there is an image memory for visual materials. Research has shown that memory for pictures is much greater than memory for words. Roger Shepard (1967, 1990), Stanford University Professor Emeritus, presented 600 pictures to students who were immediately tested and correctly identified 98% of the pictures. A week later, they still accurately identified 85% of pictures. Comparison of text and oral presentations versus pictorial presentations have found that visuals are always more effective. When information is presented orally, people recall roughly 10% when tested three days after exposure. The recall rate rises to 65% if a picture or visual element is added. So great is the advantage of visual memory that it is designated as the *pictorial superiority effect* (Brockmole, 2008).

The distinction did not matter much prior to the Internet introducing a wide range of visual resources. Because of the vast selection of visuals from Discovery Education (2013), YouTube, and other websites, educators can easily incorporate this element to optimize student thinking and learning. The *dual coding theory of information processing* explores superiority of pictures for memory tasks. This theory proposes that human long-term memory contains two distinct interdependent codes, one verbal and another visual based (Paivio, 1990). One assumption is that the two codes produce additive effects so, if data is coded visually as well as verbally, the probability of retrieval is doubled. Another assumption is that the manner in which pictures and words activate the two codes differ. Pictures are more likely to be stored visually and verbally. For example, someone might recall the title of a book and be able to remember the color or image of the cover. Words alone are less likely to be stored visually. When it comes to memory, two codes appear to be better than one.

Teachers can increase the probability of information being dual encoded for long-term memory with consequent improvement of retention, data retrieval, and transfer. Dual coding is more likely when lessons include imagery, graphics, pictorial information, or spatial mapping (Orey, McClendon, & Branch, 2006). Graphic organizers like webbing, concept mapping matrix, flow charts, and Venn diagrams help to illustrate, describe, compare, classify, and sequence concepts. Students also benefit from being referred to observation of streaming videos. A teacher's website could include advance organizers outlining daily lessons in words or notes and use visual symbols and charts that draw connections between concepts.

## An Image-Driven Environment

Education reforms to enhance visual learning can keep the benefits of customary forms of learning while also becoming capable of including ever-increasing exposure to visual lessons from media. Many students are more visually than verbally literate. Boards of education are expanding the definition of basic skills to include media literacy and make it a high school graduation requirement. *Media literacy* is defined as the ability to communicate competently in all media forms, print and electronic, as well as to access, understand, analyze, and evaluate images, words, and sounds that comprise mass media culture. Media literacy could empower people to become critical thinkers and creative producers capable of using image, language, and sound (Smith, Moriarty, Barbatsis, & Kenney, 2005).

The Center for Media Literacy in Los Angeles maintains that the convergence of media and technology for a global environment is changing how people learn about the world and challenging the foundations of education. Being able to read the printed word is no longer a sufficient source of information. Everyone should also acquire the abilities needed to critically interpret images in a multimedia culture and express themselves as well in multiple media forms. An inquiry-based theory of learning about media is proposed to merge creative communication (construction/production) skills with analytical (deconstruction) skills (Jolls, 2010).

## Visual and Verbal Intelligence

How are visual intelligence and verbal intelligence different? Mankind relied on pictures long before written words were used as communication. Verbal intelligence can be expressive (active) or receptive (passive). However, visual intelligence does not have a passive mode for thinking or learning. It seems that visual intelligence has a more prominent function than verbal ability in terms of the process of invention, originality, and discovery. That is, words come later than images in the creative process and may sometimes be inadequate for communication. Once people have language, they categorize and try to give a name to everything. This means we ignore everything that does not fit into our categorization, being in effect blind and deaf to many stimuli coming from reality. As a result, we lose some capacity to remember some vivid eidetic images because we recall only verbal categorizations (Sacks, 2011).

Every language has many words people rely on to describe their ideas, feelings, and events. Relatively speaking however, there are fewer corresponding visual prompts that are easily understood. The image of a flashing light bulb is often used to illustrate the insight experience of creative thinking, the moment of sudden revelation when a solution for a problem becomes known. It is noteworthy that thinkers who have influenced history in science, art, mathematics, and other fields commonly identify visual thinking or visual images as central to their discoveries. The language of insight is sometimes reported as visual—"I see it now." The English word *idea* derives from the Greek word *idein*, which means "to see." There are many words linking vision with thinking like insight, foresight, hindsight, and oversight (Williams & Newton, 2006).

The famous mathematician Roger Penrose observed visual thinking dominates the thinking processes of gifted mathematicians. He explains his own mathematical thought is done visually using nonverbal concepts, although thoughts are often accompanied by inane and near useless verbal commentary such as "that thing goes with this one and this thing relates to that" (Penrose, 2002). His view is corroborated by recollections of other well-known scientists. For example, Albert Einstein maintained that written or spoken words did not play an important role in his thinking processes. Instead, physical entities serving as elements of thought were seen as signs in more or less clear visual images. Einstein was able to voluntarily reproduce and combine them. He acknowledged that conventional words or other forms of expression had to be reached through struggle only in the second stage of creative thinking, after the connection of ideas was sufficiently established and could be reproduced at will (Ghiselin, 1985).

In a similar way, Frances Galton (1874) explained,

> It is a serious drawback to me in writing, and still more in explaining myself, that I do not think as easily in words as otherwise. It often happens that after being hard at work and having arrived at results that seem perfectly clear and satisfactory, when I try to express them in language I feel that I must begin by putting myself on quite another intellectual plane. I have to translate my thoughts into a language that does not run evenly with them. (p. 14)

All of us can engage our mind in imagining visually but we lack the capacity to control imagination. In verbal language we are in complete control but imagination can overwhelm us and we are left without a guide to transfer to verbal expression.

Visual intelligence and media literacy training should become more prominent in the classroom as educators recognize limitations of analogies that inappropriately equate the brain with computers. Such comparisons are based on the capacity of computers for information processing speed and access to data storage. However, what is now known about the brain places it far ahead of computers in higher-order thinking. Specifically, it is in the context of visual functioning, as contrasted to verbal functioning, that the brain is elevated to a higher status (Posner, 2012). This distinction was first recognized more than a generation ago by McKim (1980) who argued that computers are unable to see, dream, or create. Computers are language-bound. Thinkers who cannot escape the structure of language rely upon only that small portion of their brain that resembles a computer.

### Digital Images and Curriculum

The interdependence of verbal language and visual images is evident from movie experience. In Director Stanley Kubrick's (1968) film *2001: A Space Odyssey*, verbal explanations about what was happening were omitted in favor of having the viewers depend on visual thinking. By all accounts this strategy had the desired effect on audiences across the globe. In a similar way, when students are perplexed by some mathematical process introduced in algebra, there is benefit in being able to find illustrations of the progressive steps for calculating solutions by watching a presentation repeatedly. Multiple resources are available online, such as Kahn Academy (2013) available at http://www.khanacademy.org/about. Students of all ability levels become more able to comprehend than when the teacher provides a one-time demonstration for a class. The prospect of more students performing well implicates greater reliance on visuals they observe on their own time outside of school.

Merging digital images and direct instruction is increasing in schools. Discovery Education (2013), the nation's largest digital video-on-demand service for schools, offers an illustration of how greater exposure to images can support instruction. More than half of American schools utilize this service. The appeal for teachers is to choose from a library of 50,000 video content clips as brief as 2 minutes, 5,000 full-length titles, 20,000 photographs, and a gallery of 1,500 art images. Discovery videos are categorized by grade level and keyed to state department standards for subjects such as mathematics, biology, and American history. The digital materials selected are stored on the local server by subscribing schools. Teachers can upload videos to fit a PowerPoint or similar format in the classroom. New videos are continuously added to local servers for their consideration. Closed caption titles are for visual impaired learners, the hearing impaired, and students acquiring English as a second language.

There is a need for research to explore the relationship between usage of digital video and attention span of students. Think about your own experiences with movies, video games, and Internet searching. People watching movies seldom stop before a film ends and less often claim it was hard to pay attention. Why is this so for films running two or more hours in length? One speculation is that films enable spectators to remain involved because they see pictures and hear a soundtrack simultaneously. In contrast, without a stream of images or sound track, lectures yield student claims of distraction, loss of attention, and boredom. Maintaining student attention is a growing concern of teachers at all levels.

Educators lack suitable measures of attention span but estimate by observing how long students appear able to concentrate on verbal presentations. The usual conclusion is students have short attention spans for this aspect of work. Therefore, teachers have been advised to cut back on the time scheduled for direct instruction. Some observers attribute attention deficits to watching television that supposedly creates a dependency to merge pictures and sound. Multimedia presentations can combine video clips and PowerPoint, exemplifying concepts through photos, diagrams, props, or artifacts, and Internet sites. In addition to increased visual imagery, it can help to break up lectures with group activities, each lasting at least 10 minutes. This interaction minimizes monotony and encourages the students to actively process and reflect on material just covered. Students are attentive in stimulating environments while short attention spans are predictable in a nonstimulating environment. A promising explanation for teachers is to accept the challenge of providing support for visual intelligence in school and augment presentations with digital video and student engagement (Gardner, 2011).

## Media Experience Interpretation

When television was introduced in the 1950s, people thought of it as an extension of human senses, enabling viewers to travel to far away places and see events vicariously. The assumption was that spectators would be able to make rational decisions about the credibility of content that they saw on the small screen. After all, television was like photography, providing a window on reality while also disseminating information. Technology has since made changes that complicate the processing of visual learning. The common experience is that images stream past viewers so fast that viewers are unable to use reflective thinking as a basis for responding to the media-created reality. Even local news stories move quickly to emotionally involve viewers while bypassing their critical thinking. When the video satellite systems present pictures from other countries in real time, accompanied by a brief explanation, spectators must base their reactions primarily on the selected images and verbal excerpts provided them.

This prospect of observing events without training related to critical interpretation and reflection caused Marshall McLuhan to speculate that the media becomes the message in a technological environment. McLuhan explained everyone experiences more than they will ever understand but it is experience more than understanding that has the greater impact on behavior (McLuhan & Fiore, 1967). This is especially the case in relation to media where people can be unaware of the effect it has on reflective thinking.

A notable model that established a media-created reality emerged in the 1990s with ER, a television program originating in the emergency room of a hospital. Michael Crichton, designer of the show, reported that his formula for success was to speed up the pace with each episode having multiple stories and many speaking parts. This innovative format appealed to millions of viewers who found the rapid action more exciting than customary experience with in-depth treatment. This format is distinguished by a "long-take" in which the vantage points of viewers are moved incessantly, scene changes occur quickly without interruption, and visual continuity is retained by using a single camera outlook that drives through the corridors and rooms in a roller-coaster fashion. Some characters lend credibility to the action by using medical terms. Impressive sound bites substitute for dialogue. Indeed, the hurried chain of events moves along so rapidly that it is difficult for the characters to convey complex information.

Many other programs later adopted the same format. Nonstop action that imitates truth without giving any time to cognitively examine and reflect on what is happening disadvantages spectators because they are denied the active role that is necessary to weigh, balance, and make decisions about what has been seen. Continual exposure to programs in which there is no time or any recognized need to participate in reflective thinking discourages young viewers from acquiring listening habits and responding skills that are fundamental for solving problems and collaboration. If reflective activities are missing in class, students often announce their conclusion that school is a boring place.

Critical thinking is the habit of mind that resists being deceived by appearances. Everyone should be aware of the emotional power of visual images and the potential they have to exert subconscious influence, how programs as well as advertisements mimic logic while bypassing involvement with critical thought, consequences of abandoning reflection as a basis for making decisions, and implications of individual inattentiveness. Each of these concerns related to visual intelligence warrant consideration owing to a direct influence on media information processing, learning, and behavior.

## Summary and Implications

Paying attention to one thing at a time is rapidly being replaced by multitasking, a pattern of thinking people suppose helps them to get more things done in less time while improving productivity. On the contrary, experiments in neuroscience have determined that multitasking undermines learning. The education deficits related to divided attention include a decline in student ability to concentrate for a long enough time to participate in deep thinking and problem solving. The prospect of fragmented and divided attention is accelerated by extensive use of technology. Visual and verbal elements of presentations in classes should creatively merge to sustain attention and contribute to comprehension.

The most common reading preference is to skim and scroll quickly and express impatience when confronted with lengthy materials. Multitasking reflects a hold over of the traditional emphasis on independence, doing things alone without help from others. Instead, multitasking should be seen in relation to interdependence and the allocation of team resources. Unless multitasking is viewed as being a group activity rather than as an individual activity, the prospects for reciprocal learning and collective productivity are diminished. Unlike the customary practice of having all students do the same homework, individuals should select or be assigned related but different exercises to be followed by reporting what they have learned to teammates in class. Some anticipated benefits include increased motivation for self-direction, unique contributions from each teammate, greater group knowledge, less pressure to overload, and more individual accountability.

The Internet is shaping the future of education. Schools should provide students a dual emphasis on linear learning and nonsequential learning instead of placing priority on a single mode for thinking. Surfing the Internet to locate data, exploring links to learn more, and interacting online can offer benefits and has widespread appeal. In addition, all students need another set of mental assets including an ability to pay full attention to one task at a time, avoid distractions by screening them out to maximize learning, concentrate for a prolonged period of time, and think deeply as the basis for solving problems and making decisions. Encouraging both modes of thinking provides an effective design to enhance intelligence, foster mental health, and improve productivity.

The nurture of slow and deliberate reading of complex texts is bound to bring opposition from students that are habituated to skim reading and reaching conclusions in a hasty manner. Youth prefer nonsequential learning, consider linear thinking to be out-of-date, and attempt to persuade adults to give it up. This means that most students tend to dislike tasks requiring this additional realm of competence. Being assigned a lengthy document to read or listening to a lecture results in complaints of boredom by students with short attention spans. Teachers and parents should resist an inclination to relent in favor of a united effort to ensure the comprehensive cognitive perspective students will need.

# 2

# *Thinking and Internet*

**M**any people believe that being a parent in the current environment presents more challenges and opportunities than in previous generations. Growing up is also recognized as more complex because of the communications technology revolution that requires new tools for learning (Hodges & Clark, 2013). Introducing the 20 million preschoolers between ages 3 and 5 to the Internet and expected behavior in this realm is an important, unprecedented, and confusing task. Children can benefit from adult monitored Internet visits that are fun and help to begin the journey toward becoming self-directed learners. Parents are more able to support this goal when they know how to go beyond traditional school readiness activities. The emerging parent obligation is to demonstrate attitudes and skills children observe, practice, and adopt as their foundation for online learning and healthy social networking. Mothers and fathers lack guidance to help them fulfill this emerging aspect of their teaching role. The goals for this chapter are to describe creative considerations for introducing children to the Internet along with guidelines for teaching, supervision, and evaluation of learning; discuss an Internet paradigm for elementary and

*Thinking in Childhood and Adolescence,* pages 25–47
Copyright © 2013 by Information Age Publishing
All rights of reproduction in any form reserved.

secondary schools; explore social networking during adolescence; and provide guidelines for safety online.

## Parent Responsibility

### *The New Playground*

Parents bring young children to public playgrounds with the expectation that visits will present opportunities for socialization and pretending with others of their age. Children also look forward to the experience and usually express reluctance to leave the playground when they are told that it is time for them to go home. The responsibilities of adults in this environment are understood. They are supposed to act as observers that monitor all aspects of the scene to make sure that conditions are safe, there is no abuse, and every child can have fun. The appeal of playgrounds makes them popular around the world.

There is another playground, a place where children and parents interact, have fun, and learn together. In this more complex environment, parents express uncertainty about what they should expect of themselves and their children. The overall purpose is to show children how to behave online, provide corrective feedback, acknowledge learning, and maintain continuous supervision to ensure safety. Families need to know that, from now on, support for child development should include plenty of guided practice using digital tools (Clark, 2012).

The Kaiser Family Foundation conducted the first national survey to estimate the extent of media presence in the lives of infants, toddlers, and young children (Rideout & Hamel, 2006). Sources of information included 1,000 parents of children aged 6 months to 6 years old. Results showed many young children are on the computer daily. They are by themselves when they turn the machine on and are allowed to choose their own activity. These children are much too young to join social networks such as MySpace, Facebook, YouTube, Hi5, Xanga, Live Journal, or Bebo. However, large-scale providers like Club Penguin, Webkins, and Togetherville compete for this growing consumer market (Bakan, 2011).

### *Readiness Redefined*

Most families have Internet access and are eager to arrange activities that build readiness for school. Parents also wonder about the kinds of lessons that they should try to teach online. Fortunately, activity on the Internet motivates a lot of conversation. The combination of visual and audio stimulation motivates children to share their feelings, describe ideas, interpret events, express curiosity, generate guesses, detect difficulties, recognize and correct mistakes, enjoy success, and gain confidence.

There are corresponding opportunities for parents to share their own impressions, arrange discovery, demonstrate curiosity, answer questions, urge persistence, recognize achievement, correct assumptions, convey attitudes to guide conduct, support empathy, and make a unique contribution to child development of social skills. Close relationships are more possible when there is daily access to one another and mutual self-disclosure. These conditions can prevent the Internet from becoming an age-segregated forum. Concerns about family communication with older children are increasing. A decade of annual surveys of 2,000 households across the United States carried out by the Center for the Digital Future (2012) at the University of Southern California Annenberg School show that student communication with friends is increasing while communication with family members is declining. Parents report a one-third drop in face-to-face communication time with adolescents in the past several years, from spending 26 hours a week together to 18 hours a week.

Preschoolers are taught the alphabet and recitation of numbers as their preparation for kindergarten. They lack the skills needed for reading and therefore must rely on observation for much of what they learn. Between ages 3 and 6 children are in a developmental stage known as *identification*. Boys and girls in this stage are inclined to imitate attitudes and actions of adult caregivers. This factor highlights a need for parents to perform well with the unfamiliar task of providing cyber instruction (Singer & Singer, 2007).

### Concerns of Parents

Parents express concerns about what should be done to maximize the benefits of being on the Internet with their children. Some frequently asked questions are described.

1. *What should the focus of our attention be while visiting the Internet?* Many adults think of the Internet as a giant library that contains infinite knowledge. Having easy access to information is certainly a great leap forward from how people used to learn in the past. However, rather than just exposing children to as much information as possible, a more helpful approach is to emphasize cognitive processes that support creative and critical thinking. This lesser emphasis on content as a main focus seems strange in the beginning because it contradicts the customary expectation that teaching is communicating lessons that learners need to memorize. Greater benefit derives from respecting

motivation for discovery by modeling computer search skills that help children learn to find out what they want to know. Lessons that feature cognitive processes are needed because they demonstrate how to frame questions, persist with locating difficult to find data, and think critically about the truthfulness of content that is presented on the Web. The challenge is to model creative thinking by generating questions, checking hunches, exploring possibilities, judging credibility, and applying insights to solve problems.

2. *How can parents support the motivation children need for learning online?* Parents should realize some of their attitudes interfere with teaching in the new context and should be left behind. First, it is necessary to abandon a concept that was dominant when we were growing up about the relationship between pleasure and learning. Many adults still erroneously believe that, when an activity is enjoyable, it does not qualify as learning. On the contrary, educators of children should recognize that, besides providing quick retrieval of data, technology tools have enormous appeal, stimulate participation, encourage dialogue, increase attention span, and help sustain a willingness to keep trying when faced with difficulties. A common reason dropouts give for quitting school is that their education did not provide any pleasure. Educators of all age groups are recognizing that continued pursuit of learning is closely related to satisfaction. And, it is clear that children must continue to learn throughout life.

3. *How can parents contribute to the joy of learning experienced by their child?* Educators often express concern about lack of parent involvement and wish that more of them would assume responsibility for teaching. However, urging parents to help children learn is a vague recommendation that presumes all adults are equally comfortable when participating in reading, Internet searching, playing games, and having family discussion. The reality is that some parents, particularly those from low-income households, often feel uncomfortable in the culture of learning. The reason is that their years in school were mostly disappointing and led them to withdraw before finishing or receiving needed career preparation. These parents need to experience the pleasure of learning themselves before they can effectively convey a sense of enthusiasm to children. Carefully chosen Website visits can offer this experience and enable parents to share the joy of learning with their children.

4.  *What conditions should parents establish in orienting their children to the Internet?* The optimal way to acquire and apply knowledge is by having opportunities to immediately practice what has just been learned, followed by corrective guidance. Situated-learning at home often contrasts with the way knowledge is acquired at school where teachers work with many students and usually accept memorization statements as sufficient evidence of comprehension. A more practical assessment is to require that comprehension be shown in a context where the learning should be applied. Situated-learning for young children whose observation is the basis of forming concepts allows parents to model the most powerful method of instruction. The purpose of early childhood education is to help children learn how to learn. In the future, this goal will require involvement with tools of technology and careful supervision, the one-to-one encounter that can best be scheduled by parents. Staff members of day care centers and preschools are responsible for many children so they are unable to provide the individualized Internet supervision children need. Parents should take the leadership role in orienting children to Internet learning.

5.  *What difficulties can parents anticipate in teaching their children on the Internet?* Time management is a concern. The time children spend online should not be taken from the amount of time they need for physical exercise and pretend play. Each of these activities is important and should be carefully scheduled. Children cannot decide the schedule that is best to meet their needs. A related issue involves a lack of confidence in computer skills by the parent. This uneasiness can cause reluctance to spend time on the Internet with their child. Because preschoolers imitate behavior of caregivers, there is benefit if parents express their desire to become more capable of exploring the wonders of the Internet. Mothers and fathers who have an interest and enthusiasm for Internet learning can favorably shape child perspective.

## Parent Effectiveness

### Child Learning Assessment

Parents of young children do not get much external feedback on their teaching. Careful observation can make known the lessons a child has learned, detect deficits still to be addressed, and provide feedback about effectiveness of instruction. When parents have evidence that their efforts are yielding child progress, motivation for teaching grows along with self-confidence. Table 2.1 provides a set of observational criteria parents can rely on to evaluate learning.

**TABLE 2.1   Parent Observation Checklist of Child Behavior While on the Internet**

| Behaviors for Children to Demonstrate | Behaviors My Child Demonstrates |
|---|---|
| Asks questions that reflect curiosity | |
| Shows a willingness to keep on trying | |
| Talks about preferences and concerns | |
| Exhibits a sense of accomplishment | |
| Accepts challenges that are unfamiliar | |
| Listens carefully and follows directions | |
| Likes participation in repetitious activity | |
| Explains the difficulties of certain tasks | |
| Demonstrates the willingness to wait | |
| Makes guesses for experimentation | |
| Pays attention and concentrates on task | |
| Displays carefulness along with caution | |
| Reflective in trying to make decisions | |
| Manages frustration without being angry | |
| Views failure as an aspect of learning | |
| Requests help whenever it is needed | |
| Uses vocabulary terms of the Internet | |
| Predicts what is going to happen next | |
| Accepts time limits on the computer | |
| Recalls sequence of steps in a process | |
| Able to accurately interpret symbols | |
| Risks mistakes and accepts correction | |
| Summarizes a lesson that was learned | |

The left column is a list of desirable behaviors for children to demonstrate. During periodic assessment parents can place marks in the right column beside the behaviors demonstrated by their child. Parents can extend the list to include additional competencies they want their child to attain.

### Safety Practices

Most parents agree that the Internet is a wonderful resource, but are fearful their children may be exposed to situations that could endanger them. Some worrisome possibilities diminish when the following practices are implemented to provide child safety.

1. *Always sit beside a young child while s/he is doing anything on the computer.* Nonstop supervision is essential for Internet guidance and

to protect a loved one. Most children below the age of 10 do not have the critical thinking skills necessary to be online by themselves. Children will disagree with this age restriction but parents should not relent.

2. *Begin to have conversations about privacy.* Children know the frustration that happens when peers intrude on their play or do not respect their desire to be left alone. In contrast, children are inclined to trust adults and seldom question their authority. Tell the child one family rule is we never share information about ourselves with anyone else. If a website that parents believe is worthwhile encourages children to submit their name in order to personalize content, an unrelated nickname should be created that does not reveal personal information.

3. *Devise a menu of a child's favorite websites for easy access.* Young children are dependent on their parents to access websites. This practice lets the child know that returning to familiar and safe places on the Internet is easier when the computer is asked to remember the Uniform Resource Locator address, otherwise known as the URL.

4. *Young children can benefit from composing and dictating email messages.* Adults can send messages to relatives or friends and read messages received from these sources. Young children should not be allowed to participate alone in Instant Messaging (IM), chat rooms, or message boards before age 10.

5. *Recognize that Internet-filter tools cannot substitute for supervision.* Protect against offensive pop-up windows by reliance on blocker software and encourage a child to tell about any online concerns or worries. Respond to child reports by communicating positive statements, such as, "I am glad you told me about that; I would not have known otherwise." Filter software allows parents to block inappropriate content and exclude Websites that ask for personal information.

## Teaching Guidelines

Parents welcome insight on ways to meet their obligation for introducing children to the Internet. The following guidelines help define aspects of this new function.

1. *Situations that require waiting can be opportunities to model patience.* While Internet materials are loading, explain that the computer is getting things ready for play. Responding in this way conveys a lesson about learning to wait and being able to cope with the

frustration of delay. Adopting such attitudes can contribute more to the healthy adjustment of children than blaming the computer for inconvenience of having to wait. Whenever a child shows patience, this behavior should be acknowledged. Boys and girls need to know that parents prize this personal quality and consider it an achievement that helps for managing daily challenges.

2. *Respect the child's desire for repetition while exploring the Internet.* Playing a game or doing some other activity repeatedly has greater appeal to a child than an adult. These repetitive experiences provide children confidence that, in certain situations, they can tell in advance what will happen next. Being able to predict that certain things will remain the same like having a daily schedule for meals or going to bed at a regular time satisfies a need for order and consistency that is much greater in early childhood than at later stages of development (Strom & Strom, 2010).

3. *Permit the child to navigate the mouse and acquire practice without criticism.* This experience allows a sense of control rather than watching the parent as the sole control agent just because it is easier for adults and they are able to make the pace of events proceed more quickly. Sharing control with a child in certain situations is a more helpful approach than constant adult dominance. Recognize that being able to move the mouse properly is difficult in the beginning, particularly given the lesser muscle control of young children. Encourage practice. Responses like "You can do it," and "You did it correctly" are more appropriate ways to confirm achievement than is vague praise like "You are amazing," or "You are really smart."

4. *Following directions is a good way to proceed with tasks that are understood.* Parents who read aloud the directions presented online and follow them orient children to a more effective method for getting things done than resorting to trial and error. A child can be asked to explain directions to confirm understanding about the sequence of steps.

5. *Asking questions is an essential aspect of self-directed learning.* When parents show their own uncertainty by asking questions, children adopt this behavior as the way for them to confront situations that are unfamiliar. Premature conclusions and impulsive responses can be prevented by questions that motivate reflective thinking. When a child presents a question that the adult is unable to answer, one way to respond is to support the sense of wonder by searching together to find out more on the Internet.

6. *Schedule sufficient time that is unhurried for Internet exploration together.* A comfortable pace avoids hurry and confirms for children the priority they have in their parent's life. In the beginning, 15 minutes seems to be a good duration for Internet visits with children. Give complete attention to interacting with the child, and ignore distractions such as cell phone calls. Studies of Black, Hispanic, and White American families have found amount of time spent together is the single greatest predictor of parent success as perceived by adolescents and parents (Strom & Strom, 2009; Strom, Strom, Strom, Shen, & Beckert, 2004).

7. *Allow time for a child to carefully think about their answer to questions.* Parents who use this strategy support the development of creative and critical thinking. Having time to examine possibilities can motivate children to adopt deliberation as part of the thinking process they rely on in reaching decisions about what to do or say. In contrast, expecting quick responses without reflection supports a reliance on impulsive behavior.

8. *Listen carefully and respond thoughtfully to child questions, feelings, and opinions.* This practice recognizes the value of curiosity and lets the child know s/he is important enough to warrant undivided attention. When adults multitask, do more than one thing at the same time like reading while talking to a child, it is difficult to remain attentive and distractions can cause the parent to miss some things a child says. Children who conclude they are repeatedly ignored tend to seek advice from people outside the family who seem more willing to listen to them.

9. *Identify failure and provide correction as a method to motivate continued effort.* Acknowledging failure is an essential step to detect learning needs and to amend goals. Detection should be followed by remedial instruction, urging further effort to increase rate of success and provide feedback about progress. Persistence is needed to become competent and attain personal goals. Giving up when a task becomes difficult can avoid further mistakes but also prevent the success that could follow correction of behavior. A willingness to keep trying is fundamental for achievement in all sectors of living.

10. *Invite children to think about how situations might be seen by others.* Talk together about the "mental state" of characters seen on websites, television, in books, stories, and daily interactions with peers. This investment of time supports development of empathy—social understanding needed to respond to others in a compassionate way.

11. *Recognize children are more able to control their pace of learning online.* The Internet allows users to return to tasks, start some processes over again, and retrace steps. In this way, Internet activity promotes the practice needed to build confidence and problem-solving skills.

12. *Most families have access to the Internet but many poor families do not.* The widespread disparity in child opportunity to learn should motivate communities to make public resources more available. All public schools have computers with Internet access. Elementary schools could be kept open Saturdays and Sundays in neighborhoods for families without Internet access. College students who are training to become teachers of young children can volunteer to help parents introduce their preschoolers to the Internet while learning together. Recommended websites and guidelines for teaching can support progress. Fathers and other volunteers can arrange security so family exploration of the Internet at school or other after-school site is a safe activity.

## Internet Paradigm for Schools

Between early childhood and adolescence most students are continually involved with technology. When adolescents talk about being on the Internet, they usually express a wish that teachers at school would provide greater opportunities for interactive learning (Strom, Strom, & Wing, 2008). Eight strategies are described that accord with the cyber preferences of adolescents, provide the instructional environment needed to support a tech-savvy population, and qualify as essential elements in the tentative formation of a paradigm for Internet learning.

### *Linear and Nonsequential Learning*

The custom has been to depend on linear-type tools as the single method of progression to gain understanding. *Linear learning*, when applied to reading, means always beginning at the front page of a book, journal, or magazine, and continuing until the last page. Movies, programs on television, and videotapes are typically linear presentations. However, Internet learning is often non-sequential and interactive, permitting users to surf and choose links connecting to websites, blogs, or social networks to communicate with persons sharing similar interests. These sites sometimes contain graphics, audio, and video elements as well as text. Students also learn by chatting, writing electronic messages, and downloading materials. This more comprehensive perspective can accommodate differences among students in their level of knowledge, pace of development, and benefit of visual enrichment.

### Discovery and Self-Direction

This orientation encourages student discovery of knowledge to enhance direct instruction provided by teachers. So long as educators were the main source of information, it seemed appropriate for teacher training to focus mostly on ways to communicate lessons. Students continue to expect teachers to plan instruction, design and organize tasks, make themselves available to listen, and provide guidance. But students prefer to learn by doing, finding some things out on their own instead of always being told and getting knowledge secondhand. The pervasive interest in discovery means learning based on personal experience can yield greater meaning and more readily transfer to real life situations than ideas communicated by teachers.

### Obligation to Share Knowledge

This shift is needed because digital media offers exciting possibilities for working in teams. Instead of viewing discussions as a forum in which to make known only personal opinion, a broader expectation would be that everyone will share ideas and resources they locate on the Internet or local library. It is unreasonable to continue the practice of students reading only from a textbook or other materials assigned by the teacher. The potential benefit of Internet learning depends on students finding some reading sources on their own. Studies show that expecting students to bring reading materials they locate to class for peers to examine and referring to reading materials in discussion requires a reorientation to what is considered basic for members of cooperative learning groups (Strom & Strom, 2011a). This increased responsibility does not diminish teacher influence. On the contrary, teaching becomes more complex by structuring experiences that promote discovery, highlight competence, and encourage self-evaluation.

### Search, Synthesis, and Individuality

The goal of learning how to find things out has joined the traditional emphasis on memorizing information. One aspect of this broader purpose is to provide opportunities for students to gain and practice the ability to synthesize. Teammates can be assigned the task of locating the same website, reading the material there, and writing a paragraph summary. Everyone then critiques all presentations to identify how descriptions differ, note aspects that some students captured better than others, and detect relevant elements that no one mentioned in their report. Writing includes the skill of synthesizing views of others and clearly expressing personal interpretation. Being able to make connections and knowing how to build on ideas of others is an important skill. Combining the intelligence of individuals by networking can solve problems in a more efficient and less time consuming way than working alone. Instead of equating memorization with achievement, more attention should be given to honing abilities of locating data, merging information with colleagues, and synthesizing information as a basis for reaching more informed conclusions. Students who can find information, organize it, and present results in a coherent way offer credible evidence of problem solving ability.

### Durable Intrinsic Motivation

Learning in response to curiosity rather than in response to direction from someone else defines intrinsic motivation. The time available for learning in a longevity society is far greater than the past. Prior generations saw life as divided in two stages. During the growing up stage, students attended school, learned skills to get a job, and spent their adult years going to work. In contrast, knowledge increases at a more rapid rate now. The acceleration of new information motivates businesses to invest more money on the education of employees than is spent by all American institutions of higher education combined (Davila, Epstein, & Shelton, 2006). The duration of relevance that education programs can provide is also diminishing. Therefore, students should be helped to acquire intrinsic motivation so they remain eager to keep learning after graduation.

### Critical Thinking and Fact Checking

Teachers can tell students that, for particular lessons, one or more aspects of a class presentation will be incorrect. A perpetual homework task is to rely on the Internet at home as a tool to "fact-check" the lessons. Students will relearn and reinforce in memory facts from daily lessons that are accurate through Internet exploration while detecting elements that contain errors. Student reports in class can be made the next day to identify what was found by fact checking. Since adolescents enjoy finding flaws in the thinking of adults, this task motivates careful monitoring and is perceived as a reasonable process to challenge authority whenever inaccurate information is disseminated. Students may have to check several sources to find details of a lesson that are false. A sense of accomplishment usually follows as students locate "misleading" information. Rotating student assignments so two or three share the "fact checker" role daily ensures that all lessons are covered and feedback is provided for the previous day. This nontraditional principle encourages self-guided learning in cyber space and helps students gain insight about teaching. Students usually come to realize that teaching is not as easy as it looks, and educators must be prepared to back up their assertions with facts. Parents and siblings can be enlisted as helpers, thereby encouraging family interaction.

## *Differentiated Homework Tasks*

The purposes of this strategy are to increase the sources of learning by providing access to more teachers, enlarge the scope of instruction by allowing for greater data sharing, enable individuals to make a unique contribution to the growth of their teammates, and arrange interdependence to avoid overloading students while establishing individual accountability. Students can also share reactions to teacher-assigned websites. In each case, reactions reflect the perspective of individuals. Accordingly, team members can:

- Provide a synthesis of main points with examples
- Identify personal experience in relation to a message
- Challenge statements or assumed premises
- State reasons for doubts about conclusions
- Compare views on the website with personal impressions
- Describe related issues that are ignored or overlooked
- Present questions motivated by visiting a site
- Tell about some applications for the content

Students are often expected to examine articles, video clips, or other type presentations. These experiences offer greater benefit when followed by a productive team review in class. Students can be better prepared if they know the four questions that are used for each review.

- What were the main points or strategies presented by this reading or observation?
- What ideas in the presentation changed the way I think about this particular issue?
- What are the new insights from the presentation I can apply to my own situation?
- What are some things I would like to better understand about this particular topic?

## Procedures to Guide Online Research

Search skills support self-directed inquiry. There is widespread motivation to gain these skills. Most adolescents report they go online soon after getting home from school. Teachers in secondary grades can help students search more effectively using these monitoring techniques.

*Trace the cyber search path.* Most students want to learn by doing—find some things out on their own instead of gaining all of their knowledge by being told. This quest for self-direction should include the accountability to report about the cyber path taken on the Internet and sharing new knowledge that has been acquired. When the discovery approach to learning is established, it can continue to motivate and guide personal growth after students complete formal schooling. A recommendation is for students to select from a list of topics the teacher presents as relevant for some theme in the curriculum. Everyone is expected to keep a URL record of where they go on their journey in cyberspace. Teachers can use results as a road map to track student direction, retrace their steps, and recommend better pathways to reach some desired destination. Additional data teachers may require include whether an inquiry involved key words or images, reasoning for choice of search engine, and succession of links followed. When everyone on a cooperative team is assigned the same task, benefit comes from sharing the separate paths taken and gaining insights from experience of peers (Hargis, 2005).

*Evaluate significance of a problem.* Students should be expected to confirm importance of topics they choose to explore for assignments. The perceived significance of a concept can influence initial motivation and task persistence. Responses also reveal the extent to which an individual is able to bring concepts together and enlarge scope of inquiry. Sometimes students fail to recognize relevant connections. There are also times when they miss conceptual links because an assignment given by the teacher is ambiguous (Gross, 2004; McKenney, 2005).

*Provide a synthesis statement.* One sign of comprehension is processing information accurately by restating the concept, idea, or circumstance in one's own words. Knowing how to summarize is vital when others depend on us to report what has been read or heard that differs from their own experience. For each search, students should identify URLs along with a printout reflecting website content that may be posted on a classroom wall for teammates to examine. These materials should include a summary that combines data and student interpretation. This is a constructivist approach by which students create personal meaning from a lesson. Frequent practice as a summarizer supports freedom of speech encouraging students to state views in their own way. Teachers and peers can assist by editing summaries to make sure they effectively convey the outcome (Keller, 2005; Strom & Strom, 2007).

*Determine the application value.* Students should describe how data they have located can be applied to specific situations. The ability to see implications from data is an important research skill. This ability should become more common, especially among students who assume finding and copying data is sufficient evidence of learning without establishing whether they can make connections between data and applicable circumstance (Lee, 2006).

*Assess the credibility of sources.* Student should carefully examine and describe the data sources they rely on for their reports. Determining that a site provides worthwhile information is basic. The background and qualifications of individuals cited on the web should be identified along with date of posting, mission, and purposes of the website (Miller, Adsit, & Miller, 2005).

*Become familiar with computer technical vocabulary.* Teenagers commonly rely on a cryptic vocabulary for text messages many adults do not understand. There is also a technical vocabulary that computer users of all ages should comprehend. Self-evaluation of understanding and learning needs is detected by exploration of Matisse Enzer's (2011) *Glossary of Internet Terms.* This comprehensive resource helps increase knowledge about writing and conversations related to computer literacy. See http://matisse.net/files/glossary.html

## Social Networking and Relationships

Most literature on peer relationships reflect a bygone era when face-to-face interactions were a single focus of concern. Students saw each other mostly at the mall or the movies, drove around with friends, or hung out at someone's home. In contrast, friendships today are more reliant on cell phones, texting, instant messaging, email, and social networking. Consequently, during the next decade, the following types of questions about peers are likely to become a focus of investigation. How will the emerging online communication forums change the way students build and preserve friendships? What are the essential skills needed to nurture virtual friendships with age mates in other cultures? What guidance should parents provide to support online friendships and involvement with cyber dating? How can Internet friendships be linked with the goals that schools have for student socialization, communication, and cultural diversity?

### Multiple Selves and the Internet

The ability to create multiple identities on the Internet presents a new consideration for social development. While the online identities of most people will be the same as their real-life identities, some will present themselves in other ways. An interesting focus to explore Internet social interaction involves a concept of multiple selves that was originally proposed by Carl Rogers (1961). As a leader in counseling psychology, he maintained that each individual has three selves—the ideal self, real self, and perceived self. The *ideal self* is the person people would like to be, the *real self* is the one seen by others people, and the *perceived self* is the way we perceive ourselves to be.

Jamie's aspiration, his ideal self, is to become popular with peers at school. In contrast, the way peers see Jamie, his real self, is as a person who is reluctant to join them in the common challenge against aspects of adult authority. According to Jamie, his perceived self is someone whose shyness is misinterpreted as a lack of courage or assertion. Rogers (1961) indicated that the goal for counseling therapy is to help clients pursue their ideal selves while also increasing the accuracy of their perceptions of where they currently are and the extent to which their ideal self has been realized. See Figure 2.1, Congruence of Ideal, Real, and Perceived Selves as an Index of Psychological Health.

Rogers would have been intrigued by how his concept of multiple selves could be applied to people using the Internet. Adolescents who join chat rooms can have multiple aliases allowing them to masquerade, try out new roles, and discover what it is like to act differently than their typical daily behavior (Liau, Khoo, & Peng, 2005; Subrahmanyam, Greenfield, & Tynes, 2004). A teenager like Jamie who is shy might wish to act assertive on the Internet before ever showing assertive behavior in his face-to-face conversations. There are students who prefer to present themselves online as being less dominant than they are in person. Both genders claim to have learned certain courtship skills online such as finding out as much as possible about another person's interests and preferences because of conversational opportunities that may not occur in face-to-face situations. The chance to practice unfamiliar but desired roles is appealing (Kelsey & Kelsey, 2007).

Teachers should continue to remind students about accountability for social interaction online. They need to know that anything they say on the Internet could be traced and, therefore, although a sense of anonymity might be felt, it cannot be ensured. A priority goal should be to reconcile the different impressions someone chooses to make on others via the Internet with interaction that is honest, along with guarded privacy to avoid sharing sensitive information, and can be seen by anyone. In this way, misrepresentation does not happen and online selves are integrated with off-line conditions (White & Swartzwelder, 2013).

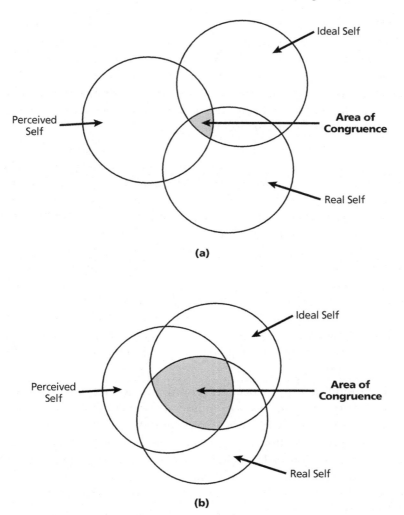

Figure 2.1   Congruence of Ideal, Real, and Perceived Selves as an Index of Psychological Health. (a) Small Area of Congruence suggests poor psychological health and the advisability of therapy to bring the selves closer together; (b) Large Area of Congruence suggests psychological health and little anxiety, and hence efficient life functioning about where they currently are and how much of their ideal self has been realized. *Source:* Adapted from *On Becoming a Person*, by C. Rogers, 1961. Houghton Mifflin, Boston, MA.

## *Underage Friends on Social Sites*

Facebook has one billion subscribers, half of whom visit this social network site daily. Most, 75%, live outside the United States. The average user has 130 friends while some have many more. This online experience provides a much greater number of contacts than young people in the past were exposed to but most are weak associations. The time required to interact with these contacts takes away from more important relationships and can cause them to weaken. Someone with 400 friends has less time to build close and durable relationship. Communication on Facebook is easier but is less personal than face-to-face interaction.

The appeal of social networks is enormous. Children across the nation are lying about their age so that they can be on Facebook. This conclusion comes from a *Consumer Reports* (May, 2011) survey entitled "That Facebook friend might be 10 years old, and other troubling news" that found over 7 million active users of this popular social network site were under the minimum required age of 13. Further, more than 5 million of the users were 10 years old or younger. Not only are kids lying about their age but they do so with the support of their parents who seem to be unconcerned by their child's involvement. Parents of the youngest group may suppose that boys and girls of this age are less likely to engage in risk taking. Only 18% of parents of preteen users made their child a Facebook friend. In comparison, 62% of parents with 13–14 year olds made their child a Facebook friend because they assume this is the age span when it is time to become concerned about taking risks.

Poor monitoring practices run counter to getting parents to become more constructively involved in online activities of children—a purpose of the Children's Online Privacy Protection Act of 1998. This legislation led to the age restriction that prohibits social network sites from knowingly disclosing identifiable information of children that makes them vulnerable to exploitation. The difficulty of finding out who is lying about being underage is complicated. Still, Facebook reports that it removes 20,000 people each day, albeit a tiny fraction of one billion subscribers worldwide (Zuckerberg, 2011).

Surveys indicate that a growing number of parents believe their children should be allowed to begin social networking before adolescence. In response, the Facebook founder, Mark Zuckerberg (2011) has expressed a willingness to support changes in federal regulations that would permit children under the age of 13 to join. He recognizes the Children's Online Policy Protection Act regulates what information websites can gather about children under age 13 and states a determination to support sensible alteration in current policy. In his view, "My philosophy is that for education you need to start at a really, really young age."

### Excessive Texting and Networking

Texting while driving is recognized as a dangerous form of multitasking for teenagers. Additional hazards may also be related to excessive involvement with texting. Professor Scott Frank (2010) at Case Western Reserve School of Medicine in Cleveland, Ohio, surveyed 4,200 high school students to determine the association between use of communications technology and health behaviors. Results indicated that excessive users of texting and social networking are much more likely to engage in unhealthy behaviors. Being a *hyper-texter* is defined as texting 120 or more messages in a school day. These activities were reported by 20% of the teens, many of whom were female, came from minority, low income, less-educated families, and from a single mother households.

Survey outcomes showed that teenage hyper-texters are

- 40% more likely to have tried cigarettes than those who spend less time texting;
- 43% more likely to be binge drinkers;
- 41% more likely to engage in substance abuse;
- 55% more likely to have been in a physical fight;
- 3.5 times more likely to have had sex; and
- 90% more likely to report four or more sexual partners.

These surprising findings suggest that when texting and other methods for remaining connected are not monitored, there could be adverse effects for health. According to the lead investigator, Scott Frank (2010), "The results should be a wake-up call for parents to not only help their children stay safe by not texting while driving, but by discouraging excessive use of a cell phone or social websites in general."

Adolescents who engage in *hyper-networking*, defined as spending three or more hours per school day on social networking sites like Facebook, is risky. Of the teenagers surveyed, about 12% reported spending more than three hours a day on social networking. This subpopulation were found to be

- 62% more likely to have smoked;
- 79% more likely to have tried alcohol;
- 84% more likely to have used illicit drugs;
- 94% more likely to have been in a physical fight;
- 69% more likely to have had sex; and
- 60% more likely to report four or more sexual partners.

The study did not conclude avid texting and networking causes unhealthy behavior but that these behaviors are associated (Frank, 2010).

### Prevention of Student Exploitation

A predictable hazard arises when students divulge personal data or photos by email or blogs. Most of what has been written about the experimentation with multiple identities on the Internet has dealt with dangerous situations that can arise whenever people exploit others. For example, pedophiles visit chat rooms and social blog sites to find and lure children to meet them. Another group of users describes or sells sexual experiences or shares pornographic images that can be downloaded. The National Center for Missing and Exploited Children (2012) released the results of its latest survey regarding the number of registered sex offenders located in the United States. The most recent survey found there are 747,408 registered sex offenders in the country, which represents an increase of 7,555 offenders since the previous survey in June 2011.

The United States Department of Justice Federal Bureau of Investigation (2013) maintains a task force to monitor the Internet for criminal behavior and protects the vulnerable—particularly minors. The FBI reports that computer sex offenders are mostly White, professional, upper middle-class males. The predators' multiple identities appear to resemble the personality polarities first described in *The Strange Case of Dr. Jekyll and Mr. Hyde,* written by Robert Louis Stevenson (1886). In this classic tale, Dr. Jekyll is the main character people believe they know well and affirm to be a model citizen. However, he is periodically transformed into the monster Mr. Hyde, whose evil deeds are seldom observed. In a similar way, when online predators are publicly identified, neighbors often express surprise stating they never observed that side of the person's dual nature. If the Internet were unavailable to these people to comfortably express themselves online, they would likely be more reclusive. Many predators have been arrested as a result of Internet electronic surveillance. The United States Department of Justice Federal Bureau of Investigation (2013) offers *The Parent's Guide to Internet Safety* online with information for parents regarding child predators.

To protect students, some school districts prohibit them from using their email address at school to register for blogs that focus on meeting others or provide cyber dating. Participants on Facebook are supposed to be at least 13 years of age but students often misrepresent themselves. Some schools offer seminars for parents about ways to protect their children online, emphasizing that it is not a matter of whether to trust daughters or sons but to show concern for safety.

Prevention of exposure to sex offenders should become a priority for schools as well as parents. A national resource that all educators should be familiar with is the website Family Watchdog (2012) (http://www.family-watchdog.us). This website provides a map of the city and state that is typed in. The map legend shows addresses where identified convicted sex offenders live and work along with locations of schools in the vicinity. In each case, there is a description of the conviction, picture of offender for ease of recognition, and indication of how close the person lives to the school or home address given in the inquiry. Bear in mind that it is a misdemeanor to harass anyone listed on the offense registry. The purpose of this national service is to make faculty and students aware of sex offenders in their community so children can be warned to avoid talking or interacting with them.

### Internet Interaction Opportunities

Robert Epstein (2010) argues against blaming brain development as the main cause for foolish risks taken by many adolescents. He suggests that instead of tracing poor judgment to delayed rate of growth in the frontal cortex, more attention should be placed upon the 24/7 immersion in the peer culture facilitated by cell phones and the Internet. Many teens are in contact with friends 70 hours a week yet lack meaningful contact with the important adults in their lives. Some spend brief periods with parents but often this is watching television, eating, or checking in by phone. In Epstein's view, American culture has infantalized adolescents, causing their isolation from adults and motivating them to communicate almost exclusively with peers.

Finding ways to improve social networking of children and adolescents should be a high priority. Consider some possibilities:

- Partnerships between the schools and businesses to help explore careers
- Students post reactions to recreational reading for classmate consideration
- Indigenous mentors answer student questions about aspects of their culture
- Question and answer site on ways to use the Internet to improve schoolwork
- Enabling students learning a language to practice interacting with others
- Have parents help their children create profiles to place on social network

- Peer counseling as a source of guidance about worries related to school
- A site where students cooperate to inform adults about concerns of kids
- Support groups for children facing similar challenges led by counselors
- School chat rooms by grade level for students monitored by counselors
- Site with options to volunteer for children often excluded because of age
- Place for children to display their drawings or pictures and get feedback

There is a need to enlarge what has become a peer-driven communication environment for social networking. More contact with trustworthy adults online and in person along with a gradual increase in responsibility for youth is essential to help build resilience (Southwick & Charney, 2012). Teachers can motivate intergenerational interaction by devising online homework that requires parent and grandparent involvement.

## Summary and Implications

A hundred years ago adults and children read to each other. As time went by they could listen to the radio together and still later watch television. Visiting the Internet can also become an enjoyable family experience as parents convey basic values at a stage when children are most ready to adopt them. Preparing children for the digital environment requires that parents assume a larger teaching role. Technology can encourage children to question, challenge, and disagree, thereby increasing their potential to become critical thinkers. Early orientation to the Internet cannot be provided in early childhood centers where the staff has too many children to provide one-on-one supervision. Accordingly, parents need to understand some aspects of technology so they can support learning in the preschool years when curiosity is high and children are easily directed to discovery tasks, search skills, and ethical attitudes for healthy social networking. Creative education programs are needed to persuade parents their children can benefit from Internet guidance and most families are capable of providing the initial instruction.

There are some things students know more about than their teachers or parents because the Internet makes it convenient to do research. This shift means direct instruction should no longer be the gateway for most learning. Instead, teachers should be facilitators who provide clues, monitor direction, provide feedback, and offer advice. These functions encourage students to become self-directed learners and can make the role of teachers more exciting. When teachers acknowledge that the technology skills students possess may exceed their own, a more equitable relationship emerges based on shared leadership and reciprocal learning.

The socialization of children and adolescents are being transformed. There is increasing reliance on technology tools to communicate with friends and strangers online. Social network sites facilitate these mostly out-of-school conversations that expose children to the opinions of others, elaborate their own impressions, report on satisfactions and disappointments, disagree over how to solve problems, and identify needs of the community (Gardner & Birley, 2012). Preventing predators from harming youth who may feel invulnerable remains a challenge for schools and parents. Although there are complaints about lack of etiquette in use of technology, there is little dispute that cell phones and the Internet have increased the number of people who listen to youth. On the other hand, periodic calls to check in with parents are not a substitute for face-to-face family conversations needed to discuss daily experiences and things that matter most. Face to face interaction will remain essential to build and sustain close relationships.

# 3

# *Thinking and Fears*

Everyone has to confront fears and worries throughout life. However, these feelings are more prevalent in childhood. One reason is that children have active imaginations and sometimes cannot distinguish fiction from reality. For them daytime includes considerable involvement with fantasy and going to sleep brings more nightmares than are reported by adults. Growing up also includes additional fears because children are being exposed to a broader range of experiences than ever before. The apprehension of parents is another influence. Television and the Internet present mothers and fathers with frequent reminders about situations that have the potential to endanger their children. In combination, these factors should motivate parents to think about ways they can help their children learn to manage fears and worries.

The goals of this chapter are to describe how children can be taught to assess risk and danger, develop a balance of caution and trust, and reduce undue pressures leading to anxiety. Knowing the stages children go through in their comprehension of death is important and can prevent misinterpretation of why war play has so much appeal to them, and avoid

*Thinking in Childhood and Adolescence,* pages 49–70
Copyright © 2013 by Information Age Publishing
**49**

attributing motives to boys and girls that do not reflect their intentions. The significant contributions of imaginative play and children's books are discussed as resources for becoming able to manage fears. Understanding how to reduce the concerns of children about school bullies and mobilize the collective influences of peers to support safe conditions are examined.

## Messages About Danger

Five-year-old Jonathan examines the milk carton in front of him while he eats breakfast cereal. He wonders if the missing boy that is pictured on the carton will be found and whether his parents will ever hear from him. Down the street 6-year-old Mark looks at a postcard that came in the mail. The card includes a photograph of a girl about his age who is missing along with printed details. Eight-year-old Denise is watching television when an Amber Alert interrupts the program. Information is given citing the license plate, color, and make of car driven by someone who abducted a young girl. Nine-year-old Jeffrey has returned from a trip to the grocery store with his mother and is helping carry packages to the kitchen. Every bag he places on the counter portrays an image of a child who has been reported missing. Jeffrey reflects on how he would escape if someone tried to take him away from his family.

No one knows how repeated exposure to these kinds of messages about missing persons impact a child's outlook on life. However, it is certain that such reports have dramatically altered the way in which many parents orient daughters and sons to relationships and guidance about interpreting their environment. Parents are naturally upset when television or written materials inform them a registered child molester has been allowed by the courts to move in their neighborhood, or media reports that children are being exploited by pedophiles they meet on the Internet. Sometimes it seems there is no end to the list of dangers children could potentially encounter (Bakan, 2011).

In response to what seems an increasingly hostile environment, some parents conclude it is necessary to warn their children against having contact with strangers. Others choose to take the precaution of fingerprinting or videotaping their children, keeping up-to-date photographs or implanting dental microdots with identification numbers filed in computer registries. The growth of these practices underscores a need for parents to consider whether they are protecting their children or just frightening them. How can parents put justified concerns in perspective so safety rather than fear dominates their behavior? Obviously, an increased awareness about potential for harm to children is bound to cause worry. Nevertheless, parents should carefully think about personal fears in relation to the evidence before they can expect to help frightened youngsters cope with situations that may be unsafe (Bourke, 2005; Pincus, 2012).

The intention should be to present a balance of concern for safety, fear, and trust. This balance is crucial because the ways parents handle personal fears determine how they prepare their children for a world in which there are many unsafe situations. One way to begin this lesson is by teaching how to assess risk—an ability that governs the extent of fear.

### Assessment of Risk

Parents whose fears cause them to believe most people cannot be trusted are incapable of teaching children how to trust others. Emotional needs of children should not be mistaken. It is essential that they have an overall impression that the world is a safe and friendly place rather than see their environment as permeated by danger and unfriendly people. Still, motivated by personal anxieties and worries, some parents discourage children from speaking to anyone who they do not know. This decision brings about a reciprocal dilemma. If children should not speak to strangers, it follows that strangers should not speak to children.

Older adults are frequently disappointed by their lack of opportunity to interact with children. Marie, a grandmother, describes one experience in this way, "I was in the drug store and decided to check my blood pressure. An elementary student was at the machine when I arrived. By looking over his shoulder, I could see the reading was 110/70 on the machine and said, "Wow, I wish my blood pressure was that low." He looked at me in an odd way, said nothing, and walked away. Whenever I try to have a conversation with children, even those living on my street, it is always they same. They do not respond. Other friends my age report similar reactions of children."

One consequence is that many safe, well-meaning grownups that children could turn to for help become reluctant to interact with them. Adults often report this response about their experience in shopping malls where a "Don't talk to strangers" practice prevents intergenerational conversation. It seems natural to smile at a child, say hello, or exchange brief comments. Yet, more and more people reason "I should not be talking to unsupervised children because I do not want to appear as a threat. They have likely been told to avoid strangers and, in effect, I am urging them to disobey their parents."

The accuracy of this perception is confirmed by the results of surveys from students in kindergarten through grade three. When asked to identify their fears, strangers are mentioned more often than any other concerns (Pincus, 2012). Children admit their parents taught them this fear. But how accurate is this scary lesson about strangers? The National Center for Missing and Exploited Children (2012) identifies each reported case as an abduction by an unknown individual, kidnapping by a parent, or a runaway choosing to be gone. Unfortunately, the specifics of individual cases are not identified by the agencies that print the warning flyers, grocery bags, and milk cartons. Thinking of missing children as a homogenous group has produced confusion and unwarranted fear. As a result, when parents lack information, many suppose strangers are the main cause of missing children (Gardner, 2009; Glassner, 2010).

The United States Department of Justice has determined that strangers are not the main cause of missing children. Every day about 22,000 children are declared to be missing, roughly 800,000 a year. The largest subgroup of 450,000 is juveniles who have run away. Of the 350,000 kidnapped, a relative without legal custody, typically father, abducts 99% of them. Only 200 children, less than 1% of the total kidnapped are taken by strangers (Office of Juvenile Justice and Delinquency Prevention, 2011). The National Center for Missing and Exploited Children (2012) acknowledges that there is unwarranted paranoia about strangers. In response, the agency shuns their previous message of years past regarding "stranger danger." The center states it no longer supports a "stranger danger" message. Children do not have the same understanding as adults about what being a stranger might mean, as this is a difficult concept to grasp. A more beneficial response is to help children build the confidence and self-esteem they need to stay as safe as possible in any potentially dangerous situation rather than teaching them to look out for a particular type of person. The "stranger danger" message is ineffective and, based on what is known about people that harm youngsters, the danger is greater from someone the children know or the family knows than from most strangers (McBride, 2011).

There are also misperceptions surrounding alleged dangers students face at school. News reports about prevalence of drugs and violence have led parents to believe that murder could be a potential threat to their child's life. On the contrary, of 55 million children in the elementary and secondary grades, on average 30 are murdered at school each year. A notable exception was the massacre of 20 students killed along with 6 faculty at Sandy Hook Elementary in Newtown, Connecticut in 2012 (Barron, 2012). During an average one-year period, parents or caretakers kill 3,000 children at home. Stated another way, children murdered at school are 1% of those that are killed at home. The illogical response to these statistics has been to increase funding for metal detection and security guards to prevent anyone from bringing a weapon on campus or coming there to harm students (Langman, 2009).

## Balance Caution and Trust

The national rate of serious crime has declined in the past five years. However, media coverage of crime increased by 600% in the same period (Bakan, 2011). Some people do not watch local news because the content tends to center on tragedy and bad situations more than favorable ones. Nevertheless, there is no reason to blame the media for our own lack of critical thinking. The fact that negative stories receive more attention on television, the Internet, and in newspapers is an insufficient reason for people to ignore objective evidence. When 99% of child kidnappings, 98% of child abuse, and 99% of child murders implicate relatives, the rational conclusion would be to pay more attention to the improvement of family life (Carrabine, 2008).

For the same reasons, it is illogical to identify all strangers, staff in childcare facilities, and community volunteers serving youth agencies as people who cannot be trusted. The errant assumption that most people would harm children is false and should be rejected. Boys and girls should be taught to trust but also to become able to recognize suspicious behavior. Let's examine some of the ways these important purposes can be achieved.

## Family Safety Guidelines

Divorced or separated parents with child custody should not identify strangers to children as being a major threat. Since 90% of all custodies in the United States are assigned to mothers, persons most likely to kidnap children are non-custodial fathers (Cherlin, 2009). This means that mothers should assess their situation before deciding what to tell their daughters and sons about missing children. It may not be in the best interest of children to inform them that non-custodial parents are responsible for most kidnappings. The idea that one of their parents would do such a thing could become an undue source of worry for children.

If a mother decides that she is not in a high-risk group because there is no custody battle and the estranged spouse has not made any threats, then her conversations with the children can focus on possible situations and ways for them to respond. On the other hand, if a former spouse appears to be a potential problem, certified copies of the legal document on child custody should be placed in a child's file at school. And, if a non-custodial parent threatens to take a child, the principal and teachers should be told so they do not allow the child to leave school with an unauthorized adult.

Parents from single and intact families should stop warning children about everyone who is a stranger. The fact is strangers are not a common danger. In the majority of cases involving crimes against children, the youngster knows the perpetrator. It could be a relative, older friend, brother of a playmate or man who lives nearby. Children can readily be taught to run away from a stranger, but teaching them to say "No" and leave adults they are familiar with or persons their parents trust is another matter.

Parents should formulate family safety rules to help protect children from dangers that are both known and unknown. Boys and girls should be told these family rules must be followed at all times. "Never go anywhere without telling Mom, Dad, Grandma, or the babysitter." This is a good rule because it prevents situations the parents would not condone. Encouraging children to trust their intuition and gut feelings about situations is important because parents will not always be around when there is a need to assess danger. Children should understand that "Anyone who tries to get you to break a family rule is a bad person. That person deserves to get in trouble, so go tell an adult—Mom, Dad, your teacher, the principal—right away if someone is bad." This rule defines bad people in terms of their behavior instead of their appearance. Children can apply the bad person rule to people they do not know and familiar faces without emphasizing danger from either source.

People who exploit children generally rely on methods that would be ineffective with adults. They use intimidation, which is most effective with children who have been taught to never challenge the authority of adults. Elementary school children that are trusted by parents to rely on their own judgment when any situation seems to present danger are less likely to do what they are told by a coercive adult. Inner strength is needed to oppose directives that children believe could jeopardize their safety. If children in the primary grades can gain confidence about making personal decisions, learn family rules on how to ask adults for assistance and feel this is the right thing to do, they will be better equipped to assess danger, cope with scary situations, and still view the world as a safe place (Lucado, 2009).

Since the terrorist attacks on September 11, 2001, Americans have been obliged to manage unprecedented fears and worries. Some parents prefer to avoid talking with children about the dangers faced by our nation. However, a more practical response assumes that the more children know, the more able they will be to cope and the safer they can feel. The Federal Emergency Management Agency (2013) recommends families discuss the need to be observant and what can be done to reduce danger. Children should be aware that the government tries to protect our family by providing media warnings when appropriate about threat levels, amber alerts, and steps are taken by airport security and air marshals who are assigned to airplanes. Despite these precautionary steps, there is a need to go beyond just training the firemen and police to deal with potential disasters. Everyone should be on guard. Families are advised to prepare a disaster kit in the unlikely event of an emergency that requires leaving home. This kit should contain water, juice, canned goods, medication, and bandages.

Parents should make sure their children know how to contact a particular person if family members were to become separated. Boys and girls should know a landline phone number to reach the contact person and understand where to go if they find themselves alone. And, of course even preschoolers should be able to tell police the full names of their parents, home address, and phone. Many parents overlook the fact they are responsible for providing children with these lessons.

Many young children are unprepared for fearful situations they may have to face. Parents should ensure their child knows essential information. These simple lessons are not learned quickly so patience and continued emphasis is needed. Practice brings the desired result. When a child can answer correctly, ask these questions in the presence of relatives and friends. Adults will tell the child that they are pleased important lessons have been learned. Young children should know:

- His or her full name, home address, and phone number
- Parents' full name and name of place where s/he works
- How to dial 9-1-1 in order to get emergency assistance
- What to do if they think that someone is following them
- How to answer the phone without letting callers know they are alone
- What to do in the case of a fire

## Child Fears

It is unfortunate when parents teach their own unfounded fears to children but dismiss the fears uniquely experienced by youngsters. Indeed, many parents are ashamed of fearful children and try to banish the fright by denial. A father recalled taking his 4-year-old son Steven to a zoo. Because crocodiles fascinated him, quite a bit of time was spent at the reptile exhibit. During that time, another little boy about the same age as Steven arrived with his family. The boy was afraid and preferred to stay at a distance from the floor-to-ceiling window behind which the crocodiles were in sight. Taking notice of his son's fear, the boy's father lifted him up, held him against the window, and said, "See, it's like I told you; they're locked in so you do not have any reason to be afraid." Imagine how confusing this situation was for the boy to be told he was not afraid when actually he was frightened. His parents, all-knowing authorities, must know more than he does. In this way some children develop alienation from their own feelings. They learn to mistrust their senses and rely on others to tell them what they should feel. It would have been better for this father to tell his child, "The crocodile is dangerous, and can make us feel afraid. We are protected behind this window and we will be careful. If we want to stand back a little ways, that's ok."

Sometimes children encounter an opposite but equally firm denial that their experiences are unique. Each of us has heard people say, "I know just how you feel." In fact, no one knows exactly how another person feels. However, this limitation of empathy—ability to participate in someone else's experience—becomes less disturbing when we realize that it confirms our assumptions about being individuals. For parents this means the fears of children should be respected if we share them or not. Our acceptance of others seems to play a larger role in determining interpersonal success than our understanding of other people. If we limit our respect to those whose experiences we understand, the quest for understanding itself becomes an obstacle to successful relationships.

Besides denial and empathy, ridicule is a common response to fear. But laughing at another person's fears does not decrease the fear. Instead, the effect is to lower that individual's confidence. Telling a child, "It's just a dream and not real," might be well intended, but inspires shame for having fears that grownups declare unwarranted. To laugh at somebody's fears or call the person a derogatory name like wimp, sissy, baby, or chicken, is to undermine a relationship. Children whose feelings are ridiculed soon stop sharing their experiences. The tragedy for parents is they reduce the chance to know their child better and forfeit an opportunity to help cope with fears and worries.

### Admission of Fears

The first step in overcoming our fears is to acknowledge them. Because children identify closely with their parents, a useful method to reduce the harmful consequences of children's fears is for parents to admit their own worries. A child who is afraid of the dark, of being alone, or starting school should be assured by adults that fear is a natural reaction and telling about fears does not make someone a coward or a sissy. Courage is not the absence of fear but instead the mastery of fear. When people lose touch with possibilities of danger, they also lose a normal sense of caution that serves to protect them.

A certain degree of fear is needed to exercise good judgment. The Greek philosopher, Plato, wrote, "Courage is knowing what to fear." And, while parents may insist there is no danger in the dark, a child observes that Mom does not go out alone late at night, and doors are double locked at bedtime. Children should not be caused to feel ashamed of expressing feelings of fear. After all, many adults have fears about becoming old, being alone, getting fat, losing a job, developing cancer, falling down, becoming a burden, and being rejected by other people. However, adults have an idea of what fear is whereas children worry long before the time they can comprehend the notion of fear.

A child whose fears are unsuspected or unshared bears an additional burden of loneliness. No other aspect of experience is more deserving of compassion, as well as attention, than a person's fears. Also, no aspect is more baffling to a child or those who want to offer assistance. Certainly children should have someone they can turn to that will hear their worries without judging them. They have this experience when their parents accept them unconditionally. No child should have to repress fear or to pretend bravery to gain esteem of parents. When worries that relatives have in common and those that are unique to each person are identified, family members are more able to help one another. Make an effort to identify the worries of your children and share some of your own fears with them.

### Use of Children's Books

One way for parents to lessen anxiety of their children is by reading books in which the main character must deal with situations that are similar to those experienced by young listeners. Talking about how a story character may feel and how these same feelings bother other boys and girls can help children realize that telling parents their fears is a way to manage them better. When people share their fears, they are no longer alone and there can be some reduction of anxiety. Consider examples of how reading about a common fear can lessen by talking with adults.

*Leela and the Watermelon* is a story about a young girl who lives in India (Hirsch & Narayan, 1971). She likes watermelons but one day ate so fast that she swallowed a seed. Her older brother teased Leela suggesting that now a watermelon would grow inside of her. Leela feels anxious because she is alone with her fear and feels helpless. Then she sees a lady at the market who has a big stomach. Had the lady swallowed a seed too? When Leela asks, the woman replies "I don't know." Leela worries about herself and she worries about the lady. Later the lady is seen again, this time announcing the birth of her baby. Again, Leela wants to find out if she swallowed a watermelon seed. Other women standing by find this funny and then they explain that having a baby does not result from swallowing a seed. When Leela tells her grandmother that her brother said a seed would grow inside her, the old woman took Leela to the bazaar to buy the biggest watermelon that was available. Leela was allowed to eat the melon all by herself and was not expected to give her brother any.

Jill is the main character in *The Alligator under the Bed* (Nixon, 1974). She hears an alligator making swishing noises with its tail under the bed so mother is called. The mother listens, suggests a bad dream was the cause, and urges Jill to go back to sleep. The same thing happens again but this time Jill's father answers her call. He advises her to avoid imagining things because it was impossible for an alligator to be under the bed. The third episode of asking for help resulted in Uncle Harry coming to the bedroom. Harry announced that he heard strange noises coming from this room. Jill said, "It's the alligator." Harry suggests that the alligator is under the bed because it makes a good hiding place and he must be lost. So Jill tells the alligator to go home, Uncle Harry opens the door, and leads the alligator out so he can return home.

Children in the elementary grades also benefit from stories in which the main character is fearful because of peer abuse and requires imaginative solutions to set matters straight. In *The Hundred Dresses* Wanda wears the same faded blue dress to school every day even though she claims to have one hundred beautiful dresses at home, all lined up. The other girls don't believe it, and when Peggy starts a daily game of teasing Wanda about her hundred dresses, everyone joins in. Maddie, Peggy's best friend, goes along with the game but secretly wonders whether she can find the courage to speak up in Wanda's defense. It is not until Wanda fails to come to school one day that classmates find out the truth about the hundred dresses, and Maddie and Peggy learn the meaning of kindness, compassion, and understanding. This heartfelt story has never been out of print since it was published 70 years ago and won the Newberry Book award. (Estes, 2004).

## Fear of Bullies at School

Elementary school students sometimes experience fear about their safety from peers that seek to bully them. Feelings of resignation that nothing can be done to stop abuse or expecting adults to deal with every incident should be replaced by a collective resolve by the students to assume their unique responsibility related to misconduct by classmates. When teachers present a structured agenda that allows students to describe impressions of peer abuse, constructive norms of response to prevent it can emerge. In a similar way, teachers should avoid assuming students who show cruelty and lack self-control are incapable of improvement so giving up on them is justified. A more promising outlook is to realize that teacher guided discussions can promote healthy group responses to frustrating situations.

Class discussions about bullying can support the motivation students need to assume their important role to ensure safety of classmates. These conversations can also improve teacher perspective. Studies have found that, compared with students, teachers and administrators underestimate the scope of bullying, consider the school as more safe, and judge incidents to be less serious (Willard, 2007). A suitable agenda invites student opinions that are seldom allowed expression and consideration in the classroom. Teachers can reinforce accurate impressions by providing summaries of findings from research studies. The following questions are recommended for periodic discussions in class with elementary school students.

- What does it mean to be a bully? (students share their definitions based on personal experience)
- How does it feel to be the victim of a bully? (encourage awareness based on hearing feelings of others)
- What can happen to someone who is bullied a lot? (effects of bullying on mental health)
- Why do you suppose people bully others? (speculation and first hand accounts about bully motivation)
- What do you think will happen to bullies when they grow up? (guesses about long-term consequences accompanied by teacher reports of research findings)
- What problems can school bullies expect to face later in life? (difficulty forming intimate and durable relationships; rejection by co-workers and neighbors in the community)
- How can bullies change to become someone that other people like? (identify possibilities for rehabilitation)
- How do you suppose their parents treat bullies at home? (conjecture about the parent–child relationships compared to what is revealed by research literature on bullies)
- What should someone do when they are picked on? (find out the best ways to respond is of great interest to students)
- What can students expect of adults to protect them from bullies? (identify ways teachers and parents can be counted on to enforce the civil rights of everyone)

- What factors should bullies consider when they reflect on their behavior? (provide healthy criteria all students should use for self-examination)
- What are some myths about bullies? (speculation followed by review of research about bullies)
- Why should students tell on a bully when they know about peer abuse (individual obligations in a civil society)
- What are some names that you do not want to be called in the classroom or outside of school?
- What results from the bully poll taken by our class do you want to discuss?

The expectation that class time should be used efficiently means teachers have choices to make about balancing instruction and giving attention to student concerns. Some educators and parents might wonder whether discussions about relationships are appropriate when the main purpose of curriculum is to prepare students for work. This perspective is shortsighted. Over the past decade, substantial evidence has revealed that students unable to get along with classmates have much higher rates of absenteeism, dropout, truancy, incarceration, suicide, and murder. Devoting class time to talking about the issues that bother students is justified (Strom, Strom, Wingate, Kraska, & Beckert, 2012).

## Preschool Soldiers

Children are curious about stories they see and hear on television, particularly scenes related to war and death. A growing number of parents report their children ask these questions: Who will take care of boys and girls whose parents are in the war? Will my father have to be a soldier? What if the enemy attacks the buses or subways in our city? No adult is fully prepared to answer these questions but parents do their best to respond. These questions relate to the fact that young children in most countries rely on fantasy play as a powerful tool for reduction of fears and worries. Parents should understand the stages of mental development that govern how children interpret the meaning of death and why they find conflict play appealing. Learning to accurately interpret child motives should motivate parents to allow them a choice of the toys and themes that guide their interactive play.

### *Child Views of Death*

Parents wonder how observing scenes of war on television might influence their child. Some are uncertain over whether to allow play with toy weapons or military games. Barbara is a 35-year-old mother who has two preschoolers. Even before fear of terrorism became a global concern, Barbara and her husband believed that violent toys could motivate lawlessness. "We knew that the decision to deny them weapon toys would be difficult for our boys to understand. It would be easy to conform to the majority opinion, but to us that would mean a lowering of our standards of integrity."

After overhearing my child tell his cowboy companions he was going to shoot and kill them, I felt compelled to say, "Donnie, you don't mean that." I reconsidered and thought maybe I should sit him down and explain that when you kill someone they are dead, and they will never breathe again. Then I wondered, if we don't let Donnie play with guns it might cause him to feel we are convinced he is so violent that he requires different toys from everyone else. Finally, not knowing what to do or say, I ignored him and went on feeling guilty.

Barbara's dilemma is common. Perhaps examining more closely just what young children mean when they talk about killing and dying can reduce the problem. The meaning of death has many interpretations and misconceptions for young children. Young children view death as a reversible process. Whether they play hide-and-go-seek or cowboys and Indians, all the dead people are expected to recover quickly and live again. The conventional television cartoon reinforces this notion when the rabbit runs and then falls off a high cliff, hits the ground with a thud, and, in keeping with the child's reversible concept of death, is brought back to life. The same thing happens whenever children watch the death of an actor on a television program who later miraculously appears as a guest on a talk show. Some time ago, when my son was a preschooler, we had this conversation:

**Son:** Dad, I'm going to dress up like an army man.
**Dad:** You look just like a soldier. I was a soldier once.
**Son:** Why?
**Dad:** The country needed me. We were having a war.
**Son:** Dad, did you die?
**Dad:** No, I was lucky.

The realization that death is permanent takes place in stages. Between ages 3 to 5, there is a lot of curiosity and questioning about death. Unfortunately, many adults suppress this curiosity, and think it is impolite for a child to ask old Mrs. Thompson when she is going to die. In contrast, several generations ago, it was quite common for children to witness at least one deathbed event, usually the death of a grandparent. Yet, the young child believes that death is not final; it is like being less alive. Just as sleeping people can wake up and people on a trip can return, so too a dead person can come back to life. The coffin limits their movement, but dead people must continue to eat and breathe. People buried at the cemetery must know what is happening on the earth, they are sad for themselves and feel it whenever someone thinks of them. Dying disturbs the young child, since life in the grave is seen as boring and unpleasant. But, most of all, it bothers the child because death separates people from one another. And, at this age, a child's greatest fear is separation from parents.

Young children are self-centered and preoccupied by present events, so they are unable to recognize how a death in the family may impose future demands including the permanent loss of someone's presence, their comfort, love, encouragement, and perhaps financial support. Because these understandings do not come until a later age, little children may not express grief immediately, or even cry like their adult relatives and friends. In fact, it is common for adults to mistakenly conclude that a child is coping well with the loss of a loved one. But, bear in mind that little children are unable to fully comprehend the situation and they can only tolerate short periods of sadness. Because it is easy for them to be distracted, they may appear to be finished with the grief and mourning process earlier than is actually the case.

Even young children recognize words are insufficient to help someone in grief and that what matters most is just being there to console them. To illustrate, four-year old Amanda did not come in from the backyard when she was first called by her mother. Later, when mother asked Amanda to explain why she was late, the little girl replied, "I was helping Judy." Mother wanted more information. "What were you doing?" Amanda said, "Well, her doll's head got crushed." Mother wondered aloud, "How could you help fix that?" Amanda had a good answer and said, "I was helping her cry."

Children between the ages of 5 and 9 tend to personify death, perceiving it as an angelic character that makes rounds in the night to start life for some individuals and end it for others. The big shift in the child's thinking from the first stage to this stage is that death is recognized as possibly being final. It is no longer seen as only a reduced form of life. This view emerges with increasing personal experiences that suggest certain separations are permanent. When the pet goldfish dies, mother buys a new one because, she says, the other is gone forever. Claude Cattaert's (1963) classic *Where do Goldfish Go?* illustrates how children can become upset by adults whose insensitive reaction to animal death is that pets can be replaced. When Valerie's goldfish dies unexpectedly no one is bothered except Valerie; yet the family is overcome with sorrow when grandfather dies, even though his death was anticipated for years. The daughter of Billy Joel asked him what would happen when he died. In response Billy wrote a song for her entitled "Lullaby, Goodnight my Angel" that can be heard on YouTube.

It is not just families that need to become more aware and sensitive to children's feelings about death. In conversations with prospective kindergarten and first-grade teachers we asked: "What would you do if some morning at school the class goldfish were found dead?" The range of responses included these comments: "I would deliver a eulogy;" "Declare a day of mourning;" "Conduct a burial;" "Discuss the virtues of the deceased;" "Consider the after-life of fish;" "Invite testimonials from friends;" "Talk about human death and its meaning;" and, "Flush the fish and say, 'Take out your books, it's time for oral reading.'"

Parents know that they cannot guarantee a long life for pets, but hope they can reduce the amount of exposure their children have to death on television. The outcome of this decision to protect youngsters usually is a refusal to allow them to watch television detective and police programs, censorship of some aggressive cartoons, and an ambivalence about viewing the local news which frequently portrays violence or death in the community.

The typical 5- to 9-year-old child believes that the cause of death is external, and they personify death as being an outside agent. Since they conceive of death as a person, children feel it is possible to avoid death if protective measures are taken. Thus, one child may claim that his grandfather won't die, because the family is taking good care of him. Children of single parents admit they worry most about "What will happen to me if my mother dies?" It is reassuring for them to know that plans have been made so they will be taken care of in the event of an unexpected death.

Finally, around age 9 or 10 children become aware that death is not only final but also it is inevitable. It will happen to them too, no matter how clever they are or how well they take care of themselves. Instead of imagining death as being controlled by an external agent, they now recognize that internal, biological forces are involved. As children begin to accept the universality and certainty of death, some changes can be observed. They begin to show concern about meaning of life, their purposes for being on earth, and ways to achieve them. This means that values become important in governing their behavior.

Many children throughout the world are growing up in the midst of death and threat of destruction. Others see death on television with such regularity that war has become a common fear. Children look to grownups for answers about death, but the attitude of adults is their most important response. Certainly parents want to explain their beliefs regarding what happens after death. However, also bear in mind that youngsters love mystery and they will adopt your sense of wonder and uncertainty if you are willing to express it (Wolpe, 2009).

## *Perceptions of Toys*

There are many playthings parents believe children could do without. Some dislike all military toys because they reflect violence. Others oppose stunt-oriented toys that encourage taking risks on skateboards. Crash cars that fall apart on impact and can be quickly reassembled are thought to disregard safety, and martial arts dolls create reliance on an irrational method for resolving conflicts. Parents with these complaints are often ambivalent because they want to purchase toys that reflect their own values but should also recognize that children require opportunities in decision making to develop their own value system. And where is it more appropriate for children to be given options than in their realm of play?

Grownups can justify making some decisions for children such as whether they will attend school, if they will go to the doctor, and when it is time for bed. Parents will determine how much money can be spent on entertainment and toys for children. On the other hand, to claim that boys and girls need coherent values but deny them practice in making some personal choices is unreasonable. So, parents are bothered about the priority they should give to feelings of children in selecting toys for them. Instead of declaring your values by choosing children's toys or by censoring the content of their fantasy, try to enact your values while you participate in pretend-type play with them. The imposition of values has less influence than illustration of values. If you feel that war tends to be glorified while the darker sides of battle are overlooked, give some attention to the aftermath of war and importance of the peacemaker role in your play.

Recognize there is a critical distinction between the fantasy wars enacted by children and bloody wars carried out by adults. This means it is a serious mistake to misread motives of the preschool soldier. Grownups who suppose that young children who play soldiers have the same purposes as the men and women at war they imitate are misinterpreting motives of children and their understanding about violence and death. Parents should strive to recognize the favorable possibilities in their children's choice of playthings.

Conflict toys and games can serve to meet certain needs of boys and girls. This kind of play offers relief from feelings of powerlessness and of dependence that accounts for much of a child's experience. Surely there is nothing strange about the desire to control others, especially those who daily exercise power over you. Children delight when asserting themselves in play and make Daddy run away or fall down because he has been shot. Then too, conflict playthings can provide a safe setting in which to express disapproved feelings like anger, fear, frustration, and jealousy. In many homes these feelings are met by punishment, ridicule, or shame. Danger play also provides an opportunity to repeatedly confront fearful issues like war, death, and injury. Although these subjects are of universal concern to children, many adults avoid talking about them and, as a result, increase the anxiety of children.

Taking risks requires practice in a low-cost setting. During danger play children can afford to take chances, to see what it is like to rebel, and to be the bad guy or the outcast. These are risks they dare not take in daily family life. In this connection, it is worth noting that war play is the only context in which some children can conduct conflict without guilt. Even though parents should teach how to settle disputes in constructive ways, some boys and girls learn instead to feel guilty whenever they oppose an authority figure. For many kids fighting off a mutual "enemy" can foster competition needs. War play also allows children to experience leadership, to take charge and command others as well as to become heroes like their favorite television characters. Finally, conflict toys and games are fun, a fact that should be appreciated by a society that values enjoyment.

### Influence of Players

Safety should always be a parent consideration when they buy toys. However, instead of overemphasizing the effect of toys, it is important to understand that the adults who play with children also can have a great influence. Otherwise, the value of playthings is exaggerated while the impact of players is underestimated. Relatives cannot fulfill their guidance role merely by purchasing the right kind of toys or forbidding the wrong ones.

Some adults complain that children are inclined to believe what they see advertised on television. Is the adult condition any better if we believe everything we read on toy packaging? For example, exposure to so-called educational or creative toys will not necessarily support child reliance on imagination. Creativity does not reside in certain toys because of their design, but mostly relates to interaction between persons that play with them. Research on creative behavior and modeling shows that parents should play with their children; they should become involved instead of limiting themselves to judging the merits of playthings. The assumption that certain toys can have a dysfunctional effect on child personality is unsubstantiated but the view that adults can have a favorable influence through play has been demonstrated.

Parents should end the practice of censoring content of children's fantasy play, except in instances of bodily danger. Once the direction of children's pretending becomes a choice of adults, boys and girls are no longer decision makers. And, in fantasy play, making choices is essential for participation. Adults can share in determining the agenda if they are willing to accept the role of play partner. It is unfair to interpret the content of children's play as representing adult motives. When an actor portrays the role of a killer in a film or a stage play, the audience may consider the performance convincing and therefore successful. However, if a pretending child chooses to play the same role, reasons for deciding to become that character may get greater attention than performance of the child. Such pessimistic interpretations of child's play can lead to unfair inferences and attribution of motives that children do not possess. The motives of children who kill each other temporarily when using toy weapons are unrelated to motivation for violent activity in adult life (Mash & Wolfe, 2012).

Parents want children to learn nonviolent methods to settle disputes. The way to achieve this goal is by a sustained long-term emphasis on conflict resolution. It is also important that mothers and fathers accept stages of normal development through which all children must grow in understanding the finality of death. Whenever the war play of children is construed to be a kind of personality fault or prelude to violent activity in adult life, the motives of boys and girls are unfairly judged. Pretending helps kids confront their common fears of war, death, and injury and gives them a vicarious sense of power to control such events. Adults should avoid censoring the focus children choose for pretending and instead encourage understanding of how to solve disputes by enacting their own values during parent–child play sessions.

## Adolescent Fears About Status

### *Body Image Concerns*

Exposure to unrealistic expectations for body models begins early for girls when they are given Barbie-type dolls with exaggerated physical proportions instead of getting American Girl dolls that resemble the shape, fashion, and child concerns of their owners. Idealized male bodies present a similar preoccupation for the boys. Youth face continual challenges to their self-esteem from television, the Internet, and magazines that portray images of physical perfection. Only 15% of girls are happy with their body and more than half feel they need to lose weight (Costin, Grapp, & Rothschild, 2011). A reflective reminder is that almost all people lack ideal measurements. In addition, caring about someone should not depend upon how tall or thin they are or the shape of their face and figure. Being capable of looking beyond physical appearance to see individuals as they really are is a sign of growing up and becoming mature.

Adults generally underestimate the scale of fear and anxiety teenagers experience about their appearance and body image. This concern is illustrated by *Real Women Have Curves*, a film featuring America Ferrera (Cardoso, 2002). Ana is an intelligent Latina high school senior torn between duty to the family and pursuing a promising future. Will she accept a scholarship to go to college or keep working in the small bridal gown factory her family owns? In one poignant scene Ana inspires overweight girlfriends to strip down to their underwear, laugh about their figure, and, at least temporarily, accept their less than perfect bodies. A related need is to recognize that girls can be both good looking and intelligent. Stereotypes regarding beautiful girls are usually inaccurate and frequently reflect jealousy that can lead to mistreatment.

### Diet and Eating Disorders

Many students skip breakfast because they think it will help them lose weight. However, any excessive diet practices including diet pills or laxatives and vomiting are unhealthy. When students avoid breakfast, they are fasting 15 to 20 hours and therefore not producing enzymes that are needed to metabolize fat and to lose weight. Avoiding breakfast is part of a patterned lifestyle of unhealthy weight management as students fear the prospect of becoming obese and prefer to look thin. Schools and parents must encourage students to understand the importance of maintaining a healthy diet.

When dieting becomes an obsession for adolescents, it can indicate an eating disorder. Eight million Americans suffer from eating disorders. The incidence has doubled over the past decade and implicates ever-younger age groups. Forty percent of 9-year-old girls report that they have dieted. Eating disorders record the highest mortality rate of any mental illness. *Anorexia nervosa* (self-imposed starving) and *bulimia* (overeating followed by vomiting and purging) are health hazards with as great a danger as rising incidence of obesity. Ninety percent of anorexic victims are females between 15 to 25 years of age (Smink, van Hoeken, & Hoek, 2012).

The cultural pressure to be thin often motivates anorexia, having body fat 15% or more below expected levels. This condition results in extreme weight loss along with complications such as anemia, hormonal changes, and cardiovascular problems. One estimate is that 10% of anorexia cases end in death, half of them attributable to suicide. The National Association of Anorexia, Nervosa, and Associated Disorders (2013) (http://www.anad.org) provides a free guide for download entitled, *How to help someone with an eating disorder.* Most studies have concluded that the cultural factor is less influential than personality disorder. The inability to cope with stress seems a dominant cause but the facade of fat provides a convenient excuse (Costin, Grapp, & Rothschild, 2011).

The half million victims of bulimia ingest large amounts of food in private before they purge themselves using laxatives, enemas, diuretics, and self-induced vomiting. The word *Bulimia* comes from the Greek language and means "huge appetite." The term is actually a misnomer because bulimics do not eat up to 50,000 calories a day because of hunger. Instead, they use food for self-medication in a similar way as those who rely on drugs to cope with their unmet personal needs. Most researchers maintain that bulimia, like anorexia, masks personality problems rooted in low self-esteem and the inability to manage stress (Wilson, Grilo, & Vitousek, 2007).

There are different personality traits associated with anorexia and bulimia. Anorexics shun food to cope with stress, tend to withdraw socially, maintain rigid self-control, deny that they have problems despite loss of up to 25% of body weight, and feel they are fat. In contrast, bulimics eat to cope with their stress, are sociable, lose self-control, recognize that something is wrong but because of their purging are able to maintain near normal weight. Another negative outcome of bulimia is significant tooth decay because of chemicals related to vomit. Treatment for anorexia and bulimia goes beyond just controlling eating habits. Body image fears, low self-confidence, and goals are also important considerations. These complexities are illustrated by reports that 25% of anorexics will become healthy, 25% will not be helped, and 50% will gain some control but remain vulnerable to recurrence (Smink, van Hoeken, & Hock, 2012).

### Families and Obesity

Children are defined as overweight if their BMI (body mass index) is in the 85th to 94th percentile and obese when they are in the 95th percentile or higher. The proportion of overweight children ages 6 to 11 tripled over the past generation, rising from 6% to 18%. During the same period, overweight children 12 to 19 year olds also rose from 5% to 18%. Approximately 25% of Hispanic and Black teenagers are overweight compared with 15% among Whites (Ogden, Carroll, Kit & Flegal, 2012).

Obesity is the greatest single threat to public health, accounting for more fatalities than AIDS, cancers, and accidents combined. The problem begins during childhood with the number of fat cells becoming fixed by age 10. Parents need to understand that childhood obesity merits immediate concern. Studies have found that 7% of children with normal weight parents grow up to be obese whereas 80% of children with two obese parents will become obese adults. There has been a large increase in gastric bypass surgery that drastically reduces stomach capacity, causing people to feel full from small amounts of food. Medical professionals are agreed that weight-loss programs do not work. A 1% success rate is the norm. Physical activity must be part of the strategy since exercise and weight management must go together (Moreno, Pigeot, & Ahrens, 2011).

What concerns health care professionals most is the cost in lives. Obese youth are three times more likely than those of healthy weight to develop high blood pressure and twice as likely to suffer heart disease. There is a saying that we are as old as our arteries, implying that the condition of arteries is more important than chronological age in evolution of heart disease and stroke. Geetha Raghuveer (2010), a cardiologist at the University of Missouri in Kansas City, led a team that examined 70 obese boys and girls whose average age was 13. Ultrasound imaging was applied to measure the thickness of the inner walls of their carotid arteries in the neck that supply the brain with blood. The intention was to gauge their vascular age, referring to the age at which level of arterial thickening would be normal. For these teenagers their vascular age was about three decades older than their chronological age. The thickness of their arteries was more typical of 45 years olds.

Additional dire predictions suggest that half of American children will develop Type 2 diabetes because of excess weight, raising the probability they will die at a younger age than their parents. An obese adolescent can expect to live 12 to 14 years less than a peer of desirable weight. The cost of medical treatment for children with obesity is three times more than treating the average child. These statistics should lead to reflection and resolve because obesity is much easier to prevent than to treat. Some implications of research are that greater attention must be given to social adjustment, the disease can be directly addressed by requiring exercise and fitness for all students at school, and everyone needs to become aware of the damaging effects on long term health (Ogden, Carroll, Kit, & Flegal, 2012).

## Summary and Implications

Children acquire some fears that parents teach them. Mothers and fathers should make sure they provide guidance about how to gauge risk rather than regard exceptional situations as normative. It is important to support a balance between the need of children for caution and their need for trust. Instead of supposing trust is a naive orientation, trust should be recognized as a basis for intimate relationships, mental health, and sense of community. By establishing family rules for responding to potential danger, guidance can be provided without adding excessive worry. As children get older, they are more able to describe fears and worries. Adults should be willing to listen to fears and anxieties while also sharing some of their own. Teachers can guide discussions related to student fears of bullies and acquaint them with the need to report face to face intimidation so that it becomes less common. When teachers arrange cooperative learning groups where children receive peer support, this orientation prevents feelings of aloneness and helplessness that produce anxiety.

Parents should understand stages of normal development in child understanding about the finality of death. When child war play is seen as a personality fault or an inclination to rely on violence to solve problems, the motives of boys and girls are unfairly judged. A common but rarely acknowledged prejudice is to misread motives of children, to suppose they have dreadful intentions when it is not the case. The developmental reality is that pretending allows children to confront universal concerns they feel about war, death, and injury. Adults should try to avoid censoring the focus children choose for pretending in favor of helping them understand how to solve disputes by enacting their own values during parent–child play.

Adolescents are more closely connected to peers than prior generations and count on one another more for communication and guidance. Dependence on peer perception can make body-image concerns a prominent fear, wanting not to be ostracized because of physical appearance. Many who want to conform to the idealized thin body image, skip meals and experiment with dieting plans that can cut calories but ignore the need for nutrients like iron and calcium. Some suffer from self-imposed starving known as *anorexia nervosa*, or *bulimia* of overeating and then purging oneself. Obesity has become the greatest public health threat with greater numbers of students categorized as overweight than ever. Parents and schools must unite to help children understand that their well-being in the future depends on current choices regarding a proper diet and getting enough exercise.

# 4

## Thinking and Stress

Student conversations often include reports about experiences they perceive as stressful. Emotional health depends on being able to manage anticipated and unforeseen stress situations, responding to daily frustration in a healthy way, and avoiding preoccupation with worries. This chapter examines the influence and effects of stress, circumstances that children and adolescents often struggle to confront, and methods teachers, parents, and peers can implement to minimize undue stress while offering support for coping with pressures commonly felt in a hurried society.

## Influence of Stress

### Stress and Personality

Hans Selye (1956), professor of medicine at the University of Montreal in Canada, was the first scientist to detect the connection between stress and health. He identified two types of stress. *Eustress* refers to pleasant events students must adapt to such as earning an achievement award, being chosen for the school basketball team, getting a diploma and being accepted by a college.

*Thinking in Childhood and Adolescence,* pages 71–92
Copyright © 2013 by Information Age Publishing
All rights of reproduction in any form reserved.

The opposite kind of pressure known as *distress* occurs when disappointing situations require adaptation. For example, distress can be experienced when adjusting to school, being mistreated by a bully, breaking up with a boyfriend or a girlfriend, and preparing to take the Scholastic Aptitude Test (SAT).

People differ in the sources of stress they are exposed to and the extent to which they are influenced by external pressures. The weight imposed by particular external stressors is not the only factor that warrants consideration. Another variable is how people perceive their situation. At one pole of vulnerability are those individuals who appear to be stress resistant, able to handle considerable pressure, and still carry on effectively. At the other extreme are persons that seem to breakdown whenever they are exposed to even slight pressure. Studies of stress-resistant people have determined some characteristics they have in common. They recognize negative forces in their environment but are not preoccupied by them, remain open to making personal changes, look at new and challenging situations as opportunities for growth, feel a need to be involved when they believe their actions can make a difference, and see themselves in charge of most things that happen to them (Blond, 2011).

### Resilience and Health

Research has revealed the way someone perceives an event or a situation can often be more important than what objectively exists. People who readily adapt to new conditions while retaining a sense of personal control have a greater tolerance for stress. *Resilience* is the ability to restore a balance following a difficult experience and integrate it into the total life perspective. Hardiness is an important element of resilience, working toward a good outcome without being overwhelmed by risks that could threaten development. Resilient people have doubts and uncertainties just as everyone else but are more able to recover quickly from setbacks and disappointments that might otherwise lead to giving up. The resilient are flexible, share faith, hope, and optimism about the future. Resilience is observed in students who come from surroundings that are mostly destructive but who, nevertheless, beat the odds and transcend their circumstance to become adults who are recognized for achievement (Southwick & Carney, 2012).

There is evidence that cognitive styles impact emotions and behavior. The key appears to be an emphasis on accurate thinking more than an emphasis on positive thinking. For example, resilience is supported in classrooms and homes by lessons about the importance of optimism, assertiveness, and flexibility. This strategy can improve personal outlook on life, enhance level of performance in the classroom, and reduce the probability of depression.

Martin Seligman (2012), a psychologist at the University of Pennsylvania, conducted 19 controlled international studies with 2,000 students from 5 to 18 years of age. Students in the Pennsylvania Resiliency Programs were taught to think more realistically and flexibly about everyday problems. Teachers focused on the benefits of slowing down the problem solving process, helping students clearly identify their goals, retrieve information without undue focus on speed, and generate alternative possibilities to attain their purpose. During the ensuing two years student optimism rates rose while risk of depression was reduced by half. The implication is school conditions that nurture emotional well-being can improve health and academic performance.

Relatives and friends should recognize the benefits of providing encouragement for one another, acknowledging setbacks, resolving to overcome obstacles, and identifying corrective behaviors to implement. This "come back" kid type of experience forms a basis for confidence that difficult challenges in the future can be seen as opportunities for success. Playing on a sports team that loses on a regular basis calls for an ability to accept defeat while also aspiring to better performance next time. Failing a course should motivate a request for tutorial help, followed by hard work to achieve necessary skills. When people try to protect loved ones from having to face adversity, these forms of protection frequently have the effect of rendering someone less capable of dealing with unforeseen challenges that are inevitably experienced by everyone. Development of resilience requires some exposure to risk and failure.

Ann Masten, professor of education at the University of Minnesota, has been conducting a longitudinal study of 205 disadvantaged children to trace their resilience over time. Thirty years after Project Competence began, it continues with 90% retention of the original sample. Marten's insightful observations have revealed the ways some participants grew up to become successful despite significant risk factors such as poverty, violence, broken families, and discrimination. An important finding has been that individuals who overcame risks they encountered early in life had access to greater protection and resources along the way than did less successful peers lacking external assets. Instead of assuming that the course of individual development is forecast by socioeconomic status, there is considerable evidence that adverse conditions can be reversed when healthy goals are supported by community intervention (Masten & Aryan, 2012).

### Cost of Sustained Stress

Individual perspective mediates how stress is perceived. However, evidence shows that sustained stress can erode capacity to cope with adversity and remain resilient. The relationship of psychological stress to biological aging was examined by Elisa Epel and Elizabeth Blackburn (2004) from the University of California in San Francisco. Their study focused on *telomeres*, genetic structures at the tip of each of the 46 chromosomes, discovered by Blackburn twenty years ago. Like caps on the end of shoelaces, telomeres function to prevent strands of DNA from unraveling and thereby promote genetic stability. Each time a cell divides and duplicates, some portion of the DNA telomeres shrink by a few basic pairs. Cells reproduce themselves often to strengthen host organs, grow, or fight disease. However, as people age, telomeres shorten and, following many rounds of division, DNA has diminished to such an extent that a cell can no longer further divide or properly carry out its function. Blackburn is credited with the discovery of an enzyme, called *telomerase*, which helps replenish a portion of telomerase lost with each division of cells (Brady, 2009). Blackburn received the 2009 Nobel Prize in Physiology and Medicine for investigations showing how chromosomes are protected by telomerase with implications for cancer and longevity.

Epel and Blackburn (2004) studied a group of young mothers who had disabled children. These mothers, who met in a weekly support group, shared a difficult caretaking task they were obliged to continue for some indefinite period. The hypothesis of the researchers was that long-term exposure to the extraordinary psychological stress these mothers experienced would in time influence the length of their telomeres. Blood samples from 39 mothers caring for a child suffering from chronic-type disorders, like autism and cerebral palsy, were compared with blood samples of 20 mothers who took care of children without disabilities. White blood cells, fundamental to the immune system response for any kind of infection, were examined with attention to telomeres. Results revealed that the blood cells of mothers who had spent years taking care of their disabled child were genetically 9–17 years older than mothers of the same chronological age who had less demanding caregiver responsibilities. The longer that mothers had taken care of a disabled child, the shorter the length of their telomeres and lower their telomerase activity.

Using a self-rating scale, mothers reported the extent to which they were overwhelmed by their daily tasks, and how often they found themselves unable to control issues of importance to them. Mothers who saw themselves as experiencing heavy stress had significantly shortened telomeres compared to those who felt more relaxed, whether or not they were raising a disabled child (Epel & Blackburn, 2004). This was the first scientific study to quantify the physiological cost of feeling highly stressed and underscores the need to discover ways to manage pressures that relieve a toll on the body. That these women who gave so much of themselves to help loved ones had to pay such a cost in terms of mental and physical health is sad.

One general implication from this research is the need to obtain relief from certain stressors that cannot be eliminated. This means arranging a schedule so that there can be attention to personal needs such as getting enough sleep, participation in a social network, physical exercise, and having time to pursue personal interests. Epel and Blackburn's (2004) continuing project with mothers of children with disabilities is evaluating a broad array of possible interventions that include meditation, yoga, and cognitive therapy to assess the effects on telomere length and perceived stress to find out what can be done to preserve the capacity for resilience. Mothers, in general, experience the combined stresses of having multiple responsibilities that include caring for their children, satisfying an employer, managing a household, looking after a husband, and sometimes caring for aging parents. Learning to relax is a lesson more parents should exemplify so their children can observe effective ways to manage stress. Cross-cultural studies have determined that parents typically overestimate their favorable influence in this context as compared to their adolescent daughters and sons who commonly fault them for failing to show how to deal with stress (Strom, Strom, Strom, Shen, & Beckert, 2004).

## Stress Management

### *Adjustment to School*

An adaptable person is able to adjust to change. Most parents know how difficult it can be to adjust to a new job or move to a new place. Sometimes adaptability does not involve a change in family address but a new environment like the school. Adjustment to being a student begins at ever-earlier ages. In recognition of the difficulty, some families try to ease adjustment by having their child attend only a couple days a week or half days in the beginning so that time with peers is balanced by time with adults at home.

Parents are usually surprised when a teacher informs them their child presents problems with self-control. How could this be when the child seems so well behaved at home? Adaptation is less difficult at home where many children get lots of attention than when they are in a group with other self-centered boys and girls who want their own way. Since adaptability involves self-discipline, a worthwhile question is: What should the success or failure of a child's beginning days at school be based on? The usual way to assess adjustment is teacher observation. As they watch each student, most teachers try to find out:

- Does the child like school? Whether a teacher can learn much about how a child feels depends upon their relationship.
- Does the child feel comfortable enough to express the entire range of feelings at school including disappointment, anger, and fear as well as pride and satisfaction? This index of security shows whether a child believes a teacher will accept all kinds of feelings.
- Does the child see the teacher as accessible and willing to give help when it is needed? Listening is always important but has even greater significance during early childhood because there are few resources for a child to access other than the teacher.
- Does the child exhibit signs of anxiety, such as nail biting, wet pants, fear or withdrawal from activities involving groups?
- Does the child feel a sense of belonging at school? This is shown by how s/he interacts with peers, makes friends, or is accepted by others.
- Does the child show a willingness to try new activities? If children consider the risks of exploration as too high, they avoid situations that add to learning.
- Does the child persist in trying to complete tasks or give up when faced with difficulty? Adults should tell children that failure is a part of learning. Parents differ in how they interpret child lack-of-success.
- Does the child feel comfortable enough to become involved with creative play by actively pretending? This can be observed on the playground or recess.
- Does the child sit still and listen to a story with pictures? Other situations can also be a focus to detect length of attention span.
- Does the child follow simple directions and finish assignments correctly?
- Does the child know letters of the alphabet, numbers up to 20, and personal information about home address, phone number, and complete name of parents.
- Does the child respond well to teacher correction and discipline or threaten to tell parents s/he is being mistreated?
- Does the child take care of personal toilet needs without adult assistance?
- Does the child show knowledge from the preschool curriculum?

Most teachers recognize the limitation of their own observations. Therefore, they rely on parents to observe a child outside of school. When parents are asked to look for certain behaviors, the resulting insight can increase understanding of a child. For example, consider the larger perspective that emerges if parents join teachers in looking for success indicators for "Does your child like school?" Children find it less threatening to tell parents about things they dislike. A teacher who supposes that children enjoy school unless they complain to her directly may overestimate willingness of students to confide in her. At home, when parents listen to the apprehension of a child about school experiences, they can probe to find out, "What did you tell the teacher about this problem?" The answer can reveal how comfortable a child is expressing feelings in class. Teachers and parents view adaptation to school as important so it is good to share observations and talk often, at least monthly in the child's first year. This takes time and improvisation of schedule. However, the benefit justifies a united effort by the teachers a child has at home and in school.

### Peer Benefits and Pressures

Peer influence on socialization and stress is shown by lessons students learn mostly from classmates. Peers provide children with the first substantial experience in equality. Everyone seeks companionship and enjoys the attention given them by others. The peer group is in the best position to satisfy these needs. When classmates behave in approved ways, the group rewards them with attention, acceptance, and emotional support. The peer group presents a separate set of standards from the expectations that are imposed by parents and caretakers. Peer norms are more attainable and often provide reasons to justify behavior that opposes adult directives. The greater resources of grownups make it difficult to declare much autonomy from them. Still, peers are consistent in listening to reports of friends about common dilemmas, and encourage one another to express their differences in the presence of grownups (Prinstein & Dodge, 2010).

The positive influence of peers should not be overlooked or undervalued. Peers provide experiences that can support social and emotional development. For example, children should have companions of their same age as a standard of self-comparison, opportunities to express themselves without fear of punishment, and chances to share leadership. They encourage one another to strive for independence and convey a sense of belonging to a group besides the family.

Children learn about friendship mostly from each other—how to get along with someone who has the same level of status. Becoming a group member requires gaining specific skills that are motivated by peers. These skills include cooperation, sharing, questing for independence, venting anger, and making up—all lessons that are more easily learned from peers than parents. They discover what friends will tolerate as well as behaviors that will not be condoned. Most children gain a sense of belonging and feel accepted in peer groups. Students find they must learn from others to handle disputes even though aggression is sometimes a pattern of behavior.

### Peer Pressure Protectors

There is a need to also recognize peers as a major source of stress. Belonging to a peer group usually requires conformity. This is fine so long as the norms a child is expected to adopt are healthy. When this is not so, individuals from early childhood onwards must be capable of withstanding pressure from peers because caving in could compromise health, integrity, and goals. Parents should prepare their children for pressures to adopt dysfunctional behavior or suffer rejection. All children need the following peer pressure protectors.

- Parents should encourage individuality by avoiding comparisons of ability, achievements, or limitations among their children. When one child becomes a standard for behavior of a brother or sister, the likely outcome is sustained rivalry and jealousy instead of life-long reciprocal support and sibling pride (Faber & Mazish, 2012).
- Encourage children to value solitude, time for reflection, self-evaluation, deliberation, and looking at things anew. Access to solitude can support individuality and creativity that children need so being with age mates for lengthy periods does not result in excessive peer dependence.
- Parents should make themselves available to listen, particularly about the difficulties of building friendships. This task demands priority, takes time, and is sometimes inconvenient. Do it anyway! Problems with classmates are likely to be continuous and, depending on the way parents respond, they may continue to be asked for advice or not at all. Children need help to get along without threatening withdrawal to force concession behaviors by others. Share your mistakes, a resource that requires self-disclosure.
- Allow and defend child privacy. Let children confide in you without insisting that everything that is going on in their lives be told to you. Trust is essential for close relationships and parents have the most prominent role in shaping this characteristic.

### Meditation and Relaxation

Stress is part of life so students should learn suitable ways to manage pressures they can expect to encounter in daily life. Stress can be partly controlled by learning to relax. *Meditation*—to empty the mind of thoughts and concentrate—is an effective way to reduce stress (Wallace, 2008). A generation ago, reports about effects of meditation were mostly anecdotal. Since then many experiments have assessed the influence using randomized controlled trials. Meditation is included in employee training at American Telephone and Telegraph, Connecticut General, Blue Cross Blue Shield, Armed Forces, and most health maintenance organizations through wellness education programs. In these settings meditation has been found to relieve tension, reduce stress, lower blood pressure, and improve physical and emotional health. Meditators typically describe an enhanced sense of well-being, reduced anxiety, improved perception, and less illegal drug and alcohol abuse.

Neuroscientist Andrew Newberg at the University of Pennsylvania scanned the brains of eight highly-skilled meditators from the Tibetan Buddhist School to identify cognitive changes during this activity (Newberg & Waldman, 2010). Following the injection of a radioactive substance that attaches to red blood cells, the "tagged" blood briefly leaves a trace that can be detected by the imaging machine. Active brain waves reflect more blood than others because neural activity is fueled by blood-borne oxygen. Single photon emission computed tomography (SPECT) identifies the brain areas working hardest by detecting concentrations of the radioactive marker. Scans reveal different patterns from those typically found in a normal state of mind. Some differences included unusually prolonged and intense concentration, reduced metabolism, less awareness of distractions, and up to 20% greater frontal lobe activity.

Should short periods of solitude, reflection, and meditation be a routine part of the daily schedule for students? Such an arrangement would seem particularly important for those from neighborhoods with high rates of crime and violence and families that over-schedule them so they lack opportunities to reflect. It is ironic that, as most people have abandoned the traditional practice of setting aside one day a week for relaxation, research is affirming restorative power that can come from meditation (Wallace, 2008).

San Francisco's Visitacion Valley Middle School serving 260 students in grades 6–8 was a place where police routinely were called to make arrests. Lawlessness in the community reflecting drug usage and violence caused students to feel fearful, anxious, and stressed. Then, in 2007, the principal mobilized faculty and parent support to establish Quiet Time, a stress reduction program of transcendental meditation as an optional activity. Twice a day, once at the first bell and again before the final bell, students sit quietly for 15 minutes. They can read, sit with their thoughts, or meditate. The time for this activity was not taken from instruction but gained by shaving a few minutes from lunch, a minute from each passing period, and half of homeroom. About 90% of students opt to learn transcendental meditation and get several hours of instruction led by teachers trained in methods to oversee quiet time (Markus, 2012).

The student population at Visitacion is mostly low income as 88% qualify for free lunch. Ethnic origins are 33% Asian, 22% Black, 16% Hispanic, 13% Filipino, 10% Pacific Islander, and 2% White. Over 40% of students are second language learners. Since the introduction of Quiet Time six years ago, truancy rates have declined 60% and suspensions by 50%. In 2011, students with unexcused absences were 7%, compared to over 20% before. School grade-point averages have risen. Students like the school, have fewer arguments, and physical fights have become uncommon. These gains have been despite little change in the violent environment outside school. In 2011, Ingleside neighborhood had 37 shootings and 10 homicides (Markus, 2012).

The implications for including meditation in secondary and higher education has been largely overlooked. If students could learn how to alter their physiological responses through meditation, they might be able to prevent stress that interferes with learning. This is a better option than excessive reliance on caffeine, drugs, alcohol, or cigarettes for coping with daily pressures. In addition, behavior problems could be dealt with more constructively by urging misbehaving students to withdraw for a time, relax, and find healthy ways of responding to difficulties inherent in modern living.

Barnes, Bauza, and Treiber (2003) at the Medical College of Georgia assessed how exposure to meditation might influence negative behavior at school. The 677 male and female Black students from two inner-city high schools were screened on three separate occasions for blood pressure. Then, 45 students were declared eligible based on systolic rates above the 85th percentile with respect to age, gender, and height. These 15–18 year olds were assigned to a meditation orientation or a health education control group for a year. Students in the meditation group met 15 minutes every day and practiced twice a day at home on weekends. Members of the health education control group attended daily sessions at school focused on lifestyle education.

A comparison of pretest and posttest data after four months of intervention found that the meditation group showed a significant decrease in school absences as compared to the control group. The meditation group also recorded a significant decline in number of school rule infractions while breaking the rules increased in the control group. The number of suspension days for misconduct also declined in the meditation group by 83%

while the control group recorded an increase in suspension time. Anger management was also more effective for the meditators. These outcomes encourage educators to consider stress reduction as a powerful strategy for improving behavior of young adults (Barnes, Bauza, & Treiber, 2003).

As of 2012, nearly 100 secondary schools in 13 states are implementing meditation. Preliminary results show that high school students practicing meditation daily have 25% fewer absences, 38% fewer suspension days, and 50% less rule infractions. Similar benefits are reported for students in grades 1–7 showing significant improvement scores on validated attention skills tests and faculty observed reduction in aggressive behavior (Markus, 2012).

### Importance of Exercise

Life is more sedentary for most adolescents now than during the past with less physical activity. Students sit at desks in school or at a computer and in front of a television set at home without getting enough exercise. In addition to giving up health benefits that come from the pursuit of fitness, teenagers in unprecedented numbers are becoming obese, a condition that contributes to a range of life threatening diseases. Choosing to exercise on a regular basis can reduce stress and improve overall health. More specifically, it enables weight control by using excess calories that would otherwise be stored as fat. Exercise also helps diminish a risk of chronic diseases like diabetes, high blood pressure, elevated cholesterol, heart disease, and osteoporosis. Other gains include building strong muscles, bones, and joints, improving flexibility and balance, warding off depression, improving mood, sense of well being, and improved sleep. Physical activity may include structured activities like walking, running, biking, hiking, basketball, tennis, golf, and other sports. It may also consist of daily tasks such as household chores, yard work, or walking the dog. Teens who adopt exercise as part of their daily activity are likely to continue the practice in adulthood, which may lengthen life expectancy (DiClemente, Santelli, & Crosby, 2009).

Less than half of all adolescents are physically active on a consistent basis. They would benefit from wearing a pedometer and arrange to walk at least 10,000 steps a day or about five miles (Hazen, Gakhar, Stitcher, Khanchandan, & Centers for Disease Control, 2013). Moderate to intense physical activity is recommended at least 30 minutes a day. An expert panel reviewed research on the effects of physical activity on young people's health and well being. Over 850 articles and 1,120 abstracts were examined. The conclusion was that youth who participate in moderate to vigorous physical activity one hour or more a day gain significant physiological, health, and psychological benefits (Siegel, 2006).

Cross-cultural studies also underscore the relationship of exercise and health. There has been speculation about the extent to which developing Type 2 diabetes is due to the genes we inherit and our environment (mainly diet and lifestyle). A National Institutes of Health study by researchers at Northern Arizona University compared Pima Indians in Arizona with Pima living in the Sierra Madre mountains of Mexico (Schulz, Bennett, Ravussin, Kidd, Kidd, Esparza, & Valencia, 2006). The Pima groups have a similar genetic heritage and, for comparative purposes, resemble identical twins that grow up apart. The Arizona Pima Indians have the highest rate of type 2 diabetes in the world; 34% of the men and 41% of the women are affected. However, prevalence of the disease for the Mexican Pima was previously unknown. When the researchers completed a physical examination of 224 Mexican Pima (77% of that population), it was found that only 8% of Pima men in Mexico and 9% of women had diabetes, a rate only slightly above the 7% for 193 other non-Pima Mexicans living in the same area. The pattern was the same for obesity rates.

What aspects of the environment protect Pima south of the border from obesity and diabetes? The diet of Mexican Pima actually contains more fat and less fiber than the Arizona Pima while similar numbers of calories are consumed. The main difference between the groups involves greater physical activity by the Pima in Mexico. Most of them make a living by physical labor and they grow their own food. They plow their fields with the help of oxen, then plant and harvest by hand. On the other hand, the Pima north of the border drive trucks or cars and farm with the aid of highly mechanized equipment. Most of them purchase their food from a grocery store. According to the researchers, the lower prevalence of type 2 diabetes and obesity among the Pima Indians of Mexico than in the United States indicates that, even for populations genetically prone to these conditions, their development is influenced mostly by environmental circumstances, thereby suggesting that type 2 diabetes is largely preventable. This investigation offers compelling evidence that changes in lifestyle associated with westernization has a major role in increasing the global epidemic of type 2 diabetes (Schulz, Bennett, Ravussin, Kidd, Kidd, Esparza, & Valencia, 2006).

## Signs of Stress

### *Worries of Adolescents*

Adolescents are continually exposed to media messages that can be worrisome. Some degree of worry is normal but the likelihood of anxiety or depression increases with perceived number of worries. Studies to improve understanding about how worry influences mental and physical health have dealt mainly with adults. This narrow focus is unfortunate, considering that excessive worry is often reported by adolescents and that adult patients suffering from excessive worry usually associate the beginning of their disorder with adolescence (Brown, Teufel, Birch, & Kancheria, 2006).

Adolescents commonly advise friends not to worry. Excessive worry can block critical thinking and preoccupy individuals to such an extent they are unable to pay attention to daily responsibilities. On the other hand, worry can have a positive side too. Worries act as a rehearsal for danger by causing us to concentrate on particular problems that we might otherwise ignore and motivate us to seek solutions in advance. Some people appear more able to benefit from focused attention that worries present because they can switch off the process and turn away from worries when it is time to attend to other obligations. People unable to snap out of it and instead remain fixed on their worries do so at considerable cost to their performance at school, home, and work (Gosselin, Langlois, Freeston, & Ladouceur, 2007).

Everyone finds it difficult to remain confident when confronted by too much uncertainty. Over the past decade there has been a significant loss of predictability. As a result, some people strive to retain some degree of predictability in life to avoid being overwhelmed by uncertainty. Some ways to attain predictability include a rigid schedule that guarantees particular events will happen when expected, being guided by values that ensure consistency of behavior, holding on to unyielding customs and beliefs, and providing relatives favorable feedback regardless of their behavior to reinforce self-confidence.

There is a protective mechanism that adolescents can learn to rely on to prevent excessive worry. A term described earlier, locus of control, refers to how people perceive forces that shape their destiny. Those with an *internal locus of control* believe they can govern the direction and momentum of their lives. Persons having an *external locus of control* hold an opposite outlook. They believe luck and influence of powerful people are why things happen. Therefore, no matter what they might attempt to do, their efforts would have little effect. For them, the rewards of life are independent of personal actions. Adolescents who look at life through the lens of an extreme external locus of control run the risk of becoming cynical and alienated since they feel powerless and suppose it is futile to spend time and energy struggling to reach goals that are unattainable (Masten & Narayan, 2012).

There has been a long-standing search for methods to acquire the capacity of extracting benefit from worry while avoiding hazards associated with it. For example, disappointment and sadness motivated by worry are low arousal states that are more likely to trigger withdrawal than perseverance. On the other hand, responding to worries by doing physical exercise generates a high arousal state incompatible with feeling down. Conversely, high-energy negative moods like anger are better dealt with by participating in relaxation and reflection activities. Adaptation calls for shifting to a state of arousal that can terminate the destructive cycle of a dominating negative mood (Darst & Pangrazi, 2008).

A confidante is a trusted person with whom personal matters are discussed. A survey of 1,000 adolescents found that those who chose parents to listen to their concerns were much less inclined to worry about being liked by classmates, school failure, their occupational future, and relationships with friends than teenagers who chose nonfamily listeners such as peers, Internet sources, or teachers (Brown, Teufel, Birch, & Kancheria, 2006). Surveys of 10–18 year olds are consistent in identifying the following most prevalent worries.

- The number one worry of adolescents is school performance, particularly doing well on state required tests and getting ready for a career (Ravitch, 2010). Relatives should be pleased that teenagers give high priority to their studies. Most students want families to be proud of them. However, many report that parents expect them to perform better than classmates even when they lack superior abilities. Pressures to meet unreasonable expectations lead to unnecessary stress. Mothers, fathers, and children should regularly discuss goals they have for one another and amend them when warranted.

- The second most common worry for adolescents is physical appearance. Most of them are preoccupied by how peers see them. A survey of 700 adolescents from five urban high schools sought to identify the personal exclusion rules they felt were fair to reject someone else. Findings indicated that perceived unattractiveness is the most prevalent reason for exclusion (Leets & Sunwolf, 2005). This is one reason teenagers are so quick to adopt new clothing styles of peers. Parents sometimes trivialize clothing fads claiming they are expensive, encourage conformity, and do not matter in the long run. A more sensible response is to realize that external conformity of dress style does not mean a student lacks individuality or can be pressured to conform in other aspects of behavior.

- The third most common worry relates to popularity. Boys and girls want to become popular, an ambition that peaks in seventh grade (Rimm, 2005). It is wise to accept this desire instead of belittling the interest in being well thought of by peers. The desire for peer approval does not signal an end to parent influence. The duration of parent influence is as long or short as the parent's willingness to encourage personal development of the adolescent. Teenagers also need to realize that their age group tends to focus more on benefits than costs of risky behavior and makes more high-risk decisions when doing things in peer groups than alone. Consequently, there may be times when popularity should be set aside in favor of discouraging group intentions or walking away from participation.

■ "I worry that my parents might get divorced or they could die." These worries are seldom expressed to parents (Umberson, 2006). Parents should anticipate these fears and describe preparations they have made in the event of their untimely death. "If Dad and I died, Aunt Joyce has agreed to be your guardian. We know she would raise you in the way we feel is best. Each year we put money in an insurance policy for your college tuition." Part of a teen's concerns deal with how his or her future would be in jeopardy. Talking about it is helpful and reassuring.

■ Students also worry about how their friends treat them. This concern reaches a peak in eighth grade and is greater among youth who are gay (Mason, 2007). The meaning of friendship and how to maintain good relationships without compromising one's values is a topic that many students wish would be discussed more often in their family. Romantic relationships are a problem for those who may break up or are mistreated by their dating partner. Parents who are willing to dialogue about these concerns are respected because it demonstrates that they realize complications that must be taken into account.

In summary, four of the five most often reported worries of adolescents implicate peers. During middle school and high school, peer influence increases and parental influence declines. Still, parent influence continues to be more powerful than peers at every level from fifth through ninth grade. Most teenagers continue to look to their parents for guidance even though Mom and Dad may suppose that because they are no longer the only source of counseling, their advice is not taken seriously.

The study of adolescent worries also reveals many want to talk about their concerns with adults who are important to them. All parents and teachers should be accessible, ready to listen, and respond to issues youth want to discuss. Talking is an effective way to relieve stress because it causes us to feel we are not alone and enables us to organize our thoughts. Whereas talking to oneself often increases stress, talking to someone else can usually reduce stress. Finally, when teachers are creative thinkers, interaction helps adolescents become aware of more alternatives.

## *Sources and Symptoms*

The sources of stress that adolescents identify implicate their life as a whole instead of being limited to particular issues (Kottler & Chen, 2011). The following list includes some of the common conditions that cause adolescent stress.

- Conflict with parents, teachers, or friends
- Rejection from classmates or felt rejection
- Anxiety concerns about abuse from bullies
- Body image (pimples, obesity, thinness)
- Dating (asking someone and being asked)
- Understanding subjects taught in school
- Sexuality (becoming involved or waiting)
- Moving (new school, neighborhood, or town)
- Being the object of prejudice from classmates
- Wearing the same clothing fashions as peers
- Breaking up with a girlfriend or a boyfriend
- Fears about possible international terrorism
- Excessive homework from multiple teachers
- Uncertainty over the choice of an occupation
- Taking illegal drugs and smoking cigarettes
- Feeling bored and lacking a sense of purpose
- Having a continually over-scheduled calendar
- Not getting enough sleep on school nights

The symptoms of stress that get the most attention by teachers and parents are aggressive behavior, destruction of property, bullying, stealing, and other anti-social conduct (Larson & Lochman, 2005). However, mental health professionals have found that these are not the primary symptoms of stress. Such overt behaviors, bothersome as they are, inform others that the perpetrators feel stressed and need help. They may be threatened or feel overburdened but continue to struggle, still try, and with assistance may overcome stress.

The more significant symptoms of stress are depression, withdrawal, and resignation. Students who exhibit these behaviors have quit. Depression is one of the most serious threats to adolescent mental health (Kramer,

2006). It is not just a matter of being moody or living in a difficult environment but these adolescents have given up hope and no longer demonstrate persistence in trying to adjust. Signs of extreme withdrawal is observed when students take illegal drugs, run away from home, skip school, drop out, or commit suicide (Herman, 2009).

When students transition from childhood to adolescence, the conditions of autonomy change. Even though adults continue to sometimes intervene for minimizing stress, teens are increasingly expected to deal with issues of stress on their own. Handling this responsibility can be promoted by discussion in middle school and high school. Students can verbalize problems, state their personal views, and hear solutions that have worked for others. Some guidelines for teachers are:

- Every student should have a chance to contribute to the discussion even when the person is not a fluent speaker or someone who does not boldly take the risk of self-disclosure.
- Situations in which students have actual experience resulting in pleasant or unpleasant emotional reactions are better topics than general issues over which youth lack control.
- The recommended size of a discussion group is three to six members so everyone has an opportunity to participate.
- Teachers should realize that they are not the decision makers or summarizers. Their role is to ensure that everyone in the groups have a chance to speak and be heard.

## Anxiety and Depression

The *Minnesota Multiphasic Personality Inventory* (2013) is a questionnaire to assess personality structure and psychopathology. This instrument has been administered to large samples of college students and adolescents since 1939. During that lengthy period, results have indicated a significant rise in the incidence of anxiety, depression, and other mental disorders. These changes seem more related to the way young people see the world than how the environment has changed. This shift implicates the concept known as locus of control conceived by Julius Rotter (1972), a personality theorist at the University of Connecticut. Rotter devised an assessment tool, the I-E scale, that measures an individual's perception of control along a continuum where internally controlled persons (I) assume their behavior and actions are responsible for what happens to them, whereas externally controlled individuals (E) believe that control is in the hands of other people or outside events.

Research has consistently found that people who score toward the internal end of the I-E Scale have better mental health than those who score at the external end. They are more likely to have work they enjoy, take care of their physical health, have an active role in their communities, and are less likely to be anxious or depressed (Davydov, Stewart, Ritchie, & Chaudiew, 2010). Between 1960–2007 the average scores for 9–14 year olds as well as college students shifted significantly from the Internal to the external end of Rotter's I-E scale. Jean Twenge from San Diego State University and her colleagues who discovered the change speculate that increases in anxiety and depression reflect a general shift from intrinsic to extrinsic goals. *Intrinsic goals* center on personal development issues like developing competence in activities of one's own choosing and formulating a meaningful philosophy for living. In contrast, *extrinsic goals* focus on material rewards and judgments of others making high income, social status, and good looks prominent concerns. The research team of Twenge, Gentile, DeWall, Ma, Lacefield, and Schurtz (2010) provide evidence that young people, on average, embrace extrinsic goals more than did previous generations. This impression is reinforced by a national annual poll of college freshmen showing that most students list "being well off financially" as more important than "developing a meaningful philosophy of life." Sixty years ago the priorities were reversed (Prior, 2007).

When certain chemicals in the brain such as serotonin and dopamine are out of balance, depression can become chronic and require antidepressants to bring chemicals back into balance (Kottler & Chen, 2011). Despite fairly equal gender rates of depression in childhood, the rates change in adolescence as girls become twice as likely to suffer (Rudman & Glick, 2010). The higher risk for females attributes partly to the hormonal changes of puberty, menstruation, menopause, and pregnancy. Fortunately, depression is responsive to intervention during early adolescence and can prevent chronic and severe depression later in early adulthood. However, even though effective treatment is available, less than a third of adolescents with this debilitating condition get care. The proportion of youth who experience depression is double the rate of their parents (Novotney, 2009).

Clinical depression, a persistent sad or irritable mood, is the most frequent mental illness among teenagers. Adults should be observant to detect depression that may be shown by one or more of the following signs: difficulty paying attention and concentrating; drop in school grades; misconduct problems in class; sleep changes leading to fatigue or loss of energy; anti-social or delinquent behavior leading to isolation; self-impression of helplessness, worthlessness, or guilt; continuous feelings of sadness; announcement of suicidal thoughts; extreme sensitivity to rejection or failure;

low self-esteem and lack of confidence; eating problems shown by appetite or weight change; and loss of enjoyment for previously pleasurable activities (Epstein, 2010).

Depressed students are more likely than classmates to engage in high-risk behaviors such as drinking, drug taking, driving drunk, and early sexual involvement (Gonzales, 2012). One of the dangers of being preoccupied by problems related to the present is an inability to place these difficulties within a longer time perspective. When people cannot disengage from their current difficulties, some become depressed and conclude that taking their own life seems to be their only option. During periods of depression, it can be motivating to look back on achievements of the past to restore self-confidence and support continued effort. Adolescents need to think about the range of possible consequences of disappointing events in a more extended time frame that involves the future and not just pain of the moment. Billy Joel composed a song for adolescents in distress, especially those contemplating suicide. His lyrics for "You're only human" illustrate how looking at events from a perspective that includes a hopeful future can enable adolescents to catch their breath and face the world again.

Each year 5,000 adolescents take their lives, making suicide the third leading cause of death among youth (Pompili, 2011). Males account for 80% of suicide completions. Gender differences in self-destruction are perplexing because females are more often diagnosed with depression and attempt to take their lives three times as often as males. But, females complete one in 25 attempts whereas males complete 1 in 3. The most common underlying disorder is depression; 30% to 70% of victims suffer from major depression or bipolar (manic-depressive) disorder. Adolescent males more often express depression by aggression, irritability, anger, and impulsiveness whereas forecast behaviors among female suicides are helplessness, hopelessness, and sadness. The suicide rate for adolescents differs by a factor of 20 between the highest risk group (American Indian/Alaska Native males) and lowest risk group (African American females). Guns account for nearly 70% of self-inflicted deaths. Households in which there are guns have an incidence of suicide that is five times greater than homes where no guns are available.

Family breakdown is the main source of stress to cause self-destruction. Over 70% of youth who attempt suicide live in single parent families (Pompili, 2011). Sexual abuse and intercourse are also factors associated with adolescent suicide. A high positive correlation exists between girls who have been sexually mistreated and those who attempt to take their own life. Deep depression can sometimes follow the breakup of a romance, especially if the couple has been sexually active. Poor self-esteem, drug dependence, absence of religious beliefs and atypical gender preference are also associated with suicidal behavior and these problems are frequently traced to the family. People who suffer sustained feelings of depression and hopelessness are more likely to think about suicide. In most cases they try to describe their feelings and need for professional help. The American Association of Suicidology reports that 80% of adolescents who consider suicide communicate their intention to relatives or other key persons in their life. Unfortunately, this signal of desperation often goes unrecognized or is not taken seriously (Goldston, Molock, Whitbeck, Murakami, Zayas, & Hall, 2008).

### *Parent and Teacher Support*

Children from all backgrounds agree that parents and teachers fail to teach them things they need to know about stress management (Strom, Strom, Strom, Shen, & Beckert, 2004). Some ways parents can help their children cope with daily stress are identified here.

- Arrange time every day for some conversation about child concerns.
- Urge reliance on reflective thinking instead of impulsive reaction.
- Demonstrate patience in waiting while others perform their tasks.
- Set aside relief time for oneself, a lesson that children will observe.
- Make certain that children learn to value having discretionary time.
- Avoid taking over so child gets to set some goals and make plans.
- Learn to observe child stress and encourage amendment of goals.
- Take small breaks so work can be placed in proper perspective.
- Participate in physical exercise so health is a prominent goal.
- Help monitor stress and approve reaching out for assistance.
- Realize a hurried lifestyle makes adults dysfunctional models.
- Teach children a vocabulary of feelings to express themselves.
- Discuss stressful situations of children in books and responses.
- Teach internal locus of control as a basis for interpreting events.
- Encourage fantasy play as a medium to retain a sense of power.
- Model anger management as a life-long asset and protection.
- View challenging situations as opportunities for development.
- Teach empathy by viewing situations from the vantage of others.
- Explain when you feel stressed and tell children how you cope.
- Show children that you are listening by focusing on them only.

Life at school can also produce undue stress for students. Educators should consider the following ways to help students cope with stress.

- Make sure students have time to process new information.
- Alter scheduled assignments when amendment is necessary.

- Use cooperative groups to enlarge the scope of instruction.
- Encourage interdependence and reciprocal learning attitudes.
- Teach Internet search skills to find and organize knowledge.
- Help make connections that bring relevance and application.
- Avoid weekend homework so students can choose activities.
- Teach calming skills like meditation and time for reflection.
- Acknowledge that creative thinking is a tool for adjustment.
- Convey importance of patience as a safeguard against stress.
- Identify and monitor common signs of school-related stress.
- Collaborate with faculty who have the same students in class.
- Detect students with skill deficits and ensure they get tutoring.
- Reduce stress by waiting for answers after questions are asked.
- Discuss the nature of stress and consider ways it can be managed.
- Poll students to determine what they regard as stressful at school.
- Schedule a calming activity such as coloring and quiet time.
- Provide referrals if needed via counselor office or administration.
- Teach study skills and social skills to cope with daily stressors.
- Emphasize prioritizing tasks based on previous commitments.

## Summary and Implications

Stress and emotional health are linked. The pressures youth experience are reflected by common reports of anxiety, frustration, uncertainty, and depression. Exceptions are resilient individuals who see setbacks and failures as opportunities to overcome obstacles and improve their behavior. The optimistic thinking of resilient people motivates them to accept challenges, consistently maintain a positive outlook, and keep on trying when situations become difficult. Resilience is not always related to poverty or contingent on having to overcome significant odds to succeed. Being disadvantaged can occur when parents try to prevent loved ones from exposure to failure in the belief that setbacks undermine self-esteem rather than contribute to personality development.

While positive adaptation is necessary for resilience, sustained stress erodes the capacity to cope with adversity. In situations where stress cannot be eliminated, it is important to arrange a schedule that allows sufficient attention to personal needs including rest, social participation, physical exercise, and pursuit of individual interests. Stresses that continue for long periods lead to elevated cortisol levels that suppress the immune system and thereby increase susceptibility to illness. Mothers are more vulnerable than other groups to high levels of stress because multiple responsibilities for taking care of children, husbands, employers, and managing the household can prevent them from properly looking after themselves. Many parents tend to overestimate their success in helping children learn to cope with daily stress. Being flexible and calm are assets that enable adjustment in situations that present uncertainty and anxiety.

Teachers should observe students for differences in the ways they respond to stress. Advocating an internal locus of control motivates confidence, persistence, and resilience. Schools that recruit mentors provide students with models who can share healthy ways of interpreting events and coping with stress. Teachers can minimize uncertainty by having goals for lessons that are easily understood, clear directions for assignments, examining possibilities and likely consequences before making decisions, and being flexible rather than rigid. Most student worries implicate peers, a situation urging teachers to promote constructive group norms. When students show signs of depression, the school and family should refer them for mental health assessment.

# 5

## *Thinking and Cultures*

Some people believe that because children and adolescents have compulsory schooling, their generation should assume the main burden for adapting to social and technological change. A more promising strategy is to obligate people of every age group to engage in certain aspects of social transformation together. This broader perspective can result in common awareness that cultural harmony and cohesion require continual adjustment by more than a single age segment of society. There is benefit in finding out how other age groups interpret events, recognizing the values they rely on to guide behavior, understanding their vision of the future, and showing a willingness to view them as a valued source of instruction. These conditions define *reciprocal learning*—mutual growth based on consideration of the feelings, ideas, methods, or perspective of another person or group.

Moving from the tradition of hierarchical relationships toward more equitable forms of interaction calls for a significant attitude change. The goals for this chapter are to describe how change influences relationships; why adults should be willing to regard children and adolescents as essential

*Thinking in Childhood and Adolescence*, pages 93–113
Copyright © 2013 by Information Age Publishing
**93**

sources of learning; ways in which reciprocal learning can yield greater productivity while improving relationships in school, at home, and the workplace; guidelines for adolescents who teach adults; and lessons that adolescents expect adults to provide them.

## Generation as Culture

The traditional way of thinking about culture is no longer sufficient because it does not take into account the enormous impact of recent technology and the consequent effect upon social evolution. There was a time when identity was influenced more by family, ethnicity, language, nationality, and religion. In contrast, because of a communications revolution, youth currently are more often exposed to similar experiences that transcend their background. Global media supports far greater influence by the peer group while diminishing the overall effect of adults. Adolescents are more reliant on peers for conversation, feedback, and advice (Kovarik, 2011).

All children adopt some aspects of the culture they are oriented to by their relatives and caregivers. However, because growing up has become so different from one generation to the next, the influence of peers is bound to be a more powerful influence. The lifestyle norms of peers are communicated and reinforced by global social networks and by entertainment media. Consequently, adolescents from Atlanta, Moscow, London, Tokyo, and Sydney may share more opinions with peers than with older members of their family. This means that most children and adolescents resemble their times more than they resemble their parents (Underwood & Rosen, 2011).

When generation is recognized as a more prominent factor in defining culture, the ideas and feelings of youth are seen as deserving careful attention. Accordingly, it seems appropriate for adults to give up their role of acting as advocates for the young in favor of encouraging them to speak for themselves. Young people in hierarchical-oriented societies are still discouraged from expressing opinions that differ from older relatives, educators, or other authority figures. In these circumstances, adolescents who express ideas, feelings, and values that conflict with those of adults are judged as lacking respect for their elders. This constraint to dialogue causes some youth to remain silent which, in turn, misleads adults to suppose the lack of opposition means there is agreement across generations (Dolgin, 2010).

A more promising outlook is to recognize that, if the voices of adolescents are heard, they may be less inclined to discount their legacy or abandon customs that might otherwise be revised and preserved. Discovering student impressions seems to be an essential requisite for uniting the goals of cultural preservation, cultural evolution, and cultural adjustment.

## *Change in a Past-Oriented Culture*

Figure 5.1(a) portrays the conditions that typify life in a past-oriented society. Trace the sphere depicting adult experience. Notice that a large por-

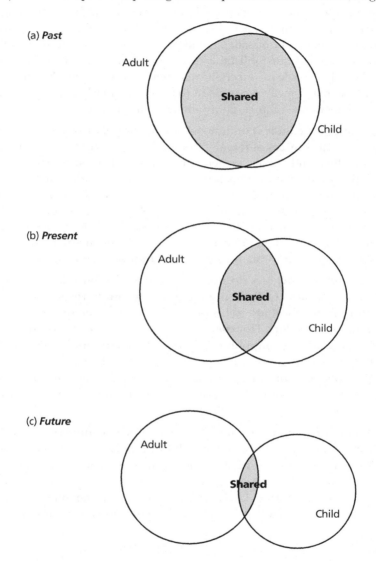

Figure 5.1    Shared Experiences in Past, Present, and Future-Oriented Cultures. (a) Past; (b) Present; and (c) Future. *Source: Adolescents in the Internet Age* by Paris Strom and Robert Strom, 2009, p. 46. Information Age Publishing Inc., Charlotte, NC.

tion of this experience is unfamiliar to children. This is because they have yet to encounter some situations that only occur in adulthood. In contrast, tracing the sphere of child experience shows the adults can remember most of what happens during the years of growing up. The experiences that generations have in common are identified as a shared sector. In a slow changing, static type of environment, parents are expected to socialize their children by conveying to them an unchallenged impression about how to live. Children believe that their future will be a repetition of the past. When things are so predictable, so free of uncertainty, anxiety is uncommon. Freedom from anxiety has great appeal to people in the present era who continually suffer from the experience of uncertainty and exposure to stress.

Past-oriented cultures continue to exist in parts of the world where adults remain the only sources of learning for children and adolescents to rely on. Visitors to the island of Bali, located in Indonesia, can observe parents as they pass on the woodcarving and painting techniques to children that anticipate making a living in the same way. The hands of time also seem to have stopped for some aboriginal tribes in Australia and New Guinea where people are dedicated to perpetuating the customs of ancestors. Religious groups in America like the Amish in Ohio and Pennsylvania retain aspects of a lifestyle that is similar to their forefathers (Kraybill, Johnson-Weiner, & Nolt, 2013).

Past-oriented societies do not recognize adolescence as being a stage in life. Instead, they celebrate initiation rites meant to recognize the transformation from childhood to becoming an adult. Some of these rites may seem cruel to outsiders. However, the result is always elevation from childhood status to the assumption of rights and responsibilities of adulthood. Initiation is no longer a tradition among technological societies where young people are typically uncertain and anxious about their place in the society and have to think about attainment of adult identity for a much longer period of time (Savage, 2008).

Reliance on identity rites and rituals continue in cultures where: (a) children can reasonably expect to have a lifestyle in adulthood that closely resembles their parents, (b) specific gender roles define the division of labor in a family, (c) cultural homogeneity is in place, (d) there is a uniform structure to socialize youth, and (e) life is relatively short with everyone having some predictable roles to fulfill. None of these conditions is common in modern America (Campbell, 2004).

### Change in a Present-Oriented Culture

Something happens when technology is introduced on a large scale and accelerates the pace of living. Social conditions change and traditional lifestyles are permanently modified. In addition, the experiences that adults and children have in common diminish and often result in misunderstandings. More of the childhood experiences in Figure 5.1(b) than in Figure 5.1(a) lie outside the memory of adults. This is because youth are exposed to novel situations that have never happened before to people of their age group. Because adults are too old to know some things firsthand about current youth experience, they need to learn vicariously what it is like to be growing up now.

Even a casual observer of age-segregated communities recognizes that younger groups regard same-age peers as their primary listeners and advisors. Certain benefits can flow from this reliance. However, the arrangement also undermines cultural continuity because it divides the population into special interest groups. As the nearly exclusive emphasis on the past is replaced by greater attention on the present, older adults lose their prominence and are less often seen by youth as sources of knowledge or sought out for advice. Instead, each generation identifies with well-known persons of their same age or next older age group and considers them as models.

### Change in a Future-Oriented Culture

Figure 5.1(c) portrays the current stage of civilization that has widespread reliance on the Internet, cell phones, text messages, instant messaging, email, and iPads. In this era, students go to school at an earlier age and continue their studies for a longer period of time. Their education features digital literacy and ease of access to knowledge that was unavailable during previous generations. Together these changes cause children and adolescents to have a different outlook. This situation urges that outdated requirements for assigning adult status like full-time work and economic independence should be abandoned. Otherwise, if adolescents continue to be denied the recognition that was granted to people of their age in the past, their quest for identity must increasingly center on the only context where it is possible to attain recognition, within their peer culture. Learning in the social context is increasingly defined mostly in terms of being influenced by peers of the same age. Adolescents face similar experiences but also share immaturity and judgment that is less well developed.

The digital divide is the most profound gulf in communication between children and adults throughout history. We proposed a paradigm to guide education and relationships to minimize the scope of the communication gulf (Strom & Strom, 2009). This imperative of teaching adolescents while learning from them is based on four assumptions:

1. Adolescents have unique experiences that qualify them as the most credible source about what going to school and growing up is like at the present time.
2. Adolescents are often more competent than many adults in using the tools of technology that will be necessary for self-directed learning during the future.
3. Adolescents and adults support mutual adjustment by adopting reciprocal learning as a practice that is essential for the development of every age group.
4. The common quest of adolescents for identity as adults is attainable if their knowledge of technology is accepted as one criterion for granting status.

## Benefits of Trading Places

*Freaky Friday* is a movie about 13-year-old Anna and her mother Tess (Gunn, 2003). They disagree on almost everything including fashion, men, and Anna's passion to join a rock band. One night the biggest freak out ever occurs when mother and daughter suddenly undergo a mysterious transformation leaving both women trapped in each other's body. Tess is planning to get married in a few days so they must hurry to find some way for switching back to their own identity. Forced to walk in each other's shoes, the pair learns a lot about one another in a short time.

### Mentors at Work

The concept of mentoring was first described in Greek mythology. When Odysseus left home to fight in the Trojan War, he asked his friend, Mentor, to take over the responsibility of educating his son Telemachus. Currently a *mentor* is defined as someone who acts as a trusted advisor, tutor, coach, counselor, and faithful friend. A common practice in business and industry is to provide new employees with a mentor, typically someone of middle age who understands company expectations, procedures, and worries of workers. This practice reflects the belief that experienced employees possess valuable insights; seniority includes a responsibility to share knowledge with newly hired colleagues; advice from veterans minimizes costly mistakes; and interdependence is communicated as essential for success of individuals, teams, and employer (Allen, Finkelstein, & Poteet, 2009).

Although employers have recognized the benefits of arranging conversations between new employees and mentors, many have given less attention to the merits of reverse mentoring. The concept of *reverse mentoring* involves turning around the usual relationship by which an older person mentors someone younger. In effect, shifting the roles or trading places is required. Reverse mentoring first received national attention after an experiment conducted by the General Electric Corporation. Jack Welch, Chief Executive Officer, realized that his senior executives were unfamiliar with tools of technology needed for effective communication in the emerging cyber environment. Instead of sending management officials back to school or arrange expensive training for them, Welch paired 500 of his top leaders with younger workers who had recently joined the company. The task younger workers were given was to teach their senior colleagues how to navigate the Internet and speed up interaction by using electronic mail (Welch & Welch, 2005). This shift in roles acknowledged the greater technology skills of young adults, confirmed for them that the company valued these assets, and called upon upper-level managers to see their younger mentors as important sources of learning. This successful experiment introduced the continuous practice of sharing expertise, and improved productivity of the company. Since then many businesses have adopted the General Electric reverse mentoring model and confirmed that it increases profitability (Grant, 2013).

Career exploration is a powerful source of motivation for most adolescents. Researching occupations, identifying skills required for positions, and thinking about relative advantages and difficulties of particular work paths should begin in middle school. The impact that middle-age mentors can have on adolescent students is strong even if the parties never meet face-to-face but interact on the Internet. A prominent example of the way influence of online mentors can foster career awareness including recognition of characteristics needed for job success is known as the Computer Clubhouse. Boston's Museum of Science and the Media Laboratory at Massachusetts Institute of Technology operate the joint venture. This center and 75 others throughout the world, provide youth in underserved communities with a rich after-school environment where they can explore career choices, acquire job-related skills, and acquire confidence about what it takes to perform well on the job. Students select a mentor after a review of biographical sketches that include visuals prepared by the adult volunteers who are willing to dialogue with them. All the mentors have successful careers, and most are middle aged. The mentors convey the importance of integrity, civility, and time management. They also emphasize the need to develop resilience as a basis for coping with disappointment, ways to support harmony, and the value of reflective thinking (Kafai, Peppler, & Chapman, 2009).

## Mentors at School

Tools of technology can motivate students to question, challenge, and disagree, thereby increasing their potential to become critical thinkers. The Internet encourages students to read, conduct searches for information, respond to messages, interact with friends or relatives, and acquire teamwork skills. Because children and adolescents enjoy being on the Internet, this tool could be used to motivate those whose dislike of school prevents them from paying attention, completing assignments, and performing well. The Internet has great potential to make life in school and homework satisfying for more students.

For the first time in history, many students possess greater skills with tools needed for learning in the future than their adult teachers. This unprecedented lag in proficiency of adults presents students with frustrating situations. Many of them report that life online after school hours is disconnected from the instructional methods teachers depend on in class. Middle age teachers, the largest cohort, grew up before the communications revolution. They commonly concede that their lesser technology skills and the prevailing emphasis on high-stakes testing combine to prevent greater use of the Internet for instruction and assignments (Rosen, 2010).

The Olympic school district located in suburban Seattle, Washington wanted to integrate technology with the curriculum at all grade levels. Teachers agreed schools have been slow to embrace innovation, mainly because the learning methods that students prefer are ignored. The solution began with a federal grant received in 1995 that was called Generation YES (Youth and Educators Succeeding). Dennis Harper, the Olympic technology leader, has been the Director of Generation YES (2012) from the outset. The project intention was to apply reverse mentoring by pairing students with partner-teachers in school. These student–teacher teams work together in planning a curriculum unit that can be enhanced by a technology application. The history of the project and opportunities for other districts to become involved is available at genyes.org. Teachers provide knowledge about a topic, awareness of learning needs, and steps to guide lessons. The student is expected to contribute some visual element to make the instructional presentation appealing and more easily understood. This collaborative creation becomes part of a curriculum presented by the partner-teacher. The process allows student partners to practice and refine computer skills for practical application while gaining interdependence experience needed for employment. The advantage for teachers is access to technology support that compliments direct instruction and the ability to learn new skills from their younger mentor.

Exciting technologies are emerging at such a rapid rate that teachers are unable to keep up. Reverse mentoring allows teachers to benefit from how fast students learn the latest technical skills and how willing the adolescents are to assume a mentor role. Professional development has relied on instructional specialists to train teachers during in service sessions in the hope that this method will translate into improved learning. The favorable experiences of the Olympia school district suggest that much more can be gained by the use of reverse mentoring (Generation YES, 2012). Allowing students to practice technology skills and enhance instruction can improve learning and reduce boredom.

The optimal reverse mentor relationship should be further explored since it could provide clues about how teacher–student interaction should evolve in the future. Each party participates in setting goals as a basis to guide their collaboration. A curriculum lesson requires both to share complimentary strengths reflecting interdependence. The teacher does not control the student but instead conveys freedom and trust that is essential for teamwork. Student and teacher alternate in taking responsibility for leadership. This sharing of dominance is a departure from the custom in which the teacher is always the leader.

Over 1,200 schools have adopted the Generation YES (2012) model for integration of technology with curriculum. This kind of on-the-job technology training in which teachers participate in reverse mentoring with tech-savvy students has proven to be an effective way for promoting education reform. Classroom experience should become more interactive, collaborative, and related to life applications. These outcomes are more likely if teachers recognize the possibilities of applying a team problem solving approach, are willing to alternate leadership, and relinquish control in favor of support for student self-directed learning. Students are the most enthusiastic advocates for reverse mentoring.

### Mentors at Home

The inversion of authority has modified some of the dialogue between adolescents and their parents. Both groups recognize that youth are more competent in using technology tools. Researchers at Carnegie Mellon University in Pittsburgh carried out an experiment to find out how this factor changes communication and relationships. There were 170 subjects from 73 middle class homes in Pittsburgh. All of the families included an adolescent and received a free computer with Internet access. None of the families had previously been connected. During the orientation, researchers explained that computers would be remotely monitored to find out how often they were used, length of time that was spent online, and sites visited but not the content. At several month intervals parents and teenagers completed surveys that described self-defined computer skills, amount of time spent together online, and how often they helped one another solve computer problems.

Monitoring detected that, on average, the time teenagers spent online was six times greater than their parents. Adolescents received ten times as much electronic mail as parents and explored the Internet to a greater extent. Another source of data were videotapes made during home visits to observe how each family used their computer. Researchers did not help when participants they were watching experienced technical difficulties. Problems were rampant in 89% of families where the usual reaction of adults reflected helplessness. Grownups offered a broad range of excuses for their inability to solve computer problems. On the other hand, teenagers seldom complained in facing difficulties and experimented until completing tasks (Kraut, Brynin, & Kiesler, 2006).

Everyone was invited to phone the Home Net line anytime to obtain assistance. However, the adults were more inclined to turn to daughters and sons for guidance. If adolescents were not home, adults usually chose to abandon a task rather than make their needs known and seek support from the Home Net. Those who phoned the help desk most often were teens, the same people who demonstrated the best performance. It appears that individuals possessing the most skill realize what they do not yet know and exhibit more confidence in challenging themselves to try ever-more-difficult tasks. Knowledge trickled upward in a majority of the families as teenagers claimed the most authority, acting as consultants to their parents.

## Principles Related to Role Shifting

### The Concept of Role Shifting

One way to reduce the risks that are associated with authority inversion is by helping adolescents acquire attributes that characterize good teachers. Possession of a skill does not necessarily mean someone is able to communicate that particular asset to others. Patience and encouragement are implicated in teacher effectiveness with students of all ages. In contrast, impatience and lack of feedback can erode the motivation of students who mentor and cause them to doubt their capacity to teach. The Home Net study revealed that adults are frequently more inclined than adolescents to give up when confronted by an unfamiliar learning situation that involves technology tools. For this reason, adolescents expected to teach grownups should understand that emotional support is essential in order for the adult learners to remain willing to keep trying after they experience setbacks and failure (Kraut, Brynin, & Kiesler, 2006).

## Challenges for Adult Considerations

Discovering opportunities for adults and adolescents to trade places in the teacher role is going to be a challenge from now on. Success requires experimentation with new methods of instruction enabling more equitable relationships. Eight challenges are presented for reflection.

1. *Reciprocal learning can enable society to grant adult identity status to youth.* There is general agreement that a well-defined role is needed to have a favorable sense of identity. This is especially important in adolescence when the common goal is working toward being accepted as an adult and gaining an individual sense of meaning, purpose, and direction (Temple, 2006). Nevertheless, permitting youth to have a significant place in society appears more difficult in a technological setting than during previous times. The customary procedure has been for society to bestow status when young people are hired for a full time job, get married, become a parent, or no longer need financial help from the family. However, these conditions occur later than in the past. The extensive schooling needed to prepare for employment along with a high cost of living often necessitates continued economic support from parents, even after young adults have a full-time position.

   Adolescents rely on technology for conversations with friends. These same tools can expand the social context for youth identity through interaction with adult mentors, relatives, community leaders, elders, and persons from other cultures. Efforts to enlarge the contextual base of identity acknowledge that the emerging social self could be too narrow if it is defined exclusively by interaction with peers online or face-to-face dialogue with one's own generation. Generally, it is appropriate to credit adolescents for having technology skills needed for learning and job performance in the future and accept this asset as a criterion for granting identity status.

   Robert Epstein shares the impression that teenagers and some young adults are unfairly denied identity status. Epstein (2010) explores fallacies in the way adults see youth as incapable of responsibility, to be shielded from tasks of adulthood, and unable to make reasoned decisions. He argues that society has forgotten how capable young people can be but adolescents are aware of their potential and feel frustrated. The new equation for identity status that youth seek considers competence with technology tools. This is more reasonable than insisting on conditions that are no longer attainable and motivate excessive reliance on peers for communication and respect.

2. *Sharing dominance is an essential aspect of reciprocal learning, allowing the other person to sometimes assume the leadership role.* Successful relationships are characterized by shared dominance instead of unilateral control based on age, gender, or rank. People who prize and rely on strengths of one another develop a partnership. Before the Internet adults were rarely in a position to consider youth as possible sources for learning. Grownups should strive to show maturity and humility recognizing that, in many situations, hierarchy is unreasonable.

3. *Listening is fundamental to reciprocal learning.* Students are told and reminded they should listen to teachers because this behavior will influence how much they learn. Ironically, divided attention and distraction of teachers is a concern. A nationwide study of achievement used results from National Assessment of Educational Progress (NAEP) measures. Results showed that students in the lowest 10% of the school population made good improvement in test scores between 2000–2007. In contrast, students in the highest achieving 10% did not improve much (Duffert, Farkas, & Loveless, 2008).

To probe for possible reasons why gains were made by one group but not the other, 900 teachers from grades 3–12 were surveyed. These teachers reported that, because of No Child Left Behind testing mandates, many school administrators have made struggling students the top priority at their school. Most teachers, 81%, agreed this meant low achievers are more likely to get one on one attention in their classroom. The teachers (92%) felt that the right thing is to give equal attention to all students, regardless of their achievement level. These contradictory views indicate that teachers are conflicted about the differences between what they believe and the way they are expected to behave (Duffert, Farkas, & Loveless, 2008). When the parents of average or higher achieving students are informed by their children that attention from the teacher is unequal, they are disappointed and sometimes transfer their student to a private institution where teachers are expected to show greater equality of attention to everyone.

4. *Teaching includes evaluation of learning.* Trusting students to participate in peer and self-evaluation of group dynamics is necessary. Teachers cannot know the interaction in multiple teams and how students teach their peers. Cooperative learning provides an ideal environment for comparison of self-impressions with the observations provided by teammates. The ability to self-evaluate helps people know when to think well of themselves and when to change behavior so their actions more closely resemble the person they wish to become. Students complete the Teamwork Skills Inventory that involves peer and self-evaluation regarding 25 team skills easily detected after interaction for a reasonable period of interaction and observation. Each student receives an individual profile with anonymous feedback from teammates on personal strengths and learning needs (Strom & Strom, 2011a).

5. *There are many adults who overestimate their willingness to learn from adolescents.* The Parent Success Indicator reports perceptions of two generations—parents and children ages 10–14. This instrument identifies views about the role performance of mothers and fathers. One item on the adult version states, "I am good at learning from my child." Optional responses include always, often, seldom, and never. The corresponding version showing adolescent observations states, "My parent is good at learning from me." Significant differences were identified in generational responses of several thousand adults and adolescents from Japan; Republic of China; and Black, Hispanic, and White families in the United States. For all these cultures, adolescents gave unfavorable ratings to their parents for learning from children while most parents rated themselves favorably as willing to learn (Beckert, Strom, Strom, Yang, & Singh, 2007; Strom, Strom, Strom, Makino, & Morishima, 2000; Strom, Strom, Strom, Shen, & Beckert, 2004).

6. *Reciprocal learning is facilitated by mutual awareness of possible benefits.* Providing feedback to adolescents on their instruction helps them realize the favorable influence they can have on others, motivates improvement of how well they teach, and encourages them to provide similar feedback to their own teachers at home and in the classroom. Teenagers are accustomed to frequent feedback on the computer so they crave this kind of response from adults. However, few recognize how feedback can motivate classroom teachers to continue their difficult tasks and sustain enjoyment in their job. Students and parents honored teachers more often in the past, a bygone custom that should be restored.

By trading places in the teacher role, adolescents can better appreciate the problems educators encounter as they try to arrange learning for individual students who collectively present a broad range of performance levels.

7. *Students should be invited to express opinions about the conditions of learning at their school.* Educators sometimes rely on focus groups as a method to gauge student views. However, focus groups can require a high risk for identified students who state negative impressions. In addition, focus groups do not fully represent the broad range of opinions in a student population. School improvement is more likely when electronic anonymous polling is applied to determine the ways of learning students prefer and perceived obstacles to achievement. Accordingly, student polling should occur on a regular basis to assess feelings of adolescents about quality of their education.

8. *Reciprocal learning should be fostered for every student when assigned homework to support interdependence.* Individuals can be assigned as one member of their team to examine particular websites. Specific tasks could include summarizing content, identifying material to augment course curriculum, and describing implications drawn from reading. These tasks appeal to students because they prefer to work online, like to share knowledge that classmates and their teacher have not acquired, recognize others depend on them to provide an accurate report, and observe greater learning occurs when each student is accountable as an educator (Prensky, 2010).

### *Guidelines for Adolescents as Teachers*

By middle school, most students gradually surpass their adult relatives in technology skills. The resulting deficit in the competence of adults should not be regarded as a put down. Instead, young people should be helped to carry out their emerging responsibility for trading places in providing instruction. Students should discuss the following guidelines to prepare for their opportunities to become effective teachers of adults.

1. *Adults prefer teachers who demonstrate patience by not rushing their lessons.* When learners feel hurried, the usual outcome is less comprehension. If enough time is arranged to practice newly acquired skills, satisfaction and success are likely to become more common.

2. *While explaining sequential steps in a task, illustrate using slow transitions between steps.* Always describe your behavior in the manner that sports commentators do when they tell fans about how a

particular play was executed. This strategy allows adult learners to observe and understand a series of actions for doing a task.

3. *Repeat examples several times to allow greater opportunity for observation.* People of all ages rely on observation as an important method for learning. Sometimes teachers who know particular processes well may think of them as simple, so they provide students an abbreviated explanation that causes the learners to become confused or suppose these processes cannot be understood.

4. *Monitor adult learner behavior and provide favorable feedback when a task is done correctly by saying, "You did it; that's the correct way."* When behavior is incorrect, ask the person to try again while you watch and figure out possible sources of error and then explain how to make the correction.

5. *Arrange situations where the adult is given enough time and opportunity to go through a process several times.* Continue to supervise the actions until the person is able to complete the task repeatedly without making any errors.

6. *Ask the adult to explain the steps in doing a task that you have taught.* Tell the person to provide reasons for each of the actions they mention. All students need to go beyond just memorizing to demonstrate understanding that can be verified by an accurate explanation.

7. *Encourage the continued effort that is needed to become computer literate and motivated to stay up-to-date.* Bear in mind that some adults may be inclined to give up after failure with technology tasks so offering emotional support to them is important.

8. *Recognize that a common problem of adolescent teachers is showing an adult how to do a task without insisting the person then perform the same process while you watch.* Modeling how to do something without engaging the learner is meant to save time but the usual outcome is continued and unnecessary dependence.

9. *Invite questions to find out what the person finds confusing or wants to know more about a specific task.* Good teachers of every age group encourage questions in order to detect learning needs that observers may be unable to see.

10. *Speak clearly and take your time because adults often process information more slowly than adolescents.* Explain terms because beginners may not know as much about the language associated with use of computers.

11. *All adolescents should be involved with reverse mentoring, including those living in hierarchical cultures where adults prefer traditional*

**TABLE 5.1 Performance of Adolescent Teachers: Feedback From Adults They Teach**

| Adolescent Teacher Performance | Feedback from Adults (Check behaviors consistently demonstrated by this teacher) |
|---|:---:|
| Encourages learner to try again after making a mistake. | ☐ |
| Carefully shows the steps needed to complete a process. | ☐ |
| Detects errors by watching learner show and explain steps. | ☐ |
| Recommends practice while continuing to act as observer. | ☐ |
| Keeps learner actively engaged instead of in a passive role. | ☐ |
| Gives honest feedback about how well the learner is doing. | ☐ |
| Accepts the pace that is most comfortable for the learner. | ☐ |
| Allows time for reflection after a question has been asked. | ☐ |
| Invites learner to judge the progress that s/he is making. | ☐ |
| Willing to acknowledge things s/he does not understand. | ☐ |
| Does not get discouraged when the rate of progress is slow. | ☐ |
| Conveys belief in learner ability to understand the lesson. | ☐ |
| Welcomes questions about aspects of learning process. | ☐ |
| Gives full attention to the learner and avoids distractions. | ☐ |
| Enjoys teaching and providing guidance to adult learners. | ☐ |
| Offers logical reasons to explain the ways things are done. | ☐ |
| Speaks clearly and uses words that are easily understood. | ☐ |
| Allows learner to set some goals that will guide teaching. | ☐ |
| Is organized and well prepared to provide the instruction. | ☐ |
| Uses visuals to urge interest and support comprehension. | ☐ |

*criteria to grant status of identity and are less willing to trade places.* In these situations, the youth strategy should be to express a willingness to teach as well as affirm their belief that adults can learn.

12. *Discover the satisfactions of teaching and find enjoyment in this leadership role.* Students of every age can tell when a teacher likes working with them.

13. *Teaching can be improved by feedback from students.* In the case of adolescents as teachers, Table 5.1 provides an evaluation form for use by the adults they mentor.

## Broaden the Scope of Learning

### *Lessons Adolescents Expect From Adults*

A growing proportion of adults who are willing to learn from adolescents is evidence of progress. At the same time, adolescents recognize their own need to learn important life lessons from grownups. Parents and teachers try to establish appropriate expectations for detection of student learning needs, assessment of development, and recognition of achievement. Reciprocal learning requires adults to find out and consider adolescent views about their educational needs. Extensive studies with the Parent Success Indicator completed by 10–14 year olds have shown that adults are not teaching certain lessons that are known to be essential for success (Strom & Strom, 2009). Adults need to improve instruction related to the following learning needs identified by students.

1. Present continuous lessons about how to manage daily stresses.
2. Be listeners who pay careful attention by avoiding distractions.
3. Illustrate self-control by showing up for appointments on time.
4. Model healthy nutrition and maintain exercise on a regular basis.
5. Discuss concerns about how to deal with friendships and dating.
6. Show goal-setting behavior that sets an example of self-direction.
7. Help with reviewing progress toward goals and amending them.
8. Encourage time alone for reflection and creative thinking.
9. Demonstrate how to disagree in a way that is civil and respectful.
10. Establish an environment that is safe, supportive, and satisfying.
11. Confirm the importance of trust as a basis for close relationships.
12. Apply teamwork skills that are needed at work and in the home.
13. Rely on reciprocal learning as a way to enrich personal relationships.
14. Dialogue about possible occupations as well as alternative lifestyles.
15. Hold youth accountable for misconduct and correction of behavior.
16. Monitor and give feedback about progress toward personality goals.
17. Confront challenges by using careful planning, hope, and optimism.

18. Detect causes of personal failure and follow up with renewed effort.
19. Give the highest priority for having a schedule to spend time together.
20. Be fair and honest to confirm the value of trustworthiness.
21. Disclose personal goals and invite youth to help evaluate progress.
22. Model the resiliency that is needed in order to overcome adversity.
23. Continue personal development so as to remain a lifelong learner.
24. Devote time to volunteer efforts in order to improve the community.
25. Respect privacy but monitor the actions and whereabouts of youth.
26. Receive encouragement, love, and show a genuine sense of caring.

## *Parent Role Requires Education*

Communities should acknowledge that parent education is needed to help improve their unique sphere of influence. One aspect of this orientation is to devise and provide a curriculum that enables families to better meet the education needs of adolescent daughters and sons as they have been defined by youth. Just as students should continue to learn beyond high school for success at the workplace, parents should also become accountable for learning that allows them to remain an effective source of guidance for their children as they progress through the grades from kindergarten through grade 12.

## *Homework for Students and Parents*

Learning from teachers and peers in the classroom should be expanded to include reciprocal learning at home with parents. This prospect depends on teacher initiatives to develop creative homework that stimulates dialogue between students and parents while learning from each other. Educators perform poorly in this context and have to improve for the benefit of all parties. Table 5.2 presents an example of a partially completed assignment for students at the middle-school level. The purpose of this assignment is for adolescents and parent(s) to find out about some historical event that took place within the parent's lifetime. Parents begin by identifying their date of birth so a student can select events from a timeframe mom or dad can remember. Student and parent then separately devise a list of three to five possible events to explore together. After they examine each other's list, one event is agreed upon for the focus. Next, the student goes online to search for data about that event and keeps a record of the URLs visited. Then the student orally presents what s/he has found out to the parent. The student also prepares three to four questions to ask the parent(s) so s/he can share personal recollections about the event. Following their interview the parent is encouraged to share additional informa-

---

**TABLE 5.2  A Partially Completed Homework Assignment for Middle Schools Students and Their Parents**

**Student Assignment**

Student Name _____ Historical Event Chosen _____

*My list of 3 to 5 possible events we could share include:*
- International access of the public for use of the Internet
- Beatles British Rock group arrives in the United States
- Women joining the workforce during the '80s and '90s
- 9/11 Destruction of the Twin Towers in New York City
- Neal Armstrong is the first man to walk on the moon

*These were the four questions used to interview my parent.*
- How old were you when this event happened?
- What were your feelings about it at that time?
- How do you view the event as you look back?
- How did the other people you knew respond?

*My parent (s) description of the event is summarized as follows:*
- Aspects of my parent's explanation that helped understand the event were:
- The things learned from my parent but not found on the Internet search were:
- The things learned from online sources that were not in my parent's report were:
- The one thing I want to remember about this event and my reasoning for it is:
- The things I was able to teach my parent that s/he did not know before were:

Parent Name _____ Historical Event _____

*My list of 3 possible events that we can explore include:*
- 9/11 tragedy of the Twin Towers terrorism in New York City.
- Martin Luther King civil rights speech on "I have a dream."
- Death of the rock and roll musical legend Michael Jackson

*This is a summary of my child's description of the event based on her/his research.*
- How do I feel about the reliability and accuracy of the online sources on which my child relied?
- What differences exist between my child's research results and my memory of the event?
- What new things did I learn from my child's presentation regarding the particular event?
- How do I feel about periodic use of this kind of homework that involves two generations?

---

tion that may not have been covered by student questions. Besides facts, parents should express opinion, memories, feelings, and reactions to the event. Students and parents complete a form the student brings to class for sharing before submission to the teacher.

## Summary and Implications

In past-oriented societies change occurs so slowly that children are able to view their future by observing the lives of parents and grandparents. Therefore, the focus for most learning is historical and adults represent the nearly exclusive source of education. In contrast, change is relatively rapid in a present-oriented society. As a result, a large proportion of the population prefer learning from their same age group or persons who have experience with circumstances that resemble their own. In future-oriented societies that are driven by technology, children and adolescents are exposed to situations never before encountered by people of their age.

Trading places offers possibilities to go beyond the limitations of traditional instruction, improve communication and respect across generations, support better adjustment to new ways of thinking and doing things, and create a society where interdependence and harmony are more common. Nevertheless, trading places can be difficult because reciprocal learning contradicts the attitudes and behaviors parents were taught while growing up and may be unwilling to abandon. Arranging opportunities for trading places at work, in the classroom, and in the home can help define a broader vision of human development and learning.

Parents are critical about the quality of schools their children attend but seem less critical of their own learning needs. Instead of complaining that adolescents spend too much of their time communicating with peers, adults should grant the identity status adolescents deserve based on competencies with technology tools essential for learning in the future. In addition, adults should expect far more interaction with youth by using current communication tools. In many homes, family members are so preoccupied by daily tasks they fail to arrange time for conversations and doing things together. Access to sensible guidelines for teaching and learning from each other can enable adults and adolescents to leave behind customary hierarchical relationship in favor of more equitable dialogue that respects the strengths and limitations of both generations. Getting to know daughters and sons is necessary to provide advice they consider relevant.

Reciprocal learning often depends on the preferences valued most by teachers. Because adolescents are highly motivated by technology, they favor mentoring in this context. The focus may include skills where the competencies of students exceed adults such as surfing the Internet, skimming text, visual–spatial skills, and multitasking. In contrast, adults often have a different set of assets that could support development. Providing a consistent example of extended attention span, concentrating without distraction, finding value in reading entire books, withdrawing from electronic stimuli to reflect and gain perspective, and processing failure to develop resilience can support acquisition of greater knowledge, inductive analysis, critical thinking, imagination, creativity, and adjustment. Perhaps the greatest value of reciprocal learning, based on differing age group orientations, can be a mutual willingness to acquire important survival attitudes and skills that are possessed by the other generation.

# 6

## *Thinking and Curiosity*

The most visible evidence that someone lacks mental stimulation is a failure to ask questions. Parents seldom recognize when the decline in this behavior begins and therefore may not help children become aware that generating questions is necessary for a good education. A common challenge of teachers is enabling students to feel comfortable in admitting confusion and being willing to seek guidance about lessons and concerns they do not understand. Solving problems often depends on asking questions and then applying rational procedures to determine answers. The French philosopher, Voltaire (1694–1778), recommended that people "Judge a man by his questions, not his answers." This advice implies that adults should help children retain their early sense of curiosity by recognizing questions as a form of achievement. By this strategy students can be credited for asking questions as well as for giving answers (Redman, 1977).

The goals of this chapter are to consider the relationship between asking questions and self-directed learning. Curiosity and doubt are discussed as being powerful sources of motivation that lead the way to logical and critical thinking. Attention is also given to the kinds of questions teachers

*Thinking in Childhood and Adolescence,* pages 117–134
Copyright © 2013 by Information Age Publishing
**117**

ask, priority for types of thinking in the classroom, and ways television can be used to support curiosity and establish a strategy for reciprocal learning.

## Role of Questions in Learning

### *Importance of Curiosity and Doubt*

Presenting students questions that motivate them to concentrate and think deeply was considered by Plato as the foundation skill for teachers (Plato & Rowe, 2012). In *The Republic,* Plato (427–347 BC) described how Socrates would provide his students a series of probing questions to engage them in critical thinking, and, eventually help them to attain understanding. The progression of steps, called the Socratic method, remains an approach used by teachers of all grade levels to evaluate student comprehension and detect lessons that have yet to be learned.

Fifteen hundred years after Plato's observations about the importance of questions, Peter Abelard (1079–1142) established the University of Paris in France. By all accounts he was an extraordinary teacher whose students included 20 cardinals, 50 archbishops, and a Pope (Celestin II). Abelard's assertion that reason and religious belief could coexist was a departure from the prevailing authority worship of his era. A book that he wrote entitled *Yes and No* presented 158 questions, all related to *The Bible* verses (Abelard, 1121/2007). For each question Abelard described conflicting views that were expressed by theological authorities. He explained that, regardless of the elevated status held by religious commentators, their words should not be believed without examining their logic. Because God is the creator of reason, then reason is the tool that he wants mankind to rely on rather than having to look to celebrities for answers. Abelard felt that when authorities disagree, deciding about the source to believe should not favor the speaker with the greatest reputation but instead the individual whose logic and reasoning is the most persuasive. Abelard suggested that common people, most of whom could not read or write, should reach their own decisions and recognize their potential to become critical thinkers, long before this expectation was thought to be possible or appropriate.

Abelard argued that truth cannot be at variance with itself. Because the truth of reason and revelation come from the same God, there must be a defect in the reasoning of mankind or some mistake in theological citations when the views expressed by religious authorities conflict. His *Yes and No* questions were viewed as offensive to the authority-loving-and-quoting scholars because it made transparent the confusion and irreconcilable statements for most of the 158 biblical questions. It was also disquieting to conservative thinkers who did not foresee that reasoning was going to be on the side of revelation.

Abelard was persecuted for stating that doubt can be valuable because it motivates curiosity, questioning, and creativity. When people ask certain questions they are more able to perceive the truth. Abelard saw curiosity as a key for personal enlightenment. In contrast, the traditional outlook was that only authorities possessed the truth. Therefore, to doubt them was considered as a sign of distrust, unacceptable to God and those who represent him in the church hierarchy.

## Taxonomy of Educational Objectives

John Carroll (1963), at the University of Chicago, challenged the notion that the rate at which students gain knowledge reflects their capacity to learn. He hypothesized that most students can learn what schools expect of them but differ in the amount of time and help that is needed to learn. Carroll speculated that if teachers were to allow enough time and made sure that time is spent on a task, instructional goals could more often be attained. When all students are expected to learn in the same amount of time, those who are slow will be unable to meet the goals. Benjamin Bloom, who was also on the faculty at University of Chicago, found Carroll's premise appealing and incorporated it into the concept of performance objectives as part of his theory of mastery learning. Bloom believed that it is possible to analyze any sequence of learning steps into specific objectives and teach them in a way that enables most students to develop their thinking capacity and meet the school requirements for graduation. Bloom and his colleagues formulated the *Taxonomy of Educational Objectives* to serve as a conceptual outline for teachers to order and reorder their tasks to ensure instruction and student thinking are not restricted to the lowest levels of the cognitive domain but also include exercise in higher order thinking (Bloom, Englehart, First, Hill, & Krathwohl 1956).

## Lower and Higher Order Thinking

Bloom's (1976) six levels of performance objectives in the taxonomy include the following:

1. *Knowledge* is the lowest level of learning outcomes, defined as the ability of students to recall facts, names, dates, principles, or other information conveyed during class or in textbooks.

2. *Comprehension* goes beyond the recollection of knowledge in being able to translate meaning by explaining concepts, interpreting data, summarizing material, and predicting consequences.
3. *Application* refers to solving new and unfamiliar problems by recognizing the implications of specific rules, methods, concepts, principles, laws, or theories provided by comprehension.
4. *Analysis* requires recognizing relationships, organizational principles, and implications. These outcomes transcend comprehension and application because they require understanding of both the content and structural forms of knowledge.
5. *Synthesis* is the ability to reconstruct data by creating a new whole portrayal such as a unique communication (theme or speech), plan (research proposal), or set of relationships (scheme for classifying information).
6. *Evaluation* is the highest level of thinking that requires ability to assess the value of material (novel, statement, report) by using internal criteria (organization) or external criteria (relevance to a purpose). Evaluation outcomes are the highest in the taxonomy because they contain elements of all other categories plus conscious value judgments based on clearly defined criteria.

The kinds of thinking that students are encouraged to practice is reflected by their tests in class. When a test covers each of the cognitive levels of the Taxonomy, students are allowed to demonstrate the full range of thinking abilities and reveal what they have learned. An example for each type of teacher question showing successive taxonomy levels is illustrated in Table 6.1.

## Assessment in the Classroom

### Teacher Questions and Student Thinking

The questions teachers ask have been the focus of many studies. Productive questions include Bloom's taxonomy levels of application, analysis, synthesis, and evaluation. Together these types of inquiry represent higher order thinking. The use of productive questions provides opportunities for students to create, apply, analyze, and evaluate. In contrast, reproductive questions emphasize only memory and comprehension. They represent lower order thinking and can frequently be found at the end of chapters in textbooks for purposes of content review.

The positive influence of productive questions on achievement has been examined. Generally, the impact ranges from 12–27 percentile points on norm referenced tests (NRT) by students whose teachers consistently rely on

**TABLE 6.1 Cognitive Levels of Bloom's Taxonomy of Educational Objectives With Teacher Questions Reflecting Lower- and Higher-Order Thinking**

| Cognitive Levels | Behavioral Evidence | Teacher Questions |
|---|---|---|
| *Knowledge* of facts, terms, procedures, basic concepts, principles, and theories | Defines, describes, identifies, labels, lists, matches, names, outlines, selects, reproduces | Who was the scholar who began the formal study of adolescence? |
| *Comprehends* and translates material, interprets graphs, uses procedures correctly | States, explains, illustrates, distinguishes, summarizes, paraphrases, infers, predicts | How does adolescence now differ from the experience of previous generations? |
| *Application* of concepts and principles to practical problems faced in unfamiliar situations | Computes, modifies, discovers, demonstrates, produces, solves, relates, justifies, operates | How should cell phones be used by teachers to improve parent awareness about behavior of students? |
| *Analysis* recognizes unstated assumptions, logical fallacies, distinguish fact and inference | Differentiates, breaks down parts, diagrams, discriminates, separates | What factors contribute to a lack of education classes for parents of adolescents? |
| *Synthesis* by a well-organized speech/paper, formulate a new method for classifying ideas | Categorizes, combines, revises, compiles, designs, generates, reconstructs, plans, organizes | Prepare a paper about polling as a method to improve the school learning environment. |
| *Evaluation* of judging how well the data supports conclusions, judging value of art or music or writing with external criteria | Appraises, compares, contrasts, criticizes, explains, discriminates, justifies, interprets, summarizes, describes, concludes, justifies | How effective is education in helping students learn to assess teamwork skills of teammates? |

*Source:* Adapted from Bloom, B., Englehart, M., Furst, E., Hill, W., & Krathwohl, D. (Eds.) (1956). *Taxonomy of Educational Objectives: The Classification of Educational Goals, Handbook I: Cognitive Domain.* New York, NY: McKay.

use of productive questions compared to those whose teachers do not regularly pose such questions. Meta-analyses have discovered that a majority of the questions asked by teachers at all grade levels fall into the reproductive category. One study analyzed 18,000 questions teachers asked: 14,400 questions, or over 75% of them, excluded opportunities for students to demonstrate productive thinking (Tienken, Goldberg, & DiRocco, 2009).

For several generations studies have consistently found that, at all grade levels including higher education, teachers overemphasize knowledge (taxonomy level 1) and comprehension (level 2) while giving inadequate attention to higher cognitive levels of application (taxonomy level 3), analysis (level 4), synthesis (level 5), and evaluation (level 6) in questions for class discussion and tests (Krathwohl, 2002). Educators should recognize that questions from students are discouraged or encouraged by peers depending on how they view learning. Teachers can explain that creativity and asking questions are linked, individuality is expressed by the questions we ask, and classmates ought to encourage curiosity by peers because this can directly support creative behavior.

Patricia King, professor of higher education at the University of Michigan, has been studying higher order thinking for three decades. Her findings show that, even after four years of college, traditional age students are seldom able to demonstrate high levels of reflection, critical thinking, and sound judgment. Most of them graduate believing that knowledge is mostly just a matter of opinion with evidence playing a minor role. Chapter 14 demonstrates how children as well as adult pre-reflective thinkers insist that seeing is believing and suppose there is a definite answer for every problem. As students advance to formal operational thinking they gradually come to recognize that uncertainty is an ally of good thinking and knowledge is an evidence-based construction. In contrast, students who remain fixed at the lower levels of thinking usually exchange ignorant certainty for intelligent on-going pondering. Given the increasing amount of distraction, there is reason to doubt whether many students can become reflective so that evidence takes on greater importance than opinion (King & King, 2012).

After the death of Benjamin Bloom in 1999 scholars who had assisted him in his formulation of the taxonomy of educational objectives held meetings over a period of five years to update the taxonomy to match current conditions in education. The outcome was a book entitled *Taxonomy for Learning, Teaching, and Assessing: A Revision of Bloom's Taxonomy of Educational Objectives* (Anderson, Krathwohl, Airasian, & Cruickshank, 2000). Currently the taxonomy gets more attention than when it was initially proposed (Krathwohl, 2002). The reason is that with rapid obsolescence of information, teaching and evaluation must go beyond the customary emphasis on remembering knowledge to include a greater emphasis on the interpretation of knowledge, application of knowledge, analysis of knowledge, synthesis of knowledge, and evaluation of knowledge.

### Curriculum Objectives of Educators

Fifty years ago, Paul Torrance, an expert on the measurement of creative thinking, speculated about the challenges of schools in the future. He forecast that the function of teachers would expand to satisfy employers that require new recruits to be capable of making discoveries, finding solutions to manage recurrent problems, and maintain a balanced lifestyle that preserves mental health. To support these outcomes, goals of educators must shift from the overemphasis on learning to also include priority for thinking. Torrance (1963) observed that college courses on Psychology of Learning were offered at many universities but courses about Psychology of Thinking did not exist. This tradition remains and, as a result, teachers continue to be trained to construct tests that only reveal what students learn in class but rarely gauge quality of thinking and self-directed learning that occurs outside school.

Teachers of all grade levels are expected to prepare syllabi for their courses that explicitly state what a student will be able to do as a result of taking the class. These course objectives are always presented in the language of learning such as students will become familiar with facts or data, conform to specific norms, and acquire correct attitudes. Teachers rarely state objectives in the language of thinking such as students will demonstrate creative thinking, critical thinking, constructive thinking, independent thinking, logical thinking, and analytical thinking. Teacher methods of instruction, the tasks they assign students, and their interaction with adolescents are primarily intended to produce evidence of convergent learning. As a result, most research about classrooms has been limited to examining learning but seldom considers the processes needed for thinking (Carr, 2006). For example, the processes of creative thinking described in Chapter 8 are seldom considered in the organization, tasks, and schedule of student work in classrooms.

The contributions of Edward de Bono are a notable exception. After training as a medical doctor and psychologist, he served on the faculties of Oxford, Cambridge, London, and Harvard. He maintains thinking is a skill that can and should be taught in schools (de Bono, 1967; 1970; 1999; 2009). He points out,

> Most universities do not have a faculty of thinking. There is no thinking classification in bookstores or libraries. Thinking is the most fundamental of all human behavior but does not get direct attention.... This needs to change. (de Bono, 2009, p. 190)

His views on the future of education and success are expressed on videos at http://edwdebono.com

## Adoption of Goals for Thinking

Paul Torrance, who was the Director of the Bureau of Educational Research at the University of Minnesota, wanted to examine teacher goals for thinking. Secondary social studies teachers across the state of Minnesota ($N = 1,297$) were invited to submit a lesson including the three objectives they considered most important (Torrance, 1963). These objectives were then classified based on mental operations students would have to engage in to attain each of them. The mental operations were originally described by Joy Guilford (1959), who at that time was psychology professor at the University of Southern California and President of the American Psychological Association.

Table 6.2 lists and defines the five mental processes of cognition, memory, convergent thinking, divergent thinking, and evaluation, along with proportion of emphasis each was given in the curriculum objectives of teachers submitted to Torrance. According to Table 6.2, little attention was given to divergent thinking (2.3%) or to evaluation (6.1%). These two mental operations are currently viewed as essential for productivity and self-direction. Recognizing that intelligence tests and classroom examinations have focused mainly on cognition and memory, there is an urgent need for traditional measures to be replaced by indicators of mental processes that match demands of the workplace and reflect the challenges adolescents must be prepared

**TABLE 6.2   Proportion of Emphasis on Mental Process Categories in the Curriculum Objectives of Secondary Social Studies Teachers (N = 1,297)**

| Mental Process Categories[a] | Definitions | Proportion of Emphasis in Curriculum Objectives[b] |
|---|---|---|
| Cognition | Calls on students to recognize, be familiar with, aware of, know about or appreciate. | 65.9% |
| Memory | Includes remembering, knowing thoroughly, and acquiring knowledge. | 5.2% |
| Convergent Behavior | Requires conforming to some behavior norms, adopting the proper attitude, and finding the single correct solution. | 20.5% |
| Divergent Thinking | Consists of tasks that call for independent thinking, constructive thinking, creative thinking, original work, questioning, inquiring, and similar activities. | 2.3% |
| Evaluation | Includes critical thinking, assessing, evaluating, judging, making decisions, comparing, and contrasting | 6.1% |

[a] Adapted from "Three faces of intellect," by J. P. Guilford, 1959. *American Psychologist, 14*, 469–479.
[b] Adapted from *Education and the Creative Potential* by E. P. Torrance, 1963, p. 5. Minneapolis, MN: University of Minnesota Press.

to meet. Toward this goal, some teachers assign discovery tasks that provide opportunities for students to become self-directed, participate in teams, and apply peer and self-evaluation (Strom & Strom, 2011a).

Educators have yet to effectively unite the full impact of combining visual images with questions. Visual images from cell phone photos, flip cameras, or other picture-taking devices can be an effective medium for acquiring question-asking strategies that can motivate thinking and evaluate comprehension of situations as they are observed by both students and teachers. Visuals can help adults achieve balance in the nature of questions to encourage reflective and creative thinking while avoiding excessive reliance on inquiries that feature lower-order thinking. Ten different kinds of questions, all related to the general theme of help, are illustrated in Table 6.3.

The teacher and students look at a set of pictures featuring children in varied situations. As each picture appears in print or on a computer screen the teacher refers to an agenda sheet containing questions to ask the child. The initial set of 20 pictures described here to practice on consecutively include: a boy with a snowman, a child's birthday party, ponies standing in a corral, a headless man and masked partner, elephants with a man, penguins walking with a boy, teacher breaking up a fight, a dinosaur statue, children in the lake, play hut builders, girls painting, children dancing for elderly spectators, kids in a swimming pool, Fort Windsor play environment, children awaiting lunch, building sand castles, a balloon parade, playing in mud, grandfather reading to a girl, and an elderly lady at her computer.

For each of these 20 pictures (or any set a reader takes) the teacher presents the same type question and then repeats the pictures to emphasize an-

**TABLE 6.3  Types of Questions Focusing on Helping Others for Adults to Ask Children**

| Types of Questions | Examples of Questions About Helping Others |
|---|---|
| Description | How do you feel when you try to help others? |
| Hypothesis | What would happen if no one helped others? |
| Inference | How do you know when a person needs help? |
| Origin | How did you learn about ways to help others? |
| Definition | What does it mean when you help someone? |
| Illustration | What are some ways that you help people? |
| Comparison | Who helps others the most in your family? |
| Advantages | What are some benefits of helping others? |
| Quantitative | How much time do you spend helping others? |
| Cause–Effect | What happens when you try to help others? |

other type of question. For example, when hypothesis questions are a focus, the inquiry for the first picture of a boy with a snowman might be: What secret do you suppose the snowman is telling the boy? In the next picture where a boy looks at his birthday cake, the hypothesis question could be: What do you suppose will happen if his wish comes true? For ponies standing in a corral, the hypothesis question could be: What do you imagine these ponies are talking about? In turn, other types of questions are presented for each picture. In addition, to be used by teachers and parents, this strategy supports intergenerational programs where older adults and young children look at pictures together on a screen. Elders find this satisfying since they feel comfortable and are able to sustain a conversation with children.

## Families and Television Questions

The place where most children learn about the benefits of asking questions is at home. Watching television is a natural context where parents have opportunities to teach. Television presents them with three major challenges. First, they have to decide about the programs their children are allowed to see. Second, they should nurture critical thinking by helping to interpret the messages conveyed by media. Third, parent willingness to ask questions and listen to their children can do much to qualify them as sources of guidance. Most parents report they watch television programs with their family on a regular basis. In fact, families spend greater amounts of time watching television than is spent on any other activity together (Singer & Singer, 2011).

### *Parent Questions for Children*

When families watch television, everyone sees the same pictures and hears the same words. However, because of distinctions in their experience, children and parents may interpret messages differently and reach dissimilar conclusions. This variance in perceptions of age groups means relatives could benefit from sharing their observations. Accordingly, one way to find out how a child interprets what s/he sees on television is asking questions that make known personal impressions. Table 6.4 presents an agenda of questions to stimulate dialogue. A couple of reminders warrant consideration. First, these questions are not intended to be in a particular sequence but instead should be asked whenever the adult determines they match events of a program. Second, you do not need to ask all of the questions, only those you feel are suitable. The purpose for each question is stated along with a more elaborated rationale. You may want to ensure easy access to these questions by making a copy and keeping it near the television or taped on the back of the remote control.

**TABLE 6.4  Television Questions for Parent–Child Conversations**

| Question | Purpose |
| --- | --- |
| 1. How would you handle this situation? | Identify alternatives |
| 2. What do you suppose will happen next? | Anticipation of events |
| 3. What parts of this program did you like most? | Expression of interest |
| 4. If you were a friend, how could you help? | Responding to needs |
| 5. What does (a word heard on television) mean? | Vocabulary development |
| 6. Do you think s/he is making the right decision? | Evaluation of judgment |
| 7. What kind of person does s/he seem to be? | Assessment of character |
| 8. What has happened in the story so far? | Sequence recognition |
| 9. How do you want the story to end? | Identify preferences |
| 10. What was learned from this situation? | Evaluation of learning |

*Source: Parenting Young Children: Exploring the Internet, Television, Play, and Reading* by Robert Strom and Paris Strom, 2010, p. 157. Information Age Publishing Inc., Charlotte, NC.

1. *How would you handle this situation?* Having the ability to think of alternatives is a valuable asset throughout life. People who can see many possibilities in a single situation are more able to negotiate, get along with others, and think of options to solve problems. These strengths are helpful when dealing with disputes and preserving mental health. By sharing interpretations, parents and children reveal the scope and limitations of their individual perception. This knowledge helps to assess child comprehension and identify aspects of a lesson that requires further emphasis.

2. *What do you suppose will happen next?* By asking questions that call upon children to guess or to hypothesize, adults motivate them to explore beyond what they can directly observe—to imagine what is unseen and express a futuristic perspective. Such an approach encourages children to talk more because the questions are open-ended, and there is no single correct answer. This strategy also allows children to express differences of opinion from the adults. When parents recognize that a daughter or son is able to think of ideas that the adults would not have conceived, respect for child thinking increases and the relationship can be enhanced. Mothers and fathers who ask children guessing-type questions also learn to feel more comfortable with uncertainty and willing to discuss issues for which they may not know the full range of responses.

3. *What parts of this program did you like the most?* This question invites a revelation of interest. One condition for building a close rela-

tionship involves striving to remain aware of things that please and disappoint the other person and, in turn, to make personal choices and preferences understood. Mutual expression of likes and dislikes provides an information base that people need to make decisions regarding compromise and sacrifice. Sharing what we like best is the easiest thing for us to talk about.

4. *If you were a friend, how could you help?* Everyone should care about other people and want to be helpful. A combination of loyalty, willingness to offer support, and ability to recognize the help that a friend needs can be taught by example and brainstorming. Relatives benefit from telling each other their friendship difficulties and methods they rely on to sustain relationships. Children begin asking for parent advice about preserving and building friendships while also maintaining independence. This topic arises early and becomes more pronounced by age 8 or 9 when pressures from peers become a strong force that influences behavior of everyone associated with a group.

    Some parents recommend to their child that, "When other kids don't treat you right, forget about them and find new friends who will be nice to you." This advice suggests that withdrawal is the best way to deal with the insensitivity of peers who, at this age, are likely to behave that way quite often. Children want to get along with classmates, even those who treat them badly. They want to improve difficult relationships and make them more satisfying. When parents do not embrace a similar goal for themselves, they are inclined to make suggestions that disqualify them as chosen sources of advice.

5. *What does (a word heard on television) mean?* Building a more extensive vocabulary should be a lifelong goal and can be helpful for conversation with other generations. Some words children hear on television may not be fully understood and should become the focus for questions like these: "What do you suppose 'danger' means? 'bystander' means? 'victim' means? 'video streaming' means? 'pod casting' means? 'entertainment' means?" Parents are amazed at the number of words for which they can provide definitions that would otherwise remain unknown to their children. There are also certain words children may know that grownups do not understand and should be identified while watching shows preferred by the children. The best way to learn new words is in context. Therefore, interaction while watching television together can augment the vocabulary that children acquire at school. This strategy calls for whoever is the more informed viewer to define words to bring meaning for others who

are watching. Everyone in the family can repeat aloud words that are not understood when spoken during a program.

6. *Do you think s/he is making the right decision?* In this case the question goal is to evaluate judgment in the actions taken by a certain character on television. Parents want their children to acquire good judgment and keep them from making serious mistakes. Sometimes harmful consequences occur before important lessons are learned. By reacting to televised versions of real-life dilemmas, families are able to simulate predictable problems and explore the worth of individual judgment without experiencing risks of disappointment, embarrassment, and other undesirable consequences. Children also need to realize that other people want to persuade them to buy things that they may not need. Families should consider together decisions about television and Internet commercials that target the young.

7. *What kind of person does s/he seem to be?* The assessment of character is an imprecise but important skill. Mothers and fathers want children to evaluate situations and be able to determine whether being with certain people is in their best interest. One way to learn how to assess character is to compare how the parent and child see particular television characters at the beginning and when the program ends. Mom and Dad may not always know best but children often conclude that parents have something of value to teach them when it comes to sizing up situations.

8. *What has happened in the story so far?* The need for recognition of sequence begins in the preschool years, ages 3, 4, and 5. A basic goal of reading is comprehension—understanding what is read. This skill calls for more than memorizing the alphabet or recognizing words. Understanding the progression of events that have been read is also important. In the books from which children learn to read, words are usually simple and the story line is often uneventful. On the other hand, most television programs have a beginning, middle, and end. Indeed, most programs are well suited for teaching sequence and can become a valuable medium for improving children's comprehension skills. At the end of a television program or during the reading of a book, ask your child to describe the main events that have happened in the story so far. You will find out what was understood, details the child considered important and the elements overlooked, thereby allowing you to provide missing insights.

Encouraging children to summarize what they experience is more important than parents may understand. Students with lots of practice in summarizing are usually able to readily describe ideas and events in their own words and therefore are less inclined to plagiarize homework, projects, or tests.

9. *How do you want the story to end?* Expressing preferences is one way to reveal values. Public polls report the opinions and priorities of adults. But the likes and dislikes of children are seldom assessed. This is unfortunate because the future that we hope the young will enjoy depends in part on helping them develop a sense of what is possible, an attitude of optimism, and a willingness to express their values. Parents have the opportunity to reinforce these behaviors in conversations while watching television.

10. *What was learned from this situation?* Television offers opportunities to be an observer of difficulties that other people encounter and witness how they try to solve their problems. Parents and children are able to identify with issues portrayed by describing related events and struggles in their own lives. There is a need to understand that the most beneficial way for children to acquire moral learning is in the role of an observer. When someone else's misbehavior is the focus of attention rather than our conduct, we are less defensive and more able to consider making the personal changes that appear warranted.

Talking to children about right and wrong decisions that characters make can be helpful. There is growing concern that the moral development of children is not keeping pace with growth of their mental abilities. One method for teaching morals that deserves consideration comes from the Athenian Greeks of long ago who received moral education at the theater. They realized that, unlike other forms of instruction, a theatrical production could hold anyone's attention and convey a profound influence. Accordingly, the nation's best playwrights were commissioned by the government to teach the public morals through drama. All Greek tragedies consist of a common format and succession of events. The leading characters are people of high social status whose departure from their admirable qualities led them to desperate situations. Later, following a renewal of commitment to one's original values, a character's reputation was restored and, with it, the esteem of the audience. Whether the plot is Oedipus Rex, Medea, Hippolytus, or other characters that are familiar, the lessons were always the same—no one, not even the most prominent persons can desert their moral code without suffering a life of tragedy and remorse.

Shakespearean tragedies, written hundreds of years later, correspond to the Greek design. Prince Hamlet, King Lear, Macbeth, and Othello are examples of heroes who turned away from their values only to find the result was great personal loss and regret. How does this concern for theater implicate moral education in the current environment? Children are daily exposed to a variety of dramatic productions on television. Parents should take advantage of this appealing context by exploring their children's values and sharing their own while watching television together.

Table 6.5 includes some additional agenda questions to try out with kindergarten through grade 3 children. For this task, the reader should develop a personal justification for talking with a child about each of the issues. The purpose of each question is given but the motivation for asking depends on your rationale for relevance and benefits.

## Skills for Lifelong Adjustment

Parents have great potential while watching television to help their child build essential skills for adjustment. All of the skills listed here contribute to achievement at school and throughout life.

1. Describe events in proper sequence
2. Identify the main points presented
3. Continue to build larger vocabulary
4. Restate the opinions of other people
5. Show curiosity by asking questions

**TABLE 6.5   Television Questions for Conversations With K–3 Students**

| Question | Purpose |
| --- | --- |
| 1. What did you like most about each character? | Perception of potential |
| 2. Why did this person do what s/he did? | Recognizing motivation |
| 3. How will that person's behavior affect others? | Influence on others |
| 4. How do you think s/he should be punished? | Scaling consequences |
| 5. Has anything like this ever happened to you? | Recognizing similarities |
| 6. What choices does s/he have in this situation? | Generating options |
| 7. In what ways are you like any of these people? | Personal identification |
| 8. Why do you think s/he made that decision? | Evaluating purpose |
| 9. How do the people in this show differ from us? | Noting differences |
| 10. Who were the important people in the story? | Significance of character |

Source: *Parenting Young Children: Exploring the Internet, Television, Play, and Reading* by Robert Strom and Paris Strom, 2010, p. 160. Information Age Publishing Inc., Charlotte, NC.

6. Listen to people with opposing views
7. Distinguish the factual from opinion
8. Review lessons offered by a program
9. Recognize right and wrong behavior
10. Anticipate what will happen next
11. Fairly evaluate character and personality
12. Determine the quality of judgment
13. Identify a range of possible solutions
14. Recognize strengths in other people
15. Comprehend similarities in situations
16. Evaluate the reasons behind decisions
17. Tell how information influenced outlook
18. Recognize how a decision affects others
19. Acknowledge personal need for help
20. Evaluate the need for moral learning

Some of these skills influence reading comprehension, such as describing events in proper sequence, identifying main points, and building a vocabulary (skills 1, 2, 3). Restating opinions of others, listening to people who express opposing points of views, and recognizing strengths of others are assets for participation in cooperative learning teams (skills 4, 6, 14). Self-directed learners share a motivation for discovery that they reveal by presenting questions, identifying similarities in situations, and reviewing their lessons (skills 5, 8, 15). Creative thinkers are able to anticipate what will happen next, generate a range of possible solutions, acknowledge lack of understanding and need for help, and tell how new information changed their outlook (10, 13, 17, 19).

Critical thinking should have high priority for education because students must be well prepared to distinguish fact from opinion, determine the quality of judgment, and evaluate reasons that govern decision-making (7, 12, 16). Emotional maturity depends on having a moral compass to guide ethical behavior shown by choosing to do what is right, being fair in judging character and personality, recognizing how a specific decision might impact others, and evaluating the need for moral learning (9, 11, 18, 20). Much of what parents want their children to learn at school also implicates the instruction they provide at home while watching television.

## *Danger of Decline in Curiosity*

Parents should recognize that preschoolers consider them their main source of learning. This is why children typically ask mothers and fathers 100 or more questions in a single day (Rothstein & Santana, 2011). The passion to figure things out reflects the powerful influence of curiosity on motivation to learn. However, only a few years later and before elementary grades are completed, many students stop asking questions of their parents and teachers.

What happens between the early childhood years and adolescence that bring about a loss of interest in discovering new knowledge, causes students to give up exploring how the world works, and eliminates fascination with mysteries of the unknown? There are no answers to fully explain the reason for this decline and on such a grand scale. However, it is clear that when a person ceases to be curious, s/he gives up the right to become a self-directed learner. Self-directed learning has emerged as a common goal because of access to the Internet. The premise is that individuals are naturally curious and will search for knowledge that interests them while also developing academic competencies everyone needs. However, people who no longer experience curiosity are unlikely to seek further knowledge. Given this possibility, preservation of child curiosity deserves high priority.

In this context, more parents should understand the need to restrict the amount of time their children spend watching television alone. A long-term study of 1,000 children in New Zealand was conducted by the Department of Medicine at Dunedin University (Landhuis Poulton, Welch, & Hancox, 2007). Researchers determined that children who watched more television at ages 5 to 7 were more likely to exhibit signs of difficulty in paying attention at ages 13 to 15. Reports of attention difficulties in adolescence were compared to the amount of time parents reported their children watched television at ages 5, 7, 9, and 11. The psychologists independently rated the attention span and the ability of each child to concentrate at ages 3 to 5. Even after gender, cognitive ability, socioeconomic status, and amount of viewing during adolescence were factored in, results showed those who watched 3 or more hours a day between 5 to 11 years of age had more symptoms of attention problems as teenagers than those who watched two hours or less a day.

An explanation for the relationship between heavy television viewing and later attention difficulties remains elusive. One theory is that the rapid scene changes that occur on television may affect development of the brain at the time it is most malleable (Small & Vorgan, 2009). Another theory is that television viewing displaces other activities and makes ordinary life seem boring. The American Academy of Pediatrics (2011) policy statement on media use by children states that screen time provides no educational benefits for children under age two and leaves less time for activities that do such as interacting with other people and playing. Parents are advised to limit daily television viewing of elementary age children to two hours.

## Summary and Implications

Potential support of the Internet for self-directed learning by having access to much information is not enough. Everyone should also retain the childhood sense of curiosity, wonder, and doubt in order to sustain a pursuit of knowledge throughout life. The benefits of self-directed learning also require generating productive questions that yield higher-order thinking. The mental operations of divergent thinking and evaluation should join memory and convergent thought as prominent outcomes assessed by classroom tests.

Presenting questions while watching television may disturb some parents in the beginning. They consider this behavior distracting and liken it to conduct that makes watching movies at a theater disappointing. They believe observers should watch quietly in order to avoid disturbing the concentration of others. Using this reasoning, the best time to discuss a program is when it is over. However, the fact is parents and children can follow a story and talk at the same time. Adults should not underestimate the capacity of family members to manage two simple tasks concurrently. Adults show this ability when they watch television while reading a message at the bottom of the screen. Children and parents easily keep up with content of a program and speak about events as they unfold. When parents make this shift, they experience the satisfaction of having children express themselves more. Adults also recognize that the benefits of conversation are greater than the entertainment offered by a program. Seeking the opinions of children influences the amount of attention they pay to comments by adults.

There is much for parents to learn about how television can be used to support creative thinking, critical thinking, and observational skills with children. Parents should expect new things of themselves to adjust to changing rules for their child's education. In particular, they should watch television with their children—this requires time. Next, they can ask questions of daughters and sons during mutual observations—this is a skill that takes practice. And, just as children are expected to express their impressions of what they see, parents should also share experiences—this requires self-disclosure. Finally, children should be allowed to select some of the programs that the family watches together—this demonstrates acceptance of child interests. Parents who subject themselves to these kinds of expectations communicate more easily with their children and establish themselves as a lasting source of guidance.

# 7

## Thinking and Discipline

Children should be taught self-control, patience, and emotional intelligence, qualities they will need for a lifetime. Evidence that these lessons are being learned is observed by how well children get along with others and the extent to which concern is shown for mutual rights. The goals of this chapter are to describe the importance of child autonomy as well as document the scale of misbehavior. Another goal is to discuss why patience and willingness to wait are essential for mental health. Implications of over-scheduling are examined. Dominion play is analyzed in connection with resolution of peer conflict. Communication strategies that unite schools and families are described as effective ways to reduce student misconduct, recognize good behavior, and share accountability.

## Success of Parents as Teachers

### Child Independence, Doubt, and Anger

The potential for independence originates with motor skills. Two and three year olds can climb stairs, push and pull objects, and throw things.

*Thinking in Childhood and Adolescence,* pages 135–157
Copyright © 2013 by Information Age Publishing
All rights of reproduction in any form reserved.

Success with these functions motivates the desire to gain independence, wanting to do certain things without help from adults. Sometimes simple tasks such as flushing the toilet, washing hands, carrying a plate from the table to the kitchen sink, and getting dressed are managed well and result in a sense of self-control. When adults urge self-sufficiency, the consequent independence causes children to believe they are able to manage certain problems on their own. Sometimes caretakers are impatient, perhaps because of a schedule. In such cases, a common response is to rush children or do for them what they are capable of and prefer doing alone. Adults who follow this path often explain "I'll do it because it takes you too long," or criticize children for spilling juice, dropping a plate, or wetting pants. In turn, this response leads children to doubt whether they are capable of controlling events.

Children need patient caretakers who allow them to do some things on their own, without an excess of supervision. If the adults are too demanding, expect too much too soon, refuse to let children do some tasks alone, or ridicule unsuccessful efforts to be independent, children become uncertain about their ability to perform well. Caretakers should provide structure, safety, and discipline. To ensure that children experience autonomy and pride instead of feeling unworthy and lacking in confidence, they must know their own limits, be aware of rules they can count on to be kept, and have assurance of a routine. Otherwise, the world seems too large, too complex, too fast, and too impersonal. Children demonstrate ambivalence in being curious and cautious, eager and fearful, and autonomous and dependent. This means that caretakers should accept child fears and worries instead of being punitive. Children seek order and need a predictable time for meals and consistent bedtime (Strom & Strom, 2010).

Anger is a child's way of stating that certain situations are seen as too difficult and produce frustration. Aggression is a violent form of anger when a child attacks someone or something in retaliation. These actions are self-defeating because they usually produce a counterattack or rejection. The word two-and-a-half-year-old children say the most often is "No." Consequently, this is the peak age for spanking from adults who say "You better get it straight that you are not the boss in this family."

Before adopting methods to help children manage their anger and aggression, caretakers should try to find out the cause of emotional upset. Observation and listening are good strategies. For example, a sullen and aggressive boy was sent to a counselor who greeted him but received no response. The counselor asked what the boy did yesterday. "I took a walk." "Was anybody with you?" "My dog." "Do you talk to your dog?" "Yes." "What did you talk about?" "My dad." This line of questioning with short answers continued slowly and soon revealed that the precipitating factor in the boy's anger was being unable to meet unrealistic expectations of his dad. When the father was informed, he began to look for commendable behaviors to acknowledge. The boy grew more responsive and more confident.

Getting children to talk about pictures they draw, coloring together, conversing on a toy phone, interpreting what is happening to someone else shown on a video or photograph are ways to solicit child impressions. It is easier to engage in these communication forums than to talk face to face with an adult who is much bigger than them. Keep in mind that the troublesome situation may not be the cause, as in the boy and dog conversation incident. Some guidelines to help children handle anger and frustration are:

1. *Discover the cause.* Exploring anger and frustration should be motivated by an intention to discover the upsetting cause rather than just to correct misconduct.
2. *Do not respond in anger.* Punishment is ineffective when it is hostile. Set limits to how anger can be expressed but explain the reasons for rules. People who suppose that venting negative feelings is the way for anger to run its course are unaware of research findings showing that venting increases anger.
3. *Remove the misbehaving child from a situation but permit a return when s/he can show self-control.* Some children find this technique sufficiently effective that they can say to a preschool teacher: "I think I better leave the play area for a while."
4. *Do not require inauthentic apologies.* This practice denies children the benefit of reflection about their behavior in favor of saying what grownups prefer to hear. Wanting to redress a hurt that we cause is an important attribute that can only emerge from reflection on our actions rather than follow politically correct ways. Apologies by many people are mingled with negative remarks like "I said I was sorry—What else do you want from me?" Instead of someone apologizing when they do not actually feel sorry, it is better to support change in their behavior (Strom & Strom, 2012).

## Preschool Expulsion and Improvement

The Child Study Center at Yale University examined 4,000 kindergartens representing all 50 state-funded programs (Gilliam, 2005). Results showed that preschool students are expelled three times more often than students in K–12. Expulsion rates are lowest in the public schools and Head Start programs, and highest in faith-based, for profit, and community offerings. Boys are expelled 4.5 times more frequently than girls. Blacks are twice as likely to be expelled as Hispanics and Whites and five times more likely than Asian Americans.

Classroom-based behavioral consultations were identified as one promising method to reduce the incidence of student expulsion. Mental health consultants were trained to provide classroom-based strategies to deal with challenging student behaviors. When teachers reported accessing the consultant, the likelihood of expulsion declined by 50%. Having a mental health consultant visit class in response to a teacher request was of greater benefit than no access but teachers sustaining a continuing relationship with a mental health consultant recorded the lowest expulsion rates. This situation existed because a teacher and consultant shared a building location or the consultant visited the classroom on a monthly basis. There is evidence that mental health consultation in early childhood can be valuable. However, this approach has not been carefully investigated and knowledge is lacking about how to establish a state system of preschool mental health consultation (Hirschland, 2008).

### Executive Function and Self-Control

The way that children spend time impacts their thinking. A long-standing practice has been for children to improvise their own activities, regulate interactions with one another, and make up their own rules applied to guide the group behavior. This custom of self-governance during play has largely vanished over the past generation. The shift may attribute to increased fear among parents about child safety that has resulted in wide support for structured play that features adult coaches and supervision (Meltzer, 2007).

Benefits of this transformation have come at a cost. The greater amount of time children used to spend in play directed by them allowed considerable practice for a set of cognitive skills that are referred to as executive function. Developing the ability to self-regulate is the purpose of executive function (Goldberg, 2009). The thought processes that govern judgment are mediated by executive function. Children with good self-regulation are able to pay attention to the teacher, follow directions, exhibit greater control of emotions, avoid misconduct, rely upon reflective thinking instead of impulsivity, and demonstrate self-discipline.

Research has determined that the capacity of children to demonstrate self-regulation is in decline. For example, one experiment conducted in the late 1940s called on 3, 5, and 7 year olds to stand still for as long as they could. The 3 year olds were able to stand still for only a minute while 5 year olds could remain still for around three minutes. The 7 year olds showed they could stand still for as long a period of time as adults requested. Sixty years later researchers repeated the same experiment for the National Institute for Early Education Research but with a different outcome. In the replication, 5 year olds stood still for the same length of time as the 3 year olds did in the original study. Seven year olds were unable to stand still as long as the 5 year olds many years earlier in the initial observation. These are disappointing results because self-regulation is an asset needed by everyone (Bodrova & Leong, 2006).

A reduction in self-regulation skills coincides with the growing incidence of students diagnosed with Attention Deficit Hyperactivity Disorder (ADHD). Poor executive function is closely associated with higher rates of school dropout, substance abuse, and involvement with criminal activity. In contrast, good executive function is recognized as a more effective predictor of academic success than intelligence test scores. Consequently, children who can manage their feelings, pay attention for lengthy periods, and concentrate are more able to learn (Frisch, 2010; Meltzer, 2007)

Unstructured make-believe and imagination-driven play facilitates self-discipline because children engage in private speech while they pretend. They talk to themselves about what they intend to do and the ways they will carry out their plans. Observation studies comparing how preschoolers behave across a wide range of activities have found that amount of private speech related to self-regulation is greatest during fantasy play. Moreover, the use of self-regulating language is predictive of better executive function. However, the more structured play becomes when adults dominate the activity, the less children are involved in private speech.

Participation on child sports teams directed by grownups provide benefit but also deny opportunities for children to practice policing themselves because they do not have to rely on self-regulation. Instead, the adults decide when the games are played, who has each position, whether pitches are balls or strikes, and if a hit is considered fair or foul. There is a loss of other conflict opportunities that implicate regulation of behavior and decisions many children are not allowed to make for themselves. The goals of adults to protect children, provide guidance about how to behave on a team, and help process experiences of winning and losing can inadvertently sacrifice activities needed to shape emotional and social development (Ripkin & Wolff, 2006).

Parents generally suppose the way to support cognitive stimulation of young children is to use literacy tasks like flash cards, early reading, and language tapes. Recent studies suggests that a better approach in preschool is to encourage engagement in active games such as Simon Says and Freeze

Tag that require high levels of executive function testing the child's ability to focus attention, working memory to remember a set of rules, and demonstration of self-control—qualities recognized as predictors of academic success. Simon Says involves 3 or more players. One child takes the role of Simon and issues directions the others must follow only if they are prefaced by the phrase, Simon Says. To illustrate, Simon says "kneel down" or Simon Says "touch your feet with your hands." The players are eliminated if they follow directions not immediately preceded by the trigger phrase, Simon says, or fail to follow an instruction that excludes the phrase, Simon says. The ability to pay attention and distinguish between valid and invalid commands, rather than physical ability, is what matters most in the game.

Megan McClelland, professor of early childhood at Oregon State University, gauges the self-regulation behavior of preschoolers using a game called Head-to-Toes. The children are told to imitate movements of their teacher as she touches her head or toes. Later, they are directed to do the opposite of the teacher, touching their toes when she touches her head. This seems to be a simple game but actually requires a high level of executive function with emphasis on paying attention, concentrating, reliance on working (short term) memory to follow rules that change, mental flexibility (to do the opposite), and self-control.

McClelland, Acock, Piccinin, Rhea, and Stallings (2013) conducted a study for the National Institute of Child Health and Human Development. The purpose was to track 430 boys and girls from age 4 until age 25 to determine factors that have the greatest influence on completing college. During early childhood parents were asked to rate their daughter or son on items such as "plays with a single toy for a long period of time" or "child gives up easily when facing difficulties." Reading and mathematics skills were assessed at age 7 by standardized tests and again at age 21.

Unexpectedly, reading and mathematics did not significantly predict whether the students would ultimately finish college. Instead, those rated one standard deviation higher on attention-span persistence by parents at age 4 had nearly 50% greater odds of earning a bachelor's degree by age 25. Attention and persistence skills are malleable and can be taught. Scheduling time in class for everyone to participate in active games like Simon Says, Freeze Tag, Red light/Green Light have been found to be effective tools to boost self-regulation and improve academic skills of students (Tominey & McClelland, 2011).

Phillip Zelazo at the University of Minnesota developed a widely-used test to assess how well children apply executive function to goal-directed problem solving at different ages (Zelazo, Carlson, & Kesek, 2008). The

Dimensional Change Card Sort directs children to sort a stack of picture cards by color, a picture of a red rabbit in one pile and a picture of a blue boat in another. Midway through the test, the evaluator alters the task and asks the child to sort pictures by shape instead. A typical 3 year old has trouble switching thinking and continues to sort by the original rule, even if s/he can repeat instructions correctly. A 4 or 5 year old typically is able to adjust and follow new rules. Zelazo believes this improvement is due to developmental leaps in self-reflection that usually occur around age 4. These leaps help children recognize that they know two different ways to sort the cards, which in turn allows them to decide deliberately which of the rules to follow.

Zelazo's work also involves training children in the process of reflection and rule use. After some training, he measures their performance and records neural activity to see whether they improved compared to tasks in which they were not trained. The results are encouraging, suggesting that it is possible to facilitate development of executive function. Perhaps in this developmental period when executive function and relevant brain regions undergo rapid change, there is a window of opportunity for intervention.

## Patience and Willingness to Wait

You may recall this conversation in *Alice in Wonderland*. Alice observes, "Why I do believe that we have been here under this tree all this time. Everything is just as it was." "Of course it is," replied the Queen. "How else would you have it?" "Well, in our country," Alice said, still panting, "if you ran very fast for a long time as we have been doing, you would get to somewhere else." "A slow sort of country," replied the Queen. "Now here, you see, it takes all the running you can do to keep in the same place. If you want to get somewhere else, you must run twice as fast" (Carroll, 1865/2004).

### *Frustration in a Hurried Environment*

Frustration is a frequent experience for those who believe they should never have to wait. Instead of realizing that frustration always magnifies impatience, they prefer to blame others for causing them to get upset. For example, customers in line at a checkout counter may be heard to complain that something is wrong with the management. After all, more registers should be open so no one would ever be inconvenienced by having to wait. When people drive behind a car that does not move as soon as the traffic light turns green, the need for greater patience seldom comes to mind. Instead, the other driver might be characterized as a person who should be banned from the road. When this process is used to interpret other kinds of events as well, frustration is seen as justified because it identifies the failure of others to act as they should. Children who observe some parents and teachers conclude that frustration and impatience are appropriate responses.

Many children endure the frustration of being rushed. When their teachers are in a hurry, students are denied sufficient time to process relevant information or to examine the range of strategies that ought to be considered for solving problems. Consequently, hasty methods of information processing are adopted. Instead of withholding judgment until all aspects of a task have been explored, hurried students that cannot wait are inclined to terminate an Internet search too soon and draw premature conclusions based on partial information. These are high prices to pay for trying to speed up the pace of learning. Efforts to rush lessons or abbreviate the time to practice newly introduced skills causes some students to fall behind and others to perform below their ability level. Time and learning are always linked. Children learn what they spend time doing and from whomever participates with them.

Some reasons why being able to tolerate frustration is important are that patience enables grownups to accommodate the immaturity of children, accept the limitations of colleagues, make allowances for personal shortcomings, and lead people to treat others with respect. It would be a mistake to abandon the pursuit of these attributes as goals that everyone should strive to attain. Parents should realize that the only persons who qualify as examples of maturity are those who consistently demonstrate patience and tolerance for frustration.

## Patience and Delay of Gratification

There is growing public concern that behaviors reflecting self-control like willingness to delay gratification and ability to show patience are in decline. A failure of willpower is seen as the root of problems such as consumer debt, obesity, addictions, relationship issues, and violence. When people adopt the belief that their needs must be met immediately, they abandon the goal of learning to manage frustrating events that require impulse control. Learning how to wait should begin early in life and is illustrated by a seminal study conducted by Mischel and Peake (1990). These researchers met a class of young children at the Stanford University Laboratory School whose parents were faculty or staff. The challenge given to four year olds was defined this way: "If you wait until I (the experimenter) go down to the school office and come back, you will be given two marshmallows to eat. If you cannot wait until I get back, come to the front of the room and you can take one marshmallow from the teacher's desk."

This task presented a lure of enjoying the immediate reward of one marshmallow or choosing to show self-restraint to get a greater reward of two marshmallows later. The experimenter left the room and came back in fifteen minutes. This probably seemed like a long time for two-thirds of the children who resorted to covering their eyes so they could not look at marshmallows, making up fantasy games to distract themselves, singing songs, or staring at the trees outside. In contrast, one-third of the children could not wait until the experimenter returned so they came forward to claim their one marshmallow.

The significance of emotional differences among children was not evident until a follow-up study was conducted fourteen years later when the students were adolescents. Dramatic distinctions were reported between those who years earlier resisted temptation and classmates who showed no inclination to be patient, wait, or demonstrate self-restraint. Those who got two marshmallows for delaying their gratification had grown up to be more socially competent, self-assertive, and capable of handling frustrations of daily life. They were less prone to getting upset when faced with unanticipated problems and did not show any signs of disorganization when pressured by peers. Teachers saw them as more self-reliant, confident, trustworthy, counted on them to assume initiative in uncertain situations, and able to delay gratification in pursuit of their goals.

In contrast, these attributes were far less often observed in the behavior of the adolescents who earlier settled for one marshmallow. This group was more often described by teachers as stubborn and indecisive, easily upset, and likely to regress or withdraw when presented with stress. They were prone to jealousy, ever ready to complain they were treated unfairly, and inclined to begin arguments by showing a quick temper. In effect, even by late adolescence, they still had not acquired self-control. An ability to postpone satisfaction, to persevere to attain a longer-term goal is recognized as essential for success in a wide range of situations from staying on a weight-control diet to completing requirements for a high school diploma.

Besides being more able to manage demands associated with daily living, those who waited patiently at age four differed in other ways as adolescents that contribute to achievement. In the estimate of their parents, they were more able to put ideas and feelings into words, listen to logic of other people, apply reasoning, concentrate, plan goals, assess personal progress, and display a zest for learning. Further, they performed better on the Scholastic Aptitude Test (SAT), a standard measure often required for admission to college. The one-third of children who most quickly came forward to get a marshmallow at age four had an average verbal score of 524 and 528 on their quantitative (mathematics) performance. In comparison, the one-third of students who waited longest earned scores of 610 and 652, a total difference of 210 points (Mischel & Ayduk, 2004; Wargo, 2009).

Marshmallow results for child delay-of-gratification at age four were twice as powerful a predictor of SAT scores in late adolescence as the IQ scores at age four. This means that the self-imposed ability to deny impulses and wait for gratification by remaining perseverant in gaining a longer-term, self-chosen goal significantly impacted academic achievement. Conversely, lack of self-control in childhood has been found to be a reliable predictor of delinquent behavior (Siegel & Welsh, 2007).

Self-control may be the most valuable human virtue and should be given higher priority in the education of adults as well as children. Roy Baumeister, a social psychologist at Florida State University, conducted experiments that demonstrated how personal will power governs behavior. Most of the problems that plague individuals such as addiction, overeating, crime, domestic violence, prejudice, unwanted pregnancy, sexually transmitted diseases, educational failure, debt, and lack of exercise implicate some degree of self-control as a central factor. Psychology has found that two main traits, intelligence and self-control, are responsible for a wide range of benefits. However, despite years of effort, psychology has yet to discover what can be done to produce lasting increases in intelligence. In contrast, studies have found that self-control by will power can be strengthened with practice and be a powerful difference in the lives of ordinary people. Will power affects most aspects of our lives from time management, to saving for retirement, getting exercise, a healthy diet, and resisting temptation (Baumeister & Tierney, (2011).

---

### Acquisition of Emotional Intelligence

Theories of learning are unable to explain why some people have a map for living well, why students with high IQs seldom become wealthy adults, why people are attracted to certain individuals right away and consider others difficult to trust, and why some individuals are able to withstand adversity and demonstrate resilience while others appear to fall apart when exposed to even slight pressure. Daniel Goleman (2006) explains that "emotional intelligence" is the answer and has documented the need for greater attention to this context of achievement. Some elements of emotional intelligence are self-control, persistence, empathy, social concern, and capacity to motivate oneself. Helping children to acquire these skills enhances maturity and relationships.

A popular misconception is that expressing negative emotions supports mental health. On the contrary, research has determined that tantrums are more likely to increase the influence and duration of anger (Savage & Savage, 2009). This is worrisome for teachers who report there is an increase in student discipline cases that reflect a lack of self-control. A sensible strategy is encouraging self-restraint as a reaction to frustration. This response helps to become more emotionally responsible than allowing tantrums to continue without interruption. The reason is that continuous stimulation of particular groups of brain cells makes them more sensitive and readily activated in the future. This is the case for brain cells required to inhibit the *amygdala*, the brain center of fear and aggression. Children who are not expected to control the emotional center of their brain become candidates for maladjustment as adults since self-restraint was not nourished at a critical stage early in their development (Vohs & Baumeister, 2013).

There is considerable evidence that a hurried type of lifestyle undermines development of patience and a willingness to delay gratification. These conditions increase the importance of arranging situations for children to practice patience and learning to wait. In each situation, the explanation for a child should focus on what it means to wait, why we sometimes must wait, and that health is preserved by not becoming upset during waiting. Telling a child how much longer some activity may take can contribute to a concept of time. In some situations, however, it is better to explain that waiting could take longer than anticipated and remaining calm is the way to react if faced with unforeseen delays. Consider some experiences that could be arranged to encourage greater emotional intelligence.

1. *Check out.* Choose a check out line in a store where you have to wait. Explain that "We are standing in line with others buying things they need, just like us. Sometimes we have to wait to get the things we want." This shows patience instead of frustration or complaining. While waiting, the child can be asked to hold some grocery items to place on the conveyer belt or counter.

2. *Taking turns.* When someone is talking, interrupting suggests his or her views are unimportant. Many television shows feature experts who routinely interrupt their colleagues. Waiting for a turn to talk is a courtesy, reflects patience, and maximizes the opportunity to learn. Children seeking to express thoughts can be told to wait until the teacher calls on them or their mother finishes what she has to say.

3. *Meal time.* The principle of anticipation, waiting for something that we want, can be practiced when a child sets the table or helps prepare a meal. Parents should explain that dinner must be made and everyone has a responsibility. People should show patience by staying seated and wait until everyone has finished their meal.

4. *Reading.* Children learn patience when their parents read books to them that require more than one visit. Unlike storybooks, chapters do not always have conclusions but build to a climax and an ending. This experience requires waiting for the next night in order to move ahead in the story. Anticipation of serial-type movies and progressive television programs are established motivators.

5. *Bathroom and Bedroom.* Children practice waiting for parents or siblings spending time in a bathroom or bedroom to get ready for the day. Boys and girls can lie in their parents' bed while talking with the adults. Parents can say, "I'll be ready in ten minutes." Point out that there is a need to wait sometimes for adults just as grownups have to wait for children.

6. *Zoo.* An example of communicating the principle of anticipation is to tell a child, "We are going to the zoo Saturday, that is five days from now." Letting the child know ahead of time provides experience in looking forward to an event while having to delay gratification. You can ask the child to keep track and count days until the time arrives for going to the zoo.

7. *Puzzle.* Assemble a large puzzle or one that has many pieces. This task provides a chance to demonstrate patience while working with a child to form a missing picture. Point out that thinking carefully about where the pieces go takes time, continued trial, and will lead to success. The value of reflective thinking should often be reinforced and portrayed as a strength that everyone needs.

8. *Saving money.* A child wants a bicycle that costs many weeks of allowance. Learning to save money by placing some in a bank is evidence of patience and delay of gratification. The child can be kept informed about the current balance and the remainder sum needed. When the total of the big purchase is reached, child and parent can go to the store and buy it.

9. *Baking.* Instead of buying cookies or cupcakes, an option is to work in the kitchen that requires patience. It is easy to open a bag of cookie dough. However, waiting for gingerbread cookies to bake and cool before they can be eaten requires anticipation, readiness to wait, and time checks.

10. *Sharing toys.* When parents arrange a play date they can tell their child the schedule. Then there can be reminders of how much longer before they are able to get together with friends. And, when the time comes, sharing toys and being willing to take turns means practicing patience. Children can be taught to wait their turn and realize that every person in the group should be treated in the same way.

## Mutual Rights and Cooperation

More children are attending group care at earlier ages than the past. One result is that they spend more time with peers, are age-segregated as never before. Day care and preschool can provide benefits but also present the challenge of teaching self-centered children to cope with conflicts. The solution involves socialization attitudes and skills that should be taught in all group settings.

### Territoriality and Dominion Play

The importance of getting along is confirmed each day of our lives. By helping children gain this ability, parents hope to improve their chances for close friendships, productive associations with peers in school and at work, a happy marriage, and peaceful coexistence. The paths to attain these broad goals are not completely known, but some clues from early childhood observations offer promise.

First, consider certain features of interaction among young children. Those who supervise 2 to 6 year olds are often disappointed by their show of selfishness and possessiveness. The usual response is to encourage more sharing and cooperation. This advice ignores a pertinent phenomenon called *territoriality*—the inclination of creatures to declare a certain space as their own. Territorial behavior is evident throughout the animal kingdom. Coyotes and wolves mark territory by leaving a scent that designates the boundaries of their space. Cats attack other cats that attempt to come in their yard.

A similar intention to protect territory is observed among people. Status is recognized by the amount of space someone commands. Wealthy individuals own larger properties surrounded by high fences with signs that warn about "No trespassing." Less affluent families establish their territory by erecting smaller fences. In businesses, the lower echelon employees often work in cubicles with minimal privacy and sense of control. Elsewhere executives of the company have their offices, the largest of which belongs to the manager or the president.

Play is the activity where young children express their desire to control territory. When they assert claim to a play space or insist on ownership of a toy, it is known as *dominion play*. This territorial-type play is normal between ages two and six. However, dominion play can sometime interfere with functioning of a group. When that happens, the adult and children should have a conversation regarding "mutual rights." Many children experience territorial situations every day at their daycare, preschool, kindergarten, or play dates.

Consider Carol and Dale. Both of these four year olds attend a pre-school. Carol, in tears, approaches the teacher to tell that Dale will not permit her to play with him. After stating she understands Carol's feelings, the teacher suggests that they go and talk with Dale. When Dale explains he is making a zoo and does not want to have helpers, the teacher turns to Carol who indicates she wants to be his partner anyway. Since Dale is not infringing on anyone's territory, the teacher defends his right to privacy by telling Carol she must play by herself or with someone else. Forcing Dale to let Carol in the zoo against his will would violate his right to privacy and fos-ter additional friction between them. In similar circumstances, the teacher would defend Carol's right to privacy. When young children cannot look to adults to defend their privacy, they develop a sense of helplessness instead of confidence.

At times dominion play can interfere with the rights of others. In such cases limitations must be set, not to deny space to someone but restrict it so others can also satisfy their needs. Jim, age four, visited a railroad round-house over the weekend. On Monday morning, as soon as he arrived at preschool, Jim decided to build a replica out of blocks. Unfortunately, he made the roundhouse so close to the block shelves that other children were unable to reach the materials they needed for play.

After observing several unsuccessful tries by Jim's classmates to have the roundhouse removed, the teacher said, "Jim, the reason everyone wants you to move your roundhouse is because they can't get to the shelves for blocks." Jim pointed out they better not touch it or the roundhouse might fall. The teacher makes another suggestion, "Jim, can you see another place in the room to move the roundhouse so other children can play too?" Jim was definite about not moving his structure. Then the teacher said, "I know that you don't want to move it but another spot must be found." Undaunt-ed, Jim stated, "Well, it's already built so it can't be moved." A location over by the window was suggested. Again, no deal. Next, the teacher proposed, "I'll help you move it by the cloakroom or you can do it yourself." Jim replied, "No." Without further comment, the teacher dismantled the roundhouse and moved it near the window so other students could access the blocks. Jim immediately resumed play with his roundhouse as though nothing had happened.

Most children will more readily accept suggestions than Jim but even when they do not, providing face-saving alternatives is a better method of teaching than using punishment, embarrassment, sarcastic remarks, or issuing commands. Boys and girls can learn how to work alongside (not in) the private space of one another. This acceptance of mutual rights is an essential basis for social competence. As a rule, when a child's right to privacy is respected, s/he is less defensive and may soon welcome play with the same classmates recently rejected.

Adults can illustrate the importance of mutual rights by reading to children a book called *This is Our House* (Rosen, 2007). The story shows how play can be a distressing aspect of school life. George will not let any kids into his cardboard house. This means no girls, no small people, no twins, no people with glasses, and no people with red hair. Then, after George comes back from the bathroom, the tables are turned and he learns what it is like to be the individual who is left out.

In time, children commonly decide that it is ok to play with one companion but no one else. By excluding all others, the pair make it known that "Two's company, three's a crowd." Adults often disapprove of this behavior and suggest that the children involved ought to like everyone. However, adults rarely meet this unreasonable expectation themselves. A more suitable response is to accept the fact that, in most situations, children should be allowed to choose their friends. Because friendships require privacy to develop, it is appropriate to honor preferences of children to be together while distant from their unwanted peers.

Parents, babysitters, and group care workers should consider these guidelines to support social development for those under age 7.

1. Respect their need for privacy, ownership, and control of space.
2. Encourage children to respect the privacy of others. Set limits for mutual rights.
3. When possible, support the decision of a child to restrict who enters personal play space. Over time s/he may welcome another person into their play situation.
4. Before rushing in to solve a conflict, take a few moments to observe what is happening. Allow time for the children to solve

conflicts in an accepted way. Support the expression of a child's feelings toward others in a civil manner.

5. If intervention is needed, offer face-saving alternatives that can restore mutual rights. This is difficult in the beginning because it requires creativity but, with practice, adults can act as exemplars.

6. Recognize that socialization requires first-hand experience for children in handling some conflicts. Generally, adults approach child conflicts as if they were policemen who will reach decisions about guilt or punishment.

7. Children need opportunities to make decisions. One aspect of decision-making that should be introduced is the importance of generating possible solutions. The ability to think of options is also an asset for reducing stress.

## Outcomes of Social Incompetence

What happens when surrogates that care for children fail to recognize the benefit of dominion play, overlook the need for mutual rights, deny privacy, force sharing, and resolve conflicts by using coercive methods? An investigation by the National Institute of Child Health and Human Development Early Childhood Care Research Network (2006) compared children who entered day care before their first birthday and continued until age five with a similar group cared for mostly in their own home. Those in day care since infancy were more easily frustrated, less cooperative, more egocentric, less task-oriented and more distractible. These children had not developed self-control and were ready to physically fight to resolve disputes.

Failure to learn "mutual rights" in child group care settings is a global concern. Barbara Tizard and Martin Hughes (2003) at Harvard University summarized eight studies on the impact of day care on social development in the United States, England, and Sweden. All of the studies concluded that young children that spend many hours a week in day care exhibit less socialization skill than those attending fewer hours. Later, in the elementary grades, social incompetence takes the form of invading peer space, distracting classmates, taking things that belong to others, and preventing conditions needed to support group learning.

Wong (2005) reported a national survey involving 350 preschool teachers. Knowing the alphabet and numbers were not seen as the most important things parents should emphasize to prepare children for preschool. This exclusive focus of many parents ignores the social skills that are needed to get along in a group. Most of the teachers, 80%, reported that parents need guidance to curb the pattern of overemphasis on academic skills while not giving enough attention to social development. Parents who help develop verbal communication, ability to follow directions, and participate successfully in groups help daughters and sons gain the most from preschool (Weigel, Martin & Bennett, 2005).

Teachers in the Horizons Corporation survey were agreed that a good way to teach social skills is exposing children to situations where they interact with age mates like play dates, playgrounds, and parent–child classes. In the opinion of these teachers, societal forces have led parents to set inappropriate priorities for child development. In a competitive environment, many parents feel pressured to push their children to get an early start on academic skills. Wong's (2005) study shows that parents can have a more beneficial effect on success at school by giving opportunities for cooperative play greater attention.

## Assessment of Group Childcare

There are 11 million American children under five years of age in group care. The size of this population is forecast to increase but the experience must dramatically improve. One aspect of the solution is providing quality care at a reasonable cost. The National Association of Child Care Resources and Referral Agencies (2011) reports that the average price of day care is greater than college tuition in a majority of the states. Specifically, full-time care of a four year old ranges from $3,900 a year in Mississippi to more than $11,000 in Massachusetts. During the past decade childcare costs have risen twice as fast as medium income of families with children.

Federal Child Care and Development Block grants help states make care more affordable but do not require that funds apply in only licensed settings. Most states require fingerprinting and background checks for childcare personnel. Nevertheless, some children receive assistance in unlicensed settings where safety may be compromised. For example, Illinois spends $700 million a year to pay for babysitting of children from 150,000 low-income families. A decade-long investigation by the Chicago Tribune determined that the Illinois State Department of Human Services poorly vetted babysitters. As a result, rapists, child molesters, drug dealers, and other felons have been paid by the state to provide care for young children (Wahlberg & Mahr, 2011).

A related need is for legitimate caregivers to earn a reasonable salary. They typically receive minimum wage, resulting in high rates of staff turnover. Child-care givers in 150 Florida centers were identified. Four years later only 2% of personnel had been retained (Jinks, Knopf, & Kemple, 2006). High rates of preschool teacher attrition continue to detract from child well being (Cassidy, Lower, Kintner-Duffy, Hegde, & Shim, 2011). To complicate the situation, high staff turnover occurs when children are most in need of continuity. Two to four year olds need a predictable routine for sleeping, eating and persons they can rely on. Stability is an essential condition as far as they are concerned. Even a family vacation poses problems when there is departure from the familiar. For example, children like Disneyland but often express a desire to sleep that night in their own bed at home instead of a hotel. This need for continuity partially explains why young children on a trip appreciate McDonald's because the menu is predictable and remains the same as the one they are familiar with at home.

## Families and Corrective Guidance

### *Teacher–Parent Communication*

Surveys of 250,000 students have found that, between grade 6 and grade 12, a decline in parent–child dialogue is common (Benson, 2010). Communication between teachers and parents also declines in middle school onwards because students no longer have just one teacher. They have four to six teachers who provide them instruction daily. In this more complex environment, faculty should share their observations about notable behavior of students they have in common with their colleagues and inform parents too. Yet, this essential kind of interaction rarely occurs.

Communication with families is poor because schools continue to rely on ineffective and outdated methods to contact parents. Most parents work so they cannot be reached during the day at home. Some do not have e-mail, answering machines, or voice mail. Others are unable to talk while they are at work or check email promptly. When parents cannot speak privately on the phone while at their job, it is unlawful for teachers to leave messages regarding student behavior with a coworker. A related problem is that misbehaving students come home before their parents, intercept the school message left on the answering machine about their misbehavior and erase it.

Teacher communication is limited. They are in classes most of the day so repeated efforts to try reaching parents is impractical. Using electronic mail during class can be difficult. Phone tag is tiring and takes too much time. Teachers are also reluctant to speak with parents who react to bad news by becoming upset and confrontational. Given these obstacles, an innovative approach is to send and receive some information without dialogue or confrontation.

An erosion of communication with parents produces unfavorable results. When schools provide information late, parents cannot provide a timely response. On the other hand, lack of information leaves parents unable to respond to misconduct or commendable behavior. Poor school communication practices motivate some parents to withdraw from a corrective guidance role and expect teachers to assume the unique family guidance role. Teachers may try to address misbehavior but, without support, most will eventually give up. No one benefits if teachers and parents ignore the observation of misbehavior. Without a synchronized effort by the school and parents, the emotional and social development needs of adolescents are bound to remain unmet.

## Collective Teacher Intervention

Most parents realize that character development depends upon being able to reinforce favorable actions as soon as possible after they occur. To explore a way to attain this goal, an experiment sponsored by Motorola involved 108 high school students, their parents, and teachers (Strom & Strom, 2009). Faculty serving these students were providing training to use a personal digital assistant (PDA) for recording events that occurred in class. The School Code of Recordable Events (SCORE) consisted of a numeric code that included 50 statements, written on both sides of a wallet-size card, to interpret classroom events. When teachers observed any criteria listed on the SCORE card, they entered the corresponding number onto their hand-held wireless organizer. Later, the information was electronically transferred to a personal computer. SCORE statements identify misconduct, good behavior, and teacher responses to incidents.

In order for results of SCORE to involve families, the Parent Alert Signal System, PASS was devised. This system informs parents about the nature of a challenge they face in guiding their child to adopt acceptable behavior or commend exemplary conduct. The teacher's numeric coded message is sent to a parent's email or cell phone. Getting a message the same day as an event occurs enables the families to focus on corrective guidance or good conduct. Once sent, a parent checks the cell or email to see the message and consult the SCORE card to identify the issue to discuss with a child. Next, the parent contacts the teacher's cell or email to confirm a message was received (Strom & Strom, 2009).

Teachers present certain lessons in school according to a planned schedule but parents usually have to teach lessons whenever they are needed in response to situations. Parents can know when certain life lessons are needed if teachers report notable events in a timely manner. The requirement of immediacy for feedback to parents about student behavior is an important condition to implicate positive/negative reinforcement and punishment.

Teachers differ in the academic subjects they provide students but every faculty member is expected to support social development. Technology can help to achieve this goal by enabling faculty collaboration. When the SCORE observations of teachers who instruct the same student are combined, a more complete picture of the behavior of that person emerges. In turn, united intervention strategies can be planned and monitored for effect. Educators who might otherwise feel helpless in coping with disciplinary situations alone can gain confidence as part of a team that shares observations with the principal and parents and identifies an action expected of families.

## Good Behavior Reports to Parents

After using SCORE/PASS most parents (98%) and students (83%) felt encouraged by getting messages from teachers regarding commendable behavior. Teachers (92%), parents (92%), and students (82%) expressed a belief that most adolescents will behave better if good conduct gets timely recognition. One mother stated the consensus view, "Before this project, I supposed that no news is good news. Now I realize that no news is just lack of information. It is a great boost to sometimes receive feedback indicating that our son is becoming mature" (Strom & Strom, 2009).

Reporting favorable student behavior as a way to encourage and maintain good conduct corresponds with research that nurturing healthy relationships at school is a better way to reduce discipline than zero tolerance policies and punitive penalties. This impression is confirmed by a national longitudinal study of adolescent health that found attachment to school is a protective factor against involvement with violence. The most significant predictor of student well-being was feeling connected with school (Franke, 2000). Other studies show that when students feel accepted by peers and vested in the institution, they engage less in risky behavior (Orpinas & Horne, 2006).

## Adolescent Self-Control Reminders

The movie that first brought recognition to Hollywood director Steven Spielberg was called *Duel* (Eckstein, 1971). Actor Dennis Weaver plays a businessman who is traveling on a deserted highway. After a few miles he was made aware that the driver of a diesel truck behind him, whose face he cannot see, is out to get him. Filmed long before the crime of road rage was familiar, this movie emphasizes self-control as a contributing factor to the maturity needed for managing unforeseen difficult situations. Self-control is defined as regulating personal behavior instead of responding to events in an impulsive manner.

Adolescents appreciate being trusted to make more of their own decisions than when they were younger and recognize this privilege means additional responsibilities. Besides having teachers report about their conduct to parents, students should monitor personal behavior and take corrective action—an indicator of growing up. Adolescents should periodically remind themselves about these behaviors that can support greater self-control.

- Use manners that respect others such as taking turns and sharing personal opinion.
- Show patience in working with others and be willing to wait for their feedback.
- Avoid blurting out answers that can interrupt the thinking process of classmates.
- Listen to teacher directions about procedures that are expected to complete tasks.
- Read stories for pleasure and learning instead of just passively watching videos.
- Know how to resolve arguments in a way that shows concern for all the parties.
- Say no to suggestions from peers to do things that may lead to harmful results.
- Establish long-term goals that are relied upon as a guide for everyday behavior.
- Consider the views expressed by others that may differ from personal opinion.
- Accept responsibility to do your share as a member of an interdependent team.
- Welcome suggestions from others on ways that can improve personal conduct.
- Refrain from put-downs or blaming others when situations do not turn out well.
- Rely on a set of healthy criteria for self-evaluation to promote personal growth.
- Acquire anger management attitudes and skills so no harm will come to others.
- Consider the perspective taken by groups other than the one to which you belong.
- Be willing to seek help if you find that negative feelings are overwhelming you.

- Share personal problems as well as possible solutions with an adult confidante.
- Know how to set goals and amend them as well as evaluate personal progress.
- Demonstrate concern for welfare of others by engaging in community service.
- Practice risk assessment to remain aware of possible consequences of actions.
- Showing up on time reflects self-control of scheduling and time management.
- Be able to persist in circumstances that may be frustrating without giving up.
- Demonstrate empathy by taking into account the views and feelings of others.
- Learn to relax and schedule time for reflection and relief from stressful events.

## Summary and Implications

A hurried lifestyle can stretch people to their limits. Some tasks should not be sped up because a certain amount of time is necessary to perform them well. When activities are accelerated that should not be, and people forget how to slow down, there is a price to be paid. Valuable assets like patience and willingness to delay gratification enrich life at every age. These aspects of emotional intelligence should be monitored because they enable people to honor personal priorities, establish suitable expectations for pace of learning, and support healthy behavior.

Self-control and self-discipline are elements of social maturity and mutually satisfying relationships. Parents are the teachers most responsible for providing basic lessons about civil behavior, concern for well-being of others, willingness to wait, and adoption of a healthy work ethic. Many families perform poorly in carrying out these responsibilities. More parents should recognize that, even though their schedule is busy, the obligation for child guidance cannot be transferred to surrogates at school.

Some observers suppose that government subsidies are the way to improve childcare. However, comprehensive changes are needed. Parents and caregivers should know psychological and physical aspects of early development. With training, caregivers can accept the social limitations of children, respect their need for the privacy of dominion play, preserve mutual rights, demonstrate how to resolve conflict in creative ways, and express anger without harming others. These strategies help children gain socialization skills essential for getting along.

Many students are not acquiring self-control and suppose that violence is a suitable way to settle disagreements. The failure of parents to teach civil behavior is seen as the most difficult obstacle in maintaining classroom discipline. Becoming emotionally upset and displaying outbursts of anger when faced with frustration is an increasingly common pattern. Student behavior often appears to imitate that of their parents whose reaction to teacher reported misconduct is denial. As a result, more schools have initiated a zero tolerance for abusive behavior. Schools cannot provide students with the corrective guidance and forms of punishments that must occur at home to set limits on self-control that can deter misconduct. Developing communication with parents can occur when teachers report same day commendable behavior and misconduct. This approach acquaints parents with aspects of development they care about, informs them their guidance is needed or succeeding, and allows them to reinforce good student behavior soon after it has been demonstrated.

# 8

## Thinking and Creativity

Parents want children to become creative adults who can adapt to change and produce unique and practical ideas. However, many families do not recognize what they can do to support these achievements. This chapter examines the shift in priority assigned to creative thinking in relation to ways teachers can improve their influence on divergent thinking. The distinction between creativity and intelligence is documented. Knowing how creative thinking proceeds is explained based on reports from individuals recognized for their outstanding contributions to society.

## Origins of Creative Thinking

### Childhood of Creative Adults

What are creative people like and what can be done to cause their extraordinary abilities to become more common? This question intrigued Donald MacKinnon (1903–1987), Director of the Institute for Personality Assessment Research at the University of California. MacKinnon (1962, 1978) and his team carefully studied the lives of over 600 mathematicians,

*Thinking in Childhood and Adolescence*, pages 159–178
Copyright © 2013 by Information Age Publishing
All rights of reproduction in any form reserved.

architects, writers, engineers, and research scientists nominated as being highly creative by experts in their fields. Assessments were able to detect characteristics that differentiated them from less creative peers.

In addition to being highly imaginative, the creative adults showed preference for solitary activities. They were able to concentrate for long periods of time and exhibit an unusual level of task persistence. How did they get to be this way? What kind of growing up experiences did they have in common? Some clues come from their autobiographical reports. Generally, they were either the eldest child in the family or were distantly spaced from their brothers and sisters. They spent more time alone and with grownups than with classmates and learned from an early age to enjoy the company of their imagination (MacKinnon, 1962, 1978).

## High and Low Daydreamers

The privacy that highly-creative adults experienced during childhood is suggestive of the environment others may need to become more creative, but the benefits of solitary play were largely overlooked until psychologists Dorothy and Jerome Singer (2011) from Yale University made some discoveries. One of their experiments involved a sample of nine year olds who were similar in intelligence, grade level, and social background. After conducting intensive interviews, the children were divided into two groups.

The "High Daydreamer" group included those reporting imaginary companions, enjoyed playing alone, and described more daydreams. Boys and girls that preferred more literal play, expressed disinterest in solitude, and reported infrequent daydreams were categorized as "Low Daydreamers." Everyone was told that, because astronauts have to spend lengthy periods of time in a space capsule without moving much or having frequent conversations with others, the goal of the experiment was to see how long the children could sit quietly without talking to the experimenter.

Results were significant. High Daydreamers could remain quiet for long periods of solitary activity and persist without giving up—factors closely related to concentration ability. High Daydreamers were also less restless, less eager to end the experiment, and seemed serenely able to remain occupied inwardly to make the time pass. Later, it was found that each of them had transformed their situation of forced compliance into a fantasy game that helped increase their ability to wait. In contrast, Low Daydreamers never seemed able to settle down. They would repeatedly blurt out, "Is the time up yet?" They continually tried to engage the experimenter in a conversation. Further testing revealed High Daydreamers also scored higher on measures of creativity, storytelling, and need for achievement.

## *Time Alone and Concentration*

Parents and teachers can confirm the Singers' (2011) findings. Children from low-income households are usually crowded together and lack opportunities to participate in solitary play. As a result, most arrive at school restless, cannot sit still, and are unable to focus on a task for very long. They are inclined to act out impulses instead of reflecting on them. Because these children lack concentration ability, much of their time is spent interrupting and distracting others. In many schools, this behavior means teachers must devote considerable effort to establish the conditions needed for learning to occur. Many educators complain that students have not developed the inner resources necessary for sustained inquiry. The forecast is not much better in higher-income homes where there are a growing number of children that complain, "There's nothing to do" if playmates, cell phones, computers, or television are unavailable.

Fortunately, when solitary play is given higher priority, boredom and inattention can become less common. This will be a difficult transition because traditionally adults have not recognized that children need privacy. In fact, children are often led to feel that being alone is a form of punishment called solitary confinement. Parents resent intrusion by their children whenever they are trying to concentrate. Nevertheless, an inclination by adults to underestimate the seriousness of children at play is nearly universal. Moreover, frustration effects of interrupting solitary play include a reduction of child persistence for mental tasks and a lowering of the ability to concentrate. The younger a child is the more vulnerable s/he is to play disturbance. This comes as no surprise to daycare and preschool caregivers who are unable to grant the request of many children seeking periodic privacy.

Sherry Turkle is a professor of science, technology, and society at the Massachusetts Institute of technology. Her book *Alone together: Why we expect more from technology and less from each other* examines how thinking in a digital society differs from the way things were in the past. According to Turkle (2011), learning to value solitude and being alone is the bedrock of early development. Parents should know they could be depriving their children of this great asset if they pacify them with a device that is used excessively to avoid being alone. Children need to be able to think independently of a device. They need to explore their imagination, reflect about events, and process ideas, and feelings without the distraction of technology. If parents don't teach their children to be alone, they'll only know how to be lonely.

### Asian View About Perseverance

The path to creative achievement can be viewed differently depending on culture.

In Asia, the emphasis on effort and relative disregard for innate mental abilities is drawn from Confucian philosophy. Confucius was mainly interested in the moral perfectibility for all of mankind. He rejected a categorization that humans are good or bad and focused instead on potential to improve moral behavior by creation of favorable environments. His view was gradually extended to include every aspect of human behavior. In effect, human beings are considered malleable and, like clay, subject to molding by the events of everyday life. Differences among individuals in innate abilities are recognized because no one can claim all people are born with the same endowments. However, more important and under the control of individuals is the extent to which they are willing to maximize their abilities through hard work. By this reasoning, deficits in academic achievement are attributed to insufficient effort more than a lack of ability or environmental obstacles (Goldin, 2011).

Generally Asians recount basic precepts of this orientation by the folktales and stories told to children. For example, famous episodes of Li Po, a poet who lived over a thousand years ago, continue to be told in all Chinese schools. One story is that Li was walking by a small stream and saw a white-haired old woman who was sitting beside a rock grinding a piece of iron. He asked what she was doing. "Making a needle," was her reply. This answer was confusing to Li so he asked how a piece of iron could possibly be ground into a needle. "All you need is perseverance," the old woman said. "If you have a strong will and do not fear hardship, a piece of iron can be ground into a needle." Li Po thought about her answer and was then ashamed. He realized that someone like himself would never make progress if he failed to study hard so, from that point on, he became a diligent student.

Many short sayings, aphorisms, portray the productive consequence of planning and hard work such as "The slow bird must start out early" and "The rock can be transformed into a gem only through daily polishing." The concept that positive efforts of hard work is not an abstract credo but rather a practical guide for daily life is shown by most Japanese and Chinese school children who believe "If you try hard you can do it." The same message is reinforced by creative individuals in other cultures who underscore the need to persevere when setbacks are encountered or new ideas fail in beginning trials. The public perception that creative people are lucky because good ideas must come to them naturally without effort is a myth that should be replaced by understanding the struggle that defines the creative process.

## Value of Creative Behavior

During the past decade China, India, Japan, Singapore, Taiwan, and other nations have determined that making creative thinking a high priority in schools is the best way to increase productivity, compete in the global market, and protect mental health (Lubart, 2010; Sahlberg, 2011). China has decentralized its curriculum allowing more flexibility. Singapore is promoting a creative environment using the principle of "Teach less, learn more." Taiwan has mandated education for parents of children from kindergarten through grade 12 so families will support reforms at school that can improve inventive thinking (Strom, Lee, Strom, Nakagawa, & Beckert, 2008). These efforts to innovate depart from the paradigm that dominated education before the year 2000 when the nearly exclusive focus was on linear, logical, and analytical thinking. Since then it has become clear that memorization alone is insufficient and must be joined by learning to process information that can be more accurately stored using technology.

There is also recognition that, as people acquire more of their knowledge from digital resources and media, it will be difficult to know what role schools have played in student learning. Encouraging the ability to generate original ideas that have value is likely to be given the same level of recognition as achievement in the curriculum subjects. The emerging paradigm reflects a premise that preservation of healthy economies will depend on greater support for the expression of divergent thinking abilities (Pink, 2009). Computing, calculating, diagnostics, and legal work skills may continue to be important but lose their value. This is because any activity that can be reduced to a set of rules and instructions is likely to become a software program like TurboTax that has replaced many accountants and migrated lower order tasks to populations in less developed countries (Kahneman, 2011).

### *Importance of Community Support*

There are conflicting impressions about ways to establish conditions that will best foster creativity. In *The World is Flat*, Thomas Friedman (2005) contends that location no longer influences creative production as in the past. Technology has leveled the global playing field, making the world flat so anyone can innovate without having to emigrate. A contrary view is expressed by Richard Florida (2012) in *The Rise of the Creative Class*. He provides lists of cities on every continent where the creative persons often move because their talents are more commonly accepted, collaborators for novel projects are easily found, and people prefer working in collaboration on interdependent productions. Florida suggests that innovations are encouraged by geographic concentration of creative persons—entrepreneurs who know that they can count on one another to allow ideas to flow freely, recommend possibilities to improve products, and implement projects sooner because creators and financial backers are in close contact. A small number of regions like the California Silicon Valley generate most of the innovative ideas and products used throughout the world.

Most young adults realize they are less creative now than during childhood when others assigned high value to their imagination that was applied in fantasy play. Creative thinking begins to decline in the early grades when schools and families urge children to discontinue their reliance on imagination (Kim, 2010; Torrance, 1995). A more promising practice is to ensure that students from every town and city find acceptance of divergent thinking without having to move to places in the nation where more favorable reaction to new ways of looking at things are the norm. What is known about the future suggests that efforts should accelerate to ensure that more children retain their creative abilities into adulthood. Creative individuals are more able to adapt to new knowledge, cope with complex situations, and think of constructive possibilities to resolve differences. They demonstrate greater ability to generate ways to improve products and situations, can make independent decisions without peer dependence, and feel comfortable living with ambiguity (Runco & Albert, 2010).

### Students That Teachers Prefer

Teachers and parents may unwittingly take away from children aspects of the gift they want to nurture. Paul Torrance (2000) wanted to find out what educators consider to be the profile of an "ideal student." Nearly 1,000 primary and secondary teachers from the United States, Germany, India, Greece, and the Philippines were given a list of 62 student characteristics. Each item was included because of previous reliability in discriminating between individuals with high and low creative ability. Teachers were directed to check the characteristics describing the kind of person they would like their students to become, double check five characteristics considered to be the most important, and cross out the characteristics that should be discouraged. The results showed the ideal characteristics teachers ranked as most important reflected a view that it is more important for students to be courteous than courageous, show obedience rather than ask questions, remember well instead of being intuitive, and accept judgment of authorities instead of challenge traditional thought. Recruiting creative thinkers to become teachers could be the single most important reform to improve schools, replacing traditional criteria that ignore such abilities.

## Assessment of Creative Potential

Much of school curriculum is designed to help students perform well on state and federal tests. Demonstrating competence on these evaluations is seen as an achievement. However, the scope of mental abilities that are included in standardized tests must expand to include creative thinking. No one knows how much cognitive potential is undetected by reliance on intelligence tests as a measure of abilities but studies have long suggested a need for revision of the views (Lehrer, 2012).

Joy Guilford (1950), a professor of psychology at the University of Southern California, devoted his American Psychological Association presidential address to document the need to broaden the definition of thinking. He described his studies with scientists nominated by colleagues for making outstanding contributions to their field. Each nominee was provided a list of 28 mental functions and invited to rank order them according to perceived importance for being a factor for success in their discipline. All but one of the traditional intelligence test factors ranked below 20th; that is, 19 of 20 characteristics that inventive leaders reported as most salient for success in their work involved abilities not measured by intelligence tests. Guilford believed the prevailing view of mental growth focused too narrowly on convergent thinking with emphasis on knowing the single correct answer for a problem and giving a speedy response. These aspects of achievement should not dominate conceptualization of mental functioning to the exclusion of other dimensions needed for creative thinking. Guilford recommended greater attention to divergent thinking—the ability to branch out and generate alternative answers for problems where there may be more than just one solution, and having the ability to perceive many possibilities in situations (Guilford, 1977).

Michael Wallach, professor of psychology and neuroscience at Duke University, and Nathan Kogan of Educational Testing Service are credited with a landmark study that changed the way scholars think about creativity (Wallach & Kogan, 1965). Their research purpose was to find out whether creative potential is measured by traditional intelligence tests or if creativity is a separate domain of mental functioning that must be gauged by the use of other kinds of measures. Creativity was defined as the ability to produce many associations among ideas and many that are unique. The 151 students in the sample were fifth graders attending a suburban public school. These students (70 girls and 81 boys) completed intelligence tests and creativity assessments resembling an earlier battery that was devised by Guilford (1950). In administering measures of creativity, speed and evaluation were de-emphasized in favor of a game-like setting without time limits.

Operationally, "intelligence" has focused on abilities needed for reading and for mathematics, subjects that are not conspicuously demanding of creative thinking. Even though creativity and intelligence domains have been established as separate, someone might earn high ratings in both sectors. One estimate is that, in a group of either highly creative or highly intelligent students, 30% would qualify in both categories. Torrance maintained that the practice of identifying gifted students as only those persons with IQs of 130 or higher results in the exclusion of 70% of the most creative students (Torrance, 1965, 1995, 2002).

Results of a 50-year follow-up on the Torrance tests of creative thinking showed that these measures have been highly predictive of creative accomplishments in adult life (Millar, 2001). Those able to generate more good ideas as children, grew up to become inventors, doctors, scientists, authors, and leaders in other fields. Plucker and Baer (2008), at the University of Indiana, reanalyzed Torrance's data and found the correlation to lifetime achievement more than three times greater for creativity scores than for IQ scores measured in childhood.

Changes in scores on creativity measures in recent years have become reasons for concern. Kyung Kim (2010), an educational psychologist at the College of William and Mary, conducted a meta-analysis of over 300,000 child and adults scores on the Torrance measures. She found creativity scores steadily rose from 1970–1990 and then progress ended. Over the past twenty years scores have declined with kindergarten through sixth grade students recording the greatest losses. These indicators are more sobering when contrasted with results from an IBM poll of Chief Executive Officers. The 1,500 leaders in business and industry identified creativity as the single most important competency that leaders will need in the future (Bronson & Merryman, 2010).

## *Enhancement of Creative Behavior*

For a long time independence was considered to be the key to success. The more recent perspective is that interdependence is also essential, requiring teamwork attitudes and skills that facilitate group achievement. Valuing the imagination of individuals while encouraging groups to avoid premature judgment of ideas is a challenge young adults must face in the workplace. Readiness to accept criticism from teammates and being able to provide constructive suggestions must become more common assets (Lehrer, 2012).

Two observations based on a decade of studies at Brandeis University provide additional clues about ways to facilitate creativity (McCabe, 1985). First, freedom has been identified as the best method to motivate creative production. Something happens when interests of individuals are respected, allowing them a chance to decide some of the goals they will pursue and ways to achieve their purposes. Having a sense of self-control increases the prospect that a person will explore unlikely paths, take healthy risks, and, in the end, produce something unique and useful. This is the reason Google, Apple, Microsoft, and other creative companies schedule time during working hours for their employees to depart from the usual assigned tasks to pursue their own hunches or dreams that are related to the mission of the company (Lehrer, 2012).

A second finding about production is that frequent evaluation smothers creativity (McCabe, 1985). This conclusion runs counter to the belief of most students that they are able to perform better if provided continuous feedback about their work. This assumption is true when the goal is to master convergent thinking tasks requiring conformity instead of a departure from conventional thinking. However, when creative thinking is the goal, people do better when their production is reviewed less often. Creative people are able to judge their own progress without having to always check with others for confirmation that their evolving ideas will be acceptable. Knowing how to accurately judge personal progress is a common characteristic among high achievers and requires confidence that is seldom attained by most people who feel compelled to continually seek the approval of peers. Those who are the most inhibited and least capable of expressing imaginative ideas are those engaged in high-pressure occupations where they experience weekly or monthly evaluations (Beghetto, 2005).

## Conformity and Divergent Thinking

Some observers of social networking and age-segregated communication patterns worry that the growing influence of peer groups in adolescence could undermine the development and expression of divergent thought. There is concern that when peer approval is the main source of identity status, motivation of students to participate in independent thinking is likely to decline. The impact of group opinion on conformity was initially explored by Solomon Asch (1952) at Swarthmore College in Pennsylvania. His experiments that lead to the study of group dynamics demonstrated how peer pressure can alter personal opinion even about obvious facts. Students in teams of six were recruited to look at a line appearing on a card and then report aloud which of three other lines—each of a different size—was the same length as the first one examined. The first five persons to report were confederates of Asch who had been instructed ahead of time to state the same wrong answer for certain trials. A sixth person, the only real subject, was always asked last to give his judgment. The tasks ensured that he would be confronted with a situation he had never experienced before. He found that the line he saw to be equal in length to a standard line is, according to colleagues, not equal at all. His peers are in a position to know yet they all disagree with him.

The experience produced tension for the subject because it was a violation of a primitive belief; group consensus was in conflict with direct evidence provided by his own senses. Asch found that most subjects continued to make independent judgments in the presence of one or two dissenters. With a single opponent the subject disagreed with his own perceptions 3.6% of the time; with two opponents the error rate rose to 13.6% of the time. Giving incorrect judgments increased significantly when the subjects were opposed by three or more persons. This indicated that size of a majority opposing them had an effect on subjects. When four opponents contradicted personal perceptions, the subjects gave up their own perceptions 35.1% of the time. The experiment continued for numerous trials after which naive subjects were highly relieved to find out about the details of their tests of nonconformity (Asch, 1956).

Asch recognized that perception and judgment were implicated when subjects announced their decisions about which lines were the same length. He could not know that years later these two cognitive functions would be found to be mediated by different circuits within the brain. In the past decade neuroscientists have been able to rely on MRI (Magnetic Resonance Imaging) techniques to map the neurobiology of processes such as emotion, attention, and memory. The question of whether groups can alter what individuals see was overlooked until Gregory Berns and his Emory University team wanted to find out how fear may distort perception as a current variation of Asch's social isolation experiment (Berns, Chappelow, Zink, Pagnoni, Martin-Skurski, & Richards, 2005).

The premise was that if others in a social setting can change what we see or what we think we see, the MRI should detect change in the perceptual region of the brain. On the other hand, if conformity is triggered at the decision-making level, changes should be detected in the brain region involving judgment. Most of the right-handed adolescents and young adults recruited by Berns and his team (2005) were confederates who had been instructed to carry out the same deception role as applied in the Asch experiments 50 years earlier. When the naive subject arrived at the lab, he saw four others he supposed had the same task. Everyone was told they would be completing visual perception tasks on the computer. Each individual would be shown the same rotating images and know the answers given by all their colleagues. The task was to decide which of two shapes were the same or different. In the warm up practice, almost all answers given by the subjects were correct. Later, when the group gave the wrong judgment as seen on the computer screen, the subject rate of correct answers dropped to 59%.

The MRI's provided the explanation. One might not think of conformity as related to a visual process but that is what was found. The group altered patterns of activation in the visual and parietal processing regions of the subjects' brains when subjects went along with them incorrectly. Whenever a subject capitulated to the group, and the group was incorrect, more activity was observed in the parietal cortex as if it was working harder. A plausible explanation is that the consensus wrong answers imposed a virtual image in the mind of the subject. In the case of conformity, this virtual image beat out the image originating from the subject's own eyes, causing the subject to ignore his own perceptions and accept the group view. Similar changes were not evident in the frontal lobes implicating judgment. Instead, the amount of activity there decreased when a subject conformed, suggesting that the group's answers took some of the load off the decision-making process in the frontal lobe (Berns, 2010).

Even when subjects stood their ground and gave the correct answer in opposition to the unanimously wrong answer by the group, changes in brain activity were detectable. However, in these instances of nonconformity, brain changes were not observed in the perceptual region but in the amygdala. When the amygdala fires, a cascade of neural events is unleashed that prepares the body for immediate action as the first stage in the so-called fight or flight system. The end result of amydala activation is rise in blood pressure and heart rate, more sweating, and rapid breathing. Many events can trigger the amygdala but fear is by far the most effective. The amygdala activation during nonconformity reinforced the upsetting experience of standing alone, even if a person had no recollection of it. In many people the brain would rather avoid activating the fear system related to social rejection and just change perception instead to conform with the social norm (Berns, 2010).

If a group is capable of changing our perceptions and to stand alone activates powerful unconscious feelings of rejection, creative behavior may be more vulnerable than generally supposed. Starting in middle school students collaborate in cooperative learning groups where consensus opinion often governs actions of all the members. In this context, students who are more capable of generating divergent ideas are often advised to demonstrate bravery and be willing to suffer rejection as the cost to avoid conformity. Creative persons frequently respond to this advice by wanting to work independently rather than in groups that dismiss their ideas without reflection. Preparing students for teamwork requires encouragement of divergent opinion and recognition that sometimes a minority of one may have a better solution than that of a unanimous majority.

## Stages of Creative Thinking

Most of what is known about creative thinking comes from anecdotal reports of famous people recognized for extraordinary achievements. These individuals agree about the process that led to their distinction (Patrick, 1955). Based on these self-reports, the respective stages in creative thinking are:

1. Preparation Stage (Figure 8.1)
2. Incubation Stage (Figure 8.2)
3. Illumination Stage (Figure 8.3)
4. Verification Stage (Figure 8.4)

### *Preparation*

People are often surprised to find out that preparation is essential for creative thinking. Instead, a common assumption is that "inspiration" just comes to certain individuals but not others. This impression makes it easier to avoid the struggle that occupies all those who create. Preparation typically begins after individuals experience vague insights and set out to examine some particular problem or realm of difficulty by literally flooding themselves with the diverse impressions reported by others. Many obstacles that undermine production characterize the preparation phase. First, the literature about a particular issue may be so extensive that the task seems overwhelming. This appears to be the case when many search engines could be applied to locate an enormous database for consideration. At this point the person might decide to withdraw from further exploration in favor of some other less complicated topic.

A second danger is that side issues can capture attention and divert interest from the original purpose. This is a familiar shortcoming among people whose indiscriminate curiosity causes them to depart from their main line of direction. They may be pursuing a particular area of inquiry but, along the way, websites they explore present links that lead them away from their intention. Remaining focused is fundamental and can be demanding when searching on the Internet or at the library.

Third, impatience that causes people to grapple with specific issues can destroy their chance for success if they prematurely come to conclusions about

Figure 8.1 Stage 1 of the Creative Process –Preparation. Search data, begin to question assumptions, brainstorm with a partner, and examine the main problems with a better perspective. This process typically takes the most time. *Source: Adolescents in the Internet Age*, by Paris Strom and Robert Strom, 2009, p. 244. Information Age Publishing Inc., Charlotte, NC.

data. This is a pervasive hazard in situations where rapid production is an expectation. When teachers set deadlines for student inquiry tasks that are too early, they unintentionally encourage superficial consideration of available data. The emphasis on doing things in a hurry is not conducive to creative thinking. It is necessary to recognize an essential aspect of the preparation phase of the creative thinking process is immersion in the ideas and insights that have already been reported by others. Awareness of these impressions produces the material on which synthesizing ability is applied. Abandoning a problem or a project at this stage is much easier than later because little effort has been invested and the degree of emotional involvement remains minimal.

Many young adults see themselves as lacking creative potential because novel ideas have not come to them without preparation. This view can be revised by reading about lives of eminent individuals who report their failures, successes, and necessity to rely on the resilience produced by courage (John-Steiner, 2006). Courage is necessary to move alone toward uncertainties, express views counter to those held by others, and do battle with personal habits of thinking to accommodate new ways of looking at things. The necessity to confront a task repeatedly calls for acceptance of the failure preceding success. More than most people, creative individuals experience failure because they do not withdraw from complexity. Many people never suffer significant failure because they are so easily discouraged that they quit projects before ever getting into them. At the same time, they can never fully succeed. Curiosity enables creative persons to sustain a question, a problem, or a task and work through to completion. The history of creative persons who have contributed the most is an account filled with endurance and courage.

### Incubation

The second step in creative thinking is incubation (see Figure 8.2). During this stage there is an irrational, intuitive encounter with the materials that were gathered in the search process. At this point people experience feelings of unrest and stress as they attempt to produce an ordering structure, a recombination of the data that can result in a unique and practical contribution. The incubating person usually becomes preoccupied with the task. One intended result of trying to avoid any distractions is that the individual sometimes fails to attend to routine tasks expected by others. As they strive to allow intuitive ideas to take conscious form, creative persons are often dissatisfied with themselves and difficult to be around. Sometimes conflicts ensue with relatives or friends who see lack of attention to them as a deliberate insult (Cain, 2012).

During the incubation stage, self-doubt presents a great hazard. Confidence is vital when unconscious activity brings up new possibilities for combination one after another. It is necessary that the conscious mind avoid disapproving of ideas as they emerge, deferring judgment until later when a range of unconscious products have become available. Feeling obliged to withhold judgment until the associative flow ends is a very difficult and demanding task that requires a high tolerance for ambiguity and frustration. Mental health is typically delicate in the incubation phase, which can vary from a few minutes to months.

Schools cannot foster creative thinking unless students have time for reflection. More homework should be for a lengthier period of time than just the next day or week. Elizabeth Blackburn (2009), a professor of bio-

Figure 8.2    Stage 2 of the Creative Process—Incubation. In-depth pondering, sketch or test ideas, get frustrated, recognize paradigm paralysis, look for one's niche. *Source: Adolescents in the Internet Age*, by Paris Strom and Robert Strom, 2009, p. 246. Information Age Publishing Inc., Charlotte, NC.

chemistry at the University of California at Berkeley and 2009 Nobel Prize winner for physiology and medicine, shared this advice with young students in her native Australia:

> I think it is important that you engage energetically in your learning but you also need time to daydream, to let your imagination take you where it can. Just do that some of the time because I have noticed that among the creative, successful scientists who've advanced things, that was a part of their life. Not that they did not work hard but we sometimes forget about the creative part of science.

Many students express discomfort or boredom when they are expected to focus on anything for very long. Instead of accepting this dysfunctional inattention by declaring it a norm, educators should strive to find effective ways to implement creative thinking. In addition, the pace of production often discourages students, that they are unable to do everything in a hurry. Teachers add to the frustration when they construe lack of speed as a lack of ability, being slow as a sign of failure. It should be understood that the amount of time needed for production depends on the individual. Mozart and Beethoven represent polarities in the realm of musical production. Mozart conceptualized quartets and symphonies in his head while traveling or exercising. After returning home he would write complete melodies. Beethoven who wrote compositions note by note, fragments at a time recorded in a booklet over years, reflects the opposite circumstance. Often his initial ideas were so clumsy as to make one wonder how, at the end, such beauty could appear (Ghiselin, 1985). Ernest Hemmingway (1964, p. 154) in his retrospective admitted, "I didn't know I would ever write anything as long as a novel. It often took me a full morning of work to write just one paragraph." This giant of literature later wrote classic novels in six weeks.

During incubation, anything that is disruptive to concentration is likely rejected. There are some individuals for whom incubation can occur on and off over a long period of time. However, for others the attempt to produce ideas leads to excessive measures to sustain touch with their unconscious in an environment that is noisy and distracting. Not everyone is psychologically capable of spending the same amount of time in the tension-producing phase of incubation. Yet, creative persons commonly prefer to work in long blocks of time so that they can be fully engaged. This is the stage when other people—classmates, relatives, and teachers—should understand the self-absorption that a person experiences. Giving up at this stage is done at great expense since creative persons typically consider not achieving the next stage, called Illumination, as total failure. Albert Einstein observed, "The intuitive mind is a sacred gift and the rational mind is a faithful servant. We have created a society that honors the servant and has forgotten the gift" (Ghiselin, 1985, p. 43).

### Illumination

If the incubation stage presents what Van Gogh referred to as a "prison" in which people are confined to internal conversation and debate, then the illumination phase is analogous to being released from jail and obtaining a full pardon. Illumination (see Figure 8.3) is seen as the inspirational moment that the artist Paul Cezanne described as liberation, the mysterious becoming external, and the time when everything falls into place (Ghiselin, 1985). It is the exhilarating triumph creative persons like so much to relive—the time that is beyond words. Charles Darwin, whose search for the theory of evolution came to an end on a dusty lane, recalled the spot on the road while traveling in his carriage that, to his joy and surprise, the solution occurred to him (Darwin & Wilson, 2005). Creative scientists, inventors, artists, and writers all tend to look back in nostalgia at this brief but cherished the moment and speak of it as mystical. Illumination lifts the burden of tension and creative persons can regain touch with those around them.

Figure 8.3   Stage 3 of the Creative Process—Illumination. "Ah-ha"—Finding the answer, loving the idea, taking the leap, and assembling the main pieces that fit well. *Source: Adolescents in the Internet Age*, by Paris Strom and Robert Strom, 2009, p. 248. Information Age Publishing Inc., Charlotte, NC.

Some creative persons, especially those who have awaited illumination for a long time, make an effort to retain their joy by sharing it. Their accounts of how they reached some new idea is less than exciting to others who view the rapid shift in personality from a total preoccupation with work and seeming depression to happiness and conscious delight as a possible sign of mental illness. They may wonder at extremes in behavior of a creative person and especially the sudden elation expressed about something others do not understand and therefore dismiss as less important than is the case. Further, in returning to a normal state of consciousness, some individuals have trouble figuring out why others have become distant toward them during the interlude (Ludwig, 1995).

For some persons, the creative process ends with attainment of the illumination stage because they have achieved the tentative answer and shed stressful tension. At this point, they may choose to move to confront another problem or interest. Persons of this inclination seldom gain recognition or contribute as much as possible since they do not go on to make the form of their invention coherent to others who could support its broader application or modify it to fit a wider range of prevailing situations.

### Verification

The stage of verification takes place after an idea or plan has emerged from unconscious activity and must then be consciously evaluated (see Figure 8.4). Some creative persons find a need for verification difficult or impossible to accept because emotional certainty regarding worth of their

Figure 8.4   Stage 4 of the Creative Process—Verification. Testing final idea to see/correct faults—"Final editing," assessment by outsiders, experience closure and recognize success via individual or social judgment criteria. *Source: Adolescents in the Internet Age*, by Paris Strom and Robert Strom, 2009, p. 249. Information Age Publishing Inc., Charlotte, NC.

ideas or products prevent them from accepting criticism or suggestions for adaptation. Nevertheless, the pleasure of illumination must give way to rational judgment as a determinant of final production. If a writer is to communicate, the inspired work must become organized and edited. There must be a coherent flow for readers to understand the message. Similarly, a successful experiment that produces elation must be clearly described (Storey & Graeme, 2005).

Unlike the brief illumination phase, verification is often lengthy, arduous, and at times disappointing to a person whose patience declines because of eagerness to get on with another project. The hazard awaiting many writers, scientists, and creators in technology and art is the temptation to avoid the steps necessary for follow through. This temptation has prevented good work from becoming public knowledge. Well-known writers such as Samuel Coleridge and Percy Shelley left fragments of unfinished work because they were unwilling to revise it, feeling their inspiration could not be improved and alteration would depreciate the illumination. Hart Crane was an exacting author. A careful look at his manuscripts reveals revisions involved as much doubt as decision. In contrast, Gertrude Stein disliked the drudgery of revision and responsibility to make her writing intelligible to the public (Ghiselin, 1985). Being willing to consider the criticism of reviewers is necessary at this stage. Sadly, most students are not taught in school or at home to find value in external criticism of their performance. This means personal growth is limited because introspection is the only source to rely on for gauging personal shortcomings. Insight during the revision process of writing can improve organization, structure, clarification, and narrative flow.

## Summary and Implications

Creativity and intelligence have been found to be separate domains of mental ability. Divergent thinking allows students to find multiple ways for solving problems when there is no single correct or convergent answer. Inventive thinkers from diverse careers report similar steps in the creative process they rely on that includes preparation, incubation, illumination, and verification. Mental operations of divergent thinking and evaluation tend to be overlooked by most educators in favor of convergent thinking and memory despite their claims to the contrary. When students have a chance to be involved with the complete range of mental operations, thinking and learning become the dual purposes for instruction and achievement.

Creativity is essential for productivity and determines winners or losers in the global competition for business. This is why the public endorsement of education for creative behavior is rising and must be accompanied by a willingness of teachers to sanction and encourage mental abilities that may differ from their personal strengths. Teachers who allow students to choose tasks and obligate them to share with peers what they have learned from the Internet and other sources contribute to the development of divergent thinking. Leadership for creative students is enhanced when they are given a helper role to assist peers. Students enjoy web site exploration, watching video clips or slides, reviewing and editing graphic organizers to fit their view of a lesson and other procedures that unite verbal and visual memory.

There are more choices for ways to spend time than were available in the past. Adults commonly try to maximize opportunities by scheduling too many things for children to do. A more appropriate strategy is to ensure that they have discretion about some events in their schedule. Teenagers should be aware that, although they enjoy interacting with friends, they also need private time for reflection about concerns of importance for them and to consider decisions requiring deliberation rather than made under the influence of peers. Spending time alone allows students to avoid becoming overly dependent on peers, enables them to stand alone if needed, and represents a condition valued by highly-creative persons. Asking questions can be discouraged or encouraged by peers depending on how they view the learning process. Teachers should explain that creativity and asking questions are linked, individuality is expressed by the questions we ask, and peers should encourage inquiry because it supports creativity.

Creativity has traditionally been associated with the inventions of individuals. Currently greater emphasis is placed on team productivity because this strategy allows people from different backgrounds to combine their expertise for solving complicated problems. Satisfying experiences with teamwork helps appreciate interdependence and motivates mutual support for creativity. Learning how to process criticism as individuals and in teams is a largely unmet need in most classes. Creativity is most prominent when curiosity is the norm, there are opportunities to practice reflective thinking, and access to imagination becomes a common asset.

# 9

## Thinking and Integrity

Choosing the values that contribute to development leads to responsibility, happiness, and maturity. When children adopt healthy values, they are less likely to be misled by people seeking to take advantage of vulnerability, confusion, and indecision. *Values* are defined as the accepted principles individuals and groups use to guide behavior. Children acquire their values from parents, other relatives, friends, classmates, teachers, clergy, musicians, sports figures, media performers, social network sites, politicians, and reality show participants. When these sources provide conflicting advice, deciding the best path to take can be difficult (Holtam, 2012). The goals for this chapter are to describe the scope of student cheating, examine motivation for deception, discuss methods teachers use to detect plagiarism, and collaborative efforts needed to educate for honesty and social maturity. Characteristics of face-to-face bullies are considered along with the emerging problems of cyber bullying. Action plans are identified to reduce these forms of abuse.

*Thinking in Childhood and Adolescence,* pages 179–199
Copyright © 2013 by Information Age Publishing
**179**

## Cheating in School

### *Prevalence of Dishonesty*

*Honesty* is the combined qualities of being fair, just, truthful, and morally upright. The Josephson Institute of Ethics in Los Angeles conducts a survey every two years to monitor the ethics of 23,000 adolescents who attend 100 randomly selected public and private high schools nationwide. All students taking the survey are assured of anonymity and results have a less than 1% margin of error. The Josephson (2012) survey shows that approximately 60% of students admitted to cheating on a test in the past year. Nearly half (45%) of boys believe that "a person has to lie at least occasionally in order to succeed." A lower proportion of girls (28%) reported this cynical attitude. Most students (76%) lied to their parent(s) in the past year about something important and 55% lied to a teacher two or more times on importance issues. Despite this evidence that moral development is in jeopardy, 93% of students still express satisfaction about personal ethics and character. Indeed, 81% stated, "When it comes to doing what is right, I am better than most of the people I know."

*Cheating* is behavior to deceive or mislead others for personal advantage. In the past it was usual to suppose cheaters had marginal abilities, causing them to resort to dishonesty as the only way to keep pace with their more accomplished classmates. However, when 3,000 students recognized in *Who's Who Among American High School Students* reported their experiences, 80% acknowledged cheating on tests (Lathrop & Foss, 2005). This high proportion of students engaging in deception reflects a 10% rise since honor students were first presented the question twenty years ago. Among the leaders that admitted cheating, 95% said they were never caught, did not feel guilty, and thought of themselves as morally responsible. At Harvard University, the administrative board in 2013 forced 70 students to leave in its largest cheating scandal involving a take home final examination for the course called Introduction to Congress (Perez-Pena, 2013). Cheating by middle school, high school, and college students has become a common concern for schools in many countries (Strom & Strom, 2011b).

### *Motivation for Cheating*

Why do students of all ages and achievement levels resort to cheating? One speculation is that academic dishonesty is just part of a broader erosion in ethics that places self-centeredness over concerns for fairness and equality. Another view is that fear and anxiety about high-stakes testing causes dishonesty among students having difficulty attaining minimal competency skills for graduation. Other observers fault the schools because evidence of character failure is ignored and students are not being held accountable. In turn, teachers maintain that many parents seem obsessed with an aspiration that their children should perform better than classmates, regardless of what it takes to get the desired results (Anderman & Murdock, 2006).

There is a way to obtain a more accurate appraisal of how students feel about this matter. Because computers are present in all schools and electronic polling can be an option, educators should make an effort to become aware of how students view life in the classroom. To increase awareness, Strom and Strom (2009) designed twelve multiple-choice polls for students to express views about conditions of learning at their school. The Cheating Poll includes items about observed prevalence, reaction to classmate cheating, punishment for test abuse and plagiarism, teacher reliance on software for detection, observation of adults who cheat, parent response to dishonesty, identifying cheating situations, circumstances that justify dishonesty, characteristics of students who cheat, and personal involvement in deception.

Every school district should have policies and procedures about cheating so faculty can respond to incidents they observe or have reported to them without experiencing fear of duress from students or parents. While 80% of students responding to the *Who's Who Among American High School Students* survey admitted to cheating, a separate survey of the parents found that 63% expressed confidence their child would never cheat. Perhaps these parents suppose that teaching the difference between right and wrong is sufficient without linking awareness with responsibility to behave ethically (Lathrop & Foss, 2005). A noteworthy example of this assumption is a college student who scored at the 97th percentile of the SAT (Scholastic Aptitude Test) used for college admission. He later took the test for six students at Great Neck New York high school, charging them $2,500 each for the deception. All seven of the individuals were arrested (Khadaroo, 2011).

A familiar outcome is that educators feel vulnerable to parent threats about lawsuits if the honesty of their child is challenged without indisputable proof. Teachers worry they may falsely accuse a student and then have to suffer dreadful consequences. Indeed, 70% of educators agree that concern about parent reaction discourages them from punishing the cheaters. An unintended result is student awareness that their misconduct rarely results in punishment and presents a low risk of detection (Whitley & Keith-Spiegel, 2002).

### Methods of Detection

Teachers are advised to be vigilant when they monitor students taking tests. A perennial form of dishonesty involves referral to messages that cheaters write on their body, clothing, or belongings. A common practice has been to remind test takers not to glance at papers of others during a test. The emergence of technological devices has spawned new and more sophisticated approaches. Students with handhelds or cell phones can "beam" or call data silently from across a classroom or, with a cell phone from anywhere off campus. During a test these tools are hidden under the table or in baggy pockets. Both devices can be equipped with text messaging, instant messaging, email, and a camera or video recorder that makes capture or transmission of answers a relatively simple task. Cell phones can have a hands-free function allowing the user to listen to sound files (i.e., prerecorded class notes). Applying this same method of sound files, others use small music devices such as iPods.

Giving open book examinations and allowing students to bring notes increases familiarity with the content of a course, improves the review process, and reduces the incidence of cheating. While some considerations described may seem unduly cautious, collectively these steps can do much to prevent dishonesty and support integrity of a test environment. Students take honesty more seriously when they see their teacher makes an effort to ensure fair assessment conditions. Fairness is an essential value that most students agree ought to be upheld by everyone.

While forms of student cheating increase in complexity, a related but unexpected threat has also become more common. Faculty and administrator salaries and career paths are often tied to test performance of students (Headden & Silva, 2011). Some teachers and principals have been fired for giving students answers to tests, prompting change in responses of students while being tested, changing answers after tests are completed and before submission to the district for processing, and allowing students more time than is specified by directions (Carey, 2011). The most high-profile case involves Atlanta, Georgia. The *Atlanta Constitution* newspaper pursued a trail of wrong doing by public school officials that date back for more than a decade. In April 2013 indictments were handed down for 35 Atlanta school principals, test coordinators, teachers, and a former superintendent of schools. The charges included making false statements, theft, influencing a witness, and racketeering. The focus of the scandal centers on educators changing responses of students on statewide examinations by erasing incorrect answers and substituting correct answers. By misrepresenting the progress of students, many educators were able to get bonus money for academic achievement that never happened (Morris & Niesse, 2013).

Many states have a contract with Caveon Test Security, the premier company monitoring annual assessments of student achievement, cheating detection, and prevention. This organization has developed data forensics, a process that searches for unusual test response patterns such as getting difficult questions correct while missing easy questions, an abnormally high pass rate for a school, and tests where incorrect answers have been erased and replaced with the correct ones. The service includes protection of instruments from fraudulent practices and applying statistical and web patrolling tools that track cheaters—holding them accountable by providing evidence to school administrators (Wollack & Fremer, 2013).

## Internet Ethics

The Children's Internet Protection Act (2000) requires schools and libraries to install filters to minimize exposure to objectionable material such as pornography. Another feature of cyber legislation, the body of law pertaining to computer information systems and networks, is safeguards for copyright material of authors and artists whose music or ideas are made available online. The national rush to make certain all age groups are online has overlooked training that everyone needs to support ethical behavior on the Internet (Gallant, 2010).

### *Students and Plagiarism*

When students lack ethical commitment needed for searching the Internet, they may suppose it is acceptable to present words and views of someone else as if it was a representation of their own thinking. Plagiarism is a major problem in middle school, high school, and college that teachers are struggling to confront (Davis, Drinan, & Gallant, 2009). Cyber law proposals defining offenses and penalties are emerging as agenda that, in the future, could be determined in the courts instead of in the schools.

Parents share responsibility for helping daughters and sons realize that looking up a topic on the web is only a first step in research, similar to visiting a library. Copying from books, journals, or sources on the Internet and portraying these products as one's own invention is dishonest and defined as cheating (Moore & Robillard, 2008). Because of broad Internet access, deceptive practices by students have been reported as moving downward to earlier grades. In 2012, the Philadelphia School Reform Commission appointed a new position called the testing integrity advisor; the state is investigating over 50 public schools, including elementary schools, over alleged malfeasance regarding student assessment testing (Graham, 2012).

——————

## *Prevention of Plagiarism*

Teachers want students to practice search skills on the Internet but are finding it difficult to cope with plagiarism. To encourage originality and prevent students from taking credit for the writing of other people, schools are contracting with a service that quickly detects work that is plagiarized. *Turnitin.com* is a plagiarism tool that identifies when more than 8 copied words in succession are used in a paper, the original source, and evidence for confronting students and parents. Public schools and universities use this resource. While 31% of the high school students' papers indicate cheating, 26% of college students' papers show cheating. For both high school and college students, *Wikipedia* and *Yahoo Answers* were the top two most popular sources of plagiarized copy (Watters, 2011).

Students are rarely asked to evaluate the practicality of classroom assignments. Another way to better understand student reaction is from conversations in which they describe their experience. Jamal, a sophomore in Montgomery, Alabama, believes it is misleading to limit the cheating focus only on inappropriate motives of students. Jamal suggests, "Maybe a bigger problem is teachers requiring students to memorize instead of teaching them to think. You can cheat if all you are going to be tested on are facts but it is harder when asked to attack or defend a position and actually write an essay."

Jamal's outlook may not reflect consensus. Nevertheless, his view that teachers could minimize cheating by devising more challenging tasks that are less vulnerable to cheating is gaining support. Assignments that motivate learning by doing, encourage reciprocal learning in cooperative groups, support self-directedness, and foster original thinking are essential shifts in teaching that allow students to become actively involved in construction of their own knowledge. Teachers have devoted preparation time mostly to instruction they present in class and little time building assignments allowing students to learn on their own.

Individual and team projects are another context for cheating. Teachers can reduce deception by considering these recommendations.

1. The purpose of every project should be clear; identify anticipated benefits; and invite dialogue about methods, resources, and products acceptable for submission.

2. Relevance should be established for students. A connection between curriculum and real life is confirmed when students are able to get credit for interaction with informants from other generations or cultures whose experience goes beyond the perspective offered by a teacher or text.

3. Encourage students to express feelings and describe the processes they rely on to reach conclusions. These presentations are more interesting to write and more satisfying to read.

4. Go beyond the customary scope of problem solving. Students are often presented questions the teacher already knows answers for or could readily locate. Yet, generating alternative solutions and then making choices is often the key to overcoming personal challenges in life.

5. Encourage varied types of information gathering. Submissions might include a hard copy of the located web data accompanied by the same information summarized and interpreted in a student's own words, results drawn from polls or interviews, and descriptions of steps in an experiment.

6. Identify criteria to be used for evaluating the quality of performance. When students know in advance the criteria that will be applied to judge work, they can focus appropriately instead of reporting at the end, "I wasn't sure if this is what you wanted."

7. Allow students to reflect, revise, and improve a project product they submit. Having access to suggestions of classmates who read their work and being expected to revise products fosters perseverance, and motivates acceptance of criticism.

8. Consider an oral critique. This method allows students to express their views verbally, permits classmates to practice giving helpful criticism, enables teachers to call for clarification if points are unclear, and eliminates use of tech tools for deception.

## Integrity and Maturity

Legalistic syllabi and tough policies are insufficient to prevent cheating. Instruction is also needed. Students are able to understand that honesty is an indicator of developing maturity. Indeed, maturity cannot materialize without the sense of obligation to treat other people fairly (Sternberg & Subotnik, 2006). Students can benefit from discussions about the need for integrity in all sectors of life. They should also be informed about the seldom considered damaging effects of cheating—gaps in knowledge and skills that adversely affect later success when the knowledge foundation needed to understand processes in higher-level courses has not been acquired (Gallant, 2010).

Academic dishonesty presents another major disadvantage. The moral compass students need to guide conduct can be thrown off course. This is the message portrayed in *The Emperor's Club*, a motion picture starring Kevin Cline (Hoffman, 2002). As a teacher and the assistant principal at St. Benedict's High School for Boys, he motivates students to choose a moral purpose for their lives in addition to choosing career goals. The story illustrates how great teachers can have a profound influence and cheating during youth can become a life-long habit.

Fairness and equality are core values families and schools expect to pass on to youth. However, neither value is conveyed in situations where students are placed at a disadvantage because others cheat. When dishonesty is common, high achievers are unable to distinguish themselves, gaps in student learning remain hidden, tutoring needs go undetected, and progress reports are inaccurate. Scandals at work and in the government continually show how unethical practices by leaders can erode public trust and motivate cynicism. Early adolescence is the time when most people establish their sense of moral direction, define commendable behavior and misconduct, and determine relationships they approve of and ways of treating others they reject. For these reasons, students benefit from guidance that leads them to choose integrity to shape behavior rather than rely on cheating to get ahead (Adams & Hamm, 2006).

## Face-to-Face Bullying

Most adults recall school bullies they tried to avoid and still wonder what caused them to torment their classmates. Similarly, opinions vary about normality of bully behavior, the kinds of individuals who become involved, and the quality of relationships they have with their relatives and friends. There is also speculation about influence of bullies on classmates who watch while they victimize others. Research has led to knowledge about some of the issues (Bazelon, 2013).

### *Misconceptions About Bullies*

When bullies stop bothering peers, schools can become safer places. One way to begin is abandon the misconception that bullying is normal, a stage that some people go through but will likely outgrow as they become adults. Studies support an opposite conclusion and suggest ways must be found to change behavior while bullies are still young. Psychologists at the

University of Michigan carried out a longitudinal study of 500 students, following them from age 8 until age 30 (Huesmann, Dubow, & Boxer, 2009). Assessments showed that bullies experienced more adjustment problems than their peers. About 25% who started fights during elementary school by pushing, hitting, or stealing belongings of others had a criminal record by age 30; the comparable record was less than 5% among the nonbullies. Furthermore, waiting longer to intervene makes matters worse.

Bullies often have unstable relationships as adults. In comparison with the general population, male bullies abuse wives more often, drive cars erratically, get fired from jobs, commit more felonies, and less often attain vocational success. Females who bully classmates in childhood are more inclined to severely punish their own children. Male and female bullies have higher than average rates of alcoholism, more often suffer personality disorders, and require greater use of mental health services (Larson, 2008).

Although bullies get attention from their teachers and principals, institutional responses seldom include instruction to improve their behavior. Later on, the same dysfunctional patterns that make bullies troublesome to classmates are portrayed on a larger scale in employment histories when rejection is the most common response of coworkers. Parents of school-age bullies should be made aware that harassing others would eventually harm the perpetrators as well as victims (Dutton, 2007). Teachers should recognize that helping students develop their own internal guidance system is a more constructive response to violence than increasing the number of guidance counselors.

Contrary to popular opinion, bullies are often intelligent, receive good grades, and express self-confidence (Huesmann, 2007). These assets cause some teachers to underestimate the dangers that may occur if such children grow up without a sense of empathy and continue to mistreat others. Policy makers encourage educators to take the problems of bullies as seriously as if they had another disability teachers feel more comfortable trying to remediate. If students experience difficulty reading, tutoring is provided with the expectation that intervention will result in improvement. However, educators less often express hope if a student is lacking in self-restraint or concern for feelings of others. In such cases, potential for learning is ignored in favor of options for punishment.

Confronting social skill deficits and emotional immaturity are matters teachers feel unprepared for when students begin to show signs of failure. Many schools give up on these individuals. Yet, classes are provided for students who have taken illegal drugs because it is assumed they are capable of recovery. This same optimistic attitude should apply to students whose emotional and social difficulties are exhibited by lack of self-restraint and empathy (Ybarra, Diener-West, & Leaf, 2007).

Low self-esteem is sometimes suggested as an explanation for motivation of bullies. Research does not support this opinion. In fact, there is a strong relationship between high self-esteem and violent behavior (Baumeister, 2005; Baumeister, Campbell, Krueger, & Vohs, 2003). People that have high self-esteem often perpetrate violence. This troublesome group includes bullies, racists, members of gangs, people associated with organized crime, rapists, and psychopaths. Intervention with these individuals that concentrates on self-control rather than self-esteem is more successful.

The favorable self-impression of bullies is usually based on lack of awareness about what peers think of them until late adolescence. While bullies are growing up, they hang out with one or two companions, often lackeys who feel constrained to help them carry out hostile wishes. Bullies mistakenly suppose that their own social situation is normal (Henkin, 2005). Owing to the social blind spot that makes them oblivious to how they are seen by classmates, bullies characteristically lack empathy and ignore views of classmates they intimidate. Acquiring empathy is an essential purpose for education of bullies (Orpinas & Horne, 2006).

Female bullies need rehabilitation too (Chemelynski, 2006). Male bullies rely on physical aggression like shoving, hitting, and kicking; females usually resort to relational aggression. To get even they spread rumors about someone so classmates will reject the victim. The way female bullies strive for domination is threatening social exclusion, "You cannot come to my party unless you . . ." Threats are made to withdraw friendship in order to get one's own way, "I won't be your friend unless . . ." The silent treatment is applied to produce social isolation. These expressions of coercion are effective because they jeopardize what girls value—their relationship with other girls. Social exclusion is especially powerful when girls transition to adolescence and are more susceptible to conflict (Goldstein & Brooks, 2012).

### Family Relationships of Bullies

Abuse is a behavior often learned at home where bullies are victims of mistreatment. Studies have found parents of bullies interact with children much differently than families of nonviolent children. Parents of bullies do not use the praise, encouragement, or humor other parent's use in communicating with sons and daughters. At home bullies often experience putdowns, sarcasm, and criticism (Dutton, 2007). The punishment of a young bully may depend more on the mood of a parent than gravity of misconduct. If a parent is angry, harsh punishment is usual. If the parent is in good spirits, the child may get away with almost anything (Centers for Disease Control and Prevention, 2011).

Dysfunctional homes sponsor an outlook that life is essentially a battleground and threats are anticipated from any direction at almost any time (Hardy & Laszloffy, 2006). Even when bullies grow too strong for parents to physically abuse them, they continue to observe mistreatment of younger siblings or a parent. The lesson is always the same—whoever has the greatest power is right. Based on erratic attacks from parents, bullies become wary and they misinterpret motives of people outside the family too. They often see hostility where there is none and this suspicion precipitates conflict with classmates (Larson, 2008). Schools must be given authority to educate dysfunctional families by giving instruction to parents of bullies as well as their children. This approach can help parents adopt constructive goals, better communication, and suitable forms of discipline. In the long-term, counseling cannot compensate for failing to offer parents the skills needed to give humane guidance (Larson & Lochman, 2005).

### Bully Influence on Peers

Students who are spared as targets of bullies can still be harmed by social lessons that are learned from them. Researchers at York University in Toronto, Canada found that bullies who do not get negative feedback about their misconduct present a dysfunctional model for classmates that suggest there are no consequences for aggression (Mishna, Scarcello, & Pepler, 2005). This observation can motivate bystanders to behave in the same way themselves. Evidence about the influence of bullies comes from studies where peers have been observers in over 80% of bully episodes at school (Lodge & Frydenberg, 2005). The willingness to remain spectators and acquiesce encourages greater intimidation (Coloroso, 2009). A study of 1,000 elementary students found that an experimental group provided guidance about ways to respond to bullies later reported enhanced bystander responsibility, greater perceived adult responsiveness, and less acceptance of bullying and aggression than peers in an untreated control group (Frey, Kirschstein, & Snell, 2005).

It is important to identify conditions that would motivate bystanders to intervene in behalf of those being mistreated. Few students challenge bullies but most who do take action have high social status. To increase peer intervention, it is necessary to make students aware of their individual responsibility to take action and demonstrate empathy for anyone being abused. In addition, students need effective intervention strategies and should be encouraged to show the courage necessary to offset a silent majority whose lack of caring can deprive victims of support while at the same time jeopardizing their own future as compassionate individuals (Beran & Shapiro, 2005).

When bully behavior is viewed as a group phenomenon, the participant role of observers is recognized and attention can be given to training them to facilitate social change by becoming willing to report incidents. Besides victims (who suffer humiliation, anxiety, and pain) and bullies (who harm others and endanger their social and emotional development), the witnesses (who are in the process of forming lifelong responses to injustice) deserve consideration. Bully behavior may begin with minimal harm but records show that it can escalate to devastating treatment of others (Salmivalli, Kaukiainen, & Voeten, 2005).

When parents and students discuss worries about school safety, the fear that someone will bring a weapon is mentioned more than other concerns. This attributes to many killings by middle school and high school students and recognition that, annually, more than 4,000 students are expelled for having a gun at school. Nevertheless, nearly half of students report they would not tell teachers or principals if they knew a classmate brought a weapon to school. The reason they give is possible retaliation—a fear the person would "Get them back." Clearly, unwillingness to report peer abuse is a perilous norm. Following cases of violence, it has often been discovered that students knew of threats but did not take them seriously or decided not to inform the faculty or parents (United States Secret Service, 2012).

The attainment of school and family cooperation can nurture development of healthy social norms that motivate students to treat others with fairness and respect and also to assume responsibility for the safety of classmates. The following peer support practices to decrease bullying and increase concern for others can assist faculty with their guidance task.

- Use healthy criteria for self-evaluation so confidence is not based on demeaning others.
- Urge students to periodically identify positive qualities that they observe in classmates.
- Portray social maturity as an achievement demonstrated by acceptance of differences.
- Help students realize that teasing shows an inability to care about other people's feelings.
- Show courage in challenging the mistreatment of others when it is observed or suggested.

- Build feelings of belonging and support for teammates from cooperative learning groups.
- Provide reminders on class walls about no name-calling, eye rolling, or laughing at peers.
- Teach students how to process teaser comments presented in many situations at all ages.
- Discuss how being teased can have harmful effects regardless of intentions of the teaser.
- Create a list of words students agree are not to be used when they talk about each other.
- Encourage students to identify the person they wish to become and set personality goals.
- Ask students about a time they teased someone, their reasons for doing so, and outcomes.
- Invite students to share an incident when they were teased and how they felt at that time.
- Enable students to learn conflict resolution skills instead of reliance on negative remarks.
- Suggest that parents talk with their child who is a teaser or was teased by someone else.

## Abuse in Cyber Space

Many adolescents possess greater skills than their teachers or parents in using tools of communication technology they will need for continued learning. This unprecedented lag in proficiency of grownups has created a virtual island where the adolescents can roam without supervision, akin to the island portrayed in *Lord of the Flies* by Nobel Prize winner William Golding (1954). His story begins as a group of boys are being evacuated during wartime. The plane they are on is shot down but no one is seriously hurt. After searching the remote island on which they are stranded, the boys realize there are no adults around to tell them what to do, make decisions for them, or punish misconduct.

Adapting to their new social environment means the boys have to develop their own rules and expectations. Some discover that control and intimidation of companions is easier if they paint their faces as a disguise, taking on a mask of anonymity while creating fear in the mind of enemies. In a similar way, adolescents who visit the virtual island called the Internet often conclude that adults are not watching, cannot know if misbehavior occurs, and will be unable to intervene when corrective action is needed. Many parents overschedule themselves and are so busy that they are unable to arrange time to explore what their children are doing on the Cyber Island.

Most students on the Cyber Island participate in healthy activities such as making and maintaining friendships; posting messages on network sites; sharing music, videos, and photos; and learning by self-directed searches for information. Students also recognize technology can be used to express the dark side (Shariff, 2008). Bullies may suppose hiding behind pseudonyms and supposedly well-disguised IP addresses can conceal their identity while victims remain unable to detect the source of threat. On this modern day Cyber Island, students can behave in shameful ways, often without accountability for their actions while their victims suffer damaging consequences (Strom, Strom, Walker, Sindel-Arrington, & Beckert, 2011).

Unfortunately, some young victims do not communicate their suffering to adults (Bauman, 2010; Kowalski, Limber, & Agatston, 2008). In addition, experts have drawn attention to a decline in meaningful communication of many teenagers with adults (Epstein, 2010). Because adults, even when present, are uninformed regarding what life is like on the Cyber Island, teenagers increasingly turn to peers as their main source of advice. A national survey by the Kaiser Family Foundation found that adolescents, on average, spend eight hours a day with media and immersed in a peer culture facilitated by cell phones and the Internet. Some youth are in touch with friends 70 hours each week but spend little time interacting with the important adults in their lives (Rideout, Foehr, & Roberts, 2010). One worrisome view is that the society is unintentionally isolating youth, causing them to communicate exclusively with peers on the Cyber Island. Creative initiatives are urgently needed so intergenerational communication can be more common and satisfying (Strom & Strom, 2011).

## *Uniqueness of Cyber Abuse*

Students have always been in contact with bullies in schools and neighborhoods but currently they must also be concerned about unseen enemies (Coloroso, 2009). The assumption that knowledge about face-to-face bullies is applicable to online bullies is unfounded. A national online survey of 1,600 students from ages 10 to 15 found that two-thirds of those who reported being harassed online did not report being bullied at school (Ybarra, Diener-West, & Leaf, 2007). Messages to undermine the reputation of a victim could do more harm than face-to-face altercations. Instead of a case being witnessed by a small group, a much larger audience become observers if cyber bullies communicate embarrassing photographs or text messages. Victims can identify their tormentors at school but cyber bullies can be difficult to trace. As a result, they avoid responsibility and do not fear getting caught or punished (Wolak, Mitchell, & Finkelhor, 2007).

Misconduct in cyberspace presents school principals with uncertainty about the boundaries of their jurisdiction. They are unable to respond when unknown parties send hate messages from a location outside school like a home-based computer or mobile phone. Some students are reluctant to inform adults about anxiety they experience at the hands of cyber enemies, fearing that parents may overreact by taking away their computer, Internet access, or cell phone. Many students are unwilling to risk having their parents choose such extreme forms of protection. The reason is without tech tools, they would be socially isolated and unable to stay in contact with friends (Rosen, 2010).

Until recently, victims considered their homes to be a place of safety—sanctuary from those who would mistreat them. This is no longer the case. Most students go online as soon as they return home from school. Some find themselves to be a target of threats, rumors, and lies without knowing the identity of persons creating fear and frustration or how to end the damage (Bauman, 2010). The following examples of cyberbullying from several countries reveal the scope and complexity of arranging safety in cyber space (Strom, Strom, Wingate, Kraska & Beckert, 2012).

Sixteen year old Denise is a high school junior in Los Angeles. She argued with her boyfriend and they broke up. The rejected boy was angry and wanted to get even. The devious method he chose was to post Denise's contact numbers, including her e-mail address, cell phone number, and street address on several sex-oriented websites and blogs. Denise was hounded for months by instant messages, prank callers, and car horns of insensitive people who drove by her house to see whether they could catch a glimpse of her. In this case, the identity of the cyberbully, Denise's former boyfriend, was detected quickly. Nevertheless, his apprehension did not eliminate the sense of helplessness and embarrassment felt by Denise.

Shinobu is a high school freshman in Osaka, Japan. When his gym period was over, Shinobu got dressed in what he believed was the privacy of the changing room. However, a classmate seeking to ridicule Shinobu for being overweight secretly used a cell phone to photograph him. In seconds, the naked boy's picture was sent wirelessly by instant messaging for many students to see. By the time Shinobu finished dressing and went to his next class, he was already a laughing stock at school.

Donna attends eighth grade at a parochial school in Montreal, Canada. Donna and her mother went to Toronto to visit her grandmother who was recuperating from cancer surgery. When Donna returned home, a cyber bully had circulated a rumor that she had contacted SARS (Severe Acute Respiratory Syndrome) in Toronto. Donna's girlfriends were afraid and unwilling to be around her or talk on the phone. Without exception, classmates moved away when Donna came near them.

Some cyber cases involve more than one bully and a single victim. Others could involve a group of bullies that persecute multiple parties. The latter occurs when students respond to online trash polling sites. These websites invite students to name individuals they feel qualify for unflattering characteristics, such as the most obese person at school, boys most likely to be gay, and girls who have slept with the most boys. The usual consequences for those who suffer from this shameful treatment are depression, hopelessness, and withdrawal (McQuade, Colt, & Meyer, 2009).

### Reassessment of Teasing

Detection and rehabilitation of cyber bullies is complicated by the way teasing is generally perceived. Many see teasing as just making fun of someone in a playful way. Teasers often explain their motivation, saying "I was just kidding." In contrast, students report that being teased is stressful. When students report physical abuse to teachers, they are encouraged to identify classmates who hurt them. However, if students report teasing, they are often given a contradictory response. The dilemma begins with a false assumption that teasers lack any motivation to harm and would stop if a person being made fun of expressed their disappointment. So, the victim may be encouraged to suck it up, view the incident as an aspect of life everyone must cope with, and consider their ordeal an opportunity to build character and develop resilience. Research regarding teasing has found that two-thirds of cases implicate name-calling, focused on a person's physical appearance or dress, followed by attention to deviance from group norms, and deficits in academic skills and other imperfections (Agliata, Tantleff-Dunn, & Renk, 2007).

Espelage and Swearer (2010) discovered a high correlation between popularity and bullying among sixth grade students. Those nominated by peers as doing the most teasing were also the students nominated as most popular and having the most friends at school. Given the reluctance of adults to condemn teasing in the same way physical bullying is renounced, it is not surprising that students adopt the same perspective. As a result, many of them trivialize such mistreatment when it is applied to harass others on the Internet. In effect, students are led to believe that to physically hurt someone is unacceptable but teasing them is relatively harmless and could even enhance the victim's ability to cope with adversity (Agliata, Tantleff-Dunn, & Renk, 2007).

There can be a high emotional cost when students call one another undesirable names. These name callers are seldom referred to as bullies even though their behavior undermines the mental health of others. When some victims of teasing respond with violence, their reasons more often relate to being teased than being physically bullied. Reports by teenage murderers who said they could no longer bear being called nasty names frequently identify ridicule as their motivation for taking such desperate actions. The United States Secret Service conducted an investigation of school shootings. The findings revealed that most attackers had experienced long-term severe peer harassment and bullying. More than 70% of them reported being persecuted, threatened, and in certain cases, injured before choosing violence as their solution. In some cases, being bullied had a significant impact on the attacker and seemed to be a factor in deciding to attack the school. More than three-fourths of school shooters were found to have announced suicidal thoughts that were ignored by their friends or family (United States Secret Service, 2012).

In 1999, at Columbine High School in Littleton, Colorado, two students used guns and bombs for killing 12 classmates and a teacher while wounding 30 others before they took their own lives. Following the massacre a suicide note from one shooter was found. In his explanation for why he and Dylan Klebold carried out their bloody rampage, Eric Harris warned against blaming the rock music they listened to like Marilyn Manson or trench coats worn by their outcast group. Instead, he repeated the message communicated to the students while the killing was going on. According to Eric's note, "Your children who have ridiculed me, who have chosen not to accept me, who have treated me like I am not worth their time are dead. I may have taken their lives and mine—but it was your doing. Teachers, parents, let this massacre be on your shoulders until the day you die" (Johnson & Brooke, 1999). When Marilyn Manson was asked what he would say to students at Columbine and the community, he replied, "I wouldn't say a single word. I would listen to what they have to say and that's what no one did" (Moore, 2002).

### Failure to Confront Parents

What happens when schools fail to confront parents about their responsibility to correct their child who is mistreating classmates? Perhaps an important lesson can be learned from England where 34 local education authorities conducted a survey to find out why the number of families deciding to home school their children was increasing at such a rapid pace. The major factors identified by parents who chose this option included a range of motivations such as a rise in the number of students in classes diagnosed with special needs and requiring more teacher attention, parents wanting to spare their child the state's school focus on testing, readily available teaching materials to use at home, guidance on the Internet, and doubling of private school fees. However, the most prominent motivation related to bully behavior. A substantial proportion of parents, 44%, cited bullying as the main reason for withdrawing their child from public school. They explained that they do not believe schools respond to problem children or hold families accountable, as should be the case. Therefore, if their child is bullied, some parents try to manage the situation themselves in a way they feel is best (Blackhurst, 2008). The extent to which American parents who transfer daughters and sons from public schools to home school, charter, private or parochial institutions based on wanting to ensure safety and psychological well being of their children is unknown.

### Anti-Bully School Legislation

New Jersey has the nation's most comprehensive school Anti-Bullying Bill of Rights statue (2011). All faculty and staff must report bully incidents on the same day they become aware of a complaint. A formal investigation must begin within a school day of an episode and completed within ten days including a resolution. All schools must appoint and provide training for an anti-bully coordinator in the school district and a specialist at each school to lead a safety team that includes the principal, teacher, and parent to review complaints. Superintendents have to report twice a year to the state department of education. A grading system ranks every school based on efficiency in combating harassment and intimidation.

This law is viewed as a game changer. During the past, using a four-letter word at school could get students into more trouble than calling someone else ugly, fat, retarded, or gay. Administrators are considered responsible for the culture of their school but the law takes away discretion of principals to ignore something that could be harmful and empowers faculty who, in the past, may have turned a blind eye to episodes knowing a principal would not act. This orientation may have flaws but promises to change what is considered normal acceptable behavior.

These extraordinary reforms were largely motivated by the bully related suicide of a freshman at Rutgers University whose roommate secretly videotaped his relationship with another man to dissemination on the Internet. Many studies have found students who depart from norms are the ones most often harassed (Mason, 2007). When 6,200 students in middle and high school were surveyed, 86% that identified themselves as gay or lesbian reported being physically abused during the past year and 44% reported physical mistreatment (Kosciw, Dias, Greytalk, 2008). The *It Gets Better Project* was established to prevent the suicide of gay and lesbian youth by giving them hope and assurance that they can have a positive future if they are able to get through middle and high school when persecution is most frequent and usually unpunished (Savage & Miller, 2012).

---

## Acceptance of Group Differences

In addition to anti-bully policies, boards of education can amend how history is presented in schools. Elementary and secondary students become more accepting of differences when they learn how groups targeted for abuse have benefitted the nation. During the 1960s schools began to acquaint students with African Americans who were previously unrecognized even though their initiatives had improved national quality of life. In the 1970s, Latinos were first portrayed to the public in a way that acknowledged the contributions by leaders in this subpopulation. The California Fair Accurate Inclusive Respectful (FAIR) Education Act (Senate Bill 48) of (2011) mandates that schools address certain gaps that still exist in current textbooks. Specifically, outstanding figures within the Lesbian, Gay, Bisexual, and Transgender community, advocates for disability rights, racial justice organizations, and other groups that have shaped history should be acknowledged in the textbooks and curriculum that chronicles the evolution of society.

Students should also be taught to recognize that fear is a valuable emotion when it motivates cautious behavior that protects us from harm. People are wise to be guided by fear of consuming illegal drugs, chatting with online predators, or traveling with drunk drivers. These kinds of dangers warrant consideration because they have the potential to threaten self-preservation. On the other hand, fear of groups whose behavior departs from norms does not serve the survival purpose, compromise safety, place the general welfare at risk, or undermine individual freedom to pursue a lifestyle of our choosing. The fact is fear of differences can only be sustained by dissemination of misinformation that is used as a basis to justify the abuse of selected groups (Strom, Strom, Wingate, Kraska, & Beckert, 2012).

In the past, a popular statement was "Sticks and stones can break my bones but names will never hurt me." We now know that statement is false because research has shown that being called names hurts and the extent of harm depends in part on the age of the victim. Prior to adolescence, students lack access to a defense mechanism called rationalization. Consequently, they are inclined to believe negative comments that others say about them. Parents struggle to convince children that such insults are false. Consider 8 year old John who, in tears, tells his mother that Roger has been calling him a "retard." John's mother may point out that "You, John, are assigned to the highest reading group in class while Roger is not in that reading group. This means that him calling you a retard is foolish." However, John is not old enough to rationalize and so remains convinced that he is whatever Rogers calls him. This sad story implicates education to treat everyone with similar respect and kindness. Being subjected to mistreatment as a child can have lifelong consequences in terms of self-esteem and confidence to achieve.

## Summary and Implications

High rates of cheating, even among honor students, shows that development of moral integrity is not keeping pace with other aspects of mental development. In response, initiatives are underway to motivate ethical conduct and define conditions of integrity to govern conduct. Explanations for why so many students cheat include erosion of ethics in society, high stakes testing, parental pressures to excel, and student desire to get ahead no matter what the cost. Schools should poll students to assess prevalence of cheating, reaction to academic misconduct, individual involvement, and ways to reduce misconduct. Technology to detect cheating, devising multiple versions of tests, teacher surveillance, and alternative assessments deserve attention.

Everyone needs training to understand ethical responsibilities on the Internet. There are websites that offer students, for free or a price, papers to submit so they do not have to write their own. Consequently, plagiarism presents teachers with situations of uncertainty regarding whether they are grading their students or achievements of someone else. Educators are reluctant to express doubts about the dishonesty of any student without proof because they fear retribution from parents and administration. To assist teachers, schools should pay for services that detect plagiarism. Another way to reduce cheating is for teachers to devise challenging assignments in which students defend or they oppose particular views and provide opportunities for reciprocal learning as generational reporters or cultural reporters gathering input from older relatives or community sources.

Use of legalistic syllabi that clearly state school policy and punishment for participating in deceptive practices can impact thinking and motivate accepted conduct. Instruction is necessary as well. Students are able to recognize that becoming mature cannot be achieved unless they demonstrate fairness and equality toward others. They should become acquainted with cyber laws, why these are needed, and situations that could place decision making on punishment for school offenses in the courts instead of the schools. There is a need to educate parents—providing agenda for family discussions about the importance of honesty, trust, and integrity.

The customary way to learn civil behavior has been to observe and imitate more mature people who are admired as models. This pattern of development does not guide how students are learning to treat others in cyberspace. They are technologically savvy, communicate more with peers than with adults, and turn to one another more for advice on interaction for using tools of technology. Adults accelerate excessive reliance on peers for communication and guidance when they refuse to listen to students about conditions of learning at school. If school improvement committees know student opinions from anonymous Internet polls, a more accurate portrayal of institutional assets and limitations in relation to cheating and civil behavior can become known.

# 10

## *Thinking and Theories*

Neuroscience can detect regions of the brain that are implicated whenever specific tasks are performed (Cozolino, 2013). These discoveries urge schools to expand the cognitive abilities emphasized when teachers are the primary source of instruction. In addition, Internet access encourages schools to give higher priority to thinking so that students can become self-directed, interdependent, and credited for achievement that occurs in the classroom and online. The purposes of this chapter are to explore mechanisms of thinking for processing information, impact of cyber technology and peers as sources of instruction, conditions for a paradigm of collaboration, and a model for evaluating advantages and limitations of particular learning theories.

## Development of Intelligence

### *Assessment of Mental Abilities*

Jean Piaget (1896–1980), a psychologist in Geneva, Switzerland, wanted to find out how children think and interpret the world. When his career be-

*Thinking in Childhood and Adolescence,* pages 201–221
Copyright © 2013 by Information Age Publishing
**201**

gan during the 1920s, he worked on test development. The tasks included administering standardized measures to children until Piaget made three observations that caused him to pursue a new direction for the assessment of mental abilities. First, instead of the usual method of calculating the number of students that get correct answers for items, Piaget examined incorrect answers to detect limitations students of the same age had in common. His conclusion was that the thinking of older children is qualitatively different from younger children. As a result, he abandoned the quantitative intelligence concept (Piaget, 1954, 1963, 1969).

A second observation caused Piaget to try new methods for studying intelligence. He thought a strategy was needed to give interviewers greater freedom than was required for standardized testing. In response to reading about Freudian psychology, Piaget tried a procedure that would allow child answers to guide the flow of questions by interviewers. However, the abnormal children he worked with had verbal deficits so this approach was not productive. Another novel feature was applied. Besides having the students state their answers as best they could, Piaget invited them to manipulate objects, thereby crediting action as evidence of thinking instead of limiting demonstration of knowledge to the use of words. Many years later other researchers found that verbal ability is greater among students from higher economic backgrounds (Eysenck & Keane, 2005).

A third way Piaget (1970) departed from other observers of development was his recognition that, because the mind seems to be an integrated unit, the best way to instruct students is by offering curriculum they can understand at their present level of thinking. His terminology is important for understanding information processing. Piaget referred to the term schemas to describe how children make sense of their experiences. *Schemas* are defined as temporary cognitive structures determining the way information is processed and situations are organized. As students encounter new experiences, their schemas must enlarge or change to allow for adjustment in a complex environment.

### Constructivism Theory

According to Piaget (1970), people rely on two processes for adaptation. First, the process of *assimilation* calls for the integration of new conceptual, perceptual, or motor information into existing schemas. To illustrate, Don is a first time visitor to the French Impressionist Exhibition at the Metropolitan Museum of Art in New York City. Before coming to the museum, he looks at pictures by Monet and Van Gogh in magazines. During Don's observation at the museum, his "Impressionist schema" has to expand to include the work of Manet, Toulouse-Lautrec, Cézanne, Gauguin, Seurat, Sisley, and Matisse—all artists who lived during the late nineteenth century and commonly explored the visual analysis of color and light. Assimilation enlarges the size of a schema, as in Don's case, but does not result in a schema change. Instead, a second process people rely on for adaptation is called *accommodation* that requires modification or replacement of a schema in order that novel conditions can be accepted.

When Don left the Impressionist gallery, he took the elevator to the next higher floor of the museum where the modern art exhibits are located. In this new context, Don was obliged to accept a different set of criteria in order to appreciate the work of abstract expressionists whose representations are more often symbolic than literal. This artistic group includes icons such as Braque, Calder, Kandinsky, Miro, Nevelson, Pollack, and Rothko. The schema Don applied to enjoy Impressionism did not enable appreciation of modern art so it was necessary to adopt a new schema. Imbalance between the familiar and the novel creates tension until new schema categories are formed.

When students sense disequilibrium, they search for equilibration through greater assimilation or by accommodation of examining unfamiliar concepts and events in new ways. Equilibration takes place when a suitable balance is struck between the amount of assimilation and amount of accommodation. If someone is engaged in assimilation only, that person would possess a few very large schemas, tend to perceive most situations as similar, and be unable to recognize differences. Conversely, someone who uses only accommodation would have many very small schemas, tend to perceive most situations as different from one another, and demonstrate an inability to recognize similarities.

*Constructivism* is the name applied to Piaget's theory that attempts to describe how students actively develop their own meaning for events based on their personal experience (Fosnot, 2005). Piaget described the way thinking evolves by succession of stages roughly associated with chronological age as shown in Table 10.1. Each of the stages are further discussed in Chapter 14.

## Importance of Support by Peers

Russian psychologist Lev Vygotsky (1896–1934) was a contemporary of Piaget. Both men agreed that the key to durable learning is for students to build some of their own knowledge instead of acquiring it vicariously by listening to teachers and through memorization. Piaget's identification of thinking stages caused him to recommend that teachers arrange opportu-

**TABLE 10.1  Thinking Abilities of Children and Adolescents**

| Ages | Thinking Abilities | Achievements and Limitations |
|---|---|---|
| **2 to 6** | Language | Speech is becoming socialized |
| | Classification | Organizes using a single factor |
| | Perception | Judgment is based upon senses |
| | Centration | Focuses on one aspect at a time |
| | Egocentrism | Unaware of how others see things |
| **6 to 11** | Reversibility | Carries thought forward and backward |
| | Logic | Solves problems in objective ways |
| | Decentration | Attends to several events at once |
| | Classification | Uses multiple factors in organization |
| | Seriation | Arranges by hierarchical order |
| **11 to 18** | Propositional Thought | Able to manipulate abstract symbols |
| | Meta-Thinking | Critically examines someone's logic |
| | Experimental Reasoning | Relies on testing to reach solutions |
| | Recognizes Combinations | Imagines full range of possibilities |
| | Understands Historical Time | Contemplates the future and past |
| | Idealistic Egocentrism | Applies excessive self-criticism |

*Source:* Adapted from *Psychology of Intelligence*, by J. Piaget, 1969. New York, NY: Littlefield, Adams.

nities for student exploration that allows personal knowledge building. Vygotsky (1978) did not propose new cognitive stages but instead emphasized collaboration as a condition teachers should encourage to enhance learning. Vygotsky saw merit in having all students perform some tasks with peers who are more competent than themselves (Smagorinsky, 2011).

Vygotsky (1978) joined Piaget in rejecting standardized testing as the exclusive method to assess intelligence. He believed that educators should go beyond detection of mental age and link processes of development with learning abilities. In order to merge development and learning, he maintained two separate levels of development must be evaluated. The *actual development level* identifies mental capacities that are shown by intelligence tests indicating what an individual can do alone without help. However, this awareness should not be the end to assessment. Vygotsky challenged the assumption that tasks students are able to do by themselves represent the full scope of their abilities. What if, as a result of dialogue with a teacher or tutoring from a more competent peer, students given questions or shown examples of solving problems become able to do so without help or can nearly finish these tasks on their own? Vygotsky's *potential development level* defines achievements students can reach with help from others. He maintained that this broader view represented a more suitable index of mental development than only what individuals can accomplish alone (Vygotsky, 1994).

The need to differentiate actual development and potential development can be clarified with an example (Vygotsky, 1998). Two students are administered an IQ test. Both are ten years old and obtain scores equivalent to being mentally eight years old. This means they can independently solve problems consistent with a normative degree of difficulty dealt with by students two years younger than themselves. Generally, since both students had the same IQ, it is assumed that their prospects for learning must be similar and it would frustrate them to be exposed to problems higher than their mental age of eight years. However, in this case, a teacher demonstrates how to solve more difficult problems, invites the students to replicate her examples, arranges for repeated observation of specific steps in the process, asks them to finish the task, encourages reflection on personal logic, and offers guidance as needed. In the end, one student is able, with assistance, to solve problems considered appropriate for nine year olds while the other student can do tasks up to the level of twelve year olds (Vygotsky, 1998).

Because performance of the two students varied to a high degree when given guidance, expectations for learning as individuals should differ. The *zone of proximal development* is the distance between the actual level of a student's development as assessed by independent problem solving and the level of potential development as found by problem solving with guidance from an adult or in collaboration with more capable peers (Vygotsky, 1994). The zone of proximal development concept shows learning can lead development. That is, the natural development process lags behind and this sequence results in zones of proximal development that call attention to the importance of tutoring, cooperative learning, dialogue with relatives, and interaction with out-of-school mentors.

A key process linked with the zone of proximal development is called *scaffolding*—techniques that are used to adjust guidance to match levels of performance. At the outset, a teacher might rely on direct instruction to introduce concepts. As the learner becomes more proficient, a gradual shift occurs so the teacher role shifts to monitoring progress, providing feedback, offering encouragement, and providing minimal correction. Middle school and high school teachers find the zone of proximal development and scaffolding concepts support better instruction.

For example, the formal operations content of math and science is cumulative so it presents difficulty for many students. Vygotsky's insights encourage peer teaching and cooperative learning in secondary school because of the greater ability of some students who could tutor others (Cukras, 2006). When students admit they are completely lost, they communicate a feeling of being outside their zone. If this occurs in a cooperative group, teammates should urge questions so a student can reconnect again. Otherwise, time will be lost for the learner and the motivation to put forth an effort may decline.

### Inclusion of Disabled Students

Vygotsky (1994) believed the social context of schooling is essential for special education students. He maintained that it is inappropriate to rely on the actual level of development, as shown by test results, as the upper limit for expectations of students with disabilities. Because mentally retarded students perform poorly on measures of abstract thinking, educators are inclined to give up on arranging tasks that require abstraction in favor of tasks that reflect Piaget's concrete stage of thinking (typical for ages 6–11). However, when instruction is limited to concrete experiences, mentally handicapped students are prevented from overcoming their limitations.

In Vygotsky's (1978) view, the most influential learning for students who have disabilities is the social consequence of rejection by normal classmates who would not behave that way in a more humane society. Forty years after Vygotsky died, the high cost of social exclusion was finally acknowledged by the Education for All Handicapped Children Act (1975) as justification for ending the long-standing practice of isolating students in special education. The replacement practice, initially called "mainstreaming," and more recently named "inclusion," is considered the best way to enable the normal population to accept student differences while also enabling those with disabilities to acquire the social skills they need by imitation of their normal peers (Farrell, 2012).

## Learning Without Adult Teachers

The premise of constructivism, originated by Piaget and Vygotsky, is that students learn best when they are allowed to build some knowledge on their own rather than being told about ideas by the presentation of their teachers. Students invent personal theories by assimilating new information into existing schema or they modify their understanding by accommodation of novel data. This section reviews cyber constructivism that has gained global attention over the past decade. Vygotsky described potential importance of peer influence on learning, but no one knows how much students could learn from peers in situations where adult supervision is lacking.

## *Appeal of Technology to Children*

A cyber form of constructivism presents children in resource-scarce environments with opportunities for cooperative learning. Leadership in this context has been provided by Sugata Mitra, a professor of Educational Technology at New Castle University in England. Before Mitra joined higher education in 2006, he was the director of research and development for India's largest software company in New Delhi. When he went to social gatherings, affluent parents often told him that their children could do computer tasks the adults regarded as very complicated and impressive (Mitra, 2003).

Mitra wondered whether these reports from parents were exaggerated, reflecting their own lack of experience with computers. If educated adults underestimate how well their children can perform with little or no formal training, perhaps disadvantaged youth can attain the same competence. Since children do not ask for or receive much instruction on computing, maybe allowing them more unsupervised use is a key to accelerating the acquisition of basic skills. To find out, Mitra put a Pentium computer with a fast Internet connection and touch pad in a kiosk located on the wall separating his company from a wasteland that people living in an adjacent slum used as an alley. The computer was always left on so that passersby would have a chance to tinker with it. All activity was monitored by a remote computer and video camera mounted in a nearby tree (Mitra, 2006).

Most adults glanced at the kiosk but did not stop to investigate. In contrast, 80 children between ages 6 to 16 and not enrolled in school, expressed curiosity. Within days, many had acquired basic computer literacy skills. Mitra had defined basic literacy as the ability to carry out window operation functions like using a mouse, point, drag, drop, copy, and browse the Internet. After three months the children had learned to load and save files, play games, run programs, listen to music, set up and access email, chat on the Internet, troubleshoot, download and play video games. Disney and Microsoft Paint were the favorite sites because everyone enjoyed drawing but no one had money for the supplies (Mitra, 2006).

When a second kiosk was placed in an illiterate rural village where no one had ever seen a computer, children helped one another gain basic skills. These "hole in the wall" projects have expanded to more than 100 sites in impoverished areas that have no schools or teachers. The cost of setting up a single kiosk and maintaining it for a year was initially about $10,000. On average, 100 children used a kiosk. Mitra's dream was to install 100,000 kiosks. He speculated that the outcome would be 10 million additional computer-literate children who would change India forever by moving themselves toward prosperity. Half of the population of India is illiterate (Mitra & Dangwal, 2010).

### Shared Exploration and Discovery

The theoretical paradigms merging to support *minimally invasive education* are unstructured collaboration and shared exploration as children rely on trial and error in opening the door to cyberspace. Because this approach to learning depends on discovery and sharing, working in groups is essential. Children teach one other and regulate the process. The ability to become computer literate in a short time seems to be independent of formal education, socio-economic background, gender, ability to read, or intelligence. The minimally invasive education concept has been adopted by other nations with a scarcity of teachers, schools, or hardware. Hole-in-the-wall kiosks have been established in Egypt, Cambodia, and six countries in Africa (Mitra, 2012a).

Learners tend to divide themselves into "knows" and "know nots." However, there is a recognition a person who knows will part with knowledge in return for friendship and exchange. The more mature participants, usually older females, commonly insist upon proceeding in a civil manner. As a result, everyone is able to enjoy the satisfaction of a social experience and a chance to learn more rapidly because they imitate one other, spur each other on, and pool their insights. When a group no longer produces breakthroughs, minimal intervention is welcomed from an online teacher who introduces a new skill for students to use in generating discoveries on their own. Studies have found that adults in the affected communities believe this method can spread literacy (85%), provide opportunity to learn about computers (80%), improve social cohesion (79%), develop confidence and pride (85%), and improve mental performance (79%) (Mitra, 2005).

### Self-Organized Learning Environments

Based on progress of children using kiosks, Mitra established 12 Self-Organized Learning Environments (SOLE) in disadvantaged areas of India. This concept requires modifying the conditions of classroom learning. Children work in small groups of four with one computer and can rely on Google and the Internet to search for information that can allow them to address hard but interesting questions such as: Do trees think? How does an iPad know where it is? Where did language come from? While supervision by adults is unnecessary, students can benefit from friendly volunteer mentors or mediators. Mitra placed an advertisement in a London newspaper asking grandmothers who were computer literate to devote one hour a week to child development. The women use Skype to help immigrant students speak and get feedback about their new language. Those who are members of the "granny cloud" provide encouragement without giving direction and they assist students at no cost to the schools (Mitra, 2012b).

These outcomes underscore the potential benefits of exposure to the Internet, the capability of students to accelerate organization of knowledge by uniting their efforts, and the need for teachers to present tasks that support opportunities for students to practice collaborative constructivism. Creation of curriculum content is no longer as important as the provision of infrastructure and access to a world of information. Minimally invasive education is a self-structured system that assumes students can construct knowledge on their own. In this paradigm a teacher stands aside and intervenes only when assistance is needed. The custom has been to expect teachers to "make learning happen." Now teachers are expected to "let learning happen." The distinction between these two expectations is illustrated by reactions of the Indian adults. Unlike children, they just stared at the kiosk and asked, "What is this for? Why is there no one to teach us something? How will we ever use such a device?" Mitra (2012a) explains previously people were led to suppose teachers should show them everything and believe they are unable to learn without them. Once upon a time, in yesterday's world, that was the case.

Alvin Toffler is a futurist, internationally recognized for his trilogy that began with the publication of *Future Shock* in 1970, *The Third Wave* in 1980, and *Powershift* in 1990. His forecasts focused on the benefits and limitations of technology. In a recent book, *Revolutionary Wealth* (2007), Toffler and his wife Heidi warn, "The illiterate of the 21st century will not be the people who cannot read or write, but those who cannot learn, unlearn, and relearn." Whenever a new way of doing something becomes necessary, unlearning is a predictable challenge. *Unlearning* is defined as a willful activity to rid the mind of strong but no longer useful habits. Unlearning can frequently be more difficult than learning something new. Indeed, many people fail to leave habitual forms of response behind. Table 10.2 contains a list of 15 behaviors that students need to unlearn to perform better when they work in cooperative teams.

## Collaboration Integration Theory

Business executives generally advocate school reform because they need to recruit workers with abilities that can match the changing work environment. Instead of showing support for top down compliance driven management, business leaders recommend that schools have more to gain from adopting methods of companies promoting transparency, engagement, shared accountability, and continuous organizational learning. For

**TABLE 10.2   Student Behaviors to Unlearn for Transition to Collaborative Teamwork**

| Traditional Behaviors | Collaborative Behaviors |
|---|---|
| 1. Limit reading to content assigned by teachers | Self-directedness means searching for materials without being told by the teacher. |
| 2. Passive listening without curiosity | Asking questions should become a norm for everyone in an information-oriented society. |
| 3. Not questioning the views of authorities | Critical thinking involves examination of logic for school policies, practices, and rules. |
| 4. Define education as in the classroom only | Growing year round, after graduation, while at work, in retirement, and until life ends. |
| 5. Leader and follower roles for group work | Differentiated roles are assigned and knowledge merged to increase learning. |
| 6. Teachers are the main source of knowledge | Students are accountable to share insights and knowledge with teammates. |
| 7. Over-reliance on use of textbooks for learning | Textbook is augmented by electronic sources, teammates, and community input. |
| 8. Defensiveness when criticized by others | Students learn to constructively process criticism to identify their needs for growth. |
| 9. Dependence upon extrinsic evaluation | Students evaluate themselves and get anonymous observational feedback from teammates. |
| 10. Gratuitous evaluation of performance for friends | Students evaluate teammates in an authentic way as expected in the workplace. |
| 11. Ignoring the intended focus of a discussion | Focus on pertinent issues and good time management reflects student accountability. |
| 12. Individual domination during discussions | Learn to limit length and frequency of comments so that everyone can be heard. |
| 13. Team suppression of divergent thinking | Peer encouragement of creative ideas is a necessary condition for group productivity. |
| 14. Inattention and distraction undermine discussions | Concentrate on agenda, determine implications and solutions. |
| 15. Uninformed opinions are a focus of discussions | Cite credible references to support personal opinions during discussions. |

*Source: Learning Throughout Life: An Intergenerational Perspective*, by Robert Strom and Paris Strom, 2012, p. 196. Information Age Publishing Inc., Charlotte, NC.

example, a number of large and small school districts across the nation in which student test scores had shown significant improvement were examined to determine the conditions they had in common. The study was conducted by the Rutgers University School of Management and Labor Relations with support from Bill and Melinda Gates Foundation. The report concluded that, contrary to the common premise of educational reformers, the factor that most often related to long term improvement of teachers, schools, and students is "substantive collaboration" at every level—the classroom, school, district, community; in short, collaboration among all of the key stakeholders (Rubenstein & McCarthy, 2010).

## Assumptions About Learning and Instruction

No one knows how to merge all the educational resources that are currently available. Bold and creative alternatives should be formulated and subjected to evaluation. Toward this goal, Strom and Strom (2009) devised a theoretical model of thinking and learning that includes specific roles for students and their involvement in the assessment of group learning. The Collaboration Integration Theory, CIT, is based on these assumptions:

1. Students need to practice the teamwork skills that are required in the workplace.
2. Perspectives are enriched by incorporating views of sources outside the school.
3. Cultural and generational differences of opinion deserve student consideration.
4. Assigning separate roles to team members increases the scope of group learning.
5. Accountability can be determined by how well students perform particular roles.
6. Observation about self and peer contributions to group work improve evaluation.
7. Individual productivity can be motivated by the anonymous recognition of peers.

## Cooperative Learning Exercises and Roles

The instructional method used to apply Collaboration Integration Theory is CLEAR, an acronym for Cooperative Learning Exercises and Roles. The goals of CLEAR are to:

- Shift the student role from passive to active learning.
- Make the collaborative process a focus of group work.
- Enable every student to provide a unique contribution.
- Reduce boredom by differentiating individual roles.
- Ensure enough peer observation to support its reliability.

This theoretical approach provides the greatest benefit when teammates have certain roles in common and additional roles based on individuals choosing tasks for which they are willing to be accountable. If teachers pre-pare multiple tasks so each team member can perform a separate role, it be-comes easier to establish individual accountability, support self-directedness, increase sources of instruction, and expand the scope of group learning.

The CLEAR model includes twelve roles that allow teams to decide about allocation of teacher tasks and the modification of guidelines for them. This approach calls on each student to make a continuous contribu-tion to the learning of teammates by taking responsibility for a particular role. The dominance that occurs when someone haphazardly takes over a group can be minimized because differentiated roles obligate each person to pay attention and listen while teammates report the results of their task. It is recommended that, for each meeting of a class, all students share three roles—discussant, reader, and review guide.

Instead of individuals participating in ineffective multitasking, CLEAR en-ables teams to practice the multitasking that is needed to expand the scope of learning and improve group production. This is consistent with the poten-tial of simultaneity provided by the Internet. It also illustrates a need to make changes in what is expected of groups and individuals. An abundance of tem-plate exercises for each of the instructional units make it possible for every student to practice a range of roles and thereby improve overall benefits of group interaction. Eventually everyone should engage in each role rather than repeatedly perform a favorite or because they do it well (Strom & Strom, 2009).

To review, tasks are differentiated so that, during a single semester each student gets to practice twelve roles to enrich group learning (Strom & Strom, 2009). Mutual understanding of purposes and anticipated out-comes for each role guides expectations of the group and clarifies account-ability that is expected of individual students. These 12 roles are defined as:

- *Summarizer* states team considerations, conclusions, and recommendations.
- *Discussant* listens to teammates and builds on ideas expressed by others.
- *Reader* shares views of outsiders and brings resources peers can examine.
- *Generational Reporter* conveys the ideas and feelings of other age groups.
- *Cultural Reporter* studies subculture and helps peers appreciate diversity.
- *Challenger* reflects an opposing view to increase the factors in a dialogue.

- *Voter* identifies the anonymous viewpoints of a particular cohort via polling.
- *Organizer* leads discussions, maintains balance, and tracks group progress.
- *Review Guide* monitors sharing of information from notes about the text.
- *Evaluator* provides evidence about peer and self-group work performance.
- *Improviser* looks into novel ways to detect possibilities and disadvantages.
- *Storyteller* conveys examples that help recognize how to apply the lesson.

### *Student Assessment of Learning in Groups*

Teacher and student discontent with teamwork skills evaluation motivated the design of the Teamwork Skills Inventory (Strom & Strom, 2011a). To help students engage in low-risk practice needed for peer and self-evaluation, this assessment tool

- gives quick automated feedback to students about their skill set,
- identifies the teamwork skills individuals consistently demonstrate,
- provides individual profiles that contain anonymous peer feedback,
- compares peer observation of performance with self-impression,
- detects skill deficits of individuals and groups to guide instruction,
- credits conscientious teammates for initiatives and contributions,
- discovers slackers that fail to do their fair share of the workload,
- provides an inflation index that reveals exaggerated evaluations,
- summarizes team skills of individuals for portfolio placement, and
- enables faculty teaching the same students to intervene together.

The inventory consists of 25 items shown in Table 10.3. The items appear in conceptually convenient clusters of five skills each to detect whether a student: (a) attends to teamwork, (b) seeks and shares information, (c) communicates with teammates, (d) thinks critically and creatively, and (e) gets along with teammates. Skills are defined in a document that is used for student referral during discussions with parents, teachers, and teammates (Strom & Strom, 2011a). Instrument items are based on studies of cooperative learning, group dynamics, creative thinking, critical thinking, and personnel evaluation methods used in business and industry (Moore & Parker, 2008; Myers & Anderson, 2008; Roseth, Johnson, & Johnson, 2008; Runco, 2006; Tapscott & Williams, 2010a; Torrance, 2000).

---

**TABLE 10.3   Criteria for Evaluation of Teamwork in Cooperative Groups**

**Attends to Teamwork**
1.  Demonstrates reliability by keeping a record of good attendance
2.  Shows dependability by arriving on time for group participation
3.  Focuses attention on the team task so there is no waste of time
4.  Fulfills rotation roles such as summarizer, discussant, and improviser
5.  Can be counted on to do a fair share of the team-assigned work

**Seeks and Shares Information**
6.  Admits uncertainty when in doubt about what should be done
7.  Asks questions that help to understand and complete class lessons
8.  Teaches peers by explaining or reviewing concepts and assignments
9.  Brings relevant reading materials for teammates to examine in class
10. Refers to reading materials as a basis for enhancing the discussions

**Communicates With Teammates**
11. Can be counted on to disclose feelings, opinions, and experiences
12. Speaks clearly and uses vocabulary that can be easily understood
13. Limits the length of comments so other people have a chance to talk
14. Listens to everyone in the group and considers their points of view
15. Encourages teammates and recognizes contributions of individuals

**Thinks Critically and Creatively**
16. Explores viewpoints and suggestions that may not be liked at first
17. Uses logic to challenge the thinking and work methods of the team
18. Practices reflective thinking and avoids making hasty conclusions
19. Combines and builds upon the ideas that are expressed by others
20. Discovers different ways of looking at things and solving problems

**Gets Along in the Team**
21. Responds well whenever peers disagree or express their criticism
22. Avoids blaming and judging teammates for difficulties or mistakes
23. Accepts compromise when it is the best way to overcome conflicts
24. Keeps trying even when the task or situation becomes demanding
25. Expresses optimism about the team being able to achieve success

---

*Source: Teamwork Skills Inventory,* by Paris Strom and Robert Strom. Copyright © 2012. All rights reserved.

## *Teamwork Skills Inventory Software Features*

The online Teamwork Skills Inventory includes the following software features:

- *Student responsibility for evaluation.* Teachers are supposed to evaluate student teamwork skills and deficits but cannot be present to observe all group interactions. TSI results augment teacher insights from the vantage point of the students.
- *Anonymous evaluation by teammates.* Students want social status protected. Feedback from peers appears on an individual profile revealing only the proportion of teammates that observed consistent demonstration of each teamwork skill.
- *Understanding assessment criteria.* When students want to review a definition for any teamwork skill used to assess peers, they click the line for that specific skill and a pop-up message appears providing a definition of the criterion.
- *Convenient summary of responses.* Students complete the inventory online. Responses are automatically tallied immediately and available to individuals in profile format as soon as all members of a team finish with their peer and self-evaluations.
- *Detects Inflation ratings.* If a student credits anyone with 20 or more team skills, a popup states—"Are you sure? This is a very high rating." The reminder is to prevent deceptive evaluation that keeps others from learning how to improve.
- *Inflation Index of student ratings.* A reminder that a very high rating was given urges reflection. The number of high ratings that individuals give appears on the profile as an inflation index to identify those requiring guidance about authentic assessment.
- *Enabling teacher collaboration.* Teachers of all curriculum subjects are expected to support social development. Access to profiles of individual students across their classes offers a larger picture and enables the faculty to apply united interventions.
- *Encouraging student goal setting.* After getting formative feedback from their peers, individuals should identify teamwork skills they want to work on. Progress toward these goals can be detected by comparing the formative and summative outcomes.
- *Determine needs for intervention.* Teachers have access to individual, team, and class profiles. This information recognizes student assets, progress, learning needs, and opportunities to arrange practice for team skills that have yet to be acquired.

▪ *Parent involvement as teachers.* Parents need to know how team-work skills of their child are perceived by teammates. Keeping parents informed of progress in this social context enables them as coteachers to reinforce skills needed for success.

▪ *Portfolios and social development.* Individual student profiles kept in portfolios become a school record of progress in this realm of accomplishment. Portfolios can help students monitor gains, amend goals, and recognize levels of achievement.

▪ *Threat assessment index.* Consistent peer perceptions that detect individuals with profiles of concern might forecast danger and motivate intervention. A school safety committee can regularly review TSI profiles to identify students for faculty consideration.

## Considerations in Choice of Theory

Decisions about whether to use Constructivism Theory as a guide for instruction depends on several factors: (a) cultural orientation, (b) application to current conditions, and (c) type of learning. Each of these factors should be given careful consideration.

### Cultural Orientation

Nicholas Negroponte (2013) established the One Laptop per Child Association (OLPCA) in 2005 with the mission to provide a low-cost machine and software that allows children across the globe new opportunities for learning. Three million free units have been given to low-income children, mostly in South America locations such as Uruguay, Peru, and Argentina; and nations in Africa including Rwanda, Ethiopia, and Sierra Leone. Distribution has also taken place in Cambodia and cities like Birmingham, Alabama in the United States.

The constructivist perspective of OLPCA is that children learn best by doing rather than passively listening to teachers. This theoretical orientation has also been a source of conflict. The education system governing many countries are founded on the premise that the way for students to gain knowledge is to have it passed on to them by teachers who monitor progress and provide correction. Negroponte (2013) soon found out that educators in China and India, the two most populated nations, were reluctant to support self-directed learning for students. Instead, longstanding cultural reverence for authority figures led the Chinese, Indians, and other nations to conclude that the orientation children need most is effective reading and writing habits instilled by teachers instead of student involvement with laptops. Some critics refer to the OLPC movement as a form of cultural imperialism, an arrogant attempt to impose American views about learning. You Tube has continuing reports about Negroponte's initiatives that describe progress and obstacles.

Negroponte (2013) had supposed providing children access to technology tools would be universally embraced but he underestimated the amount of resistance that emerges when educators are asked to merge their direct instruction with student self-directed learning. Accordingly, the movement has undergone a shift so that, even in countries that welcome OLPCA, the initial focus is on training teachers to view student use of the computer as an additional way of learning without supplanting the important lessons that are conveyed by teachers in classrooms.

Western educators defend their aspiration to make learning meaningful to students so they can remain motivated to continue learning after formal education is completed. However, it is important to recognize that most learning theories are based on democratic and egalitarian assumptions that are not accepted in cultures guided by other political ideologies. The American way of thinking is to encourage learners to explore ideas on their own but it is relevant to keep in mind that western logic is not universal and what appears to us as natural is a product of our independent way of life.

*Constructivism* with a learner-centered and self-directed instruction model is promoted as a way to develop higher-order thinking skills, innovation, and to increase productivity of learners of all backgrounds, cultures, and countries. Recognizing the power of western technology as the basis for global competition, affluent populations in the Arab world like Dubai and Abu Dhabi have invited American universities to establish educational programs for them. A prominent obstacle is that many of the students have problems meeting the admission standards.

The Arab world tends to remain nocturnal, based on the pre air conditioning era when people would sleep during the hot afternoon and picnic in the park with all family members after midnight when it is cool. One result is that getting up for morning classes can present difficulties for students. Research has found that constructivist approaches like cooperative learning and project-based instruction seldom succeed in Arab nations that are welfare societies with youth having a sense of entitlement and apathy toward work and education (Dahl, 2010).

## *Application to Current Conditions*

Researchers in the physical sciences rely on immutable theories. This means using established principles that are not subject to change. These indisputable principles are the building blocks for further investigation. There is no need to go back and try to confirm something that has already been proven. These conditions allow successive generations of investigators to add cumulative knowledge that will promote incremental progress. A different situation exists within the social sciences where theories are time bound instead of timeless. The outcome is continuous disputes by advocates asserting that a theory they prefer has greater worth than others. This situation is productive if scholars recognize when a theory they subscribe to no longer accords with current conditions and should be revised or abandoned. In this way the insights of theorists are recognized along with the realization that authors can rarely see beyond the events of their time.

For example, theories featuring adolescent identity have not kept pace with social change. Consequently, educators continue to explain adolescent development using theories that were originally proposed in the 1950s (Erikson, 1950; Havighurst, 1950). The common assumptions of these theories were that having a high school diploma represented enough education for most careers, full-time jobs were found at an early age, and almost all girls would abide by customary gender expectations. In addition, the workforce would be mostly men, almost everyone would get married, two-parent families would continue as the cultural norm, and the average lifespan would be 55 years. None of these assumptions accurately describe the current environment.

Learning theories should be evaluated periodically to determine whether the well-being of students is supported by a continued implementation. Instead, the common practice in higher education has been to expect students to memorize theories without challenging their current validity. This situation can improve by applying the Strom Model for Evaluation of Learning Theories, illustrated in Table 10.4, to assess the current relevance of particular theories such as Creative Thinking, Social Cognition, Behavior Modification, Moral Development, Dual Coding of Information Processing, Mastery Learning Theory, Constructivism, Cyber Constructivism, Collaboration Integration Theory, Structure of Intellect Theory, Hierarchy of Needs, or others.

The evaluation model, shown in Table 10.4, includes 10 criteria used to judge a theory. For each criterion, the reviewer answers questions. Responses can be keywords, phrases, or full sentences. If some questions are difficult and raise doubts about a response, the reviewer relies on intuition and acknowledges the opinions given are speculative. The greatest benefit occurs when teams of students examine a particular theory they have chosen and share what is learned with teammates and later provide a handout as part of a presentation to classmates.

**TABLE 10.4   Strom Model for Evaluating Theories of Learning
Name of Chosen Theory:**

| Criteria | Questions | Answers |
|---|---|---|
| 1. Cultural & societal change | What changes became common since this theory was proposed? | _____ |
| 2. Technological resources | How well does the theory include the use of current technology? | _____ |
| 3. General assumptions about learning | What are the assumptions about learner and teacher roles? | _____ |
| 4. Specific instructional methods | What specific instruction strategies flow from this theory? | _____ |
| 5. Assessment procedures | How can the impact of this theory be determined? | _____ |
| 6. Sources of teaching or guidance | What sources (parents, teachers, peers) implement this theory? | _____ |
| 7. Educational environments | What are the environments for which this theory is intended? | _____ |
| 8. Learning schedule | How is pace addressed for low, average, and high achievers? | _____ |
| 9. Learning goals | What stated education goals and levels of thinking are reached? | _____ |
| 10. School goals | What school goals does this theory help to achieve? | _____ |

## Type of Learning

Constructivism urges individual students to acquire information that has intrinsic interest to them by searching the Internet. However, if a person's goal is to stop smoking, lose weight, manage anger or other self-regulation issues, behavior modification could be a better theoretical option to apply. Similarly, when the purpose is to become competent in performing mathematical procedures, mastery learning might be the theory of choice. Overcoming moral shortcomings is less likely attained by suffering the consequences of bad behavior than in a preventive way by learning as an observer. Retention of learning may be less successful using role memorization than application of dual code of information processing that features superiority of the pictorial effect for visual learning. Decisions regarding the best way to learn require the considerations included in the Strom criteria for judging efficacy of theories. Readers should refer to Table 10.4 as a guide while they reflect on the best theory to apply for improvement of student thinking.

## Summary and Implications

The instructional principles most American teachers rely on are drawn from Constructivism Theory. School observers agree that when students get to learn some lessons on their own rather than always depending on teachers as a source of insight, comprehension and ability to transfer training to everyday problems are enhanced. Encouraging self-directed learning also supports the motivation of individual students to discover satisfaction at school and continue personal development after formal education is completed. Piaget described the specific potential and limitations of thinking at various cognitive development levels associated with chronological age. His qualitative view of intelligence has influenced curriculum so school tasks reflect the stage of student thinking. Vygotsky discovered that providing disabled children a chance to work with more competent peers increases learning, supports a sense of belonging, and presents general education students as models of behavior for those in special education to observe and imitate.

Cyber Constructivism combines the orientations of Piaget, Vygotsky, and Mitra by linking self-directed learning with learning from more experienced peers and participating in collaboration. The "hole in the wall" experiments demonstrated that students can learn without adult supervision and computer access in resource scarce environments is a creative way to sustain and guide motivation. Collaboration Integration Theory outlines a comprehensive shift that seems necessary to make room for powerful influences like computers, the Internet, satellite television, and personal digital assistants and incorporates cultural, ethnic, and generational resources students should rely on for learning outside school. Twelve differentiated roles are defined that individuals can choose from or be assigned by a team. These roles make each student accountable to share with peers the separate learning they each acquire and enlarge the scope of group achievement.

Cultural orientation is a powerful influence in determining whether theories of thinking and learning are acceptable. In nations where respect for authority overrides individual freedom of choice, self-directed learning is considered to be unimportant and potentially dangerous. In the United States where civil rights has high priority, individuals can pursue their dreams and amend them as necessary. Teachers should realize that social science theories are time bound so the duration of their relevance depends on the pace of change. Instead of supposing a specific theory will be relevant throughout time, it is more helpful to periodically evaluate how well it accords with contemporary conditions. The Strom model includes a set of criteria and questions that can be applied to assess the worth of a theory. Finally, the type of learning desired should guide teacher choice of theory because no single perspective can meet the entire range of learning needs.

PART **III**

*Planning and Direction*

# 11

## Thinking and Goals

The school headmaster Albus Dumbledore in *Harry Potter and the Chamber of Secrets* suggests to Harry, "Always remember it is our choices that show what we truly are, far more than just our abilities." (Rowling, 1999, p. 333). Students have more lifestyle options and career choices now than in the past. When parents and teachers are familiar with the goals of individual students, they are more able to offer relevant advice and give feedback about progress toward their aspirations. The goals of this chapter are to examine how the common goal of adolescents to be seen as adults and to begin exploration of choices for a career can be attained. Some issues include revision of the criteria that is applied to grant adult status, importance of experiencing satisfaction at school, reasons to encourage achievement within the social context, benefits of adopting personality goals, school provision of career exploration, and recognizing when goals should be amended. Goals associated with academic achievement are described in relation to use of criterion-referenced tests, norm-referenced tests, and school reports provided to students and their parents.

*Thinking in Childhood and Adolescence,* pages 225–246
Copyright © 2013 by Information Age Publishing
All rights of reproduction in any form reserved.

## Adolescent Identity

### *Quest for Adult Status*

Having a well-defined social role and feeling respected are elements of identity (Leary & Tangney, 2012). Adolescents want to be accepted as adults with a sense of purpose and direction. However, the more common experience that they report is feeling stuck between childhood and adulthood. Although they enter puberty at a younger age than ever, youth find it more difficult to obtain adult status than their predecessors. One reason is the continuation of the practice of granting adult status only after young people are hired for a full-time position, get married, become a parent, or no longer need further economic assistance from their family. These conditions of independence are met at a later age now than was the case in the past. The extensive schooling required for employment along with a high cost of living combine to lengthen the period of financial dependence on relatives, sometimes well after someone has full-time employment.

The adolescent dilemma is further complicated because views about formation of identity have not kept pace with technological change, social evolution, and longevity. Instead, dominant assumptions reflect theories of development initially proposed sixty years ago when conditions for being accepted as an adult were very different (Erikson, 1950; Havighurst, 1953). At that time the public supposed that earning a high school diploma was enough education to prepare most students for their career, full-time employment could readily be found at an early age, and most females would adopt traditional gender roles. In addition, it was assumed that the work force would be composed mostly of men, getting married would be the path chosen by nearly everyone, two-parent families would remain the norm, and the average lifespan would be 55 years. These assumptions are no longer accurate.

### *New Criteria for Recognition*

If the criteria for being recognized as an adult are outdated, how should they be revised? Most adolescents rely on technology devices to remain in continual contact with their friends. If they more frequently used these devices for communicating with adults, age segregation might decline, and older age groups could better understand the needs of youth. Family concerns about limitations of communication are rising. A decade of annual surveys of 2,000 households across the United States by the Center for the Digital Future (2012) at the University of Southern California Annenberg School have shown that communication with friends continues to increase for adolescents while their communication with family members is in decline. Parents report this worrisome trend, a drop in face-to-face communication time (from 26 to 18 hours per week) in Internet households over the past several years.

Efforts to improve adolescent chances for attaining adult identity should recognize that the emerging social self of teenagers is too narrow when it is defined only in relation to peers. Many adolescents believe their friends are the only people able to understand them. Parents should challenge this false premise and attempt to convince their children that, at every age in life, it is a mistake to choose peers as the single audience to rely upon for processing personal concerns. Limiting the discussion of important issues to peers restricts adolescent perspectives and forfeits the opportunity to practice communication skills that they will need for relating to teammates from other age groups in the workplace. The ideal support group consists of loved ones who make themselves available to listen, attempt to understand feelings, offer emotional support, discuss options and possible consequences, recommend issues for reflective thinking, and provide help in hard times. Relatives and friends who act in these ways are usually seen as trusted advisors (Strom & Strom, 2012).

Robert Epstein (2010) suggests that adolescents are being unfairly denied adult status. He explores fallacies in the way in which many grownups view youth as incapable of responsibility, to be shielded from adult tasks, and unable to make their own reasoned decisions. He refers to an artificial extension of childhood by which teenagers are isolated from the people they are about to become, trapped in a meaningless world controlled by peers and media figures that cater to them. Epstein contends society has forgotten how capable young people can be even though adolescents recognize their own potential and feel frustrated when their strengths are overlooked.

A new set of criteria for granting adult identity status could include the development of further competence with technology tools along with evidence of personal development in the social context. This seems more sensible than to perpetuate unattainable conditions leading to alienation and causing adolescents to affiliate with peers for nearly all of their communication. The growing amount of student involvement with social network friends on *Facebook* and cell phone texting reflects the dependence on peers for conversation as society shifts to greater age segregation. Talking to peers is easier because it is based on equality—a condition less common when speaking to adults. Computer skills are generally valued so people that possess these assets deserve adult status, should have responsibilities, and interact with other cohorts in order to support social harmony and mutual understanding (Strom & Strom, 2012).

Schools have an important role in helping students attain adult identity through further development of their technological competence. For example, the United States Bureau of Labor Statistics (2013) predicts that, by 2020, there will be one million more jobs available in computer science than there will be students studying for this degree. Less than 3% of college graduates have a computer science degree even though jobs in this field offer the highest beginning salary and are available at twice the rate of other kinds of positions. The shortage is compounded by the fact that, in 41 of 50 states, software coding classes in high school are an elective and do not count toward the graduation requirements in mathematics or science. Nine in 10 high schools do not even offer courses in computer programming.

To address this resource deficit and accelerate curriculum change in schools, a nonprofit foundation was established by technological entrepreneur Hadi Partovi called Code.org (Barret, 2013). The mission is to ensure that every student in every school has an opportunity to acquire coding skills and enable computer science and computer programming to become a part of the core curriculum throughout American schools. The message that this addition is essential is disseminated directly to youth. Code.org (2013) produced a 5-minute video called *What most schools don't teach.* This video features famous individuals like Facebook founder Mark Zuckerberg, Microsoft chairman Bill Gates, Jack Dorsey, cofounder of Twitter and other well known figures in technology who share their thinking about the need to learn software coding. The video informs adolescents that learning how to code is the new literacy, there is a global shortage of computer programmers and software developers, and well-paid jobs will be plentiful in the future for students who earn a degree in computer science or computer engineering.

### Personality Goals and Identity

Parents and teachers know that goals can support identity as well as motivation to learn. Also, they are concerned about ways that adolescent goal setting can be supported without sacrifice to academic success. Certainly, students cannot choose all the subjects they study at school. However, they could be encouraged to select personality goals before making decisions about career goals. This sequence of establishing personality goals first and career goals later means students can focus initially on the kind of person they want to become, the way they want to behave, and kind of influence they aspire to have on others. These aspects of maturity can be observed well before there is evidence indicating the kind of career a student may one day be qualified to perform. When students adopt personality goals and enact values they reflect, achievement in the social context can become more prominent.

The problems some people have in getting along with others, as demonstrated by a record of abuse, prejudice, being fired, or criminal activity more often relate to poor emotional health and to immaturity than to lack of competence in academic subjects (Vohs & Baumeister, 2013). Reading, writing, and mathematics will continue as essential skills for everyone, and these skills should be recognized as the easiest lessons in life to learn. In addition, students need education that equips them with resilience to confront adversity and cope with stress at school, pressures from peers, and family conflict (Ginsburg, 2011). Parents should recognize their goal should be to bring up children who will be successful when they are 40 years old and beyond. This means that getting good grades is not enough. Parents should also strive to help shape emotionally and socially intelligent individuals able to recover from disappointment and forge ahead through life.

Individually selected personality goals can be a worthwhile focus for self-evaluation. Personality is the key to identity—the way we see ourselves and how others perceive us. Personality and identity are closely linked since both are lifelong concerns, whereas having a career is not. Family and school support for personality goal setting by adolescents convey a message that social and emotional development is an important context of achievement along with cognitive performance.

When adults identify the personal attributes they want to be remembered for by family and friends, they typically mention noncognitive qualities that endear people to one another. These attributes become more common when they are chosen as goals. The example that adults set is important. They can acknowledge personal shortcomings to younger relatives, describe any plans they have for improvement, and ask for feedback to help them gauge progress. This means that, in addition to helping adolescents establish short-term and long-term goals, adults review personal goals and make them known. Everyone should try to improve their personality for as long as they live.

Table 11.1 presents a list of personality goals that students can be encouraged to consider (Strom & Strom, 2009). Achieving any of these interpersonal skills is bound to enhance success no matter which career a student may eventually choose. Some goals are briefly elaborated here as reminders about their relevance for preparing students to deal with important challenges of growing up and adulthood.

- *Get along with classmates.* A 14-year-old granddaughter of an 82-year-old African American grandmother told her, "Grandma Flora, I want to be just like you when I grow up." Flora replied, "Why? I have so little in the way of material things and did not make much

**TABLE 11.1  Personality Goals and Achievement for Consideration by Adolescents**

| Goals for Individual Consideration | Achievement Perceived by Parents | Achievement Perceived by Self |
|---|---|---|
| Get along with classmates | | |
| Treat people around me fairly | | |
| Show a willingness to help others | | |
| Look at the bright side of things | | |
| Make time for what is important | | |
| Develop a healthy sense of humor | | |
| Make feelings known to relatives | | |
| Learn to become a better listener | | |
| Settle arguments in a peaceful way | | |
| Ask questions if I don't understand | | |
| Avoid unkind statements about others | | |
| Keep trying as things get difficult | | |
| Ask for help when it is needed | | |
| Be patient in dealing with others | | |
| Be a person who others can rely on | | |
| Keep mind and body healthy | | |
| Reflect on behavior to improve self | | |
| Seek and accept criticism of others | | |
| Have self-control and self-discipline | | |
| Become a self-directed person | | |

*Source: Adolescents in the Internet Age,* by Paris Strom and Robert Strom, 2009, p. 96. Information Age Publishing Inc., Charlotte, NC.

of myself." Her granddaughter said, "Grandma, you have more real friends than anyone I know." What a nice compliment.

▪ *Treat people around me fairly.* Society is struggling to get this right; it is an important lesson to learn and a difficult one to teach.

▪ *Show a willingness to help others.* This is what growing up and maturity are all about, moving from being self-centered to showing concern for the welfare of others.

▪ *Look at the bright side of things.* Being able to see possibilities in others and situations is a valuable asset. Few things are worse for adolescents than being around cynical adults who cause them to lose hope for the future.

▪ *Make time for what is important.* Identifying the things that matter most and assigning priorities is usually acquired with age. This vital lesson could be learned earlier.

- *Develop a healthy sense of humor.* As people mature, they discover that laughing at themselves can be an effective path to balance mental health.
- *Settle arguments in a peaceful way.* Many youth are not learning this lesson and parents should not expect schools and teachers to be the only adult sources of instruction.
- *Avoid making unkind statements about others.* Teenagers report relatives teach them values indirectly by how they react to characters on television, or gossip regarding the neighbors or people featured in the media.
- *Show patience in dealing with others.* Impatience is becoming more common and typically has the effect of undermining productivity at work and in intimate relationships.
- *Be a person others can rely on.* This is one of the greatest accomplishments anyone can achieve.
- *Become a self-directed person.* The ability to make independent decisions and to perform tasks without outside control shows internal locus of control and maturity.

Mary Ann Evans (1819–1880) was a 19th century English writer who believed people underestimated women by supposing they could only write stories about romance. She wanted her work to be taken as seriously as if written by a man. Therefore, she used the male pen name George Eliot. Her insights about paths to self-improvement are described in the classic novel *Silas Marner: The Weaver of Raveloe* (Eliot, 1861/2010). She suggested that it is never too late to be who you might have been. There is still time, no matter what our age, to set more mature goals and in pursuing them become someone with a more favorable influence. At a workshop for parents on ways to define success, one man shared this observation, "All my life I said I wanted to be someone. Now I can see I should have been more specific."

Some indicators of adolescent success include trophies, certificates, high grades, and competitive test scores. These signs are evidence of growth; however, they also reflect a narrow definition of achievement. In addition, social skills like adaptability, patience, flexibility, and collaboration are essential. Many parents tell their children, "This is America so you can be whatever you want to be." Perhaps they might also add, "You can be the kind of person you want to become, and we will make an effort to help." Adolescents can reflect about the goals listed in Table 11.1 and add others that seem most appropriate for them. Some goals teens have suggested include defending the rights of others, showing greater empathy, assuming more responsibility, becoming willing to compromise, and strive to demonstrate integrity. Monitoring personality development is a long-term challenge that can be supported by respectful observation and authentic feedback from parents and educators.

## *Satisfaction With School*

The school selects some of the goals that students are expected to reach. School includes two cultures, an instrumental culture and an expressive culture. The *instrumental culture* consists of academic requirements every student should meet for graduation. Instrumental goals include curriculum areas like mathematics, science, and English. These are compulsory subjects because each contributes to skills, knowledge, and values stated as the purposes of education. Students participate in the instrumental culture to attain satisfactions they desire in the future like getting a diploma, being admitted to a college, and finding a job (Jennings & Likis, 2005).

The *expressive culture* at school includes activities students participate in for the pleasure of involvement (Mahoney, Larson, & Eccles, 2005). Art, drama, music, and athletics are aspects of the expressive curriculum. Although involvement with the expressive culture often increases knowledge and skills, this result is not considered as important as for the instrumental culture where everyone has to pass state examinations in mathematics, reading, and science. Students enjoy singing in the choir, working with clay in art, helping with a theatrical performance, or playing volleyball. The criterion for success in the expressive culture depends more upon how much a person enjoys the participation than how well s/he performs.

Sometimes the instrumental culture has an expressive impact such as when a student gains satisfaction from science experiments, reading novels, or doing algebra. In a similar way, there can be an instrumental outcome in expressive activities when students gain considerable skill and knowledge about art, music, and drama. But, students generally distinguish between the expressive and instrumental cultures. Because most students find satisfaction in the expressive culture, competition is deliberately minimized in this context making it the most viable venue in which to teach values, such as appreciation for learning, commitment to individual growth, and valuing collaboration with peers. Parents can more easily be involved in the expressive culture.

The motivation to stay in most situations usually depends on satisfaction. People will endure disappointment if satisfaction remains a part of their overall experience. This means that some experiences in school must be satisfying so students are motivated to stay and graduate rather than withdraw and drop out. Various combinations of satisfaction with instrumental and expressive cultures can sustain involvement or motivate withdrawal. Table 11.2 shows that a high level of satisfaction in both cultures defines academic achievers that also feel good about their extracurricular activities. A high instrumental and low expressive combination portrays someone who gains satisfaction from results of academic tests but does not care about extracurricular activities. A low instrumental and high expressive combination identifies those who have mediocre test scores but feel satisfaction from the extracurricular activities. Such a person has difficulty in mathematics or English but shines on the basketball court or football field. In this situation, the single incentive to stay in school is the pleasure and favorable self-impression from being involved with athletics, band, or drama (Rathvon, 2008).

Some students do not find satisfaction in the expressive or instrumental culture. They dislike the required courses and refuse to engage in expressive opportunities. They consider school to be a place of disappointment so they want to drop out when they reach the minimum age to leave. Feelings of alienation motivate them to withdraw and hope they can find satisfaction in some other environment. Schools have to discover better ways to appeal to these students so they can find satisfaction within the institution and prepare for the future (Goldstein & Brooks, 2012).

Unlike dropout prevention programs or remedial education to overcome academic deficits, extracurricular activities can support adjustment

**TABLE 11.2  Level of Student Satisfaction With the Instrumental and Expressive Cultures at School**

| Culture and Satisfaction | Example of Student Reported Experience |
|---|---|
| High Expressive<br>High Instrumental | Renaldo enjoys the math courses he has taken and wants to become an engineer. He also likes playing trumpet in the school marching band. |
| Low Expressive<br>High Instrumental | Melinda likes the curriculum and has a part time job. Her busy schedule means that there is no time left to participate in extracurricular activities. |
| High Expressive<br>Low Instrumental | Jason is 6 feet, 8 inches tall, lives for basketball, and is the top scorer for the conference. He struggles with required subjects but is grateful to get tutoring. |
| Low Expressive<br>Low Instrumental | Avery does not like school and feels that his classmates look down on him. His friends left before graduating, and he thinks this would be the best choice for him too. |

*Source: Adolescents in the Internet Age*, by Paris Strom and Robert Strom, 2009, p. 99. Information Age Publishing Inc., Charlotte, NC.

to school demands by promoting individual interests and satisfaction. Creative use of the expressive culture can make school a place of greater satisfaction for more students and improve their results in the instrumental culture. This was shown at a junior high school in Harlem, New York. Black and Puerto Rican students were involved. The top half of the 1,400 students were chosen for a Higher Horizons Project (Morrissey & Werner-Wilson, 2005). These students typically scored two years below grade level for reading and mathematics. The principal told them, "We realize most of you don't like mathematics or reading but it doesn't change the fact that these skills are important for your future. However, instead of increasing the time that you spend on these subjects by cutting back on other curriculum like art, music, and physical education, we plan to take the opposite approach." So, motivating influences from the expressive culture were introduced to increase satisfaction and motivation to learn. Students were taken to sporting events, concerts, and movies. They visited parks and museums, went on sightseeing trips while also continuing exposure to instrumental subjects.

Follow-up studies found project members who went on to senior high school graduated in substantially greater numbers than those in the same junior high during pre-project years. Then too, 168 graduates advanced to attend higher education, compared with 47 in three classes preceding the experiment. It seems that expressive activities offered enough satisfaction to motivate students to stay in school instead of leaving. Effects included higher instrumental performance (Morrissey & Werner-Wilson, 2005). This is why middle and high schools devote considerable attention at the beginning of the year to encouraging student involvement with extracurricular activities and after school programs. Lack of involvement in the expressive culture renders some students less able to cope with pressures and more vulnerable to stress (Christie, Jolivette, & Nelson, 2005).

## Career Decisions

In *Alice in Wonderland* (Carroll, 1865/2004), Alice comes to a crossroad and asks for advice from a cat. "What road should I take?" The cat replied, "That depends upon where you want to go." She admits, "I don't know where I want to go." The thoughtful cat says, "Well, then any road will do." Students currently have more roads to choose from than in earlier times. They welcome having options but overchoice is also a reason to feel anxious and stressed about choosing a future career. Adolescents are unsure about how long to wait and where to begin in exploring their alternatives. Many express disappointment about what is perceived as a lack of guidance other than encouragement to attend college and persevere in attaining their dream.

## Career Exploration Poll

To gather insight on the perceptions of adolescents about their important task of choosing an occupation, 288 students in grades 9–12 from a rural high school were invited to complete the online Career Exploration Poll (Strom & Strom, 2011c; Whitten, 2011). These 14- to 19-year-old females (51%) and males (49%) were White (55%), Black (27%), and Hispanic (11%). The sample was 78% of the entire population of students at the school. Poll items identified sources of influence on career choice, steps taken to explore possible occupations, types of education needed for a desired job, advice from friends and relatives, frequency of dreaming about a career, ways school could assist with orientation, experiences that shape career planning, stress of decision making, and degree of certainty.

Most of the students identified relatives (78%) as the source they prefer to talk to about job opportunities. Friends (65%) and educators (44%) were also seen as valued advisors. When describing the steps they had already taken to find out about careers, the most frequent student response (55%) was searching the web to determine educational requirements for particular jobs. Almost everyone (96%) reported that they often dream about what it will be like to be involved with their future career. A majority of 67% acknowledged that trying to figure out the occupation to pursue is accompanied by considerable doubt, uncertainty, and worry. Many worry the society is changing so fast that a job they prepare for may no longer be available when they finish their studies. A minority of 39% reported that they had definitely decided on the kind of work they wanted while 61% admitted they have not yet identified the best career path for them (Whitten, 2011).

The factors students considered most important in the choice of a career are salary and benefits (74%), satisfaction with the work (52%), and having a reasonable time schedule (28%). The order of these factors departs somewhat from suggestions given by preferred advisors who encouraged students to give the highest priority to an occupation that will provide satisfaction (76%) ahead of a job that pays well (48%). Experiences that have influenced career outlook so far included family advice (69%), talking to people in the desired occupation (50%), and characters watched on television, movies, and the Internet (32%) (Whitten, 2011).

Most students (53%) reported that getting a college degree is required for the occupation they prefer. Only 5% saw technical or trade school curriculum as a suitable preparation for them. The career exploration activities preferred were scheduled observations of people in the desired line of work (51%), guidance to improve career data searching on the web (38%), and orientation nights at school presented by guest speakers representing a wide range of possible careers (36%). Overall, the age, grade level, and ethnicity of students did not reveal any significant differences in perceptions about careers. However, significant gender differences were found for four items: (a) girls were more certain than boys about their career choice; (b) girls more often searched the web for occupational information; (c) girls were more interested in a school career exploration program; and, (d) girls more often chose to work in the rapidly growing field of healthcare (Whitten, 2011).

## Support for Career Planning

The Career Exploration Poll results by Whitten (2011) suggest that a well-defined role for parents can make a school career exploration program more effective. Other investigations of occupational aspiration confirm that parents are the main source adolescents rely on most for guidance about careers (Fitzpatrick & Constantini, 2011). In one study of 700 Black, Hispanic, and White mothers of 10- to 14-year-old students, the mothers were asked to rank order a list of 60 ways that might help to improve their influence. The choice ranked second highest out of 60 was "I need more information to help my adolescent explore careers" (Strom, Strom, & Beckert, 2008).

In most families tuition costs and conditions associated with student loans should be a focus of conversation along with issues related to living at home or on campus. The Project on Student Debt (2012) reveals, by state, the average debt of college graduates, the proportion of students with debt, and resident tuition for each higher education institution. More than 90% of the 18.5 million college students take out loans. In 2012 the average graduate from a four-year public university owed nearly $27,000. Americans owe more money for student loans than for credit cards (Martin & Lehren, 2012). Debt is a concern for many adolescents who do not want to burden their parents with having to pay for education, particularly when the students have yet to decide on a career goal. One half of students in the upper one half of their graduating class in high school choose not to attend college right away because of concerns about debt (Fitzpatrick & Constantini, 2011). Schools can assist parents by identifying the broad scope of conversation that is needed for making decisions on higher education. Table 11.3 can be a discussion agenda.

Career education at school should make students aware that indecision about occupation is normal in adolescence and underscores the need for continued exploration. Premature career choice is a mistake many adults admit as they look back on their work life. If given a chance to do things over, some adults say they would choose differently (Strom & Strom, 2012). A faculty committee could assume the task of preparing a list of websites to guide student Internet visits about occupations along with some explanation about benefits offered by specific websites. For those students who are not self-starters, this kind of resource could motivate them to begin searching and enrich the career conversations they have with relatives.

The low rate of students (5%) who viewed short-term programs in community colleges or trade schools as appropriate may reflect a growing misperception that good paying jobs will be limited to college graduates. The United States Bureau of Labor Statistics (2013) contradicts this impression and indicates secondary students do not have enough exposure to the potential of technical or vocational training. Planning visits for students

**TABLE 11.3  Career Exploration Discussion Agenda**

| Questions for Discussion | Considerations |
| --- | --- |
| How long does it take to prepare for this occupation? | Time and money are important factors. |
| Am I informed about the requirements to reach this career goal? | Know the necessary steps. |
| Would I enjoy the tasks involved with this career? | Awareness is crucial. |
| What are my reasons for wanting this job? | Personal motivation should be clear. |
| Do my goals include intellectual, social, and emotional growth? | Balance is a key to personal success. |
| Is this goal being pursued for myself or for other people? | Believe in your own sense of direction. |
| What do trusted adults see as benefits and drawbacks? | Weigh the judgments of others. |
| Does this career provide opportunities for advancement? | Explore promotion possibilities. |
| Will this job offer the income needed for my desired lifestyle? | Calculate the match. |
| What resources will I need to achieve this goal? | Search for needed information. |
| Is this a realistic and attainable career goal? | Seek feedback about your capabilities. |
| How are my original career goal and amended goal different? | Be specific and understand your reasons. |
| Am I aware of the stresses and demands related to this career? | Think about necessary adjustments. |
| How can achieving this goal affect my happiness? | Discuss it with people in the field. |

to gather information about future opportunities should include technical and vocational institutions along with colleges and universities. If the poll responses of these students characterized the communities in which they live, there would be a severe shortage of electricians, carpenters, electronic technicians, plumbers, health care providers, and transportation workers.

Some career paths involving less education are ignored like skilled labor in construction. If trained construction workers cannot be hired, the quality of road systems is bound to decline, businesses will have difficulty expanding facilities, and the need to build new homes will be unmet. One might expect that opportunities in this sector would be communicated to adolescents. However, because most students are only urged to attend college, many of them see employment in the construction trades as a last resort. In contrast, the United States Bureau of Labor Statistics (2013) forecast for 2010 to 2020 shows that opportunities in construction will increase by 33%, adding nearly 2 million jobs. This growth will occur while goods producing industries such as agriculture and manufacturing experience negative growth.

Career education is becoming a prominent obligation for middle schools and high schools. One option is to convene periodic school meetings that host professional, technical, and trade sector representatives. Their goal would be to acquaint students and parents with training required for specific jobs and details about work. An alternative is for national public television to provide career orientation. This innovation would combine the work preparation purpose of schools with the general awareness purpose of media to inform families of current and future job prospects.

### Need for Goal Amendment

The need to amend goals is often overlooked as an aspect of decision-making and career planning. Steven, age 14, informed his parents the occupation he wanted to pursue was to be a commercial airline pilot. The family had conversations on appealing features of the job including the satisfactions of flight, promising economic future, chance to visit places across the globe, and responsibility for ensuring safety of passengers. Then Steven found a newspaper advertisement on flying lessons. The cost of $500 included 20 lessons with solo flights and landing experience needed to qualify for a basic licensure to operate a small aircraft. The parents agreed that taking lessons would enable Steven to find out what is expected of aviators and whether this occupation would be satisfying for him.

Steven was not old enough to have a license to drive a car; therefore, his father drove him to the airport for each lesson. After finishing the second lesson, Steven returned to the lounge where his father was reading. Steven looked pale but said nothing. The same sickly appearance was evident at the end of the third and fourth lessons. The day before lesson five, Steven said, "My lessons are not turning out as I supposed. Flying the plane is easier than I thought but I get sick to my stomach each time we go up. At first I thought it was something I ate, but it continues to happen."

Further conversation revealed that Steven wanted to end the lessons. However, he said, "I know you spent a lot of money to give me this chance so I will keep going if you want me too." The father said, "No, the tentative goal that you had to become a pilot is no longer appealing. The money was well spent since the result showed that flying is not the right occupation for you. Finding that out is a good thing because you might otherwise have continued to believe being a pilot had greater promise than is the case. Many adults dislike the career choice they made and wish it were possible to change. Fortunately, you can amend the goal to be a pilot and consider other careers."

Goals in every sector of life should be evaluated periodically; they should be modified when they cannot be attained or when they are less appealing as awareness of other possibilities emerge (Creed & Hood, 2013). Many adults make a mistake in thinking that it is wise to always encourage young people to persevere in reaching whatever goals they may have chosen. At times some people choose unrealistic goals. In such cases individuals do not need cheerleaders who encourage them to continue pursuing inappropriate goals. Most people do not want to be seen as a quitter. There are times when taking a different path is the smartest thing to do.

The processes that facilitate goal amendment should be better understood. This issue is becoming more important as adolescents are exposed to many occupations. Students may have been given grades in school that do not accurately reflect their competence. Wise amendment of goals is necessary to adjust to previously unrecognized requirements, underestimated difficulties, and opportunities that may have been overlooked in other sectors of employment. The following questions support reflection by adolescents about whether to amend some goals.

1. *Have I written my goals so they are specific and could be conveyed to a confidante?* It is difficult for relatives or friends to provide feedback about ambiguous goals.
2. *Have I set goals in all sectors including mental, social, emotional, physical, spiritual, career, and family?* If goals are too narrow, growth is limited in a corresponding way.

3. *How long will it take to achieve each goal that is on my list?* Unless a reasonable time limit is assigned, it is difficult to know when specific aspirations should be amended.
4. *What are my reasons for pursuing these goals?* Writing down motives for each goal encourages reflective thinking.

When there is evidence that academic goals cannot be reached, it is necessary to modify and redirect goals. It is appropriate to amend goals and make a commitment to achieving the revised purposes. People who consider amending their goals should be aware of several common obstacles. First, adults often discourage students from abandoning an original career goal because they believe it can be attained with greater effort. Second, subtle pressures may be felt when one gender or the other dominate a particular career path, frequently an issue for women who want to become engineers or men who choose to be nurses. Third, there may be fear of being overwhelmed by the conditions that must be met. Perhaps training takes longer than expected, there is more competition than supposed, and trying to belong in the new group of colleagues may be challenging. Fourth, there could be a lack of initial success. When something new is tried, failure may occur and unless individuals are prepared for setbacks, they may conclude that success is impossible. Fifth, there can be unrealistic expectations. Many high school athletes dream of becoming professional athletes. Understanding the probability can help them develop realistic backup plans (Stone & Lewis, 2012).

## Student Progress Assessment

In the past the main purpose for school testing was to compare students so that the most talented could be identified and admitted to college. However, because college has become an expectation for almost everyone, the purpose of testing has changed to monitoring individual competence in basic skills. This emphasis, referred to as *mastery learning,* began with Benjamin Bloom (1976) at the University of Chicago. Bloom believed that, by continually tracking progress of every student, teachers could detect deficiencies early and provide the remediation needed to meet minimal school goals. Mastery learning has been the dominant approach since the 1990s when allegations arose that the high school diploma was losing credibility since many students were being allowed to graduate without demonstrating the basic skills of reading, writing, and mathematics. In response, all states and local boards of education adopted stringent policies. The new focus was on minimal competency tests that require students to show that they possess basic skills before being approved for graduation (Loveless, 2005).

## Criterion-Referenced Testing

Table 11.4 is an example of a criterion-referenced test (CRT), the most appropriate measure to assess competence in the basic skills. In a criterion-referenced test the required performance level is decided ahead of time before anyone takes the test so results are not influenced by how well other students in a class or grade perform. Mastery at the 75% to 90% level is the typical minimal standard chosen. For example, if there are four items on reading comprehension, a student must get three out of four items correct to reach 75% mastery. Whatever standard is set, it is the absolute criterion against which the performance of every student is compared. Because a criterion-referenced test is diagnostic, it is intentionally success-oriented. Most students are expected to pass, if not the first time, then on a retest following remedial instruction. In this context, a student who does not reach the required standard for a basic skill is not considered as a failure. Instead, the student is identified as someone able to learn the skill and pass the test but has yet to do so (Thorndike & Thorndike-Christ, 2011).

## Norm-Referenced Testing

A norm-referenced Test (NRT) compares performance of individuals with performance of some specified group, such as students from the same grade in a school district, state, or nation. A student whose percentile rank of 60 on a mathematics test knows he scored as well or better than 60% of the group that took the same test. However, this information does not provide diagnostic information about what the student already understands or has yet to learn in mathematics. Norm-referenced tests as shown in Table 11.5 are not designed to detect particular strengths or weaknesses. They are designed to produce scores revealing an individual's relative position in a specific group so that education decisions based on performance differences can be made.

To illustrate, selection of a limited number of students for an accelerated mathematics honors program proceeds more fairly when it is recognized that Tom's 60th percentile rank score is much lower than Michelle's score placing her at the 96th percentile rank. To allow for such comparisons, there must be some reasonable spread of scores that would not happen if a test were so easy that everyone was able to perform well. For this reason, norm-referenced test items that do not contribute to variance are subject to change. Consequently, the items about concepts and skills considered to be basic will, over time, be eliminated from a norm-referenced achievement test. The ideal item to maximize variance is one that only half (50%)

## TABLE 11.4   A Sample of Minimal Competency Criterion-Referenced Test Reports on Basic Skills

**Student Number:**          **Student Name:**          **Date:**

*Reading Skills Areas*—The high school reading basic skills requirements are that each student demonstrates 75% proficiency in each skill area prior to graduation. X indicates proficiency.

| **Comprehension Skills:** | **Reading** |
|---|---|
| 1. Identify stated main idea | Part 1 |
| 2. Identify stated detail | Part 2 |
| 3. Identify stated cause/effect relationships | Part 3 |
| 4. Identify inferred main idea | Part 4 |
| 5. Identify inferred cause/effect relationships | Part 5 |
| 6. Identify inferred sequence | Part 6 |
| 7. Identify inferred conclusions | Part 7 |
| 8. Identify fact/opinion statements | Part 8 |
| 9. Identify relevant/irrelevant data | Part 9 |
| **Study Skills:** | |
| 10. Follow written directions | Part 10 |
| 11. Extract information from diagrammatic/pictured materials | Part 11 |
| 12. Use dictionary, index, table of contents | Part 12 |
| 13. Identify prefixes, suffixes, roots | Part 13 |
| 14. Use context clues | Part 14 |
| | *Proficiency Met* |

*Mathematics Skills Areas*—The high school mathematics basic skills requirements are that each student demonstrates 75% proficiency in each skills area prior to graduation. X indicates proficiency.

| | **Mathematics** |
|---|---|
| 1. Adding whole numbers | Part 1 |
| 2. Subtracting whole numbers | Part 2 |
| 3. Multiplying whole numbers | Part 3 |
| 4. Dividing whole numbers | Part 4 |
| 5. Adding fractions | Part 5 |
| 6. Subtracting fractions | Part 6 |
| 7. Multiplying fractions | Part 7 |
| 8. Dividing fractions | Part 8 |
| 9. Adding decimals | Part 9 |
| 10. Subtracting decimals | Part 10 |
| 11. Multiplying decimals | Part 11 |
| 12. Dividing decimals | Part 12 |
| 13. Finding percent of a number | Part 13 |
| 14. Interpreting scales, graphs, charts | Part 14 |
| 15. Equivalent expressions for measurements | Part 15 |
| | *Proficiency Met* |

**TABLE 11.5 A Sample of Norm-Referenced Test Reports on Basic Skills**

| School: | | Student No.: | | Student Name: | | | Form: | | Date: |
|---|---|---|---|---|---|---|---|---|---|
| **Percentile** | | **Below 5** | **5–10** | **11–22** | **23–40** | **41–59** | **60–77** | **78–89** | **90–95** | **96 & above** |
| **Stanine** | | 1 | 2 | 3 | 4 | 5 | 6 | 7 | 8 | 9 |
| **National Norms** | | **Below Average** *Promedio Bajo* | | | | **Average** *Promedio* | | **Above Average** *Promedio Superior* | | |

| | | | | | | | | | |
|---|---|---|---|---|---|---|---|---|---|
| Reading Vocabulary *Vocabulario de lectura* | | | | | | | | | |
| Reading Comprehension *Comprension de lectura* | | | | | | | | | |
| Spelling *Deletreo* | | | | | | | | | |
| Language Mechanics *Expresion escrita* | | | | | | | | | |
| Language Expression *Uso de la lengua* | | | | | | | | | |
| Mathematics Computation *Computaciones de matematicas* | | | | | | | | | |
| Mathematics Concepts *Conceptos de matematicas* | | | | | | | | | |
| Mathematics Application *Aplicacion de matematicas* | | | | | | | | | |
| Reference Skills *Uso de libros de consulta* | | | | | | | | | |
| Science *Ciencia* | | | | | | | | | |
| Social Studies *Civismo* | | | | | | | | | |

the students answer correctly. An item that is answered correctly by 80% or more of students is often eliminated because it does not spread out the range of student scores (Ceci & Papierno, 2005).

An important distinction between the two types of tests is that the criteria for judging success on a criterion-referenced measure are pre-established—determined before the test is administered to anyone. Ideally, everyone will pass, if not on the first try, then later after tutoring. In contrast, the criteria for success on a norm-referenced test cannot be decided in advance. Instead, the success of an individual depends on performance of the particular group taking the test. The range of scores becomes a basis for determining the standing of individuals in relation to one another. Generally, the purpose of stated mandated criterion-referenced tests, sometimes called high stakes testing, is to assess minimal competence. This type of evaluation is recommended only when the emphasis is on limited academic objectives and mastery is viewed as a reasonable expectation for all students. Neither condition obtains for advanced learning. Then broad educational objectives are implicated, calling for integration of concepts and ideas from different subject matters. For such complex achievements, it is necessary to rely on norm-referenced testing. The important reminder is that educators do not have to choose between the use of criterion-referenced tests and norm-referenced tests as being the best for every situation. Both types of measures are needed because they serve different but complementary purposes for evaluating development.

### Student and Parent Reports

Parents want to be informed about the progress of their child. Table 11.4 illustrates a Minimal Competency Criterion-Referenced Test Report on Basic Skills with the information received by the parents of high school students. All of the reading and mathematics skills required for graduation are stated, the minimal performance standard is specified (75% mastery), and sections of the test that have already been passed by the student are identified. Minimal competency tests that include writing skills are usually administered annually starting in grade four. All required subjects have to be passed before students receive a diploma.

Besides results of minimal competency tests, parents want to know how the achievement scores of their child compare with classmates in the same grade. Such information, as provided by norm-referenced tests, can be helpful in career planning. Percentile ranks that are used in norm-referenced tests are the most informative way of reporting comparative achievement, provided two characteristics are made clear to students and parents: (a) the norm group is identified (city, state, national); (b) *percentile score* is defined as the percent of the norm group whose performance a student has equaled or surpassed. Percentile ranks range from 1% (lowest possible standing) to 99% (highest standing surpassing almost everyone).

Table 11.5 is an illustration of a Norm-Referenced Test Report on Basic Skills about performance on a comprehensive test of skills. This report provides several ways of looking at performance in comparison with other sophomores in high schools in the district. Percentile ranks are given along with test *stanine*, dividing students in achievement groups with one as the lowest and nine as highest. A below average, average, or above average rating is also portrayed. The Family Educational Rights and Privacy Act (1974) allows parents access to all their child's school records.

## *Education of Immigrants*

Congress has expressed its intention to soon decide about the future status of 11 million illegal immigrants in the United States and the path to citizenship that might be established for them. Thinking about national concerns in new ways can sometimes produce better solutions. Suppose the Congressional plan was to include the formation of a Department of Immigrant Education. The effectiveness of this department might be determined by an outside source of evaluation. Some possible benefits of implementing this strategy might be:

- Maintaining uniform records of student progress across states and districts
- Providing accurate rates of failure and dropout across states and districts
- Relying on federal economic support instead of local property taxation
- Conducting research to compare effects of competing instructional methods
- Tutoring for members of the population that has a high dropout rate
- Requiring English language training expected for every generation
- Providing assistance by indigenous volunteers for students in the classroom
- Engaging parents and grandparents to support student progress
- Training sufficient numbers of teachers for their subject and communication
- Maximizing software development by companies of instructional materials

What other advantages can you think of that would be a result of this proposal? Perhaps you disagree with the idea of establishing a federal department to provide education for immigrant children, adolescents, and adults. What are some disadvantages you anticipate and ways to overcome them?

## Summary and Implications

The common goal of adolescents to be granted adult identity status is more difficult to attain in the present environment because extensive education is necessary for employment but criteria for being granted adult status reflects the past. There is a need to revise criteria so they reflect the contemporary setting. Teenagers benefit when the grownups in their lives trust them and encourage setting some of their own goals. The opportunity to engage in career exploration in a low-risk setting can help students shape a future of their choosing, become more responsible, and experience satisfaction.

Adolescents should be encouraged to adopt personality goals that will contribute to their maturity. Physical appearances are difficult to change but the kind of person someone aspires to become is a matter of choice. Personality goals are the realm in which adults have the greatest opportunity to be seen by adolescents as models for imitation.

Students should be urged to participate in extracurricular activities that can support the expressive as well as instrumental aspects of school. The social context is an important place to build connections with others who have similar interests. Participation in the expressive culture can result in greater satisfaction at school, lower dropout rates, and foster healthy adjustment to offset disappointment that happens in other sectors of living. These benefits are reinforced by evidence that expressive involvement can support coping with pressures, make students less susceptible to stress, and better able to choose appropriate models for relief.

Students have an abundance of career alternatives and need guided experiences to process the choices. When teenagers choose goals that can disappoint them, reflective conversations with trusted adults is a better strategy than expecting a student to endure disappointing consequences. Parents should join their children as participants in a school program that allows them to explore a range of career options.

Learning how to revise aspirations is generally overlooked as an aspect of decision-making that allows someone to figure out when a change in personal direction is warranted. Teachers ought to avoid recommending persistence in every case because some students may need additional exploration to identify career goals that are more appropriate for them.

All students should have the goal of achieving minimal competence in the basic skills. When this goal seems difficult to attain, there is a need for remediation by free tutoring that is provided through the school and commonly encouraged by faculty, parents, and students. For students whose career path is uncertain there can be benefit in comparing norm-referenced test results with usual expectations for candidates wanting to pursue particular career paths.

# 12

## Thinking and Reflection

**P**eople who can rely on reflective thinking and imagination are more able to conceive of solutions for problems and demonstrate good judgment when making decisions. These assets should be identified as a priority for long-term education that begins during early childhood. The goals for this chapter are to discuss how learning to value time alone can influence thinking and the acquisition of time management skills. Adult participation in pretend type play with children is discussed as a factor that reinforces the importance of imagination. Suggestions focus on how to help adults feel comfortable while engaged in play with children, recognize the limitations of praise to motivate creative behavior, and understand how both generations gain from pretending together.

## Lifestyle and Solitude

### Arrange Time to be Alone

Learning to get along with peers is a socialization skill children can acquire in school. However, learning to value solitude and spending time

*Thinking in Childhood and Adolescence,* pages 247–264
Copyright © 2013 by Information Age Publishing
All rights of reproduction in any form reserved.

alone will probably begin at home or never happen (Cain, 2012). Obviously, the number of children in a school and frequency of interruptions combine to make solitary activity a low priority in classrooms. Then too, once school begins, organized groups like the Girl Scouts, Little League, Soccer, Boys and Girls Clubs, and after-school programs become options. These experiences can be beneficial but parents should recognize their obligation to ensure the schedule of their child includes some daily time alone. This is a difficult task, especially for parents who are unable to schedule uninterrupted time for their own leisure activities.

Parents should show they value solitude and arrange time alone for themselves. In a two generational study, the self-impressions of 1,545 Black, Hispanic, and White mothers and their 10 to 14 years olds were examined. The purpose was to determine what each generation saw as assets and shortcomings of the parents. Mothers reported that being able to set aside time for personal leisure was their most difficult task, ranking 60th out of 60 situations. Adolescents also detected the inability of their mothers to arrange personal leisure by ranking it 57th of 60 items (Strom, Strom, Strom, Shen, & Beckert, 2004).

This common difficulty should be seen in a broader context than maternal sacrifice. Children need mothers to show them how to deal with stress by setting aside time for relief and demonstrate ways to manage time so they have balance and personal control of their life. There is evidence that many employed mothers suffer from stress produced by multiple role responsibilities that typically include child care, responsibilities toward a husband, offering support for aging parents, satisfying an employer, and managing a household. These combined pressures can motivate mothers to overschedule their children, thus depriving them of free time that provides a needed sense of control over life and chance to decide what things they want to do alone.

Similar results were found in studies of 517 Black and White fathers along with their early adolescent daughters and sons. These fathers reported that, like mothers, their greatest difficulty was being able to schedule leisure time for themselves. This inability to demonstrate time management—to plan for personal discretionary time—has an influence on most contexts of parental guidance. When parents are stressed out or fatigued, the time they spend with children often includes more nonproductive conflict and a reduction of mutual satisfaction. Most fathers accept less responsibility than mothers do for childcare and supervision. Consequently, it seems improbable that a father would be able to teach children how to cope with multiple demands on their time when he is unable to arrange moments for personal relief and renewal. Many children conclude their parents have yet to learn how to deal with the pervasive pressures that cause feelings of being hurried and a sense of helplessness about lack of control of their time. As a result, some decide they have to turn to sources outside the family for guidance on coping with stress. Some of these external sources provide unhealthy solutions (Strom et al., 2000; Strom, Beckert, Strom, Strom, & Griswold, 2002).

Consider what takes place in many homes. Mom and Dad have been at work throughout the day and, after dinner, engage in a brief activity with their child. Then, to ensure their own privacy, parents may direct the child to get ready for bed even if the time may be earlier than is necessary. A more helpful approach for parents to arrange personal time alone is to tell a child, "It is time for you to be alone, doing things you enjoy. Mom and Dad will do the same. The light in your bedroom will be left on so you can decide whether you want to quietly look at pictures, color, draw, play with dolls, action figures, other toys, or something else that is interesting. In 30 minutes, we will come to tuck you in and turn out the light so you can sleep." This strategy helps a child to realize everyone needs time alone and it can be an enjoyable experience with benefits that cannot be found in other ways. By arranging time for solitude, parents avoid depriving a child of the self-encounters everyone needs to nurture imagination and self-evaluation.

Sherry Turkle is a professor of science, technology, and society at the Massachusetts Institute of Technology. Her book *Alone together: Why we expect more from technology and less from each other* examines how thinking in a digital society differs from the way things were in the past. According to Turkle (2011), learning to value solitude and being alone is the bedrock of early development. Parents should realize they may be depriving their children of this great asset if they pacify them with devices that are used excessively in order to avoid being alone. Children need to be able to think independently of a device, to explore their imagination, reflect on events, and process ideas and feelings without the ever-present distractions of technology. If parents fail to teach their children ways to enjoy being alone, children will equate solitude with being lonely.

### Imagination and Solitary Play

When children engage in solitary play, they fantasize more than during play with friends or parent–child play. Nevertheless, although parents recognize solitude is the best condition for fantasy practice, some worry about the child who prefers to play alone. This apprehension relates to the high value that society assigns to extroversion and sociability. Most people are unaware that two-thirds of highly creative individuals are introverts (Cain, 2012). Some parents express reservations about whether solitary play is healthy. One father observed, "Playing alone may be fine in some cases but my 4 year old seems to be a victim of hallucinations. He refers to talks with Roy, a fantasy companion." If this father had listened more carefully, he would recognize that during solitary play it is the child who controls imaginary friends. In fact, total control over the fictitious companion may be what bothers some parents. Perhaps they suppose the power that comes with being boss is not good for children since it could cause them to be uncooperative in relating to adults. The fact is that cooperation implies a sharing of power. Children who feel powerless are unable to cooperate and instead can only acquiesce.

If imaginary companions appear at all, children between ages three and six create them and these products of fiction seldom remain after the age of 10. Bear in mind that these are not also lonely, timid, or maladjusted children. They are normal, found in families of all sizes and social status. Estimates from 20% to 50% of boys and girls are the proportion that experience fictitious companions. Studies have found that highly-creative children are more likely than less creative peers to interact with fantasy companions. These findings have been corroborated by retrospective studies of creative adults who share similar memories of playing with imaginary companions (Taylor, 1999).

Consider this scenario. A highly-competitive money manager becomes aware that his desire for a promotion will depend upon providing better economic forecasting than another candidate for the position. He soon determines that it is wise to turn to his 7-year-old daughter and her imaginary companion for guidance. Eddie Murphy is the part-time father and full-time executive, in *Imagine That* (Kirkpatrick, 2009), a movie where viewers are helped to discover all you need is imagination, enough time to spend with each other, and a lot of love to achieve the most in life.

During solitary play children govern the behavior of everyone involved in their stories. This expression of imagination is normal in early childhood. There will be times when children report on conversation with imaginary companions that parents consider to be disturbing. For example, 4-year-old Derek reports he did not pick up the toys in his room as directed by parents because Ollie, his fictitious friend, told him he did not have to do it today. Some parents respond with punishment or a reminder that lying is unacceptable, and want the child to stop making up stories. This reaction is intended to reinforce differences between right and wrong and support development of moral character. However, Derek's mother looked at the situation differently as shown by her reaction. She said, "Tell Ollie that your mother is the person who decides how our house is taken care of and what chores are expected of everyone in the house including Derek." Mother did not refer to Derek as being a liar nor did she discourage a relationship with his imaginary friend. Instead, she called attention to the fact that Derek can make up stories but she will not approve excuses for not doing assigned chores.

## *Parent Support for Reflection*

Children learn at home the importance parents attach to reflective thinking. Preschoolers typically ask many questions throughout the day. When parents encourage continual expression of curiosity, they cause children to recognize questioning is considered to be an important way to learn. Similarly, waiting for a child to answer questions reinforces the priority parents assign to reflective thinking. Some parents can misinterpret silence that follows questions presented to a child. Perhaps they suppose this is an indicator of a lack of understanding. Some teachers act the same way by assuming that waiting takes too long or students will be unwilling to wait for classmates to reflect before responding. Adults who judge the thinking of children in this way also tend to modify their questions or resort to providing clues about the expected answer. This practice of rushing children leads to a premature response and ignores the pace of decision-making called cognitive tempo. The term *cognitive tempo* refers to the speed at which a person processes information, reaches judgments, and solves problems.

Psychologist Jerome Kagan (2007) of Harvard University who devised the Matching Familiar Figures Test (MFFT) provides an example of cognitive tempo. On this test children are asked to select, from six pictures that seem to be similar, the one that is identical to the model. Boys and girls demonstrating an impulsive tempo tend to act on first impressions without pausing to evaluate the quality of their replies. Thus, they react quickly but make many errors. By comparison, children with a reflective tempo take more time in examining each picture. Because they think before acting, reflective children are more accurate and make fewer mistakes. Cognitive tempo is evident by age 2 and fairly stable by age 4. Researchers have found that cognitive tempo seems related to early patterns of interaction between mother and child.

Children sometimes approach a parent asking: "Guess what?" This is the phrase children use in hopes of involving parents in the guessing or hypothesis behavior that triggers creative thinking. But many parents refuse the invitation and reply by asking—"what?" This response indicates that guessing is not the way that parents want to learn: They prefer to learn by being told. Parent reluctance to engage in the creative thinking they want to support can be observed early. The authors conducted an observational study of 30 couples, all of which had a young child (Strom & Strom, 2010). Each family was given a Fisher Price toy airplane along with colorful wooden passengers and suitcases. Time samplings of family play conversations in each of the homes were recorded. When the 800 questions parents asked during play were analyzed, it was determined that 469 or 57% called for classification thinking. For example, "Which suitcases are square? Which passenger is wearing a blue suit? Another 270 parent questions or 33% were descriptive—"What sound is made by an airplane? "What does a stewardess do on an airplane? Together classification and description questions accounted for 90% of the total. Even though all the parents had stated a desire to encourage creative thinking, only 14 questions, less than 2%, invited their children to hypothesize or speculate—the first steps that are necessary in solving science problems.

Although society cherishes reflective thinking, the results showed these parents expected their children to give immediate reaction to questions. The mothers waited a minimum of 5 seconds for an answer to their question 60% of the time. Fathers, who had a greater need for closure, waited 5 seconds in only 40% of the cases. In contrast, children respected deliberation the most, waiting 5 seconds or more in 86% of cases when they asked a question of parents. We recommend applying the 5-second rule when presenting questions to your child instead of urging hasty answers that have not been reflected on. When children are given time to reflect, they are more likely to value critical thinking.

Related studies in elementary science classes have shown that when teachers extended the wait time after asking their question, all of the following increased: (a) the length of student responses; (b) the number of unsolicited but appropriate student responses; (c) number of questions asked by students; (d) the number of experiments students proposed; (e) number of times students made inferences and supported them; and (f) number of contributions made by slow learners (Feynman, 1999).

Daughters and sons want to please parents and can tell when adults are impatient and unwilling to wait for answers. Parents should demonstrate patience or they disadvantage their children. Waiting long enough for answers seems to be an important skill in presenting questions and encouraging reflective thinking. The only way children can become reflective is when they are given time to think. By insisting answers be given without delay, parents encourage impulsive behavior. School success requires an ability to reflect, and the need for this ability increases as a student moves up through the grades.

## Social Awareness

### *Empathy and Social Skills*

The way mothers talk to their preschoolers about understanding feelings of other people, referred to as empathy, can have a lasting effect on social skills. Social understanding develops by reflecting on how others may see things, taking into account how events could be interpreted from the view of someone else. Researchers at University of Sussex, England, examined child ability to recognize and appreciate the perspectives of other people (Ruffman, Slade, Devitt, & Crowe, 2006). A longitudinal experiment tracked 57 children from age 3 to 12. At the outset, half of the mothers were provided guidelines for talking with their children about feelings, beliefs, wants, and intentions of others; the remainder group of mothers was given no recommendations to shape their conversations.

Researchers visited the homes to observe how each mother talked to her children while looking at a series of pictures together. For example, successive pictures of a young girl showed her favorite toy was broken, she visited swings and slides at a playground, and the high tower she has built out of blocks was deliberately pushed over by a boy. The children whose mothers talked with them about the mental state of characters in these as other pictures performed better on tasks of social understanding that were administered every year. The relationship between conversations that dealt with mental states and social understanding was strongest in early childhood and independent of mother IQ or level of social understanding. Mother influence waned between ages 8 to 12 when children were less dependent on them and spent more time with peers, teachers, and other adults (Yuill & Ruffman, 2009).

One measure of social understanding that was applied with children age 8 and older involved watching clips from *The Office*, an NBC comedy television series (Daniels, Klein, Silverman, Gervais, & Merchant, 2005). The main character, David Brent, typifies individuals who are inclined to incorrectly interpret social situations. Adult viewers realized that the reason David so often embarrassed coworkers was his lack of social understanding. Children also detected David's social skill deficits in explaining why he seemed oblivious to how he continually made others uncomfortable. Every parent should take advantage of television viewing to talk with children about how characters on programs might be feeling as a result of actions or events as they unfold. Labeling the way other people might feel—identifying their mental state—is an important step toward achievement of social maturity.

There are also daily opportunities to reinforce this lesson based on how children interact with companions. For example, when a child grabs a toy from a playmate, the observing parent could use this incident to point out that "When you took the airplane away from Terry, it made him feel sad." This interpretation provides the child with insight and offers greater benefit than saying, "Give it back now or you will be punished." Parents should help their children develop a vocabulary of feelings so they learn how to express emotions, use words to explain how they suppose other people are feeling, and establish empathy as a consistent personality pattern.

### Children as Social Observers

One method to help children acquire a sense of empathy and social perspective about the feelings of peers is by expecting them to report their daily observations of interaction and activity. Mothers and fathers often ask their children, "How was school today?" Even though children are away from home for much of the day, many of them have little to report about what happens at school. Young children are egocentric and self-centered, characteristics they need to grow out of to be able to get along well with their peers. Social awareness can enlarge child perspective so that it includes continuing concern about the way other people feel. Parents can support this process by asking questions that implicate the child in the observer role. Being an observer broadens the outlook of a child to go beyond just telling parents about things that happened to them and also recognize that the experiences of other people are also important.

Teachers can recommend that parents use the practice described here with the following directions. Place a check beside the questions you ask your daughter or son each day and note the questions that are repeated. Enrich the agenda with other relevant questions and follow up.

I asked my child these questions during our conversations today:

1. What examples of students helping others did you observe?
2. What mistreatment of peers did you see while at the school?
3. What teacher lessons caused you to see things differently?
4. How did you comfort someone who was in need of support?
5. What was the most satisfying thing that happened today?
6. Looking back, what things would you have done differently?
7. What arguments could you have managed in a better way?
8. What actions did you take that show you are growing up?
9. What goals did you choose and make some effort to reach?
10. What did you learn that our family could benefit from?
11. What criticism or compliments did you get from others?
12. What problems did you have getting along with others?

### Practice With Self-Evaluation

Parents and caregivers evaluate children daily but rarely provide opportunities for them to practice self-assessment. Self-control can become more common if children acquire healthy self-evaluation practices. High achievers share the ability to accurately evaluate their limitations, an asset that alerts them to personal assets as well as learning needs. Consider some contexts that adults can arrange for children to practice self-evaluation and get feedback that either confirms or challenges self-judgment. For each situation, it is helpful to provide questions to rely on as a basis for self-evaluation.

*Swimming lessons.* After a lesson, children can reflect on these questions: How well did I listen to what was said by my coach? Did I understand and follow the directions I was given? Did I encourage others in my group to swim better? How did I act when other swimmers did well? How do I feel about my progress as a swimmer? How well do I swim compared to others taking lessons with me? The agenda allow for expression of feelings, estimation of progress, and detection of problems. A child can also gain a sense of obligation by this kind of dialogue.

*Play date.* After a date, each child can answer these questions: How did I get along with my friends? Did I share playthings with others? Did I take turns when it was the right thing to do? How did I handle arguments? Did I have a good time? Did everyone have fun? Did I say something mean to anyone? Did I help anyone? Parents can then ask themselves: Do I agree with a child's assessment of progress and achievement? Share your observations with the child.

*Getting dressed.* A child should be able to recognize whether s/he is suitably dressed in the morning and know if anything is missing with the clothing. Questions can include: Does the shirt I picked go with my pants? Do the clothes I have chosen match the weather? Will my outfit be too cold, too warm, or about right? Have I chosen clean clothes to wear today? What did I do with my clothes that are dirty? How do I feel about deciding what to wear?

## Teaching Through Play

Parents want children to become creative adults who adapt to change and produce unique and practical ideas. But, few families know what should be done to facilitate these achievements. Play is the universal activity of children. Parents say that they would like to respect motivation of their children to play but doubt if engagement with fantasy activity offers any benefit. They also wonder whether it is reasonable to encourage reliance on imagination as preparation for getting along in the real world. Other parents have mixed feelings about how they should respond when their children invite them to become partners in fantasy play (Brown & Vaughan, 2010).

### Parent–Child Pretend Play

Many parents of young children are uneasy about becoming involved with the pretend play of their children. Some questions parents ask about what to do in this context are presented along with answers based on large-scale family studies (Strom & Strom, 2010).

1. *How should I respond when my child asks me to participate in play?* When a child invites you to join in play, the best response is to agree. Even though play is the favorite way boys and girls like to spend their time, adults are unsure about its value and reluctant to engage in pretending themselves since it causes them to feel silly. Feelings of embarrassment reflect an unfortunate view that the only justifiable time to engage in fantasy is during early childhood. A more beneficial perspective is to think about your child and yourself as partners. In a partnership, there is no competition because the strengths of each partner are used to advantage both parties. Your child has more access to imagination but you possess greater language, values, and maturity. When these assets are combined, both parent and child are bound to benefit.

2. *How long can I remain interested while at play?* A casual observer will notice that going shopping has little interest for young children. Usually they ask their mother to go home well before she is ready. Mothers recognize that what boys and girls complain about as "a long time" is actually just a few minutes. This attention deficit is reversed in fantasy play. For example, we invited 300 families with young children to be part of an experiment. As each family arrived they were greeted by a host who invited the parents to play with their child for a while using a box of toys until our staff was ready to meet them. They were unaware that the length of playtime was being measured. Later they were told, "We are glad that you kept busy playing until we could see you. By the way, how long did you play?" Most parents guessed they had been playing 20 minutes even though the actual time was 6 minutes.

   When someone says another person has a short attention span, it really depends on the activity. For many parents this means that initially they can expect to play for about 10 minutes or less without becoming bored or distracted. Because it is unwise to play beyond your point of interest, tell the child, "It's time for me to stop. I cannot play as long as you can." When you take this approach, you experience satisfaction, become less inhibited, and your attention span for pretending will increase.

3. *How important is my influence during play?* There are unique benefits of parent–child play. The children gain a broader perspective than when playing with friends or playing alone. Whatever play theme children choose, parents can help to enlarge vocabulary by defining new words in context. The more words boys and girls understand because of play, the greater their comprehension will be for reading. Plan to play at times when you are energetic and insightful rather than the times when you are intolerant and fatigued. Sometimes tired parents read to their child supposing the effort supports literacy, but reading in a monotone voice provides little benefit. In contrast, if you express emotion and act as the character you are reading about, enthusiasm for spending time with books is a likely result.

Much of what boys and girls learn before they enter the elementary grades comes from asking questions, playing, exploring, and observing. These activities match most definitions of the creative process. Because children prefer to rely on imagination, all parents should place high priority on preservation of this asset. Creativity is fostered when adults join children in play. Children often base their self-esteem on the extent to which parents get involved with activities that they enjoy. Therefore, it is not surprising that parents who engage in fantasy play are the ones establishing a closer relationship (Brown & Vaughan, 2010).

4. *Should I praise my child during the time we play together?* Children seek recognition but it is less for praise than for acceptance. In this sense, acceptance is the greatest reward that we can offer children because then they can retain their imagination into adult life. Although praise is well intended, it is often used to shape behavior in ways that can deflect normal development. Normal development would be the continuation of creative behavior. If praise were the way to sustain creative behavior, schools would not contribute to a decline in creativity because most teachers spend a great deal of time praising students. It is when we want to develop initiative, creativity, and problem solving that praise fails us most. To liberate these qualities in others, we need to rely on internal motivation to enable people to feel free of our control.

Children at play experience the intrinsic satisfaction of play so there is no need to praise one another. They may sometimes try to control playmates and playthings but praise is not a tool they rely on. However, praising adults ignore the intrinsic satisfaction of play and instead insist on acting like a judge whose function is to verbally reinforce certain behaviors. If parents find pleasure in play, they can sustain attention for this activity. On the other hand, when parents lack enjoyment during play, it usually shows up as a short attention span and reliance on praise as an extraneous reward system.

Adults who rely on praise are easily distracted from play and tend to lapse into a pattern of near constant compliments and favorable feedback. Consider four-year-old Darin playing submarines with Jill, his grownup play partner. When Darin announced they were getting close to the island of monsters, Jill replied, "OK, you keep on watching the controls." Immediately Darin shouted, "Oh, oh, we're out of gas." Without delay, Jill answered, "Good, just keep going." Darin, who was obviously the only player aware of the imaginative dilemma declared, "Good, what do you mean good?" Many children could ask Darin's question of distracted parents who use praise as a substitute for giving their full attention.

Being an observer also implicates praise. Suppose your child comes to you with a picture s/he has colored. You are busy with other activities and don't have time to talk so you say, "That's a wonderful job," "That's great," or, "I like it better than the one that you did before dinner." Soon s/he returns to show the next product and solicit your praise. Change your strategy by sitting down and watching the act of coloring. Now the child realizes that what is being done has sufficient importance to warrant your full attention so s/he no longer has a need to seek praise. When children are young, it is not only listening to them that matters. Observation can also have a great effect by reinforcing what parents consider to be important behavior.

When people of any age become dependent on praise, they have to look outside of themselves for confidence and thus remain incapable of judging their own behavior. The need for undue praise happens most when grownups impose inappropriate expectations. For example, parents who pressure four year olds to read find it necessary to praise them more often. The unintended result is that the child becomes overly reliant on praise in situations requiring perseverance. When Scott was in second grade, he asked, "Dad, why was I good at football right away?" "Because we started to play catch with the football when you were six years old instead of four years old." At age four, Scott was less coordinated and would have required frequent praise to stay involved. To support favorable self-concept without the high cost of dependence on continual praise, emphasize the main motive and strength of young children—imagination expressed through play. Watch children at play and you will discover they never praise one another. Praise discourages independence, a quality that people need when they become involved with long-term and difficult tasks. Should parents ever praise children? Certainly, but avoid praise to make comparisons such as, "You did that better than your brother," or to indiscriminately commend trivial behavior.

5. How can I encourage creative abilities in my child? Research has found that the single most important factor that distinguishes creative children from less creative peers is family support of imagination (Singer & Singer, 2011). Play is the method most children prefer to express imagination. Therefore, parents are encouraged to watch their children play. By watching them as they pretend, approval of this activity and the acceptance of imagination is shown. In this environment, boys and girls realize that they do not have to change what they enjoy doing in order to get attention. They must feel that creative play is worthwhile before they can conclude that the ability to pretend is important to retain. Adults must learn to value the qualities in children that we want them to retain beyond childhood.

## *Multitasking and Reading*

Some of the worries parents express about play are related to multitasking and reading.

1. *Is it ok for me to multitask while I am playing with my child?* No. Parental inattention is a major obstacle to successful teaching and close relationships. This common obstacle is shown by a father's observation of his 3-year-old daughter:

> When she seeks my attention and wants me to look at something she created, finds interesting, or has questions about, I (especially when preoccupied with other matters) offer confirmations like "uh huh," "oh, yeah," or "that's neat," without turning my head to look. It is in these moments when her tone becomes more insistent, and she tells me, "Daddy, look with your eyes." It sounds

so basic, but it is her method to request my undivided attention in the only way she knows how to confirm it—when I'm looking directly at her.

2. *Should I read to my child as well as play together?* Yes. Reading is important and provides benefit if these guidelines are considered:

   (a) Read to a child when you are fresh and energetic. Don't give a son or daughter the time when you are tired and lacking in enthusiasm. Arrange time together because it reflects the high priority children have in your life.

   (b) Reading children's books is fun but make certain the child also gets to see you read alone for pleasure or lessons you try to convey about the joy of reading will have much less impact.

   (c) Reading is more exciting and can lead to greater learning when the process includes stopping to ask questions, talking about a story, and commenting on related events.

   (d) Recognize that during reading the adult is in the power position because the child is unable to read. This means you should also spend time playing together where your child can share dominance by demonstrating strengths of imagination.

## Parent Unique Opportunities

Being aware of personal limitations can motivate better behavior. All parents have assets but they sometimes overlook the advantages that may be provided by their unique circumstance.

1. *What are the difficulties I experience when pretending with my child?* Several hundred parents and teachers were surveyed to identify the top ten difficulties in playing with young children. Their responses, presented in Table 12.1 are listed in rank order with 1 being the greatest problem and 10 the least. Look over the list and rank order the problems based on your own experience using the My Rank column. This reflective task can help to recognize personal shortcomings and target goals to become a better play partner with your child (Strom & Strom, 2010).

2. *How do my opportunities to teach using play compare to play at school?* Examine Table 12.2 to learn how parent opportunities are different from teachers. Given these distinctions between home and school, it is obvious that the parent has greater potential for using play for teaching—the learning context children prefer most.

**TABLE 12.1  Rank Order of Parent and Teacher Difficulties Playing With Children**

| Difficulties Playing with Young Children | My Rank | Parent Rank | Teacher Rank |
|---|---|---|---|
| Staying interested in the play | | 1 | 2 |
| Cannot arrange enough time for play | | 1 | 9 |
| Trying to control the play process | | 3 | 1 |
| Boredom because of the repetition | | 4 | 5 |
| Feeling silly or embarrassed about pretending | | 4 | 14 |
| Orientation to completion and order | | 6 | 2 |
| Cannot think of ideas to focus play | | 7 | 5 |
| Put up with child dominance during play | | 8 | 11 |
| Needing to control the noise level | | 9 | 5 |
| Substituting praise for involvement | | 10 | 4 |
| Interruptions from other children | | — | 5 |
| Conflicting claims of toy ownership | | — | 10 |
| Accepting play themes child chooses | | 10 | — |

Source: *Parenting Young Children: Exploring the Internet, Television, Play, and Reading*, by Robert Strom and Paris Strom, 2010, p. 116. Information Age Publishing Inc., Charlotte, NC.

3. *Am I willing to arrange time for fantasy play with my child?* Many parents are in a constant state of fatigue. They come home tired or late, and often excuse themselves from interactive play until the weekend. Nevertheless, the child's need to play with parents is continuous rather than a Saturday or Sunday phenomenon. A better plan is to amend the daily schedule so 10 minutes can be devoted to playing together. Recognize that unscheduled play may sometimes be necessary too. Occasionally every child will make demands or provide other clues that extra attention is needed—"Watch me," "Look at this," "See what I did." In such cases, a few minutes of play can prevent frustration or conflict. Successful parents have in common the attitude that family members always come first.

4. *How worthwhile am I as a model for leisure?* Children need to observe how parents use leisure time; become aware of the activities Mother and Dad enjoy when they are not working. Some parents give this explanation: "I sacrifice my free time so you can have things and opportunities I never had as a child." This gratuitous statement implies the child should be grateful to their parent for doing without leisure.

**TABLE 12.2  Twenty Differences in Using Play to Teach at Home and at School**

| Teaching With Play at Home | Teaching With Play at School |
|---|---|
| 1.  Ideal teacher–child ratio | 1.  High teacher–child ratio |
| 2.  Activities can be left unfinished | 2.  Activities must be finished |
| 3.  Child can be spontaneous | 3.  Turn taking is important |
| 4.  Child speaks without permission | 4.  Child gets permission to speak |
| 5.  Teaching is one responsibility | 5.  Teaching is main responsibility |
| 6.  Creativity can have priority | 6.  Memory usually has priority |
| 7.  Opportunity to share dominance | 7.  Teacher usually dominates |
| 8.  Child participates continually | 8.  Child participation is variable |
| 9.  No comparison with peers | 9.  Some comparison with peers |
| 10.  No peer pressure to conform | 10.  Peer pressure to conform |
| 11.  Learning can be unscheduled | 11.  Most learning is preplanned |
| 12.  Emphasis on ways to learn | 12.  Emphasis on learning facts |
| 13.  Continued feedback on learning | 13.  Variable feedback on learning |
| 14.  Child privacy can be arranged | 14.  Less possibility for privacy |
| 15.  Play is accepted use of time | 15.  Play may have low priority |
| 16.  Parent is seen in all conditions | 16.  Teacher may be little known |
| 17.  Individual space and movement | 17.  Less space and movement |
| 18.  Child can choose playmates | 18.  Child may be assigned groups |
| 19.  Time limits are seldom needed | 19.  Time limits are usually needed |
| 20.  Children choose play activity | 20.  Children are told what to play |

*Source: Parenting Young Children: Exploring the Internet, Television, Play, and Reading,* by Robert Strom and Paris Strom, 2010, p. 117. Information Age Publishing Inc., Charlotte, NC.

On the contrary, one of the responsibilities of parents is to show how to arrange for leisure time. Parents need to recognize that the time and interactions they share with children are more valuable than the material things they can give them. Happiness is one of the most elusive goals sought throughout the world. When parents make an effort to consistently model how to maintain a life consisting of balance, a schedule that includes time for pleasure as well as for work, their children become rich if not affluent beneficiaries.

Parents whose main goal is to provide greater family income may not be around enough to demonstrate healthy pathways to find or realize satisfaction and happiness. In these situations, children often turn to either their peers or risky experimentation to discover how to experience enjoyment. When the preferred lifestyle parents communicate includes only how to work hard while excluding examples of how to experience satisfaction, the model is too narrow to support development.

## Summary and Implications

Productive use of privacy is a lesson that can be more effectively learned at home than in any other environment. Young children seldom decide on their own to withdraw from the presence of others. Parents decide how daughters and sons spend their time and can arrange a schedule that includes time for solitude each day. However, this practice contradicts the lifestyle of families where adults admit they find setting time aside for personal leisure is their most difficult task. Another group of parents insist on privacy for themselves but do not recognize children also need privacy. Reflective thinking calls for solitude and is a factor in making decisions. Society tolerates the results of a broad-based failure to schedule children so they have uninterrupted time for solitary activities and reflective thinking. Hyperactivity, disruptive behavior, impulsivity, inattentiveness—teachers and parents reluctantly feel obliged to accept these problems. A more promising future is likely if more parents recognize that solitary play is a basis for problem solving by its direct influence on the development of concentration, task persistence, self-control, and delay of closure.

Play is the dominant activity of young children; the method of learning they prefer most. Some adults consider pretending an insignificant activity; tolerable for children only. The fact is imaginative play contributes to creativity and mental health at every age. We are accustomed to thinking of adults as giving leadership in most sectors of life. However, children are the models that we should look to for how to play. Recognizing the importance of reciprocal learning is the way to establish a respectful relationship.

Encourage children to reflect on information they find while searching the net. Young children soon become accustomed to fast communication online. This expectation for immediate access to games and ideas should not carry over to the more complicated task of information processing. Reflective thinking calls for solitude and is the basis for good judgment. Remind your child that to act on information in a hasty way without reflection is often the cause of poor decisions in every sector of life. Analyzing out loud what to do before taking a course of action involves reflective thinking. Alternatives should be weighed as part of a process for identifying the most suitable response.

Arrange uninterrupted time for imaginative play with a child. Young children have much to gain when they can count on regular playtime with parents. Plan to have the play sessions when you are energetic and insightful rather than fatigued or intolerant. Recognize that some unscheduled time may also be necessary. Occasionally almost every child will make demands or give other clues that extra attention is needed. In such cases, a few minutes of play may avoid unproductive conflicts. Your child possesses greater imaginative strength while you have more mature values, extensive command of the language, and power of approving and reinforcing creativity. By merging these assets, reciprocal learning in your family could begin with play and continue in elementary school when technology becomes an added medium for sharing.

Maintain a lifestyle that balances work and play. An increasing number of adults accept more responsibilities than can be managed in the expected period of time. Some consequences for individuals who behave in this way are feelings of anxiety, stress, resentment, helplessness, anger, and loss of self-confidence. Learning to say no when others make requests that would erase family leisure time or asking for a later due date when unreasonable expectations are proposed is more sensible than hurried or last minute efforts to finish tasks. Children should learn to gauge personal limits from examples given by parents.

# 13

## *Thinking and Decisions*

**M**aking decisions should begin early and focus on daily concerns of preschoolers. The ability to demonstrate good judgment and reach reasonable conclusions are essential steps in growing up that call for low cost practice at home and in the classroom. Some children are denied such experiences because their parents or caregivers suppose they know best and are justified in deferring opportunities for children to make some of their decisions. Grownups usually justify dominance by claiming that allowing children to make poor choices could have disappointing consequences. Therefore, "I am doing this for your own good." A more helpful strategy is to permit children to make some of their own informed choices. This strategy fosters greater child control, helps to develop a sense of personal direction, supports motivation to pursue personal goals, and enables boys and girls to become less vulnerable to unfavorable sources of external influence.

This chapter examines several contexts where children and adolescents should be encouraged to make decisions and ways adults can maximize opportunities for thinking. Each context involves situations that everyone can expect to experience throughout life. Specifically, the emphases are on be-

*Thinking in Childhood and Adolescence,* pages 265–282
Copyright © 2013 by Information Age Publishing

coming an informed consumer, building friendships, preserving intimate relationships, and managing disagreement in a civil way.

## Consumer Behavior

### *Need for Critical Thinking*

Young children pay attention to the advertisements that are directed to them on television and the Internet. Their cognitive abilities are not developed enough to detect the motives of others, a limitation that makes them more vulnerable to unreasonable suggestions. The increasing amount of child exposure to media means that education about critical thinking should begin in the preschool years.

Advertisements try to appeal to the youngest consumers. Children ages 2 to 7 watch 14,000 television commercials a year (Bakan, 2011). Many parents resent the corporate sponsors for what they consider to be exploitation of their children. Other parents believe their best response is to help children acquire critical thinking skills so they will be able to make intelligent choices that are needed in a consumer driven society. This discussion will show why parental guidance is necessary to help children process messages of persuasion by the media and reasons why some family conversations should focus on daily advertisements directed to children.

*Critical thinking* is defined as the exercise of good judgment. Children have to learn to judge events and situations for themselves so they can make good choices and become less subject to misdirection from others. Most parents are aware that critical thinking is necessary since children are making more choices at earlier ages than ever before. For the same reasons, the critical thinking skills needed as a basis for informed conclusions are being assigned higher priority at school. The traditional evidence of understanding, memorization, is being challenged in favor of an emphasis on critical thinking.

### *Media Efforts of Persuasion*

Four-year-old Haley was watching cartoons presented by Metropolitan Fun Fruits Company. After a commercial, Haley asked her mother, "Can I have it?" Her mom Jean replied, "No, Haley, it will spoil your dinner." The little girl looked thoughtfully at her Mother and said, "TV makes you want things, doesn't it?" Mothers and fathers can count on their children to solicit them for whatever products they find appealing while watching commercials. Parents can choose to blame advertisers, dislike the products, become upset about power of the media or view these predictable situations as chances to help children think critically about how commercials make you want things.

When young children lack adult guidance they cannot comprehend the sponsor motivation behind commercials. They should watch commercials critically and become aware of how others try to persuade them to want to buy things. An important aspect of providing instruction to children is helping them learn to interpret concepts, events, and situations. This important role involves clarifying what the family and community value. Parents should communicate how companies attempt to appeal to children as consumers.

### Child Health and Advertisements

During the past decade public concern has grown about marketing strategies that target ever-younger children. Cereal companies provide on-line games that motivate children to persuade their parents to purchase sugary cereals and salty snacks featured in the games. At the same time, certain foods that contribute to obesity have become a subject of warnings to parents (Singer & Singer, 2011).

To gain greater perspective, the Kaiser Family Foundation (2006) examined 77 United States food company websites. Regulators have no authority to call for change on these sites because the information is considered editorial rather than advertising. It was determined that 85% of food brands targeting children with television ads used branded websites also that could have even greater influence because no time limits are imposed for the exposure as is the case with a commercial limited to 30 seconds. Three-fourths of all the food websites offered "Advergames" featuring company products. Adver-education occurs when advertisements provide children with related information that appears to add to their basic knowledge. Based on national Nielsen Net Ratings, the websites Kaiser surveyed received over 12 million visits from children ages 3 to 11 within a period of three months. The reader is recommended to visit the website www.YouTube.com, General Mills Total Mind Games comedy skit on a Blueberry Pomegranate Total cereal. This presentation illustrates the difficulties of becoming an intelligent consumer.

In 2008 eleven major food companies including McDonald's, General Mills, and Coca Cola stopped airing commercials to children under age 12 years for potato chips, cookies, and sugary cereals that do not meet a particular nutritional standard. These voluntary efforts were seen as a preemptive measure to head off government regulation to curb the present epidemic of childhood obesity. However, the companies continue their commercials on programs that cater to "families" rather than just children. That qualifier amounts to a major loophole, given the media habits of children. For example, Sponge Bob Square Pants is seen by a million children between age 6 to 11, according to Nielsen Media Research, and falls within the category of shows that are off limits to ads for junk food. However, "American Idol" that qualifies as a family show, attracts over 2 million children in this age group (Bakan, 2011).

*Consumer Reports* (2008) conducted a study of the 27 top breakfast cereal companies that spend over $200 million each year on advertising to children. With the exceptions of Cheerios, Kix, and Life that had relatively lower sugar and higher dietary fiber, most other brands had substantial amounts of sugar, some as high as 50%. The study also found that, on average, children served themselves 50% more than the suggested serving size. Parents feel a need to protect their children from a barrage of advertising that encourages them to adopt poor eating habits. In their words, "We are always playing defense, trying to resist a broad range of bad influences as we attempt to raise responsible children."

A study to examine the advertising influences on young children's food choices versus parental influence was reported by Ferguson, Munoz, and Medrano (2012). Seventy-five children, from ages 3 to 8, were randomized to watch two cartoons with a commercial between each cartoon. Half the children saw a commercial about apple slices with dipping sauce and half were shown a commercial on French fries. After their viewing, children were allowed to choose a coupon for one of the advertised food items, with input from their parents. Half of the parents were told to encourage their children to select the healthy food and the other half were told to remain neutral. Among the children that had seen the French fries commercial, 71% chose the coupon for French fries if their parents remained neutral while only 55% opted for the French fries if they were encouraged by parents to select the healthy food. Of the children who had seen the apple slices commercial, 46% chose the coupon for French fries if their parents remained neutral while 33% elected a French fries coupon if encouraged by parents to make the healthy choice. Clearly food advertisements are persuasive with children but parents can moderate the influence by saying no when poor options are selected. Not only do parents choose most of what children eat but also they can model good food choices.

### Discussions About Commercials

Parents have the daunting responsibility of preparing children to think critically about the many advertisements they will be exposed to that seek to shape their buying habits. As boys and girls get older, the products they are urged to buy or persuade their relatives to purchase for them become more expensive. One way to allow practice and reinforce the good judgment children should attain is to establish a continuing dialogue that draws attention to motives, methods, and consequences of commercials. Consider a several week homework assignment we prepared for parents of children in the primary grades. This activity includes three sets of questions about commercials. Choose any of the questions you want to talk about while watching commercials together. Remember that your purpose is to support becoming a critical thinker and consumer.

1. *The Purpose of Commercials.* Explain to the child that the purpose of a commercial is to get you and other people to buy something that the company makes (such as food, toys, cars, and clothes). Here is a lead-in question to ask your child before you start to watch television together: What commercials do you like the most, and why do you like them?

   – Why do you suppose that we have commercials on television?
   – What are some good things and bad things about commercials?
   – How would television be different if there were no commercials?
   – What commercials seem to make a difference in how you feel?
   – What commercials are repeated so often that you get tired of them?
   – Why do you suppose commercials sound louder than programs?
   – What programs do you think should not have any commercials?
   – What songs or jingles do you remember from commercials?

2. *Positive and Negative Messages.* Here is a lead-in question before you watch television together: What are some commercials that you feel do not really tell the truth?

   – What commercials for children do you really like and want to watch?
   – What kinds of commercials should not be shown on television?
   – What commercials have you watched that contradict each other?
   – What are some hidden messages that appear on commercials?
   – How do you show your disapproval of commercials that are bad?
   – What do you think of commercials used to promote lots of sugar?
   – What are your views about infomercials appearing on television?
   – How do commercials about public health and safety influence you?

3. *Effective Commercials.* The goal is to become aware of what makes some commercials effective or ineffective. Common techniques

include music, slogans, and endorsements by celebrities. Consider this lead-in question before you begin watching television: Who are some famous people you recognize in commercials?

- What are some ways commercials get you to want something?
- What approaches do you like and dislike in the commercials?
- How can you tell whether some television commercial is a success?
- Which food commercials make you feel hungry and want to eat?
- What is it that you enjoy the most about your favorite commercials?
- What are things that commercials have caused you to want to buy?
- Which commercials do other members of your family ever mention?
- What commercials do you like to see rather than leave the room?

## Friendship and Dating

### *Early Sexual Maturation*

*Puberty*, the time when sexual reproduction becomes possible, is the biological onset of adolescence. The age of puberty in girls has declined in the past several decades. Frank Biro, Director of Adolescent Medicine at the Cincinnati, Ohio Children's Hospital and his research team studied 1,239 girls between 6 and 8 years of age from three regions of the nation (Biro et al., 2010). By 8 years of age, 27% had begun puberty. Specifically, this was 18% of the White, 43% of the Black, and 40% of the Hispanic samples. The proportion of girls who had breast development is greater than that reported from studies of girls 10 to 30 years ago. Generally, the development of breasts in girls occurs anytime between ages 8 to 13 years. The falling age of puberty among females is commonly attributed to an increase in average body weight. Excess body fat increases the blood levels of estrogen that promote breast development.

Girls need to be aware that the two breasts do not typically grow at the same rate. Even when the breasts are fully developed, they are unlikely to be exactly the same size. When breast growth is underway for about a year, the overall physical growth reaches its peak. A year after this spurt, girls experience the *Menarche*, their first menstrual period. *Menstruation* is a monthly process of discharging blood and other matter from the womb and occurs between puberty and menopause in women that are not pregnant. Menstruation signals a need for parents to begin the discussion of sexual behavior and contraception (Santelli & Crosby, 2009). Parents of daughters that are entering puberty should engage them in conversations, encourage questions, and contribute to the reduction of anxiety.

Puberty for boys has been thought to arrive between age 9 and 14, later than for girls. The male body prepares for the biological transformation by creating additional androgen hormones. These hormones, made primarily by the testicles, produce physical changes of puberty. A familiar sign of change is pubic hair at the base of the penis. There is enlargement and darkening of the scrotum. These alterations occur well before the time physical growth reaches its peak. Although a penis can become erect from infancy, it is not until two years after the onset of puberty and one year after a penis begins to lengthen that it becomes capable of ejaculating semen. Initial ejaculation can be spontaneous in reaction to fantasy, nocturnal emission, or masturbation (Paley, Norwich, & Mar, 2010).

According to Marcia Herman-Giddens and colleagues at the University of North Carolina School of Public Health, boys are also entering puberty earlier but it ends about the same time. Boys start to sexually develop six months to two years earlier than the standard that has been reported in medical textbooks. A sample of 4,100 boys from ages 6 to 16 were examined by 200 practitioners across the country to record information on boy's genital size, early testicular volume, and the appearance of pubic hair. An overall concern is that by hastening puberty, childhood is shortened. The real impact is not just on future fertility but that puberty is a physiological change in the brain. Parents should be aware their son is likely to enter puberty at an earlier age than they did so discussion is needed to explain body changes (Herman-Giddens et al., 2012).

### *Formation of Friendships*

When children become adolescents, between ages 10 and 13, some corresponding change occurs in the worries that preoccupy parents. Mothers and fathers continue to be concerned about the motives of strangers but also friends, particularly boyfriends and girlfriends. Adolescents place friendship and dating at the top of their list of concerns (Rubin, Bukowski, & Larson, 2011). Friendships are relationships based on mutual feelings of trust and affection. The ability to form friendships is vital for socialization. *Dating*, to go out with someone as a social partner, enables adolescents to practice building friendships and explore romantic connections. A majority of students between 12 and 18 years of age report they have experienced a romantic relationship. By age 16, many adolescents interact more often with their romantic partner than they do with parents, siblings, or friends (Egan, 2013).

Some students never learn to build healthy friendships because their parents ignore the sequence of attitudes and knowledge that is needed to achieve this goal. The orientation that parents provide on dating should emphasize equality, mutual respect, and consideration of a dating partner's goals. Instead, parent fears of possible sexual involvement and pregnancy often motivate some to ignore communicating principles about friendship building as a focus for lessons in favor of warnings about premature sex and discussions about condoms. These concerns of parents are reinforced by health reports that annually three million teenagers are diagnosed with a sexually transmitted disease (STD) and one million adolescent girls become pregnant (Centers for Disease Control and Prevention, 2012). Parents are also frustrated by scenes of intimacy that appear on television, especially situations where couples become sexually involved quickly after their first time meeting. The fear is teenagers will conclude a sped up level of involvement is acceptable and incorporate it as part of their expectations for dating.

### Sexual Harassment and Abuse

One problem adolescents and young adults encounter is *sexual harassment,* unwanted sex-related advances toward someone. Touching a person improperly or making suggestive remarks are examples of harassment. Students that are disabled, gay, or lesbian appear to suffer the most from suggestive and pejorative remarks (Ryan & Ladd, 2012). Girls have reported comments or improper touching by boys who excuse themselves saying, "I was just kidding," or "She is my friend so it's alright." Most schools have sexual harassment policies but seldom provide instruction about the issues. Lessons could help curb the problem. In addition, communities should increase the after school, no-cost places where students can hang out, talk, play games, dance, and have guided discussions about healthy relations and daily concerns. Most after-school programs are too goal-oriented, too competitive, and too gender-segregated (Ryan & Ladd, 2012). Teenagers benefit from opportunities to practice being around and feeling comfortable talking to persons of the other gender. Adequate time spent together in enjoyable wholesome activities and discussions about respect can establish a foundation for what can become genuine, caring friendships and dating.

*Dating abuse* is when someone resorts to a pattern of violent behavior by means of verbal, physical, or sexual intimidation to gain power and control of a partner. Some adolescent boys suppose that it is cool to call girlfriends bad names or mistreat them in the presence of guys they wish to impress. These put-downs make further mistreatment of the girls easier to justify (Maas, Fleming, Herrenkohl, & Catalano, 2010). Many adolescent boys get conflicting and harmful messages about what constitutes being a man. They need better advice about how to treat girls. Parents and teachers should become informed and more accountable for their responsibility to teach gender respect to boys and girls from an early age (Kindlon, 2006).

Zweig and Dank (2013) of the Urban Institute conducted the nation's largest survey of middle school and high school students about their experiences with sexual harassment and abuse in the digital context. The 5,600 adolescent respondents reported on social networking sites, texts, cell phones, and email. Results of the study showed that those who were victims of digital intimidation were 2 times more likely to be physically abused, 2.5 times more likely to be psychologically abused, and 5 times as likely to be sexually coerced. The proportion of teens in relationships who reported ways they were abused and harassed through technology are shown in Table 13.1.

## Dating Rights and Responsibilities

Some of the dating orientation that adolescents need should occur in the classroom during teacher-guided discussions with peers. There is a

**TABLE 13.1   How Teens Get Abused and Harassed Through Technology (N = 5,647)**

| Ways of Abuse and Harassment in Technology | Proportion of Teens |
| --- | --- |
| Used my social networking account without permission | 8.7 |
| Sent me texts/e-mails/etc. to engage in sexual acts I did not want | 7.4 |
| Pressured me to send a sexual or naked photo of myself | 6.8 |
| Sent threatening messages to me | 6.1 |
| Sent me so many messages it made me feel unsafe | 5.5 |
| Posted embarrassing photos of me online | 5.5 |
| Wrote nasty things about me on his or her profile page | 5.1 |
| Spread rumors about me using a cell phone/e-mail/networking site | 5.0 |
| Made me afraid when I did not respond to my cell phone/texts/etc. | 4.2 |
| Sent sexual or naked photos I did not want | 3.8 |
| Used information from my social networking site to harass me | 3.7 |
| Sent me instant messages or chats that made me feel scared | 3.4 |
| Used a cell phone/text/etc. to threaten to harm me physically | 2.7 |
| Took video of me and sent it to his/her friends without my permission | 2.6 |
| Threatened me if I did not send a sexual or naked photo of myself | 2.6 |
| Created a profile page about me knowing it would upset me | 1.3 |

*Source: Teen Dating Abuse and Harassment in the Digital World: Implications for Prevention and Intervention* (2013 February) by J. Zweig & M. Dank. Washington, DC: Urban Institute. Retrieved from www.urban.org

need to understand that driving a car, playing on an sports team, and dating each involve a set of rights and responsibilities. The Washington State Attorney General (2013) provides the following healthy dating guidelines for application by middle school and high school students in Table 13.2.

Most teenagers have questions about dating and want to prevent exposure to mistreatment. For example, "I thought my boyfriend really did care for me until he started to call me a lot on my cell. Now he wants me to tell him all the time what I am doing and where I am. This kind of behavior reflects possessiveness, trying to control the behavior of someone else. This is similar to jealousy but it is more extreme. A controlling attitude is apparent when one person dominates a relationship and makes all the decisions. The person dominated is not permitted to have separate opinions. Some controlling persons dictate how their partner dresses, others they are allowed to talk to, where they can go, and what activities they can do. Frequent phone calls are a way to maintain control, always being aware of what the other person may be doing and their whereabouts. Sometimes a boyfriend monitors the chat room or e-mail activities of his girlfriend. If this

**TABLE 13.2   Dating Rights and Responsibilities for Adolescents**

| Dating Rights:<br>I have the right . . . | Dating Responsibilities:<br>I have the responsibility . . . |
|---|---|
| To be treated with respect always | To not threaten to harm myself or another |
| To my own body, thoughts, opinions, and property | To encourage my girlfriend or boyfriend to pursue their dreams |
| To choose and keep my friends | To support my girlfriend or boyfriend emotionally |
| To change my mind at any time | To communicate, not manipulate |
| To not be abused physically, emotionally, or sexually | To not humiliate or demean my girlfriend or boyfriend |
| To leave a relationship | To refuse to abuse physically, emotionally, or sexually |
| To say no | To take care of myself |
| To be treated as an equal | To allow my boyfriend or girlfriend to maintain their individuality |
| To disagree | To respect myself and my girlfriend or boyfriend |
| To live without fear and confusion from boyfriend or girlfriend anger | To be honest with each other |

*Source: Dating Rights and Responsibilities by* Washington State Office of the Attorney General, 2013. Retrieved from Washington State Office, April 20, 2013, http://www.atg.wa.gov/ Reprinted with permission.

is the predicament that any girl finds herself in, she needs to speak with a teacher, parent, or other trusted adult to seek guidance.

### Family Conversations About Dating

The purpose of dating should be to get to know someone while having fun at the same time. No one has to convey false impressions or commitments beyond "getting to know you." Nevertheless, concerns that youth may rush sexual relationships distract many parents from their responsibility to provide a healthy orientation to dating. *Empathy* is the ability to identify with and understand another person's feelings or difficulties. Some ways of showing empathy in dating include listening to hurt feelings and considering the other person's goals and aspirations. Building trust and respect are vital ingredients for emotional ties that are durable and mutually satisfying.

Some parents defer lessons on dating until their adolescents reach the age at which the adults were first allowed to date. In contrast, studies of American girls have confirmed that puberty and menstruation arrive earlier than during the past. The time of first intercourse occurs earlier too, at age 16 (Egan, 2013). Family dialogue on these issues should begin in grade four since some girls enter puberty as young as age 8. Studies involving 2,000 Black, White, and Mexican American parents of adolescents and their adolescents (ages 10–14) were conducted to rate parental guidance. Both generations agreed parents are not involved to the extent they should be in discussing dating (Strom, Strom, Strom, Shen, & Beckert, 2004).

## Conflict Management

There are 95 million adults raising middle school, junior high, and high school students. These adolescents, who at younger ages seemed so agreeable, now appear to have issues that provoke daily debates. Arguments usually center on procrastination for not completing chores, cleaning a bedroom, monopolizing the bathroom, scheduling transportation, spending more than was budgeted, and agreeing on time for curfew. Adolescents consider these topics suitable to leverage their independence. The resulting hassles motivate parents to renegotiate how they communicate with children in more equitable ways (Barkley & Robin, 2008; Cherlin, 2012).

### Parent–Child Disagreements

Family disputes usually involve resources, needs, and values. Issues on resources like the car, television, cell phones, and computers are easiest to resolve by negotiation, additional purchases, or having someone be a mediator who establishes a schedule for sharing use of limited resources. Arguments focused on personal needs for status, esteem, and power are more difficult because the reasons precipitating these differences are often unclear. A problem solving approach that allows adolescents to state their hopes and express discontent is usually effective as a way to settle such disagreements.

## *Guidelines for Disputes*

The best method for adults to address disagreements with adolescents is to always take the high road and show maturity. Getting back at the other party should not be seen as an option. A Chinese proverb informs us that "Those who pursue revenge dig two graves." Conflicts over values present the greatest difficulty. When the benefits and the goals that generations prize are challenged, they might feel their sense of self is at risk. Conflicts that involve values necessitate careful listening along with realization that the people we love may adopt certain beliefs with which we disagree. Since youth values deviate from parent values more than in the past, these guidelines for both generations can help in conducting family conflicts.

1. *Respectful relationships are based on self-disclosure.* Every person should express his or her view so fair consideration can take place. Parents need to be aware of the adolescent perspective to offer guidance that is relevant. In turn, adolescents should feel obligated to enable fulfillment of this goal by providing continuous insight about how they see and feel about events and ideas. The resulting dialogue ensures that a certain amount of disagreement is inevitable because it meets the necessary conditions for getting to know each other.

2. *Establish ground rules together that will be used to guide arguments.* Put downs, shouting, and sarcasm should be out of bounds because they contradict the goal of both parties to demonstrate self control, an agreed upon indicator of maturity. The speaker/listener role can be applied so while one person talks, others listen and do not interrupt. Listeners should restate what a speaker says to confirm that what was expressed has been understood. Adolescents should avoid statements like "Everyone else's parents let them do it . . ." Parents should avoid making comments like "When I was your age . . .".

3. *Agree on a definition of the issues so conversation has a common focus.* It can be frustrating to find out at the end of a lengthy talk that both

parties are still unaware of the main concerns felt by the other. For a daughter, an argument over curfew may be a challenge to her maturity whereas the parents see it as a matter of safety. There is a great difference between telling an adolescent "I don't trust you" and saying "I am afraid for you because most car accidents happen after midnight." Parent fears, worries, and concerns always warrant expression and deserve to be heard.

4. *Set aside uninterrupted time to discuss bothersome matters.* Most arguments arise in response to particular events but certain disputes are continuous. These issues require attention when neither party is distracted and is able to spend time in a serious conversation. If anger surfaces, either person should call time-out and bring the topic up again later. At every age, anger makes us temporarily unable to access divergent thinking or show consideration for the needs and feelings of others.

5. *Examine options that you may not like at first consideration.* Building an addition to the house so an adolescent has more space could be a parent response to the frustration of continually viewing a crowded bedroom. However, this situation could also motivate practical options such as wall shelves to add storage or donation of old clothes to a charity. Almost every solution to an argument is more difficult for one party than for the other. If either person feels their position has not been fairly assessed, the search for more solutions should continue until there is agreement. The best resolutions often involve more than a single strategy. Finding storage space in some other room and showing restraint in comments about how teenagers maintain their bedroom could combine to minimize a dispute. Agree on a schedule for evaluating whether trial options are succeeding or new ones are necessary.

6. *Acknowledge the existence of disagreements.* Parents who do not spend enough time with adolescents tend to ignore conflicts by making concessions. This denial of disagreements overlooks the benefits parents can offer adolescents by giving them opportunities to practice emerging debate skills in a safe and constructive environment. The family should be the ideal setting for learning to disagree with others since parents love their children and generally are able to show greater maturity. This should enable adults to respond with restraint instead of anger. Greater maturity also allows the grownups to enact important social skills such as listening, empathy, negotiation, compromise, and independent think-

ing. Parent and adolescent disputes also confirm that people can disagree and still love each other.

7. *Encourage constructive behaviors you have yet to master.* Acting as a model does not imply having knowledge about how to succeed in all situations. Instead, people qualify as models by being further along the path toward achievement. Adolescents who recognize that parents can be effective teachers while they also improve themselves understand this condition. A powerful way to help adolescents go beyond the example of older family members is encouraging them to set conflict learning goals and monitor their attainment.

8. *Everyone's views should be heard without interruption.* Some Native American tribes solve some problems by use of a talking circle. At Good Samaritan Hospital in Phoenix, a Navajo family let us observe this procedure. In the hospital room, the leader of the circle began by holding an arrowhead above his head. Then he said, "Sometimes older people in our tribe must come to the city for medical care. This is a time of worry and feeling bad because they lack spiritual support of their traditional medicine man. What can be done to help the Indian who is disoriented when placed in the hospital, recuperation center, or nursing home? How can others help during this time of difficulty?" Then the leader passed the arrowhead to the person standing on his right. That person then had the opportunity to speak and make suggestions. In turn, each person in the circle was given a chance to comment. The order of speakers was determined by their seating and they always held the arrowhead, passing it on only when s/he was finished talking.

This practice differs from television programs where experts invited to state their views routinely interrupt one another and try to dominate the conversation. Some of the talking circle speakers expressed agreement with the views of others who had spoken before them. Often the speaker supported a position or elaborated some idea that had already been stated. Sometimes a novel solution was presented. At the end, the initial speaker summarized what those in the circle had proposed. When an elder is at the hospital, it would be possible for the medicine man to visit, conduct ceremonies on the reservation in absentia, bring religious artifacts that were blessed by the medicine man, play video or audio messages recorded by the medicine man, and use the hospital computer center for patients to have iChats with loved ones from the reservation.

9. *Rely on search skills to resolve factual disputes about people, places, and things.* Knowing the correct answers for issues that relate to dates, locations, events, and outcomes can trigger disagreement. Before access to the Internet it was common practice to challenge the view of an opponent by asking, "What do you want to bet?" as if determination of the correct answer should cost one party something instead of resulting in mutual benefit. A better strategy is to begin the family practice of going to the Internet to look up matters of fact or confirm events that represent the disagreement. This encourages curiosity and searching for answers as the key to reciprocal learning and settling differences.

10. *Recognize that conflict can provide opportunities for everyone to learn.* Parents can be more motivated to pursue opportunities for modeling if they realize that family disagreements can yield benefits for both parties. Adolescents are acquiring the ability to examine logic so they carefully monitor the reasoning of others. They tend to practice this newfound ability mostly by debating with parents and teachers. Parents report continual challenges to their ideas can be exhausting. Mothers and fathers who do not recognize these daily arguments as chances to share feelings and engage in reciprocal learning usually attribute their turmoil to the undesirable influence of their child's peer group (Cherlin, 2012). A more accurate appraisal is that youth are motivated to initiate conflicts so parents can show them how differences can be dealt with in a civil way.

11. *Take initiative for reconciliation that can restore harmony.* This guideline is based on research of Franz de Waal (2009), professor of biology and Director of the Yerkes Primate Research Center at Emory University. Before his studies, primatologists were reluctant to assert that animals are capable of thinking. There were exceptions such as Wolfgang Kohler (1925) who documented that chimpanzees are able to recognize cause and effect by showing insights needed for problem solving. Gordon Gallup (1982) found that chimpanzees could recognize themselves in a mirror. Jane Goodall (1986) observed animals that used self-made tools to hunt for food below ground. Nevertheless, most primatologists had followed the conclusion of Behaviorists that, because mankind cannot know what animals feel or think, there are no good reasons to talk about it. Most investigations of chimpanzees tracked them in the wild with a limitation that the animals could not be continuously seen. Thousands of social contacts took place in the dense undergrowth or in

trees where the animals could not be observed. Consequently, the few interactions that were witnessed served as a basis for describing behavior that was much more complex.

In contrast, Franz de Waal (2009) went to the only place in the world where a colony of chimpanzees had been confined and could be observed at all times. Over a six-year period, he took daily notes and photos to detail the social life of 23 chimps living on two acres of forest surrounded by a moat at Burgers Zoo in the Netherlands. His observations revealed how closely the social organization of chimpanzees with their continual struggle for power resembles the organization patterns of humans. The data that de Waal collected about conflict determined that after all of their frequent and loud disputes the chimps quickly resumed contact to reconcile. As a rule, this took only a few moments before they would come together, kiss, embrace, and begin to groom one another. This pattern was universal even when the process was delayed for several hours. Until the combatants reconciled, both parties demonstrated observable tension. These findings, corroborated by subsequent primate studies, illustrate how reconciliation fulfills a necessary purpose of repairing valuable relationships between individuals with close ties and a cooperative partnership.

Consider this question: Can people learn lessons about relationships from the chimpanzees? Some adults seem uninformed about how they can repair damage in their important associations. On the other hand, adolescents are often reminded that, when they become angry, say hurtful things or mistreat others, they should try to make amends. Grownups who refuse their obligation to model reconciliation forfeit valuable opportunities to teach children to accept expression of differences and retain harmony. Everyone can make progress toward maturity by considering the chimpanzee example demonstrating reconciliation, starting over, and building bridges.

---

## Goals for Living With Conflict

Children need to learn more than they are taught about living with conflict. When this goal is stated in general terms, it seems vague and overwhelming. However, when we divide the goal into a larger number of manageable tasks, a more complete picture of conflict learning begins to emerge. In addition, it becomes clear that certain lessons should be dealt with at school and other lessons should be learned at home. In both environments, the way that parents and teachers can begin is by choosing the objectives they are willing to pursue. Examine the following list of conflict goals and identify the ones you are currently trying to reach. Share this information with other family members so they are aware of your goals and can provide observational feedback using examples of your behavior as a gauge for progress. Invite them to make known their conflict goals from this list in order to help one another move toward greater maturity.

1. Recognize that people who love each other may experience conflict.
2. Helping others may require becoming involved where there is conflict.
3. Decide to talk things over instead of trying to settle issues by fighting.
4. Be able to accept changes in people that we would wish to prevent.
5. Know that self-conflict is essential for moral behavior (conscience).
6. Develop the ability to respect others by willingness to compromise.
7. Be able to accept defeat when this is the outcome of a competition.
8. Have will power to stand alone when it appears necessary to do so.
9. Accept that living with a certain amount of uncertainty is necessary.
10. Find ways to disagree on things without a loss in status or affection.
11. Be willing to apologize after making hurtful comments about anyone.
12. Understand there might be certain differences that are irreconcilable.
13. Learn to share possessions as well as take turns with other people.
14. Realize that respect for personal property is a way to reduce conflict.
15. Listen to others when they express contrary feelings or opinions.
16. Analyze conditions that are needed to result in mutual reconciliation.
17. Share dominance and demonstrate an ability to be cooperative.
18. Cope with complex situations that present unfamiliarity and anxiety.
19. Learn to assert personal opinion without having feelings of guilt.
20. View differences as possible opportunities for reciprocal learning.

## Summary and Implications

Parents are frequently in the position of having to persuade their children to do things they may not want to do such as going to the dentist, cleaning a bedroom, or eating vegetables. The persuader role is reversed when the child sees appealing products advertised and must try to convince mom or dad to purchase them. This common situation is where children learn the effective and ineffective methods of motivating their parents to behave in a desired way. When parents recognize these conversations as opportunities to practice critical thinking, a child can learn that sometimes our family does not buy things because they are not good for us or we cannot spend that much money right now. There are also times when we buy things because they are good for us and we want them. Each choice to purchase is different and requires critical thinking. The way children are taught about being a consumer will carry over to influence the way they respond to advertising as they grow older and the price of products rises. The way to protect children from exploitation is to teach critical thinking. In this way parents help children prepare for a predictable lifelong role as consumers and spectators that necessitate decision-making skills appropriate for a media-driven environment.

Being able to build and sustain friendships is essential for getting along with others. Dating provides a context for the practice of friendship skills and exploration of romantic connections. The concern of many parents about potential early sexual involvement of children leads them to overlook fundamental lessons they should teach about healthy relationships. One outcome is that teenage dating violence is a greater health and social problem than is estimated by most parents. Girls and boys express frustration that, even at school, there are few opportunities to have friendly conversations with the other gender. Some education about dating should occur in the classroom during discussions. All students should understand dating rights and responsibilities and recognize where to turn if they are abused or know someone is being mistreated.

Emotional tension and arguments with parents are normal in adolescence and can facilitate the transition to adulthood. This awareness does little to ease the anxiety of parents who sometimes believe their teenager has a mission to engage them in perpetual conflict. Reliance on practical guidelines to conduct conflict can allow both generations to feel comfortable expressing differences of opinion while they each acquire a broader perspective.

# 14

## *Thinking and Perspectives*

The purpose of educational reform is to improve conditions of learning at school. Until recently it was supposed that adults knew when it was time to make changes and could update practices without conferring with students. However, access to the Internet, cell phones, satellite television, iPads, and computers, have transformed the experiences of childhood and adolescence. Consequently, adults are too old to know some things firsthand because they are not growing up in the current era. They cannot remember how they managed certain challenges that youth encounter because some of the situations did not exist in the past or were less prevalent. For these reasons, students should be recognized as the most accurate sources to express their opinions on what they value in school and identify helpful experiences they feel are missing.

The goals of this chapter are to describe the stages of thinking children and adolescents go through as a basis for identifying appropriate expectations for the tasks they are assigned in school, at home, and in the community. Another goal is to realize the technological transformation of society should include the consideration of student views about their schooling. On-

*Thinking in Childhood and Adolescence*, pages 283–304
Copyright © 2013 by Information Age Publishing

line polling is examined as a method that can ensure adolescent voices are taken into account by faculty and school boards when making decisions on ways to change practices and policies about instruction and evaluation.

## Piaget's Stages of Thinking

Parents and educators should be aware of progressive changes that occur in the ways normal children view and interpret situations as they get older. This knowledge helps to establish reasonable expectations for thinking, prevents imposition of undue pressure, and takes advantage of opportunities for growth. Jean Piaget (1969) discovered that cognitive abilities emerge in a predictable sequence of stages, roughly associated with chronological age. These stages are called preoperational (ages 2–6), concrete operations (ages 6–11), and formal operations (ages 11 to adult). *Preoperational* refers to the thinking that precedes use of logic. The logic used by *concrete operational* thinkers is restricted to involvement with concrete materials and situations. Unless concrete thinkers have some direct experience with a particular situation or the material is tangible, they are usually unsuccessful in solving abstract problems. Students at the higher thinking stage of *formal operations* can reach solutions without using props, manage hypothetical situations, and manipulate abstractions. Evidence of formal operations appears between ages 11 to 15 for most students, somewhat later for others (during their 20s), and never for some (Piaget, 1970).

### Thinking of Preschool Children

The preoperational stage of thinking among two to six year olds is defined by the processes outlined in Table 14.1. Each process is briefly described.

*Language.* Meaningful words that people outside the family can understand are initially spoken around 12 months of age. Most of the words ac-

**TABLE 14.1  Piaget's Preoperational Thinking Stage of Preschool Children**

| 2 to 6 Years Old | Achievements and Limitations |
| --- | --- |
| Language | Speech is becoming socialized |
| Classification | Organizes using a single factor |
| Perception | Judgment is based upon senses |
| Centration | Focuses on one aspect at a time |
| Egocentrism | Unaware of how others see things |

*Source:* Adapted from *Psychology of Intelligence,* by J. Piaget, 1969. Littlefield, Adams, New York, NY.

quired between age one and age two identify a child's favorite objects or events like doggie, cookie, milk, and toys. Two-word phrases like "all gone," "big truck," and "more water" are evident. The basic information is there but verbs are not. In the third year the number of words children are able to comprehend increases to nearly a thousand. The vocabulary children understand is far larger than their spoken vocabulary. At this age they experiment with three- and four-word sentences like "I want more milk." A typical 4 year old asks 300 questions a day, leading parents to temporarily feel omniscient. Four year olds begin to grasp the rules of grammar but falsely suppose they are consistent. So, they sometimes say things that adults consider humorous such as "Mama telled me," or "I drinked my milk." At age 5, most irregular verbs of grammar are in place, and by age 6 all letter sounds including s, r, and th can be spoken (even by those who lisp). First graders are capable of conversation with any age group (Strom & Strom, 2010).

Many children are more likely to have poor speech models than during the past. This is because children then spent more time with older children or adults. A far higher current rate of maternal employment modified the situation. Because language is learned mostly through imitation, children at day care and preschool naturally copy the speech of immature companions and thereby acquire and reinforce poor communication habits.

*Classification.* The ability to classify is essential for organizing things and solving problems. Preschoolers can sort objects in groups based on a single factor like color, size, or function. Limitations should also be recognized. When 4 year olds are asked whether there are more boys or children in their preschool class, they say, "There are more boys than girls." This response shows lack of understanding that a person can belong to two groups at the same time. It will not be difficult to understand by age 7, when children recognize that Tom classifies as a boy and a child. In one day preschoolers can see a number of short, tall, fat, and thin Santa Clauses at different malls but not have their belief about Santa shaken since they consider every Santa Claus to be one and the same.

*Perception.* Preschoolers rely on sight more than ability to reason so they can be easily misled by problems of conservation. The term *conservation* means understanding that, unless something is added or taken away from an object, the quantitative aspects of that object remain the same despite changes in appearance. Consider the conservation of substance. Before age 6 a child will observe that two balls of clay are of equal size and then, several moments later, declare the piece that they have just seen transformed into a long, thin strip has more clay than the ball-shaped clay. In a similar way, preschoolers believe that the same amount of liquid is greater when it appears in a tall, narrow glass than when it appears in a short, wide container.

*Centration.* Failure to understand the conversation of volume attributes to another limitation of thinking in early childhood. *Centration* limits attention to just one aspect of a situation at a time. Thus, the preschooler tends to focus on either height or width of the container and fails to notice the other is also changing in a compensating way so volume remains the same. Centration is also evident while watching television as a child misses some things noticed by adults. Grownups can enlarge the scope of what children see by asking them questions that draw attention to details they would otherwise overlook. Wise parents realize that because children can focus on only one thing at a time, the directions they give should be simple, clear, and repeated as often as necessary.

By age 6 some children attain the concept of conservation, but by age 7 one-third of them have still not acquired the concept. Even by age 10 there may be 15% who do not understand that quantity stays the same regardless of altered appearance (Piaget, 1970). This means it is probable that slow learning children do not understand some school work and just go through the motions when assigned rote tasks involving habit and repetition. Instruction can go beyond a child's level so s/he counts and writes without grasping the lessons. This is why tutoring is important and leads to higher achievement. Tutoring allows the ability of an individual rather than level of the peer group to set the focus of instruction. The benefits of one-to-one tutoring have been confirmed by studies of home-schooled children whose parents teach them instead of attending schools. On average, home-schooled students score higher than children at school in part because the parent has the ideal pupil–teacher ratio to detect errors and follow up with correction to a greater extent than educators in class working with groups of students (Cook & Honeycut, 2013).

*Egocentrism.* The thinking of preschoolers is limited by egocentrism. This is not a derogatory term but instead describes excessive reliance on personal viewpoints with the consequent inability to be objective. Egocentric people of any age group find it difficult to comprehend how anyone can see things from a different perspective than themselves. Therefore, in their mind, they are "always right." This outlook ensures continuous conflict in day-care, preschool, and other group settings.

Egocentric children lack ability to distinguish between their own views and views of someone else. A preschooler may shake his head indicating yes or no while on a cell phone as if the caller, who may be many miles away, can observe these gestures. First-grade teachers often report that when a child is speaking to them, another student comes along and starts a conversation with the teacher, disregarding the other child who is also talking at the same time. A mother complains, "When I try to get Michelle ready in the morning, she dresses slowly and does not understand the urgency for me to get to work on time." It is this insensitivity that adults try to banish when they urge children to show empathy for playmates that are crying or feel they have been left out. However, young children are unable to demonstrate desired qualities beyond their maturity.

Nearly half of the speech preschooler's use is egocentric (Singer & Singer, 2011). Collective monologues can be witnessed in collective settings where boys and girls are expected to participate in a similar activity. Each of them describe what they are doing but none seem to listen to others. Everyone is talking aloud to themselves in front of peers. This same behavior can be observed in the backyard as young children engage in parallel play. Many kindergartners and some first graders are egocentric and need help to enlarge their perspective. These students benefit from daily dramatic play requiring role taking, identifying alternatives, and listening to others share their feelings. Such activities are a better base for developing empathy than adults appealing to children to feel guilty for being self-centered (McAfee & Leong, 2010).

Adults often view egocentrism as a selfish trait that inconveniences caregivers. Although this is an accurate assessment it is also important to recognize that egocentrism makes preschoolers more vulnerable to family crises. For example, mistreated children seldom recognize that lack of self-control by an abusive adult is the cause of their harm. Instead, they are likely to feel at fault; to interpret a beating as something that must have been deserved. This inclination to credit self as the cause of most events can also account for preschoolers feeling they are the reason for parent separation or divorce even though they are told "it was not your fault." Because there is a potential for crisis in any family, children should be urged to share feelings and talk about things that bother them.

### Thinking in Elementary School

The stage of thinking that elementary school students engage in was first described by Piaget (1969). Characteristics of this stage, known as *Concrete Operations* (ages 6–11), are summarized in Table 14.2.

*Reversibility.* The most important mental ability that differentiates elementary school students from preschoolers is reversibility. Having the capacity to carry thought backward as well as forward is a requirement for arithmetic reasoning since addition and subtraction are the same operation carried out in opposite directions. Second graders can learn that 4 + an unknown number = 7 and use reversibility to determine the answer (7 minus 4 = the unknown). As early as third grade children can play the hand bean game in

**TABLE 14.2  Piaget's Concrete Operational Thinking Stage of Elementary School Children**

| 6 to 11 Years Old | Achievements and Limitations |
|---|---|
| Reversibility | Carries thought forward and backward |
| Logic | Solves problems on tangible things or involving familiar situations |
| Decentration | Attends to several aspects of a problem at once |
| Classification | Uses multiple factors to organize or categorize; class inclusion |
| Seriation | Arranges things in order by sequence or according to some quantitative aspect |

*Source:* Adapted from *Psychology of Intelligence,* by J. Piaget, 1969. Littlefield, Adams, New York, NY.

which a student counts out a required number of beans. The teacher puts these beans in both of her hands. Then she closes one hand, hiding some of the beans, while opening the other hand to show the beans there. Regardless of the bean combinations, children know that the total will always be the same. This is not magic; it is reversibility. When faced with a liquid conservation task where children must judge whether a tall slender vessel contains more liquid than a wide, short container, elementary students are able to rely on reversibility by pouring the liquid back into the original container to see whether the two quantities take up the same amount of space. In this way they try to solve problems by retracing conclusions.

The concepts of reversibility and conservation take on additional meaning as the children mature. During the upper elementary grades, they begin to apply reasoning to specific problems. When faced with a discrepancy between thought and perception as in conservation tasks, they make logical decisions rather than perceptual decisions. As logic is acquired, boys and girls move from egocentric thinking toward objectivity. They no longer see the world exclusively from their own view and become capable of looking at situations from the perspective of others. When this ability is exhibited with regularity, typically by age 9 or 10, children are ready to shift from doing most of their schoolwork alone to also working in small cooperative groups.

*Logic.* Elementary logic becomes more evident. Students are able to solve story problems in mathematics by choosing the right arithmetic process to apply instead of computing answers by rote or asking the teacher for directions. By fourth grade (age 9) students learn how to figure percentages and can understand that parts of an object make a whole. Fifth graders are expected to predict story endings. Logic is needed for this activity because the ending is a rationale extension of events that have been presented.

*Decentration.* The ability to *decenter*, focus on more than one aspect of a situation at a time, is witnessed during play. "Battleship" is a favorite game that calls for locating and destroying enemy ships. Players find their opponent by guessing and deduction using board grid numbers and letters in combination such as B6 or G4. Children can recite numbers and letters before third grade but usually cannot handle them simultaneously. This is why board games indicate the recommended mental (not chronological) age. For Battleship, a mental age of 8 is the minimum for players.

When 7-year-old Kathy plays checkers, she knows positions for each of her pieces. Because she is able to focus on more than one set of circumstances, Kathy is capable of developing a strategy for winning the game. Playing the piano or another musical instrument also calls for decentration, as the musician has to pay attention to several aspects of a situation, including reading of notes and taking timing into account.

*Classification.* As children advance in the elementary grades, they improve in ability to classify objects and events. When second graders are given eight pictures of animals with slight differences, most students are able to identify the two pictures that are alike. An increasing need for competence in this context is tested by assignments at school like recognizing vowels in a word, deciding whether each has a short or long vowel sound, and deciding which ones are silent. By the third grade students learn to group animals into classes such as mammals and reptiles. Fifth graders can subdivide by classes and tell which numbers are divisible by 5 (out of, for example, 15, 19, 12, or 20) and which numbers are divisible by 3 (out of, for example, 15, 19, 21, or 33).

*Seriation.* Elementary students can seriate. In reading they may be expected to examine separate events of a story and then put them in proper sequence or arrange pictures in correct order. Third graders have learned to place groups of 5 words that all begin with the same letter into alphabetical order. They are able to apply the seriation concepts of "more" and "less" and the symbols for "greater than" (>) and "less than" (<) when comparing pairs or groups of numbers. When asked to seriate the states by size, as determined by square miles, they indicate Alaska is biggest, then Texas, and California. In contrast, although preschoolers can count, arranging numbered cards in order usually defeats them; they are unable to seriate.

## Thinking in Secondary School

The brain is no longer growing physically in size during adolescence but alterations continue as more complex thinking begins to differentiate students (Cozolino, 2013). The logic of some students remains limited to their involvement with concrete materials, situations, and contexts. Unless they have direct experience with a situation or if the material is intangible, concrete operations thinkers (ages 6–11) are unsuccessful in abstract problem solving. Other students that have attained a higher stage are called formal operations thinkers (Piaget, 1970). They can solve problems without props, deal with hypothetical situations, and manipulate abstractions. Evidence of formal operations initially appears between the ages of 11 and 15 for a majority of students, somewhat later for others (in their 20s), and never for some people. Table 14.3 defines elements of formal operational thinking.

*Propositional thinking.* Formal thinkers are able to apply reasoning for solving problems verbally or propositionally without the presence of objects. They are no longer restricted to concrete thinking, working only with what they can see and feel. Students learn to use symbols, as in algebra. Their reasoning permits them to transcend current situations and think about future possibilities. Even propositions that may be contrary to fact can be examined as if they were true. Formal operation thinkers can consider propositions like "Let's suppose that snow is black." In contrast, concrete stage thinkers cannot accept any premise that contradicts their own experience so they would dismiss this proposition by pointing out that "Snow is white, snow is not black." The ability to consider merits of opposing views increases reliance on scientific methods, decreases self-centeredness, and improves relationships (Piaget, 1970).

*Metacognition.* Adolescents appreciate their new ability of metacognition, the process of critically examining logic. The benefits of metacognition are

**TABLE 14.3   Piaget's Formal Operational Thinking Stage of Secondary School Adolescents**

| Ages 11 to 20 Years Old | Achievements |
| --- | --- |
| Propositional Thought | Manipulates abstract symbols; addresses propositions, even those contrary to fact; and understands metaphor |
| Metacognition | Thinks about and analyzes the reasoning process of others and oneself |
| Experimental Reasoning | Relies on tests to reach solutions on separation of variables and their relationships (proportional, inverse, etc.) |
| Understands Historical Time | Contemplates the future and past |
| Idealistic Egocentrism | Identifies ways to improve life |

*Source:* Adapted from *Psychology of Intelligence,* by J. Piaget, 1969. *Littlefield, Adams, New York, NY.*

evident when someone seeks a professional counselor, relative, or friend to help monitor their thinking about concerns. There is an obvious risk when adolescents limit themselves to guidance from peers just because they share experiences. Classmates may be unable to engage in metathinking to examine the logic of a friend or fear a loss of friendship if they seem critical. Teachers usually lack many experiences of students but their ability to monitor logic and provide feedback is applicable in most situations (Dunlosky & Metcalfe, 2008).

When adolescents first acquire their capacity for metacognition, they practice this skill by arguing about almost everything. They are motivated to detect the weakness of logic that adults use at home or school. This response can be seen by the challenge of seventh and eighth graders to any school policies they consider unfair. It is fun to catch teachers or parents in faulty propositions. Some parents express disappointment with the transformation of their children from passively accepting adult ideas to challenging how authorities view things. A more accurate interpretation is that the adolescent has arrived at the stage of formal operations and deserves encouragement for independent thinking.

*Experimental reasoning.* This asset enables a student to go beyond personal observation as a basis for reaching conclusions. New information can be deduced from a generalized set of data when subjected to testing. In Biology, Chemistry, and Physics students form hypotheses, test variables, and discover probable consequences. Unlike classmates at the concrete thinking level whose reasoning is limited to direct experience or what they call "reality," formal operations thinkers can consider potentiality—conditions that do not yet exist but might occur in the future (Mayo & Spanos, 2010).

*Understanding historical time.* This strength is seldom in place in the elementary grades when most students rank social studies as their least preferred subject. However, things begin to change as some students move to formal operations thinking and are able to comprehend historical time. For them the distant past assumes meaning, possible futures are contemplated, life in other cultures seems intriguing, and history is regarded as interesting rather than boring (Tally & Goldenberg, 2005).

*Idealistic egocentrism.* Because formal operations thinkers can look ahead and identify possibilities, they often feel frustrated when comparing the world as it could be with the existing conditions that often appear inequitable. The idealistic perspective can get students in trouble with adults who do not share their ability to function at the formal operations level and are therefore limited to seeing only things in the present. Such persons label idealistic teenagers exhibiting formal operations as dreamers and often recommend that they become realistic (Lesko, 2012).

Adolescents who reach formal operations thinking usually direct their newfound ability for criticism and judgment on themselves. They may set standards and aspirations beyond their ability. Consequently, they feel unsuccessful while at the same time friends and relatives describe them as performing well. Excessive self-criticism is nourished by the egocentric assumption among teenagers that everyone is observing their faults. This phenomenon is called the *imaginary audience*. For example, a high school cheerleader detects a pimple on her chin before going onto the field to perform at a football game. Moments later, while doing cheer routines in front of the fans, she supposes they are looking at her pimple. Teachers should know that adolescents are more defensive in processing evaluation comments than are older age groups (Wormeli, 2006). Capacity for introspection and idealism that emerges in adolescence can be essential assets that should be supported by training in how to process criticism.

An important reminder is that a student might function at formal operations level in some classes but not others. Tom's spatial intelligence enables him to perform as a formal operations thinker in three-dimensional drawing for advanced art class. However, Tom struggles and cannot function at formal operations in mathematics. Piaget (1970) estimated that perhaps two-thirds of adolescents and half or more of adults do not use formal operational thinking. He also determined variance in the scope of application. Some people can use formal thinking across school subjects while others seem limited to formal thought in a single domain like mathematics, science, or art.

## Student Views About Their Education

Communities want to know how well public schools perform (Darling-Hammond & Lieberman, 2012). Students share this concern and have unique insights about the classroom based on daily observations. Inviting the opinions of students can make known forms of instruction they prefer, obstacles they encounter, and factors that support or detract from their motivation. Finding out how they see conditions of learning can help educators reach more informed decisions about ways to change school policies and practices. Everyone should recognize students are the stakeholder group with the most to gain or lose from education reforms.

### *Construction of School Polls*

Input to discussion on school improvement has been restricted to adults, making them the only population whose observations guide change. A better approach would be to reflect an intergenerational perspective. When the opinions of students and adults are considered together, a more accurate picture can emerge of institutional strengths and limitations. However, educators express uncertainty about how to gather the opinions of students while also protecting their privacy. Adolescents feel comfortable stating views in an anonymous context. They consider polling to be a safe method of self-disclosure based on personal experience. Television talent programs feature polls so that viewers are able to influence decisions on winners and contestants for elimination. Television shows like American Idol, Dancing With the Stars, America's Got Talent, Nickelodeon, and VH1 invite their observers to phone in or log on and vote. A chance to be part of the action motivates viewers more than when they are passive spectators. More than other school reforms, online polling communicates a message to adolescents that school boards, principals, faculty, parents, and the community want to understand their opinions.

Paris Strom and Robert Strom (2009) devised a strategy to assess student thinking by electronic polling. Each poll contains 15 to 20 multiple-choice items and an open-end fill-in response for answers not presented by the given options. Focus groups of middle school and high school students from rural and urban school districts examined initial drafts of the polls. Their obligation was to judge relevance of poll topics, ease of understanding content, and suitability of response options. Based on focus group feedback, the polls were modified, examined by students again, and checked for readability level. The resulting 12 polls to examine student-perceived conditions of learning are: (1) Internet learning, (2) attention, (3) tutoring, (4) time management, (5) stress, (6) peer support, (7) career exploration, (8) cyber bullying, (9) frustration, (10) dress code, (11) cheating, and (12) boredom. Students provide demographic data about their ethnicity, gender, and grade level which is used to assess how each of these variables influence perceptions of school.

Student sampling differs from common practices of public opinion assessment. Gallup, Harris, Rasmussen, Roper, and other national polling organizations caution that findings they report can generalize to a larger population within some specified margin of error, typically 3 to 5%. In contrast, the purpose of student polling is to discover opinions of students at only one school. This more narrow focus makes generalization of results to populations of students at other schools unnecessary. School-specific polling maximizes relevance of outcomes and motivates greater response from *stakeholders* (faculty, students, parents, community) because results implicate their school. By repeating a poll after intervention, the effects of change can be assessed.

Applicability of poll results is found by calculating percentage of invited students that completed a poll. For example, 2,000 students from Edison

High School were invited to provide opinions. Results showed that 1,700 students or 85% of the school completed the poll. This high rate of response along with results for each option on all the items is available to every stakeholder group including students, faculty, parents, and the general community. For the example, the opinion of nonrespondents, accounting for 15% of the students, remain unknown because anonymous polls protect individual identity. School response rates have been 75% or higher for polling of 6,000 students (Strom, Strom, Walker, Sindel-Arrington, & Beckert, 2011; Strom, Strom, & Wing, 2008; Strom, Strom, Wing, & Beckert, 2009; Strom, Strom, Wingate, Kraska, & Beckert, 2012).

### Procedures for Online Polling

Teachers bring their classes to the computer lab where students are given password protected entry data to access particular polls, a school code, and random individual code. This procedure guarantees anonymity so students feel free to express their views without being identified. The school principal who has immediate access to data monitors voter turnout. Within a few days after the polls close, each principal receives a report that shows the overall student responses for his or her school by percentages for all items and options. Separate breakdowns are also provided by grade, gender, age, and ethnicity.

Student answers are depicted by bar graphs so that stakeholders can consider each reform based upon specific responses provided by students. Feedback also includes student comments for each question under the "other" option. In order to protect the anonymity of anyone who might be identified from their comments, write-in responses are rephrased and presented as concept maps.

### Need for a Process Model

Some limitations of student polling have been detected. Most principals agree that all stakeholder groups should have access to the outcomes of polls and some mechanism to suggest changes based on their interpretation of results. However, the task of reporting to such a broad audience and processing their reactions is a new challenge for educators. Follow up discussions with participating principals identified the following elements of a process model for trial in future studies (Strom, Strom, & Wing, 2008).

1. Principals should select some of the polls administered, particularly ones that they consider relevant for their school based on

achievement data, district mandates, local concerns, or directives related to state and federal accountability.

2. School leaders should be provided a rationale for each of the polls to disseminate along with other information they believe reflects the uniqueness of their school. This strategy can help everyone better understand why certain poll topics were chosen, generate interest among students, and foster ownership in resolving issues identified by poll results.

3. Students should complete their polls within a specified period such as 2 weeks. A suitable schedule for the computer lab can be publicized that enables all students to complete their polls within an expected time frame.

4. Administrators should be able to monitor the polling process daily at their online website and update students with reminders of how many persons have already completed each poll.

5. Final reports by independent variables should be quickly provided to principals.

6. Stakeholder groups (faculty, students, parents, and community) should be able to go online and find out the results of polling.

7. After stakeholders deliberate they should use their interpretation of polling results as a basis for making recommendations to the school improvement committee.

8. The school improvement committee should make decisions about possible tentative changes in policies or practices that should be implemented for trial.

9. A designated period should be identified to monitor effects of recommended changes. Effects of trial changes can be determined in part by having students complete the poll a second time.

10. The school improvement committee should decide whether trial changes should be adopted, revised, or abandoned.

## Use of Poll Results for School Reform

### *Implications for the Classroom*

A distinction between two kinds of reports disseminated to stakeholder groups requires an explanation. An illustrative study involved 956 middle and high school students who self-administered the Internet learning poll (Strom, Strom, Wing, & Beckert, 2009). A common practice of business executives is to expect staff to assist them in interpreting the meaning of data that is meant for presentation. In a similar way, scholars who write journal articles are expected to go beyond reporting the analysis of data and also provide a discussion of how results could affect policy or practice.

This same kind of advisement can benefit school stakeholder groups. They are given access to complete poll results by items and options along with a summary of implications to guide deliberations about reform. A summary of implications that identify notable results from the Internet Learning Poll study are as follows:

- 64% of students are on the Internet more than one hour each day.
- 12% of teachers require Internet homework daily.
- 43% Internet homework helps to better understand the topic.
- 34% Teachers need training to organize team Internet searches.
- 8% of Internet homework requires sharing with other students.
- 44% of students want instruction on methods to improve Internet search skills.

The related discussions draw stakeholder attention to (1) student motivation for Internet learning, (2) benefits of Internet homework, (3) Internet research skills, (4) teacher readiness for their changing role, (5) optimal use of school resources and obstacles, and (6) possible ways to increase parent involvement (Strom, Strom, Wing, & Beckert 2008).

1. *Motivation for Internet Learning.* In reporting the amount of time they spent on the Internet, 64% of students chose options greater than one hour a day; only 9% reported that they did not visit the Internet on a daily basis. The appeal of being on the Internet was reinforced by responses making known "the way(s) I learn best." Students expressed interest in multiple ways of learning that include discussion with classmates (24%), direct instruction from the teacher (24%), books and other print sources (13%), and watching television programs or DVDs (14%). The option most often selected was learning from the Internet (25%). These student preferences contradict the ways instruction is arranged in many classrooms and urge increased involvement with technology.

   Students justify the high priority they assign to Internet learning. In their opinion, Internet learning is beneficial because it allows individuals to proceed at their own pace (29%). Teachers also realize the importance of pace, particularly for the 8 million slow learners with 70–85 IQs that do not qualify for special education but pose a great risk for failure in subjects and dropout from school (Heward, 2012). Students reported that the Internet helps them discover information (26%) and this supports autonomy. The knowledge that students gain from being online can contribute to learning for their teachers (12%). Faculty who value learning from students report that this satisfaction motivates them to remain in a profession that has high turnover (Strom & Strom, 2008).

2. *Benefits of Internet Homework.* Students consider Internet homework helpful because such assignments increase their understanding of curriculum topics (43%), facilitate independent learning (25%), and allow practice with research skills (24%). These benefits justify greater experimentation with innovative homework. In describing how often their homework requires them to go online, twice a week was reported by 11% of the students and daily by 12%. Never (23%) was the dominant choice.

   Another response suggesting the goals of traditional homework should expand was that only 8% of students reported their teachers expect them to share knowledge from the Internet with peers. Homework often centers on convergent thinking with students expected to show they understand correct answers. However, when divergent thinking is the goal, sharing answers with peers before submitting an assignment to the teacher can enlarge student perspective. Data sharing can also have the effect of causing students to become more accepting of divergent ideas and creative classmates who are able to generate new ideas. The national goal to elevate priority for creative thinking should include encouraging opportunities for higher-level divergent thinking, and recognizing possibilities in everyday situations where there may be no correct answers but the ability to recognize options are needed to guide judgment (Strom & Strom, 2007).

   Methods of cooperative learning were developed prior to the Internet. Some of these methods should be revised in order to match conditions of the modern classroom. Working in cooperative groups is more productive when students feel obliged to bring Internet materials to share with teammates and, during group discussions, refer to reading they have found on their own without being told what to read by the teacher. This orientation adds to team learning and prevents excessive reliance on personal opinion as the information base for group discussion. When the learning that individuals gain from the Internet is shared with cooperative teammates and the teacher, the benefits of social interdependence become evident and strategies can be devised to work together online.

3. *Internet Research Skills.* Students seek Internet training and recognize their need to practice more complex information processing

skills than the review of a single source such as a textbook. This need is clear from the broad admission of confusion about ways to proceed. In the process of doing Internet homework, some students (32%) find it difficult to decide on websites they should explore while others (31%) get sidetracked as they try to carry out their search. Identifying key words to begin a search is problematic (20%), as is the temptation to plagiarize (18%).

Homework should enable students to understand curriculum topics and to improve Web search skills, critical thinking, and decision-making. The authors have devised a set of practical techniques that are used by middle school and high school teachers to help students do research. One of these strategies is called tracing the cyber path. Students choose from a teacher-provided list of topics relevant to the curriculum objectives. Everyone is expected to maintain a record of where they travel on their journey in cyber space. Teachers use the results as a type of road map for tracking student direction, retracing steps, and suggesting better routes to reach the desired destination. Additional data can indicate whether the search begins with key words or images, selection of search engines, and succession of links. If all members of a team pursue the same topic, new ideas will emerge from sharing independently taken paths and collective experience.

4. *Teacher Readiness.* The public is familiar with reports from educators on student lack of readiness to perform tasks expected in school. In a similar way students have concerns about readiness of teachers to design instruction involving the Internet. They suggested that teachers need training to organize team Internet searches (34%). Recall that only 8% of students reported teachers expect them to share what they learn on the Internet with peers. Online teamwork tasks broaden group learning, reinforce importance of data sharing, and motivate individuals to improve communication skills.

Students realize that their possibilities for active learning depend on a major shift in the way teachers use their preparation time. In the past, when teachers were the main source of learning, it made sense to devote most of their time to preparation and presentation of lessons. However, since the Internet is now the major source of information, students believe teachers should spend more time preparing assignments to facilitate self-directed learning online (29%). This shift requires a new focus in teacher preparation and in service professional development.

5. *School Resources and Obstacles.* Students would like to see their schools have more supportive structures to foster Internet learning. The option chosen most often for ways schools can become more supportive is by making online courses available (34%). When students have access to classes online, they can overcome school schedule limitations, faculty shortages, take classes of personal interest, recapture missed credits, and perhaps graduate early. Students also want school computer labs kept open during evenings and on weekends (29%). They also feel that school-wide policies should be adopted to ensure that instruction for all subjects include greater involvement with the Internet (25%).

Students (37%) feel that Internet learning on campus is limited by excessive filtering restrictions that prevent comprehensive searches. They want computers and printers located in classrooms to facilitate cooperative work instead of kept in the computer lab (25%) only. This improvement can foster collective search in class, dissemination of data among peers, editing team documents, and practicing group work skills. A related concern is the reluctance of teachers to prepare and assign Internet activity (23%). Lack of a home computer presented a problem for 15% of respondents. This is a reminder that the school is supposed to be a community resource with its access to the Internet 24/7. The computer lab schedule should be extended so that it allows evening and weekend access to low-income students and parents. Students suggested additions to curriculum. In response to "I wish my school offered Internet instruction," students replied: (a) "to improve research skills" (44%), (b) "to evaluate credibility of websites" (29%), (c) "to understand how to block inappropriate material" (15%), and (d) "to know how to deal with cyber bullies" (12%).

6. *Parent Involvement.* Students agreed parents could support their Internet learning most by having a computer available at home (39%). Schools can increase this prospect when some homework encourages family discussion of information students find on the Internet (23%). Such conversations allow practice in communication skills while parents solicit clarification and elaboration before giving feedback on effectiveness of adolescent reporting. The parent role could also include assisting students in research by identifying key words and choosing paths to pursue (21%). Monitoring the places students visit online by inspecting their site history is a necessary aspect of parental supervision (16%). Novel initiatives that enable parents to learn with and from their chil-

dren are needed and should be encouraged. Parents can benefit from understanding how to fulfill their teaching and guidance obligations related to the Internet.

### Considerations for Principals

Administrators often identify out-of-school circumstances over which they lack control like poverty and crime as factors that place students at risk for failure. In addition, institutional practices that cause students to fail should be recognized as risks that educators could control. One risk concerns the extent to which schools adapt to using the Internet as a tool for learning. Principals have a key role in this transition. Mobilizing the faculty to accept their responsibility as a team rather than act as isolated professionals is essential to modernize the operation for an entire school. This site-specific challenge requires that principals lead a sustained and self-critical collective effort to address the following agenda questions.

1. How can faculty be more responsive to student motivation for learning on the Internet?
2. How can Internet homework help students learn interdependence through data sharing?
3. How can students be taught search skills and progress to being self-directed learners?
4. How can poor families be given supervised Internet access at school on weekends?
5. How can students be persuaded to bring materials to share with teammates in class?
6. How can student discussions refer to reading done without assignment by the teacher?
7. How can teacher and student reciprocal learning become a common goal at school?
8. How can school better serve students with virtual learning by using external resources?
9. How can teachers develop better Internet assignments for individuals and teams?
10. How can assignments more often involve parents with student tasks on the Internet?

### Distinctions of Student Polling

Some anticipated benefits of online student polling have been confirmed such as an increased sense of empowerment among students, school improvement committee addition of more appealing forms of instruction and online homework, increased access to tutorial help, and opportunity to practice the democratic process. Other less obvious advantages provided by this nontraditional form of gathering student opinion include (1) motivation to stimulate school change, (2) community involvement in decision-making, and (3) determining the impact of school reforms in policies and practices.

1. *Motivation to stimulate school change.* A major obstacle that prevents many individuals and institutions from making improvements is failure to be self-critical—to identify shortcomings as well as accomplishments. When reports that schools send to families and communities include descriptions of student achievement only and leave out limitations and unmet goals, the parents are misled and the community does not detect issues for reform. In addition to the need for greater transparency in school reporting, a related factor that can inhibit change is the inclination of parents to assume their local school performs better than schools in general. Surveys have consistently shown parent agreement that poor national performance of students and teachers are unacceptable but the school their child attends is a positive exception (Shumow, 2009).

   How can local schools more accurately gauge effectiveness, acknowledging aspects of poor performance along with evidence of progress and success? Student polling is a new way to attain a more comprehensive intergenerational perspective about the quality of instruction. If school improvement committees are informed about elements that students value in their education and aspects they feel are missing, there is greater readiness to consider innovation. Because students often have higher expectations for schools than other stakeholders, their opinions should be known and taken seriously.

2. *Community involvement in decision-making.* There are 14,000 school districts in the United States, each led by elected boards of citizens that are given considerable autonomy in making judgments on academic standards, curriculum, instruction, and evaluation. The reason for allowing independent boards to oversee 95,000 schools and 3.2 million teachers rather than operate from a central authority reflects the popular belief in local control by citizens having a vested interest and awareness of community needs. This system worked well during the past. However, as the proportion of families with children declines in most districts, a growing proportion of taxpayers are uninformed about their schools and

less willing to support them. Then too, community involvement is eroding at even the most basic level as an increasing number of families come to believe that holding schools accountable should be the sole responsibility of government.

New mechanisms are needed to engage more segments of the community in active oversight of schools. One strategy to compensate for the misleading practice of schools reporting only favorable news involves acquainting all stakeholder groups (students, parents, faculty, taxpayers) with student poll results and implications for change in practices and policies. Each stakeholder group should reflect on and share interpretations that lead to recommendations for the school improvement committee. This process enlarges the school mission from an exclusive emphasis on seeking parent involvement to also expecting greater community involvement. Providing a good education for children is the responsibility of all adults. Every school should expand its communication network to include the entire community on a regular basis rather than limit contact to mailings when bonds are up for voter consideration. This broader scope for dissemination ensures everyone is informed and feels empowered to help improve the quality of local schools.

3. *Determining the impact of school reforms.* Innovation should be tried before any decisions are made to adopt them. This practice reflects a popular opinion that every school is unique in certain ways and ought to respond to its own needs rather than replicate approaches credited for success in schools elsewhere. No Child Left Behind directives have led underperforming schools to imitate other institutions when it was more sensible to determine, with help from students, the best ways to transform their learning environment. External pressures to modify the culture of a school seldom succeed (Bauer & Brazer, 2011). Student polling offers the only internal observation source likely to identify limits of school and needs for change.

People become a community when they are aware of and responsive to the needs of their entire population including the diverse subgroups. If these conditions are overlooked, the concept of community ceases to have meaning. In modern America, communities should expect stakeholders to become informed of student poll results, reflect on policy implications, and make recommendations for improvement to a school improvement committee. This process motivates trial reforms that can be evaluated by inviting students to retake polls that led to the tentative change. Teachers and parents should also share observations about the advantages and limitations associated with reforms. Finally, decisions about whether to modify, adopt, abandon, or extend duration of trial reforms should be made known to the community so all citizens are assured that their school retains its capacity for effective adjustment.

## Summary and Implications

The main reason for Piaget's eminent standing and popularity almost one hundred years after his contributions is because his methods to assess thinking abilities enable educators to rationally determine assignments individual students can benefit from. He emphasized the wisdom of using each child's stage to guide teaching. Children should perceive, talk about, and manipulate objects in order to develop their mental abilities. First-hand experience, however time consuming, is the key to stable learning. Therefore, a fundamental responsibility of adults is to provide tasks that permit children to acquire understanding. What matters more than verbalizing rules or committing facts to memory is involvement in activities that require problem solving, critical thinking, and creativity.

A passive role for students in the learning process should be left behind. Personal engagement with learning is necessary to maintain personal growth needed in the Internet age. Unlike the past, adults can no longer "give students an education." Students are the stakeholders with the most to gain or lose in the national effort to transform the public schools. When adolescents share perceptions about conditions of learning at their school by using anonymous polls, they can identify forms of instruction they prefer, factors that support or inhibit motivation, and suggest alternatives for change. Adolescent polling can provide a more accurate picture of school effectiveness, identify ways to foster student engagement, and offer insight to local school improvement committees.

The continuing project on school polling is motivated by several shifts in American education. First, a common goal is to ensure that, while local control of the schools is retained, students and schools in every state should reach high levels of performance. Second, the national emphasis on encouraging all students to stay in school requires awareness of how they perceive relevance and effectiveness of their instruction and responsiveness of faculty members to their learning needs. Third, every public school has computers available that could allow students to express anonymous opinions about their experience. Fourth, student expectations for their schools continue to rise. Together these factors urge adults to acquire a broader view of education than their predecessors and solicit student opinion about conditions of learning to serve them better.

Americans want every student to have equal opportunity for success. This goal must be met by independently governed school districts that are not obliged to share a common curriculum or centralized administration as is the case in many other nations. This daunting task requires collaboration that combines the observations of adults and students about suitable instruction. Electronic polling is a viable method that motivates adolescent self-disclosure about school and an effective way for adults to appreciate the significant benefits that can be acquired by reciprocal learning.

# 15

## Thinking and Risks

Taking a risk means that there is a chance something could go wrong and result in damage, injury, or loss. A risk can also yield benefits that would not happen otherwise. Adolescents are more willing to take risks than people from other age groups. Helping teenagers exercise good judgment is a purpose that unites parents and teachers. Everyone makes decisions about risks that can contribute to or detract from their health, safety, and achievement. Learning to recognize risks worth taking and identifying those to avoid is a challenge through life. The goals for this chapter are to consider the importance of risk assessment, the reasons to monitor how well students gauge risks, identify growth-oriented risks to support, discuss the influence of praise and encouragement on risk-taking, and understand how lack of institutional honesty can pose a significant risk for the future of students.

### Risk Assessment Practices

Taking risks is more common during adolescence than at any other stage in life (White & Swartzwelder, 2013). Some of the dangerous risks include preg-

*Thinking in Childhood and Adolescence,* pages 305–324
Copyright © 2013 by Information Age Publishing

nancy, sexually transmitted diseases, substance abuse, visiting predators online, lack of sleep, smoking, truancy, quitting school, joining a gang, involvement with crime, bringing a weapon to school, cheating, lying to parents and teachers, procrastination in doing school work, not studying for tests, lack of exercise, poor nutrition choices, failing to get help when it is needed, and running away from home. Additional risks include reckless driving or being the passenger of a driver who has been drinking. Readers can access episodes of the MTV program called *Scarred* that demonstrate adolescents and young adults involved with risky stunt behavior along with the physical consequences that follow (Perry, 2013). Costs of adolescent risks are also described by the Centers for Disease Control and Prevention (2013), search Youth Risk Behavior Surveillance System website at www.cdc.gov

## *Origins of Risk Analysis*

Some observers of schools believe that teachers should discourage students from taking any risks. An opposite conclusion comes from research about how risk influences behavior. First, being able to accurately gauge risk is a skill that everyone needs to learn because it helps to prevent foolish choices. Consider what happens when individuals are unable to accurately assess whether some risks are suitable or believe their courage is confirmed by involvement with situations shunned by others as being too risky.

During the Korean Conflict in the 1950s, military leaders began a new practice to protect soldiers at war. Risk analysis is the practice of monitoring the ability of individuals to accurately gauge the risks they face. Psychological teams were formed to conduct risk analysis with air force squadrons (Torrance & Ziller, 1957). The purpose was to identify fighter pilots who should temporarily be withdrawn from the battle zone. Prior to this strategy, the only consideration for relief from war environment had been the completion of a particular number of combat missions. This policy was amended to include risk analysis for pilots who flew too low or too close to the enemy response system so they jeopardized the lives of crew members, aircraft, and the mission. Because of the severe stress associated with their task, some pilots took on characteristics of high-risk takers. They were no more courageous than fellow airmen but seemed to lose the common fear necessary to carry out successful bombing runs. Therefore, whether they flew a minimum number of flights to justify a furlough, those pilots detected by risk analysis as needing relief were reassigned to Hickham Field in Honolulu where they received mandatory recuperation. The reason for removing them from the battle scene was to help pilots recover their usual sense of caution, the normal degree of fear essential to effectively perform their dangerous task (Torrance, 2000).

This risk analysis strategy implemented by psychological teams has been credited with saving many lives. It also revealed that individual capacity to accurately gauge risk is a fundamental survival skill that can sometimes cease to function, even among highly intelligent people (Vose, 2008). This aspect of adolescent behavior should be continually monitored by adults who are concerned about their well-being. Schools do not present dangers comparable to a battlefield but can present significant risks. The students who drop out are more likely to become casualties than survivors. Just as American fighter pilots required external feedback to detect when their ability for risk assessment was impaired, teachers and parents should provide risk analysis for adolescents. In particular, it is necessary to challenge the personal fable that causes teenagers to suppose they are exempt from consequences of certain risks that others choose to avoid. The broad range of behavior implicated by the personal fable is evident from these comments by ninth graders, "I will not get a sexually transmitted disease because my boyfriend told me he has never done it with anyone else." "The television warnings are wrong; tobacco does not have to be a tumor causing, tooth staining, smelly puking habit because I am an occasional smoker, not a chain smoker."

Driving a car presents another example of unreasonable risk taking by many adolescents. Teenagers typically surpass adults in their physical ability to respond quickly. Yet, they are responsible for a disproportionate number of car accidents. The leading cause of death among 16 to 20 year olds is car accidents. Poor judgment is the main reason for most fatalities. A related outcome is that insurance rates are higher for teenage drivers than for adult drivers. Rates for boys, who take greater risks behind the wheel than girls, remain more expensive until age 24 when risk taking moderates and similar rates obtain for both genders (Medina, 2009).

Many teenagers are reluctant to ask adults for advice before they take risks that could carry a high price. Discussions about gauging risk can be more helpful than trying to create fear or assure adolescents that they are trusted unconditionally. There is greater benefit when, in a low-risk setting with adults who care about them, teenagers can calmly reflect on possible outcomes of actions that have not been taken yet than to consider the damage from poor decisions after the fact (Reyna & Farley, 2006). A teacher, relative, or friend who has a reputation for a willingness to listen is often allowed by adolescents to review problematic options and anticipated costs linked with each choice. These dialogues offer an opportunity for adults to monitor the risk assessment ability of the adolescent and urge that their choices always consider the effects on long-term plans. When students have a commitment to long-term goals, it is easier to avoid foolish risks (Benson, Scales, Hamilton, & Sesma, 2006). In the event teenagers find themselves in a crisis, like the 2 million who run away from home each year, there are sources of help such as The National Runaway Switchboard (2013) at http://www.1800runaway.org

When students recognize the possible rewards that can come from taking growth-oriented risks, they become more willing to take such risks. For example, setting goals is a risk that can provide someone with a sense of purpose, guide behavior, and minimize boredom. Asking questions in class presents a risk of admitting ignorance but holds the promise of being better informed. Providing authentic feedback to cooperative learning group teammates is a risk that can enable awareness and preserve honesty. Giving advice is a risk that reveals the scope and limits of personal perceptions. Becoming a volunteer is a risk that requires helping others whose needs could be ignored. Self-assertion is a risk that involves acquainting others with the way we stand on matters of importance. Sharing differences of opinion poses the risk of conflict but can promote mutual learning. Taking elective courses on unfamiliar topics risks exposing novice frames of reference but also offers new perspectives. Trusting friends and relatives is a risk that could be a basis for reciprocal support. And, risking spontaneity requires departure from a routine but might offer worthwhile experiences that could not be planned (White & Swartzwelder, 2013).

### Mistakes and Perseverance

Teachers and parents should encourage students to risk the making of mistakes as a necessary aspect of learning. Sir Ken Robinson (2011) has described how many modern nations are beginning to view creativity as important as literacy and deserving the same support from early in life. He tells the story of a primary school girl who generally paid little attention in class but was highly motivated when it was time for art. During an art period the teacher approached her desk to ask what she was drawing. "I am drawing a picture of God," the girl replied. The teacher reminded the girl nobody actually knows what God looks like. The girl said, "They will in a minute." This story illustrates how young children feel comfortable looking at situations in new ways, ready to engage in activities they may have never done before, and show a willingness to take chances that are motivated by curiosity. They are not bothered by the fact that the path they choose might turn out to be wrong.

Unfortunately, many schools and families orient children to believe they should always avoid mistakes; a decision that can cause them to stop generating original ideas. As students advance through the grades, the fear of being wrong means making mistakes and taking a risk is unacceptable. In contrast, creative children and adults recognize that they may have to be wrong repeatedly before the solution to a problem is discovered. They do not become discouraged by mistakes but instead are motivated by eliminating options that do not lead to solutions.

Robinson (2011) points out, "If you are not prepared to be wrong, it is unlikely you will ever come up with an original idea." The path to creative thinking typically includes side roads that lead nowhere and requires backing up, revising thinking, and mapping out a new way to reach the destination. Robinson identified prominent people such as Terrance Tao at UCLA, a recipient of the Fields Medal for Mathematics (the highest possible award in his field). Tao explains mathematics is a continuous process of trial and error. Someone comes up with a wrong idea and pursues it for a time until realizing that it does not work. Then, another idea is generated and subjected to trial. Eventually, by the process of elimination, a solution is achieved. Nobel Prize winning chemist Harry Kroto from Florida State University expresses a similar description of how problems should be pursued. When asked how many of his experiments are failures, he estimates 95% but indicates, "Failure is not the right word. You are just finding out what doesn't work." Albert Einstein observed, "Anyone who claims to have never made a mistake has never tried anything new" (Heath, 2009).

What happens when students who no longer feel comfortable with being wrong are placed on a cooperative learning team with creative teammates who see mistakes as directional signs for improvement? A predictable result is that the ideas of creative team members may be dismissed because they do not accord with the group consensus. This disappointing response can lead creative students to dislike being on a team—a condition that must change to facilitate greater group productivity. The willingness of less creative students to listen to divergent thinkers is vital for novel ideas to emerge (Lehrer, 2012).

## Cost of Making Mistakes

Many airline pilots gain their navigation skills by flight simulator practice. This experience allows beginning aviators to learn from their mistakes without being exposed to the costly consequences that might occur during an actual flight. In effect, pilots get to assess the risk of certain maneuvers and then correct their errors without expense. In this way, they can make mistakes without also making headlines. Simulator training was used to prepare astronauts and is implicated in video games where the players pretend they are drivers of race cars or downhill skiers who take risks and then correct poor judgment without being exposed to physical injury (Wagner, 2012). Because the cost of mistakes is certain to be low and feedback about performance is constant, flight instruction using simulators requires less time, costs less, and results in better performance ratings.

The principle of keeping the cost of making mistakes low at school would seem appropriate. However, it conflicts with a strongly held and contrary teacher belief about self-esteem. According to this view, mistakes could place the self-confidence of students at risk and undermine their motivation to learn (Twenge & Campbell, 2010). Students in the authors' classes affirmed the view that mistakes are seen as undesirable. Curious as to how prospective teachers saw student mistakes, we included the following item on a true–false quiz: "Student mistake making in class should always be discouraged." Most of the soon-to-be-teachers agreed that the statement was true. On the contrary, there is abundant evidence that making mistakes is essential for development. From the time infants take their first tumble when they begin to walk, mistakes are an essential aspect of living and the experience of anyone willing to approach tasks that are new or difficult. Making mistakes is the way people discover what they are able to do and have yet to learn.

Continued effort following mistakes has been confirmed as a factor in improved performance. The pleasure of success occurs when previous defeats are overcome. In addition, exposure to mistakes can generate courage, stamina, and resilience (Warrell, 2008). Progress through history has been dependent on sustained efforts of individuals who made mistakes repeatedly but did not consider their setbacks as a sign of inability. Instead, they recognized the value of staying engaged with a task to pursue solutions rather than giving up. The success that follows mistakes triggers continued motivation and hope to keep trying during the next difficult venture.

Teachers do not have the power to prevent students from making mistakes but they can usually control the cost related to mistakes. The reason the cost must be low is that some amount of mistakes are needed for learning to happen. When students fear making mistakes, they avoid exploring methods that could bring about changes in their thinking. The view that success is possible without making any mistakes contradicts experience. Students are more willing to make mistakes when they are allowed to explore tasks without getting a grade, choose unfamiliar topics for projects, and try new ways of reporting using formats such as photographs or pod casting. In these situations students are willing to take a chance, mindful that the mistakes they are bound to make can be corrected, will probably lead them to success, and will not threaten their course grade.

When teachers make the cost of mistakes low enough so students are comfortable looking at things in new ways, there is corresponding increase in achievement. Teachers demonstrate a willingness to correct mistakes when they: (a) revise the scale of a task, (b) extend the deadline for an assignment, (c) take the same tests they expect students to complete and post their own responses to the test items, (d) discuss obstacles that delay a project, and (e) amend team goals that appear to be unattainable. In classrooms where all students anticipate making mistakes and accept lower success levels in the beginning, they become less defensive about errors and more inclined to learn from their mistakes (Dweck, 2006; Pink 2009).

Parents have a role in supporting this realistic orientation about mistake making in the classroom and outside of school. If they accept the notion that denial of failure is the way to protect their child and preserve self-esteem, they unintentionally prevent experiences that are needed to grow up and cope with events when first tries are not good enough and quitting is a poor choice. The capacity to succeed in school tasks and relationships requires the detection of mistakes, resolve to correct them, renewed effort using more appropriate steps, and remaining confident about the eventual outcome. These kinds of responses to failure help youth view new and unfamiliar tasks as opportunities for learning instead of evidence that they are incompetent. Resilience to overcome problems in life cannot be gained without practicing patience. This means encouraging mistakes, controlling costs of errors, and getting corrective feedback are worthwhile.

Sharing our own experiences reinforces the hopeful attitude needed to process failure. Many adults suppose that the memories they describe should feature personal achievements with rare mention of mistakes. However, the willingness to acknowledge failure causes adolescents to see these adults as capable of understanding their struggles. Because most people fail often, there is a wide range of situations to choose from in sharing experiences with teenagers about these questions.

1. In what activities will you risk failure to learn something new?
2. What situations are the ones where you are most likely to fail?
3. Of all your failures, what was the most difficult one to accept?
4. Who usually helps identify your failures and ways to recover?
5. Which friendship failures would you now handle differently?
6. What are some of your plans that turned out to be unsuccessful?
7. What failures bother you less than they bother other relatives?
8. How do you respond to relatives when they experience failure?
9. What failures have you looked back upon with some pleasure?
10. How do family members react when they find out you failed?

President Barak Obama (2009) gave this advice to students at Wakefield High School in Arlington, Virginia:

> You won't succeed at everything the first time that you try. That's ok. Some of the most successful people are those who had the most failures. The first *Harry Potter* book by J.K. Rowling was rejected twelve times before publication. Michael Jordan was cut from his high school basketball team, and he lost hundreds of games and missed thousands of shots during his career. Jordan said, "I have failed over and over again. And that is why I succeed." These people succeeded because they understood you cannot let your failures define you. Instead, let failures teach you what to do differently next time.

## Importance of Soft Skills

Academic and technical skills that can be taught and measured are referred to as hard skills. In contrast, soft skills are defined as behavioral competencies usually called interpersonal or social skills. These more difficult to measure social intelligence aspects include friendliness, listening, communication, optimism, and manners that characterize respectful relationships. Employers value soft skills because they improve the level of customer satisfaction and increase team productivity. People with soft skills are more able to motivate others to trust and rely on them. The importance of helping students to acquire soft skills is illustrated by changes in the admission process of medical schools. Doctors are trained to save lives but some show arrogance in the way they treat nurses, fail to listen to patients, and prefer to work alone rather than to collaborate with a professional team of colleagues. Consequently, soft skills have recently been included among the criteria considered for selection of student applicants to medical school.

Stanford University and the University of California at Los Angeles are among the medical schools that have discontinued the traditional total reliance on grades, test scores, and a single 60-minute interview. According to Dodson, Crotty, Prideaux, Carne, Ward, and De Leeuw (2009), candidates that can present acceptable academic credentials (hard skills) participate in a process that resembles speed dating. Nine brief interviews are held that force them to show that they possess social skills that are needed to navigate a complicated health care system in which communication is essential. The Multiple Mini-Interview (MMI) process begins as candidates stand with their backs to the door of an interview room. When a bell rings, they turn around and read a sheet of paper taped to the door describing an ethical challenge. In two minutes the bell rings again indicating it is time to enter the room where an interviewer is waiting. After introductions, candidates are given eight minutes to discuss the challenge they have read that relates to that particular room. Then they move to another room for another surprise challenge and different interviewer who scores applicants with a number and notation.

The tradition of using a single lengthy interview has provided a poor assessment of social skills because it reflects the view of only one interviewer. There can be greater reliability when views of multiple observers are combined. Secret questions used in the interviews are intended to find out how candidates think on their feet and assess their willingness to work in teams. The most important responses are not to the challenges stated on the doors because they have no right or wrong answers but rather to learn how the individual responds when someone disagrees with them, something that happens on a regular basis for members of a professional team.

Potential students who rush to conclusions, are easily distracted, do not listen well, and are unwilling to admit uncertainly get poor marks because these behaviors are known to undermine the effectiveness of professional teams. In contrast, those who respond to emotions and ideas of an interviewer and ask for more information perform better since these tendencies support reciprocal learning with colleagues and patients. The MMI detects students that look good on paper but lack soft skills needed for success. Development of the process was motivated by studies showing interviewers rarely changed their scores following the first five minutes, use of multiple interviews removes random bias, and interviews that focus on situations rather than the individual more often reveal character flaws. In fact, MMI scores are highly predictive of medical license scores 3 to 5 years later that evaluate decision-making, patient interaction, and cultural competence. A majority of the medical schools in Canada, Australia, and Israel use multiple mini-interviews (Dodson, Crotty, Prideaux, Carne, Ward, & DeLeeuw, 2009).

Several trends account for serious consideration of soft skills by medical schools. First, as many as 98,000 preventable deaths in America each year are blamed on poor communication by doctors who may be technically competent but socially inept. When a licensing body reviews the performance of a physician following patient complaints, the most frequent concerns are related to noncognitive factors such as interpersonal skills, professionalism, and ethical-moral judgment. Second, medicine is moving away from an individual practitioner model to a team model approach. Doctors cannot remain isolated professionals working for a large health care system. They have to be trained for team-based care with colleagues from allied disciplines (Dodson, Crotty, Prideaux, Carne, Ward, & DeLeeuw, 2009). In a similar way students in secondary schools need to enjoin their quest for personal achievement with interdependence and develop respect for the competence of others whose strengths can compliment their own.

## Influence of Praise

What we become depends on the feedback we get about our behavior. If feedback is always praise instead of corrective criticism as well, children do not acquire the ability needed to gauge personal progress or to advance toward maturity. Adults should consider how to motivate students to participate in growth-oriented risks without overpraising them. Certainly praise in response to poor performance should not been seen as a gift. Encouragement supports persistence in trying to do difficult tasks but praise should be reserved as a method to confirm progress. It is necessary to strike a balance in telling children that we love them but offer them praise if deserved and criticism if warranted. The good news for daughters and sons is to know that the love of their parents is unconditional while their praise is conditional.

Some parents admit to bribing children for not causing a scene in public, sleeping all night in their own bed, or completing homework for a designated period of time. Often the rewards parents provide are for behaviors their own parents expected of them without recognition. A 35-year-old mother says "I am sure my parents would be appalled if they knew how my husband and I bribe our children." The consequence is that many children feel insecure unless they are being complimented most of the time. There is also praise inflation. Positive traits can be so exaggerated that words become meaningless. It may not be enough to describe a girl as being "pretty" unless she is portrayed as "drop dead gorgeous" or someone is not just "smart" but a "genius." It is necessary to distinguish between encouragement and praise. It is helpful to encourage when performance is mediocre and offer praise when performance shows improvement. Praise should be specific so children understand what they do well.

### *Praise of Ability or Effort*

Carol Dweck (2006), professor of education at Stanford University, studied the effects of praise on 400 fifth graders attending 20 elementary schools in New York City. Previous to her experiments, it was commonly supposed that praising children for their intelligence could give a boost to self confidence. Dweck suspected this strategy would backfire when children had to confront failure. Her team administered nonverbal IQ tests composed of puzzles that were easy so everyone performed well. Following the test students were individually told their scores and given a single line of praise. Randomly divided into groups, some students received praise for their intelligence and were told "you must be smart at this." Others were praised for their effort such as "You must have worked really hard."

Students were given their choice of test on the second round. One option was to take a more difficult test that the children were told would help them learn a lot. The other option was to take another easy test similar to the first one. Of the children earlier praised for effort, 90% chose to work on a harder set of puzzles. Of those praised for intelligence, the majority chose to complete another easy test. In effect, the "smart kids" chose not to accept a challenge. The inference was that when children are praised for intelligence, they learn to look smart and not risk making mistakes. During the next experiment, no one was given a choice. This was a difficult test, designed for students two years beyond their grade. Predictably, everyone failed. However, the two groups divided at random when the study began responded differently again. Those praised for effort on the first test assumed they hadn't focused enough on this challenge. They got involved to try every solution for the puzzles. This was not the case for those praised for being smart. They assumed their failure was evidence that they were really not smart after all.

Having artificially induced a round of failure, Dweck (2006) gave all children a final test as easy as the initial one. Those praised for effort significantly improved on their first score by 30%. Those who had been told they were smart did worse than they had in the beginning by 20%. Dweck suspected that praise could backfire but she was surprised at the scale of effect. Emphasizing effort gives children a variable they can control so they are able to see themselves in control of success. By contrast, emphasizing intelligence takes success out of a child's control and provides no recipe for responding to failure.

In follow up investigations it was found that students who think intelligence is a fixed trait, and therefore the key to success, begin to discount the importance of effort. Making an effort appears to be proof that a person cannot perform well based on their natural gifts alone. Repeated experiments have confirmed that this effect of praise on performance is true for students of all socioeconomic backgrounds and both genders. Even preschoolers are not immune to the inverse power of praise.

## Praise and Self-Esteem

Nathaniel Branden (1969/2001), author of *The Psychology of Self-Esteem*, maintained that self-esteem is the single most important quality of a person and should be carefully nurtured. Before long the belief that we must do whatever is required to support self-esteem became a movement with broad influence across the nation. By 1984 the California legislature created an official self-esteem task force reflecting a view that improving self-esteem would do everything from lowering rates of dependence on welfare to decreased pregnancy among teenagers. These arguments made self-esteem a powerful initiative, especially for children. Anything that might potentially damage their self-esteem was eliminated. This meant that competition became frowned upon. Soccer organizations stopped recognizing only the best team and instead gave trophies to every team. Teachers stopped using red pencils and criticism during class was replaced with ubiquitous, often undeserved praise.

Jean Twenge is a professor of psychology at San Diego State University. In her books *Generation Me* and *The Narcissistic Epidemic*, she concludes that an excessive focus on self-esteem in the past generation should be replaced by emphasis on humility and empathy. The fixation on praise has economic, labor, and social implications. Overpraised children grow up to become adults who remain narcissistic on the job and their personal relationships. Narcissists do not do well crediting others for achievement which makes for problematic marriages and troublesome interaction at work. Twenge's studies indicate that young adults are more self-centered than in the past. She administered the Narcissistic Personality Inventory that includes statements like "I think I am a special person" to 16,000 students in college. She found that scores have risen 30% since the test was initially given 30 years earlier (Twenge 2007; Twenge & Campbell, 2010).

Over the past decade, more challenges have been raised about the contention of the self-esteem movement that praise, self-esteem, and academic performance rise and fall together. Between 1970–2000, more than 15,000 articles on self-esteem appeared in journals. Results of these studies were largely contradictory or inconclusive. In response, the Association for Psychological Science asked Roy Baumeister, social psychologist at Florida State University, to review the literature. He concluded that most of the studies were flawed science (Baumeister, 2010). Typically the 15,000 articles asked people to rate their self-esteem and then rate their intelligence, career success, relationship skills or other variables. The self-reports were extremely unreliable because people with high self-esteem often have an inflated perception of their abilities. Only 200 of the 15,000 studies applied acceptable methods to measure self-esteem and its outcomes. After reviewing the 200 articles, Baumeister concluded that high self-esteem did not improve grades or career achievement, did not reduce use of alcohol, nor lower violence. Highly aggressive and violent people have a favorable self-impression, debunking the theory that people are aggressive to make up for low self-esteem. Baumeister believes the continued appeal of self-esteem is tied to parents' pride in children's achievements and is so strong that when they praise daughters and sons, it is not far from praising themselves (Vohs & Baumeister, 2013).

A generation ago the German psychologists Meyer, Bachmann, Biermann, Hempelmann, Ploger, and Spiller (1979) studied 500 students, age

8–19, as they watched other students being praised. Results showed that, by age 12, children believed that praise from a teacher is not a sign a student has performed well but actually a sign that a student lacks ability and the teacher believes some extra encouragement is needed. Educators adopted this pattern of deception so students falling behind are often drowned in praise. Meyer found that teenagers discounted praise to such an extent they believed it is the criticism of teachers, not their praise that really conveys a positive belief in a student's capacity for success. Daniel Willingham (2010), a cognitive scientist at the University of Virginia believes that a teacher who praises a student may unwittingly be sending the message that the student has reached the limitations of innate ability while a teacher who provides criticism conveys a belief that the student is capable of improvement.

Carol Dweck (2006) believes the biggest mistake most parents make is to assume their children are not savvy enough to recognize the true intentions of adults. Just as grownups can recognize a backhanded compliment or a disingenuous apology, children are able to scrutinize praise for a hidden agenda. Only the very young, those below age 7, take praise at face value; older children are just as suspicious as adults. Brushing aside failure and focusing just on the positive is not a norm around the world.

Florrie Ng and her colleagues reproduced Dweck's paradigm in Illinois and in Hong Kong while adding an interesting dimension to the experiment (Ng, Pomerantz, & Lam, 2007). Instead of having children take the short IQ tests at school, the children's mothers brought them to the campus in Champaign Urbana and University of Hong Kong. While moms sat in the waiting room, half the children were randomly given the really hard test, where they could get only about half correct, thereby inducing a sense of failure. At that point the children were given a 5-minute break before the second test, and mothers were allowed in to the testing room to talk with their child. On the way into the testing room mothers were told their child's actual raw score and then a lie that this score was below average. Hidden cameras recorded the 5-minute interaction between mother and child.

American mothers avoided making negative comments. They remained upbeat, and positive with their child. A majority of moments were spent talking about something other than the testing at hand, such as what they might have for dinner. But the Chinese children were likely to hear: "You did not concentrate while doing that first test" and "Let's look over your test." The majority of the break time was spent discussing the test and its importance. After the break, scores of the Chinese kids on the second test rose by 33%, more than twice the gain that was made by Americans. The trade off would seem to be that the Chinese mothers acted harsh or cruel but that stereotype may not reflect parenting in

Hong Kong. Nor was it quite what Ng saw on the videotapes. Although their words were firm, Chinese mothers actually smiled and hugged their children as much as the American mothers and were no more likely to frown or to raise their voice.

Offering praise has become a panacea for anxieties of modern American parents. Away from their children from breakfast to dinner, mothers and dads turn it up a notch when they come home. In the few hours they have together, parents want the children to hear things they cannot say during the day, that we are on your side, we are here for you, we believe in you, etc. In a similar way, parents place their children in pressure environments, seeking the best schools and then rely on constant praise to soften the intensity of those environments (Ng, Pomerantz, & Lam, 2007).

## *Guidelines for Criticism*

Student willingness to risk acceptance of criticism from teachers, parents, and peers is necessary to be successful in working with teammates (Fee & Belland, 2012). However, few adolescents are taught to process criticism and participate in civil critiques of work by their peers. Consequently, defensiveness is common and progress is limited because individuals rely on themselves alone to detect their needs for further growth (Drucker, 2005). Teachers have opportunities to provide timely feedback on assignments that reflect lower levels of thinking, tasks that are inadequately prepared, submissions for which directions were not followed, and work that should be revised. This formative feedback can motivate improved effort without influencing the course grade. Giving criticism is difficult but can be helpful when using these guidelines.

1. Clarify for a student the reasons why you are offering them criticism.
2. Place emphasis on a clear description of what should be improved.
3. Focus on particulars of an assignment rather than abstract behavior.
4. Invite discussion of possible consequences instead of giving advice.
5. Keep judgments tentative, indicating that this feedback is formative.
6. Present criticism in a way that allows the student to make decisions.
7. Focus criticism on behaviors that a student is capable of changing.
8. Include the recognition of positive outlook in your critical feedback.
9. Avoid providing an overload of concerns for the student to process.
10. Engage in perspective taking by inviting the student to respond.
11. Encourage reflection and state your willingness to provide help.

For students to benefit from teacher criticism, they should be willing to process the observations of others. These guidelines should be discussed during class and posted as a reminder for students about the worth of considering external criticism.

1. Recognize the potential value of receiving constructive criticism.
2. Engage in perspective taking from the viewpoint of an observer.
3. Acknowledge criticism that focuses on behaviors you can change.
4. Listen carefully so that you fully understand the focus of concern.
5. Ask questions to clarify any aspect of the criticism not understood.
6. Welcome criticism to improve behavior instead of being defensive.
7. Seek constructive changes to the behavior that is being criticized.
8. Recognize that behavior change is a function of your own choice.
9. Arrange time to reflect on the criticism without any distractions.

## Risks by Educators

### *Inflation of Student Achievement*

At the beginning of the new millennium evidence emerged that there were many teachers who did not expect enough of students. Grade inflation was soon acknowledged as a pervasive problem from kindergarten through graduate school (Hunt, 2009). Giving high marks to low-achieving students presents a serious risk because it prevents the detection of learning needs, condones mediocrity, and ignores accountability for students and their schools. When grades cease to be reliable signs of academic achievement, other methods should be applied to detect competency, progress, and learning deficits. Some school districts are discontinuing the use of letter grades in favor of standards-referenced grading procedures that identify level of mastery a student has attained in specific subjects (Hanover Research, 2011).

Common expectations about skills needed for proficiency is important because standards set by each state shape the curriculum and dictate how instructional time is spent. Parents seek assurances that the state where they live has high standards instead of low expectations that could make students and schools seem more successful than is the case. Parents are confused when told that the students in their child's school are making progress while poor performance is usual among other schools and districts. Concern over whether administrators are willing to be transparent in making known the limitations of their schools is reinforced by public interest groups encouraging citizens to demand accurate data about student achievement, quality of schooling, and reforms.

Reports of exaggerated progress has motivated action groups to provide a wake up call to the public by issuing their own report cards that implicate local institutions. To address the concerns of parents and other stakeholders, two common obstacles warrant attention. First, a way must be found to reconcile differences in state and federal estimates of student achievement. Second, it should be possible to make comparisons between the performance of students in different districts and states.

## Comparisons of State Tests

Recognizing how states vary in defining proficiency and how the nation performs in competition with other countries requires usage of comparable measures. One way to determine differences among the states is by comparing the performance of students on state tests with their performance on the *National Assessment of Educational Progress* (United States Department of Education, National Center for Education Statistics, 2013). NAEP evaluation is respected because its standards compare with achievement tests developed by other nations. Student proficiency scores on the NAEP have similar meaning and share credibility with the indicators used with students in Asia and Europe. Based on NAEP scores, 31% of American 8th grade students score as being proficient in mathematics as compared to 73% of 8th graders in Finland, the highest ranking nation (Sahlberg, 2011).

The Educational Policy and Governance unit of Harvard University compared *National Assessment of Educational Progress* (NAEP) scores of students with state scores for a period of six years. Only three states—Massachusetts, Missouri, and South Carolina—received the report card grade of A. This grade does not refer to how well students performed but to the high expectations these states set for mathematics and reading proficiency. None of the three states convey an impression that students perform so well that school improvement is unnecessary. Instead, the honest appraisal that only 25% of 8th graders in South Carolina are proficient on state tests was shared with the parents. Georgia received an F grade because the state set a standard lower than the National Assessment of Educational Progress. About 88% of Georgia students are reported proficient on state test scores but only 26%, a similar proportion as South Carolina, score at or above NAEP proficiency level. Fifteen states were assigned report card grades of D or F, underscoring a need to raise expectations of students and to accelerate the pace of school reform (Peterson, 2010; Peterson & Hess, 2008).

The United States Secretary of Education Arne Duncan (2009) stated, "I think we are lying to children and families when we tell students they are meeting standards and, in fact, they are woefully unprepared to succeed in high school and have almost no chance of going to a good university." The implication for secondary education is to make certain that students and their families receive honest reports about academic achievement.

In 2011 students in grades 4 and 8 from 60 countries took the same reading, mathematics, and science tests. The National Center for Education Statistics compared student state scores on the National Assessment of Education Progress (NAEP) with results on the international test. American participants were from 1,000 schools in nine states. Figure 15.1 and Figure 15.2 present comparative results for mathematics and science. Overall, students from Asia performed better than the Americans. Massachusetts, North Carolina, Minnesota, and Connecticut performed the best on mathematics among the states represented. Massachusetts, Minnesota,

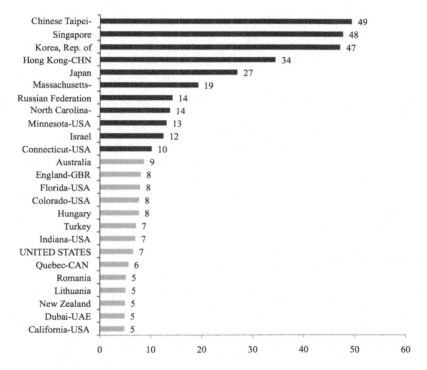

Figure 15.1   Eleven systems had higher percentages of 8th graders reaching advanced than the United States in math. *Source: Highlights from PIRLS and TIMSS 2011*, by J. Buckley, December 11, 2012, p. 43. National Center for Education Statistics, Washington, DC.

*Note:* Education systems with lower percentages of students reaching the Advanced benchmark than the percentage of U.S. students reaching the Advanced benchmark are not included in figure.

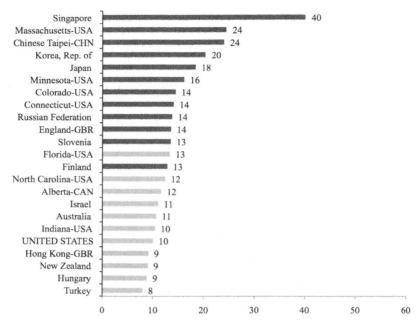

Figure 15.2   Twelve systems had higher percentages of 8th graders reaching advanced than the United States in science. *Source: Highlights from PIRLS and TIMSS 2011*, by J. Buckley, December 11, 2012, p. 66. National Center for Education Statistics, Washington, DC.

*Note:* Education systems with lower percentages of students reaching the Advanced benchmark than the percentage of U.S. students reaching the Advanced benchmark are not included in figure.

Colorado, and Connecticut performed better than other states on science (Buckley, 2012).

## High School Graduation Rates

Another indicator of how well students and schools perform is the high school graduation rate. These figures have often been in dispute because of differences in the way that states calculated rates. Many observers have warned that inaccurate reporting masked the scale of a national dropout crisis estimated to be 1.2 million students a year. Arne Duncan (2012), the United States Secretary of Education, argued that 50 states doing their own thing could lead to reduction of standards. He observed a better outcome would require being transparent about school problems, developing appropriate reforms, and having a common method for determining graduation rates.

The United States Department of Education (2012) released details of state graduation rates of high schools for 2011, the first time all states used the same common, rigorous measure. The varying methods previously used made any comparisons between states unreliable, while the new, common metric is intended to enable the states, districts, and individual schools to promote greater accountability and develop strategies to diminish dropout and increase graduation rates across the nation. In the preliminary reports using the common metric, 26 states had lower graduation rates and 24 remained unchanged or were higher. Iowa reported the highest rate at 88% and Nevada the lowest at 62%. Rates of graduation for the states can be found at www.eddataexpress.ed.gov—search graduation rate (United States Department of Education, 2012).

The uniform formula states now rely on defines the four-year adjusted cohort graduation rate as the number of students who graduate in 4 years with a regular high school diploma divided by the number of students who form the adjusted cohort for a graduating class. From the beginning of 9th grade, students entering that grade for the first time form a cohort to be adjusted later by adding students who transfer into the cohort during the 9th grade and the next three years and subtracting students who transfer out, emigrate to another country, or die in that same period.

## Summary and Implications

The adolescent experience typically involves risks that could threaten or enrich development. Deciding in advance how much risk is acceptable in particular situations clarifies the true range of choices available and eases decision-making. Interpretation of risks and responding in constructive ways requires the capacity to accurately gauge and consider possible costs associated with situations. This ability is often overridden by the personal fable that causes teenagers to suppose they are invulnerable and will not suffer the harmful consequences that might affect others who take the same risks. Students can make better decisions about lifestyle when adults help them monitor their ability to think about possible consequences of certain behaviors. Being a careful listener qualifies adults to provide their more mature perspective than the feedback adolescents get from peers.

Encouraging adolescents to pursue growth-oriented risks like mistake making and continuing to grapple with difficult tasks should be seen as an obligation by teachers. When students feel comfortable trying unfamiliar ways to solve problems, realize failure is an essential aspect of the learning process, and know they can explore without cost to their grade point, there is greater learning. As students experience the rewards that come with such risks, they become more willing to take them. In contrast, people of every age who stop taking potentially beneficial risks become less able to cope with change, demonstrate more rigid behavior, and show less flexibility in thinking.

Adults rely on praise much more than they do on encouragement as a method to motivate thinking and learning of children and adolescents. This risky orientation often causes students to overestimate their abilities and skills, undervalue the need for hard work and persistence, develop unwarranted confidence, and resist the consideration of external criticism about personal shortcomings or advice on ways to improve behavior and relationships. A more promising strategy is to encourage students to include adults among their confidants, grownups who can be counted on to assist with risk assessment and provide honest feedback.

# References

Abelard, P. (1121/2007). *Yes and no.* Charlotte, VT: Medieval MS.

Adams, D., & Hamm, M. (2006). *Redefining education in the twenty-first century: Shaping collaborative learning in the age of information.* Springfield, IL: Charles C. Thomas.

Agliata, A., Tantleff-Dunn, S., & Renk, K. (2007, January). Interpretation of teasing during early adolescence. *Journal of Clinical Psychology, 63*(1), 23–30.

Allen, T., Finkelstein, L., & Poteet, M. (2009). *Designing workplace mentoring programs: An evidence based approach.* New York, NY: Wiley-Blackwell.

American Academy of Pediatrics. (2011). Media use by children younger than 2 years. *Pediatrics, 128*(5), 1040–1045. Retrieved from http://www.pediatrics.aappublications.org

American College Testing. (2006). *Reading between the lines: What the ACT reveals about college readiness in reading.* Iowa City, IA: ACT.

Anderman, E., & Murdock, T. (2006). *Psychology of academic cheating.* San Diego CA: Academic Press.

Anderson, L., Krathwohl, D., Airasian, P., & Cruickshank, K. (2000). *A taxonomy for learning, teaching, and assessing: A revision of Bloom's taxonomy of educational objectives.* Boston, MA: Allyn & Bacon.

Anti-Bullying Bill of Rights Act, State of New Jersey. (2011, January 5). Retrieved October 12, 2012, from http://www.njleg.state.nj.us/2010/Bills/AL10/122_.PDF

Asch, S. (1952). *Social psychology.* New York, NY: Prentice-Hall.

Asch, S. (1956). Studies of independence and conformity: A minority of one against a unanimous majority. *Psychological Monographs General and Applied, 70*(9), 1–70.

*Thinking in Childhood and Adolescence,* pages 325–346
Copyright © 2013 by Information Age Publishing
All rights of reproduction in any form reserved.

Bakan, J. (2011). *Childhood under siege: How big business targets children.* New York, NY: Free Press.

Barkley, R., & Robin, R. (2008). *Your defiant teen.* New York, NY: Guilford Press.

Barnes, V., Bauza, L., & Treiber, F. (2003). Impact of stress reduction on negative school behaviors in adolescents. *Health and Quality of Life Outcomes, 1*(1), 10.

Barret, V. (2013, February). Super investor Hadi Partovi on bringing back the American Dream. *Forbes.* Retrieved from www.Forbes.com

Barron, J. (2012, December 14). Nation reels after gunman massacres 20 children at school in Connecticut. *The New York Times*, p. 1.

Bauer S., & Brazer, S. (2011). *Using research to lead school improvement.* Thousand Oaks, CA: Sage.

Bauerlein, M. (2010). *The dumbest generation: How the digital age stupefies young Americans and jeopardizes our future.* New York, NY: Penguin.

Bauman, S. (2010). *Cyberbullying: What counselors need to know.* Alexandria, VA: American Counseling Association.

Baumeister, R. (2005). *The cultural animal: Human nature, meaning, and social life.* New York, NY: Oxford University Press.

Baumeister, R. (2010). *Social psychology and human nature.* Belmont, CA: Wadsworth.

Baumeister, R., Campbell, J., Krueger, J., & Vohs, K. (2003, May). Does high self-esteem cause better performance, interpersonal success, happiness, or healthier lifestyle? *Psychological Science in the Public Interest, 4,* 1–2.

Baumeister, R., & Tierney, J. (2011). *Willpower: Rediscovering the greatest human strength.* New York, NY: Penguin.

Bazelon, E. (2013). *Sticks and stones: Defeating the culture of bullying and rediscovering the power of character and empathy.* New York, NY: Random House.

Beckert, T., Strom, R., Strom, P., Yang, C., & Singh, A. (2007). Parent Success Indicator: Cross-cultural development and factorial validation. *Educational and Psychological Measurement, 67*(2) 311–327.

Beghetto, R. (2005, Spring). Does assessment kill creativity? *The Educational Forum, 69*(3), 254–263.

Benson, P. (2010). *Parent, teacher, mentor, friend: How every adult can change kids' lives.* Minneapolis, MN: Search Institute.

Benson, P., Scales, P., Hamilton, S., & Sesma, A. (2006). Positive youth development: Theory, research, and applications. In W. Damon & R. Lerner (Eds.), *Handbook of child psychology* (6th ed.). New York, NY: Wiley.

Beran, T., & Shapiro, B. (2005). Evaluation of an anti-bullying program: Student reports of knowledge and confidence to manage bullying. *Canadian Journal of Education, 28*(4), 700–717.

Berns, G. (2010). *Iconoclast: A neuroscientist reveals how to think differently.* Boston, MA: Harvard Business Press.

Berns, G., Chappelow, J., Zink, C., Pagnoni, G., Martin-Skurski, M., & Richards, J. (2005). Neurobiological correlates of social conformity and independence during mental rotation. *Biological Psychiatry, 58,* 245–253.

Biro, F., Maida, P., Galvez, L., Greenspan, C., Succop, P., Vangeepuram, N., et al. (2010). Pubertal assessment method and baseline characteristics in a mixed longitudinal study of girls. *Pediatrics, 126*(3), e583–e590.

Blackburn, E. (2009, February 18). *Daydreaming.* A presentation to Moriah College, Sydney, Australia.

Blackhurst, R. (2008, June 22). A class apart. *Financial Times,* 1–2.

Blonna, R. (2011). *Coping with stress in a changing world.* New York, NY: McGraw-Hill.

Bloom B. (1976). *Human charactistics and school learning.* New York, NY: McGraw-Hill.

Bloom, B., Englehart, M., Furst, E., Hill, W., & Krathwohl, D. (Eds.) (1956). *Taxonomy of educational objectives: The classification of educational goals, Handbook I: Cognitive Domain.* New York, NY: McKay.

Bodrova, E., & Leong, D. (2006). *Tools of the mind: The Vygotsky to early childhood education.* Upper Saddle River, NJ: Prentice-Hall.

Bourke, J. (2005). *Fear, a cultural history.* London, England: Virago Press.

Brady, C. (2009). *Elizabeth Blackburn and the story of telomores: Deciphering the ends of DNA.* Cambridge, MA: Massachusetts Institute of Technology Press.

Branden, N. (1969). *The psychology of self-esteem: A new concept of man's psychological nature.* Los Angeles, CA: Nash Publishing.

Branden, N. (2001). *The psychology of self-esteem: A revolutionary approach to self-understanding that launched a new era in modern psychology.* San Francisco, CA: Jossey-Bass.

Brockmole, J. (Ed.) (2008). *The visual world of memory.* New York, NY: Psychology Press.

Bronson, P., & Merryman, A. (2010, July 10). The creativity crisis. *Newsweek, 156*(3), 44–49.

Brown, S., Teufel, J., Birch, D., & Kancheria, V. (2006, October). Gender, age, and behavior differences in early adolescent worry. *Journal of School Health, 76*(8), 430–438.

Brown, S., & Vaughan, C. (2010). *Play: How it shapes the brain, opens the imagination, and reinvigorates the soul.* New York, NY: Penguin.

Buboltz, W. (2012, February 16). *College student cell phone usage: How much is too much?* Presentation to the American Association of Behavioral and Social Sciences Annual Conference, Las Vegas, Nevada.

Buckley, J. (2012, December). *Highlights from PIRLS and TIMMS 2011.* Washington, DC: Center for Education Statistics.

Cain, S. (2012). *Quiet: The power of introverts in a world that can't stop talking.* New York, NY: Crown.

*California Fair Accurate Inclusive Respectful Education Act.* (Senate Bill 48) (2011, July 14). Retrieved from Legislative Information Website available at http://www.leginfo.ca.gov/pub/11-12/bill/sen/sb_0001-0050/sb_48_bill_20110714_chaptered.html

Campbell, J. (2004). *Pathways to bliss: Mythology and personal transformation.* Novata, CA: New World Library.

Cardoso, P. (Director). (2002). *Real women have curves* [Motion picture]. United States: HBO Independent Productions.

Carey, K. (2011, July 19). *The good news in the Atlanta and D.C.'s schools cheating scandal.* Retrieved March 1, 2012 from Education Sector, Washington, DC, http://www.educationsector.org.

Carr, N. (2006). New rules of engagement. *American School Board Journal, 193*(4), 66–68.

Carr, N. (2010). *The shallows.* New York, NY: W. W. Norton.

Carrabine, E. (2008). *Crime, culture, and the media.* Boston, MA: Polity.

Carroll, J. (1963). A model of school learning. *Teachers College Record, 64*(8), 723–733.

Carroll, L. (1865/2004). *Alice in wonderland.* London, England: Macmillan.

Cassidy, D., Lower, J., Kintner-Duffy, V., Hegde, A., & Shim, J. (2011, January–March). The day-to-day reality of teacher turnover in preschool classrooms. *Journal of Research in Childhood Education, 25*(1), 1–23.

Cattaert, C. (1963). *Where do goldfish go?* New York, NY: Crown.

Ceci, S., & Papierno, P. (2005). The rhetoric and reality of gap closing. *American Psychologist, 60*(2), 149–160.

Center for the Digital Future (2013). *Surveying the digital future: Year eleven.* Los Angeles, CA: University of Southern California, available at http://www.digitalcenter.org/

Center for the Digital Future (2012). *America at the digital turning point.* Retrieved February 3, 2013 from University of Southern California Annenberg School http://www.digitalcenter.org

Centers for Disease Control and Prevention (2011, April 22). Bullying among middle school and high school students. *Morbidity and Mortality Weekly Report, 60*(15), 1–3.

Centers for Disease Control and Prevention (2012). *Sexual risk behavior: HIV, STD, and teen pregnancy prevention.* Atlanta, GA: CDC.

Centers for Disease Control and Prevention (2013). *Youth Risk Behavior Surveillance System.* Retrieved from www.cdc.gov

Chemelynski, C. (2006, July 18). When mean girls turn to female violence. *School Board News,* 8.

Cherlin, A. (2009). *The marriage-go-round.* New York, NY: Random House.

Cherlin, A. (2012). *Public and private families.* New York, NY: McGraw-Hill.

Children's Internet Protection Act (2000). Public Law No. 106-554 USC.

Children's Online Privacy Protection Act (1998). Retrieved April 15, 2013, from http://www.ftc.gov/ogc/coppa1.htm

Christie, C., Jolivette, K., & Nelson, M. (2005). Breaking the school to prison pipeline: Identifying school risk and protective factors for youth delinquency. *Exceptionality, 13*(2), 69–88.

Clark, L. (2012). *The parent app: Understanding families in the digital age.* New York, NY: Oxford University Press.

Code.org (2013). *What most schools don't teach* [Video]. Retrieved from Code.org.

Coloroso, B. (2009). *The bully, the bullied, and the bystander.* New York, NY: William Morrow.

*Consumer Reports* (2008, November). Better breakfasts? Some cereals are more than 50 percent sugar. Retrieved from http://www.accessmylibrary

*Consumer Reports* (2011, May). That Facebook friend might be 10 years old, and other troubling news. Retrieved from http://www.ConsumerReports.org

Cook, S., & Honeycut, S. (2013). *Homeschooling with insider information.* Seattle, WA: Amazon Digital Services.

Costin, C., Grabb, G., & Rothschild, B. (2011). *8 Keys to recovery from an eating disorder: Effective strategies from therapeutic practice and personal experience.* New York, NY: W. W. Norton.

Cozolino, L. (2013). *The social neuroscience of education.* New York, NY: W. W. Norton.

Creed, P., & Hood, M. (2013). Disengaging from unattainable career goals and re-engaging in more achievable ones. *Journal of Career Development, 40*(2), 1–19.

Cukras, G. (2006, Winter). The investigation of study strategies that maximize learning for underprepared students. *College Teaching, 54*(1), 194–197.

Dahl, M. (2010). *Failure to thrive in constructivism: A cross-cultural malady.* Rotterdam, The Netherlands: Sense Publishers.

Daniels, G., Klein, H., Silverman, B., Gervais, R., & Merchant, S. (Producers). (2005). *The office* [Television series]. New York, NY: National Broadcasting Company.

Darling-Hammond, L., & Lieberman, A. (2012). *Teacher education around the world.* New York, NY: Routledge.

Darst, P., & Pangrazi, R. (2008). *Dynamic physical education for secondary school students.* Boston, MA: Benjamin Cummings.

Darwin, C., & Wilson, E. (Ed.) (2005). *From so simple a beginning: Darwin's four great books.* New York, NY: W. W. Norton.

Davila, T., Epstein, M., & Shelton, R. (2006). *Making innovation work: How to manage it, measure it, and profit from it.* Upper Saddle River, NJ: Pearson.

Davis, S., Drinan, P., & Gallant, T. (2009). *Cheating in school.* New York, NY: Wiley.

Davydov, D., Stewart, R., Ritchie, K., & Chaudiew, I. (2010). Resilience and mental health. *Clinical Psychology Review, 30*(5), 479–495.

de Bono, E. (1967). *New think: The use of lateral thinking in the generation of new ideas.* New York, NY: Basic Books.

de Bono, E. (1970). *Lateral thinking: Creativity step by step.* New York, NY: Harper & Row.

de Bono, E. (1999). *Six thinking hats: Edward de Bono.* New York, NY: Little, Brown.

de Bono, E. (2009). *Think! Before it's too late.* London, England: Vermillion.

de Waal, F. (2009). *Primates and philosophers: How morality evolved.* Princeton, NJ: Princeton University Press.

DiClemente, R., Santelli, J., & Crosby, R. (Eds.) (2009). *Adolescent health: Understanding and preventing risk behaviors.* San Francisco, CA: Jossey-Bass.

Discovery Education. (2013). *Inspiring curiosity.* Available at http://www.streaming.discoveryeducation.com

Dodson, M., Crotty, B., Prideaux, D., Carne, R., Ward, A., & De Leeuw, E. (2009, January). The multiple mini-interview: How long is long enough? *Medical Education, 43*(2), 168–174.

Dolgin, K. (2010). *The adolescent: Development, relationships, and culture.* Upper Saddle River, NJ: Prentice-Hall.

Drucker, P. (2005, January). Managing oneself. *Harvard Business Review,* 1–10.

Duffert, A., Farkas, S., & Loveless, T. (2008). *High-achieving students in the era of No Child Left Behind.* Washington, DC: Thomas Fordham Foundation.

Duncan, A. (2009). *Key policy letter to chief state school officers.* Washington, DC: United States Department of Education.

Duncan, A. (2012, November 16). Duncan sketches out second-term agenda. Presentation to Council of Chief State Schools Officers, Washington, DC. Retrieved from http://www.parentsunited.org

Dunlosky, J., & Metcalfe, J. (2008). *Metacognition.* Thousand Oaks, CA: Sage.

Dutton, D. (2007). *The abusive personality: Violence and control in intimate relationships* (2nd Ed.). New York, NY: Guilford.

Dweck, C. (2006). *Mindset: The new psychology of success.* New York, NY: Ballantine Books.

Eckstein, G. (Producer), & Spielberg, S. (Director). (1971). *Duel* [Motion picture]. United States: Universal Studios.

*Education of All Handicapped Children Act* (1975). Pub. L. 94-142, 20 USC 1400.

Egan, R. (2013). *Becoming sexual: A critical appraisal of the sexualization of girls.* Malden, MA: Polity.

Eliot, G. (1861/2010). *Silas Marner: The weaver of Raveloe.* London, England: Bibliolis Books.

Enzer, M. (2011). *Glossary of Internet terms.* Retrieved from http://matisse.net/files/glossary.html

Epel, E., & Blackburn, E. (2004). Accelerated telomere shortening in relation to chronic stress. *Proceedings of the National Academy of Sciences, 101,* 17312–17315.

Epstein, R. (2010). *Teen 2.0: Saving our children and families from the torment of adolescence.* Fresno, CA: Quill Driver Books.

Erikson, E. (1950). *Childhood and society.* New York, NY: W.W. Norton.

Espelage, D., & Swearer, S. (2010). *Bullying in North American schools.* New York, NY: Routledge.

Estes, E. (2004). *The hundred dresses.* New York, NY: Harcourt.

Eysenck, M., & Keane, M. (2005). *Cognitive psychology.* Philadelphia, PA: Psychology Press.

Faber, A., & Mazish, E. (2012). *Siblings without rivalry.* New York, NY: W.W. Norton.

Family Educational Rights and Privacy Act, 20 U.S.C. § 1232g (1974).

Family Watchdog. (2012). *Awareness is your best defense.* Retrieved from http://www.familywatchdog.us/

Farrell, M. (2012). *New perspectives in special education.* New York, NY: Routledge.

Federal Emergency Management Agency. (2013). *Build a kit.* Washington, DC: United States Department of Homeland Security.

Fee, S., & Belland, B. (2012). *The role of criticism in understanding problem solving.* New York, NY: Springer.

Ferguson, C., Munoz, M., & Medrano, M. (2012, March). Advertising influences on young children's food choices and parental influence. *The Journal of Pediatrics, 160*(3), 452–456.

Feynman, R. (1999). *The pleasure of finding things out.* Cambridge, MA: Perseus Books.

Fitzpatrick, C., & Constantini, K. (2011). *Counseling 21st century students for optimal college and career readiness: A 9th–12th grade curriculum.* New York, NY: Routledge.

Florida, R. (2012). *The rise of the creative class revisited (2nd Ed.).* New York, NY: Basic Books.

Fosnot, C. (2005). *Constructivism: Theory, perspectives, & practice.* New York, NY: Teachers College Press.

Frank, S. (2010, November 9). *Hyper-texting and hyper-networking: A new health risk category for teens?* Presentation to the American Public Health Association Annual Conference, Denver, Colorado.

Franke, T. M. (2000). Adolescent violent behavior: An analysis across and within racial/ethnic groups. In D. de Anda & R. Becerra (Eds.), *Violence: Diverse populations and communities* (pp. 47–70). New York, NY: Haworth Press.

Frey, K., Kirschstein, M., & Snell, J. (2005, May). Reducing playground bullying and supporting beliefs: An experimental trial of the "Steps to Respect" Program. *Developmental Psychology, 41*(3), 479–490.

Friedman, T. (2005). *The world is flat: A brief history of the twenty-first century.* New York, NY: Farrar, Strauss & Giroux.

Frisch, S. (2010). Ready, set, learn. *Connect,* Summer, 12–16. University of Minnesota College of Education and Human Development.

Gallant, T. (2010). *Creating the ethical academy: A systems approach to understanding misconduct and empowering change.* New York, NY: Routledge.

Gallup, G. (1982). Self-awareness and the emergence of mind in primates. *American Journal of Primatology, 2,* 237–248.

Galton, F. (1874). *English men and science: Their nature and nurture.* London, England: Macmillan, p. 14.

Gardner, D. (2009). *The science of fear: How the culture of fear manipulates your brain.* New York, NY: Plume.

Gardner, H. (2011). *The unschooled mind: How children think and how schools should teach.* New York, NY: Basic Books.

Gardner, S., & Birley, S. (2012). *Blogging for dummies.* Hoboken, NJ: Wiley.

Generation YES (Youth and Educators Succeeding). (2012). *Free resources from Generation YES.* Olympia, WA: Generation YES. Retrieved from http://www.genyes.com/freeresources/

Ghiselin, B. (Ed.). (1985). *The creative process.* Berkeley, CA: University of California Press.

Gilliam, W. (2005). *Prekindergarteners left behind: Expulsion rates in state prekindergarten systems.* New Haven, CT: Yale University Child Study Center.

Ginsburg, K. (2011). *Building resilience in children and teens.* Elk Grove, IL: American Academy of Pediatrics.

Glassner, B. (2010). *The culture of fear: Why Americans are afraid of the wrong things.* New York, NY: Basic Books.

Goldberg, E. (2009). *The new executive brain: Frontal lobes in a complex world.* New York, NY: Oxford University Press.

Goldin, P. (2011). *Confucianism.* Berkeley, CA: University of California Press.

Golding, W. (1954). *Lord of the flies.* New York, NY: Riverhead Books.

Goldstein, S., & Brooks, R. (2012). *Handbook of resilience in children.* New York, NY: Springer.

Goldston, D., Molock, S., Whitbeck, L., Murakami, J., Zayas, L., & Hall, G. (2008). Cultural considerations in adolescent suicide prevention and psychological treatment. *American Psychologist, 63*(1), 14–31.

Goleman, D. (2006). *Social intelligence: The new science of human relationships.* New York, NY: Bantam.

Gonzales, L. (2012). *Surviving survival: Art and science of resilience.* New York, NY: W.W. Norton.

Goodall, J. (1986). *The chimpanzees of Gombe: Patterns of behavior.* Cambridge, MA: Harvard University Press.

Gosselin, P., Langlois, F., Freeston, M., & Ladouceur, L. (2007). *Cognitive variables related to worry among adolescents: Avoidance strategies and faulty beliefs about worry.* Amsterdam, The Netherlands: Elsevier.

Graham, K. (2012, March 6). Amid cheating allegations, district appoints "Integrity advisor." Retrieved March 8, 2012 from *The Philadelphia Inquirer* available at http://www.philly.com

Grant, A. (2013). *Give and take: A revolutionary approach to success.* New York, NY: Viking.

Gross, E. (2004, November). Adolescent Internet use: What we expect, what teens report. *Journal of Applied Developmental Psychology, 25*(6), 633–649.

Guilford, J. (1959). Three faces of intellect. *American Psychologist, 14,* 469–479.

Guilford, J. (1950, September). Creativity. *American Psychologist, 5*(9), 444–454.

Guilford, J. (1977). *Way beyond the IQ.* Buffalo, NY: Creative Education Foundation.

Gunn, A. (Producer), & Waters, M. (Director). (2003). *Freaky Friday* [Motion picture]. Burbank, CA: Walt Disney Studios.

Hallinan, J. (2010). *Why we make mistakes.* New York, NY: Broadway.

Hanover Research. (February, 2011). *Effective grading practices in the middle school and high school environment.* Retrieved from http://www.hanoverresearch.com

Hardy, K., & Laszloffy, T. (2006). *Teens who hurt: Clinical interventions to break the cycle of adolescent violence.* New York, NY: Guilford.

Hargis, J. (2005). Collaboration, community, and project-based learning: Does it still work online? *International Journal of Instructional Media, 32*(2), 157–161.

Havighurst, R. (1950). *Developmental tasks and education (3rd ed)*. New York, NY: David McKay.

Havighurst, R. (1953). *Human development and education*. New York, NY: David McKay.

Hazen, A., Gakhar, M., Stitcher, A., Khanchandani, & Centers for Disease Control & Prevention (2013). *Working with schools to increase physical activity among children and adolescents in physical education classes* (Kindle Edition). Seattle, WA: Amazon Digital Services.

Headden, S., & Silva, E. (2011, December 1). *Lessons from DC's evaluation system*. Retrieved March 1, 2012 from Education Sector, Washington, DC, http://www.educationsector.org

Heath, R. (2009). *Celebrating failure: The power of taking risks, making mistakes and thinking big*. Pompton Plains, NJ: Career Press.

Hemmingway, E. (1964). *A moveable feast*. New York, NY: Charles Scribners, p. 154.

Henkin, R. (2005). *Confronting bullying*. Portsmouth, NH: Heinemann.

Herman-Giddens, M., Steffes, J., Harris, D., Slora, E., Hussey, M., Dowshen, S., et al. (2012). Secondary sexual characteristics in boys: Data from the Pediatric research in office setting network. *Pediatrics, 130*(5), e1058–e1068.

Herman, K. (2009). Childhood depression: Rethinking the role of school. *Psychology in the Schools, 46*, 433–446.

Heward, W. (2012). *Exceptional children*. Upper Saddle River, NJ: Pearson.

Hirsch, M., & Narayan, M. (1971). *Leela and the watermelon*. New York, NY: Crown Publishers.

Hirschland, D. (2008). *Collaborative intervention in early childhood: Consultation with parents and teachers of 3- to 7-year olds*. New York, NY: Oxford University Press.

Hodges, C., & Clark, K. (2013). *Web-based presentation tools: Tech tools for learning*. Columbus, OH: Linworth.

Hoffman, M. (Director). (2002). *The Emperor's Club* [Motion picture]. United States: Universal Studios.

Holtam, B. (2012). *Let's call it what it is: A matter of conscience*. Boston, MA: Sense Publishers.

Huesmann, L. (2007). The impact of electronic media violence. *Journal of Adolescent Health*, S6–S13.

Huesmann, L., Dubow, E., & Boxer, P. (2009). Continuity of aggression from childhood to early adulthood as a predictor of life outcomes. *Aggressive Behavior, 35*(2), 136–149.

Hunt, L. (2009). *Grade inflation: Academic standards in higher education*. Albany, NY: State University of New York Press.

Jackson, M. (2009). *Distracted: The erosion of attention and the coming dark age*. Amherst, NY: Prometheus Books.

James, W. (1890/2013). *The principles of psychology*. New York, NY: Cosimo classics.

Jennings, L., & Likis, L. (2005, March). Meeting a math achievement crisis. *Educational Leadership, 62*(6), 65–68.

Jinks, C., Knopf, H., & Kemple, K. (2006, Summer). Tackling teacher turnover in child care. *Childhood Education, 82*(4), 219–226.

John-Steiner, V. (2006). *Creative collaboration.* New York, NY: Oxford University Press.

Johnson, D., & Brooke, J. (1999, April 22). Portrait of outcasts seeking to stand out. *The New York Times,* pp. 1–26.

Jolls, T. (2010). *Literacy for the 21st century: Theory/overview of media literacy (2nd ed.).* Los Angeles, CA: Center for Media Literacy.

Josephson Institute of Ethics (2012). *The ethics of American youth: 2012.* Los Angeles, CA: Josephson Institute. Retrieved from http://josephsoninstitute.org/

Kafai, Y., Peppler, K., & Chapman, R. (2009). *The computer clubhouse.* New York, NY: Columbia University Teachers College Press.

Kagan, J. (2007). *An argument for mind.* New Haven, CT: Yale University Press.

Kahn Academy (2013). *Practice your math skills.* Available at http://www.khanacademy.org. Mountain View, CA.

Kahneman, D. (2011). *Thinking fast and slow.* New York, NY: Farrar, Straus & Giroux.

Kaiser Family Foundation (2006). *It's child's play: Advergaming and the online marketing of food to children.* Menlo Park, CA: The Foundation.

Keller, J. (2005, May). The new tech tutors. *Technology and Learning, 25*(10), 15–17.

Kelsey, C., & Kelsey, C. (2007). *Generation MySpace: Helping your teen survive online adolescence.* New York, NY: DeCapo Press.

Khadaroo, S. (2011, September 28). SAT cheating scandal. *Christian Science Monitor,* 1–2.

Kim, K. (2010). Measurements, causes, and effects of creativity. *Psychology of Aesthetics, Creativity, and the Arts, 4*(3), 131–135.

Kindlon, D. (2006). *Alpha Girls: Understanding the new American girl and how she is changing the world.* Emmaus, PA: Rodale.

King, M., & King, P. (2012). *Assessing meaningmaking and self-authorship.* San Francisco, CA: Jossey-Bass.

Kirkpatrick, K. (Director). (2009). *Imagine that* [Motion picture]. United States: Paramount Pictures.

Kohler, W. (1925). *The mentality of apes.* New York, NY: Vintage.

Konnikova, M. (2012). *Mastermind: How to think like Sherlock Holmes.* New York, NY: Viking.

Kosciw, J., Dias, E., & Greytalk, E. (2008). *The 2007 national school climate survey: The experience of lesbian, gay, bisexual and transgender youth in our nation's schools.* New York, NY: Gay, lesbian, and straight education network.

Kottler, J., & Chen, D. (2011). *Stress management and prevention.* New York, NY: Routledge.

Kovarik, B. (2011). *Revolutions in communication: Media history from Gutenberg to the digital age.* New York, NY: Continuum International Publishing.

Kowalski, R., Limber, S., & Agatston, P. (2008). *Cyberbullying: Bullying in the digital age.* Malden, MA: Blackwell Publishing.

Kramer, P. (2006). *Against depression.* New York, NY: Penguin.

Krathwohl, D. (2002). A revision of Bloom's taxonomy: An overview. *Theory Into Practice, 41*(4), 2002, 216–218.

Kraut, R., Brynin, M., & Kiesler, S. (2006). *Computers, phones, and the Internet: Domesticating information technology.* New York, NY: Oxford University Press.

Kraybill, D., Johnson-Weiner, K., & Nolt, S. (2013). *The Amish.* Baltimore, MD: The Johns Hopkins University Press.

Kubrick, S. (Producer). (1968). *2001: A Space Odyssey.* United States: Metro-Goldwyn-Mayer.

Landhuis, C., Poulton, R., Welch, D., & Hancox, R. (2007). Does childhood viewing lead to attention problems in adolescence? Results from a prospective longitudinal study. *Pediatrics, 120*(3), 532–537.

Langman, P. (2009). *Why kids kill: Inside the minds of school shooters.* New York, NY: Palgrave Macmillan.

Larson, J. (2008, January). Angry and aggressive students. *Principal Leadership, 8*, 12–15.

Larson, J., & Lochman, J. (2005). *Helping school children cope with anger.* New York, NY: Guilford.

Lathrop, A., & Foss, K. (2005). *Guiding students from cheating and plagiarism to honesty and integrity: Strategies for change.* Englewood, CO: Libraries Unlimited.

Leary, M., & Tagney, J. (2012). *Handbook of self and identity.* New York, NY: Guilford.

Lee, S. (2006, March/April). The learner center paradigm of instruction and training. *TechTrends, 50*(2), 21–22.

Leets, L., & Sunwolf (2005, September). Adolescent rules for social exclusion: When is it fair to exclude someone else? *Journal of Moral Education, 34*(3), 343–362.

Lehrer, J. (2012). *Imagine: How creativity works.* New York, NY: Houghton Mifflin Harcourt.

Lesko, N. (2012). *Act your age: A cultural construction of adolescence.* New York, NY: Routledge.

Liau, A., Khoo, A., & Peng, H. (2005). Factors influencing adolescent engagement in risky Internet behavior. *CyberPsychology & Behavior, 8*(6), 513–520.

Liu, Z. (2008). *Paper to digital: Documents in the information age.* Westport, CT: Libraries Unlimited.

Lodge, J., & Frydenberg, E. (2005, Fall). The role of peer bystanders in school bullying: Positive steps toward promoting peaceful schools. *Theory Into Practice, 44*(4), 329–336.

Loveless, T. (2005). Test-based accountability: The promise and the perils. *Brookings Papers on Education Policy*, 7–45.

Lubart, T. (2010). Cross-cultural perspectives on creativity. In J. Kaufman & R. Sternberg (Eds.), *The Cambridge handbook of creativity* (pp. 265–278). New York, NY: Cambridge University Press.

Lucado, M. (2009). *Fearless: Imagine your life without fear.* Nashville, TN: Thomas Nelson.

Lucas, G. (2005). *Teaching communication*. Retrieved March 1, 2012 from Edutopia, San Rafael, CA, available at http://www.edutopia.org

Ludwig, A. (1995). *The price of greatness: Resolving the creativity and madness controversy*. New York, NY: Guilford Press.

Maas, C., Fleming, C., Herrenkohl, T., & Catalano, R. (2010). Childhood predictors of teen dating violence victimization. *Violence and Victims, 25*(2), 131–149.

MacKinnon, D. (1962, July). The nature and nurture of creative talent. *American Psychologist, 17*(7), 484–495.

MacKinnon, D. (1978). *In search of human effectiveness*. Buffalo, NY: Creative Education Foundation.

Mahoney, J., Larson, R., & Eccles, J. (2005). *Organized activities as contexts of development*. Mahwah, NJ: Erlbaum.

Mark, G., Voida, S., & Cardello, A. (2012, May 7). A pace not dictated by electrons. Presentation to the Association for Computing Machinery's Computer-Human interaction conference in Austin, TX.

Markus, D. (2012, February 22). *Risking peace at a troubled school*. Retrieved from Edutopia, San Rafael, CA, March 1, 2012, available at http://www.edutopia.org

Martin, A., & Lehren, A. (2012, May12). Degrees of debt. *The New York Times*, p. 1.

Mash, E., & Wolfe, D. (2012). *Abnormal child psychology*. Belmont, CA: Wadsworth.

Mason, G. (2007). *Spectacle of violence*. New York, NY: Taylor & Francis.

Masten, A., & Narayan, A. (2012). Child development in the context of disaster, war, and terrorism: Pathways of risk and resilience. *Annual Review of Psychology, 63*, 227–257.

Mayo, D., & Spanos, A. (2010). *Error and inference*. New York, NY: Cambridge University Press.

McAfee, O., & Leong, D. (2010). *Assessing and guiding young children's development and learning*. Upper Saddle River, NJ: Pearson

McBride, N. (2011). *Child safety is more than a slogan*. Retrieved from the National Center for Missing & Exploited Children http://www.ncmec.org

McCabe, E. (1985, August 1). Creativity. *Vital Speeches of the Day, 51*(2), 628–632.

McClelland, M., Acock, A., Piccinin, A., Rhea, S., & Stallings, M. (2013). Relations between preschool attention span—persistence and age 25 educational outcomes. *Early Childhood Research Quarterly, 28*(2), 314–324.

McKenney, S. (2005, Winter). Technology for curriculum and teacher development. *Journal of Research on Technology in Education, 38*(2), 167–190.

McKim, R. (1980). *Thinking visually: A strategy for problems solving*. Los Angeles, CA: Dale Seymour.

McLuhan, M., & Fiore, Q. (1967). *The medium is the massage: An inventory of effects*. Corte Madera, CA: Gingko Press.

McQuade, S., Colt, J., & Meyer, N. (2009). *Cyber bullying: Protecting kids and adults from online bullies*. Westport, CT: Praeger Publications.

Medina, J. (2009). *Brain rules*. Seattle, WA: Pear Press.

Meltzer, L. (Ed.). (2007). *Executive function in education.* New York, NY: Guilford.

Meyer, W., Bachmann, M., Biermann, U., Hempelmann, M., Ploger, F., & Spiller, H. (1979, April). The informational value of evaluative behavior: Influence of praise and blame on perceptions of ability. *Journal of Educational Psychology, 71*(2), 259–268.

Millar, G. (2001). *The Torrance kids at mid-life.* Westport, CT: Greenwood.

Miller, S., Adsit, K., & Miller, T. (2005, November/December). Evaluating the importance of common components in school-based web sites. *Tech-Trends, 49*(6), 34–41.

*Minnesota Multiphasic Personality Inventory.* (2013). Minneapolis, MN: University of Minnesota. Retrieved from http://en.wikipedia.org/wiki/Minnesota_Multiphasic_Personality_Inventory

Mischel, W., & Ayduk, O. (2004). Willpower in a cognitive-affective processing system: The dynamics of delay of gratification. In R. Baumeister & K. Vohs (Eds.), *Handbook of self-regulation: Research, theory, and applications* (pp. 99–129). New York NY: Guilford.

Mischel, W., & Peake, P. (1990). Predicting adolescent cognitive and self-regulatory competencies from preschool delay of gratification. *Developmental Psychology, 26*(6), 978–986.

Mishna, F., Scarcello, I., & Pepler, D. (2005). Teachers' understanding of bullying. *Canadian Journal of Education, 28*(4), 718–738.

Mitra, S. (2003). Minimally invasive education: A progress report on the "Hole-in-the-wall" experiments. *British Journal of Educational Technology, 34*(3), 367–371.

Mitra, S. (2005). Self-organizing systems for mass computer literacy. *International Journal of Development Issues, 4*(1), 71–81.

Mitra, S. (2006). *The hole in the wall: Self-organizing systems in education.* New Delhi, India: Tata-McGraw-Hill Publishing.

Mitra, S. (2012a). *Beyond the hole in the wall: Discover the power of self-organized learning.* New York: NY: TED Books.

Mitra, S. (2012b, March 26). *Sugata Mitra–Keynote Speaker.* Presented at the 21st Century Learning Conference in Hong Kong. Retrieved April 10, 2012, from YouTube, http://www.youtube.com

Mitra, S., & Dangwal, R. (2010). Limits to self-organizing systems of learning: The Kalikuppan experiment. *British Journal of Educational Technology, 41*(5), 672–688.

Moore, B., & Parker, R. (2008). *Critical thinking.* New York, NY: McGraw-Hill.

Moore, M. (Director). (2002). *Bowling for Columbine* [Motion picture]. United States: United Artists, Alliance Artists, and Dog Eat Dog Films.

Moore, R., & Robillard, A. (2008). *Pluralizing plagiarism: Identities, contexts, and pedagogies.* Portsmouth, NH: Boynton/Cook.

Moreno, L., Pigeot, I., & Ahrens, W. (2011). *Epidemiology of obesity in childhood and adolescence.* New York, NY: Springer.

Morris, M., & Niesse, M. (2013, April 2). Suspects in Atlanta schools cheating scandal surrender. *The Atlanta Constitution*, p. 1.

Morrissey, K., & Werner-Wilson, R. (2005, Spring). Relationship between out-of-school activities and positive youth development. *Adolescence, 40*(157), 67–86.

Myers S., & Anderson, C. (2008). *Fundamentals of small group communication.* Thousand Oaks, CA: Sage.

National Association of Anorexia, Nervosa, and Associated Disorders. (2013). *How to help someone with an eating disorder.* Retrieved from http://www.anad.org

National Association of Child Care Resources and Referral Agencies. (2011). *High cost of child care.* Arlington, VA: The Association.

National Center for Missing and Exploited Children. (2012, January 23). *Number of registered sex offenders in the US nears three-quarters of a million.* Retrieved February 21, 2012, from The National Center, Alexandria, VA, available at http://mcmec.org

National Institute of Child Health and Human Development Early Childhood Care Research Network. (2006, February/March). Child care effect sizes for the NICHD study of early childhood care and youth development. *American Psychologist, 6*(2), 99–116.

National Runaway Switchboard. (2013). *National Runaway safeline.* Retrieved from www.1800runaway.org

Negroponte, N. (2013, March 19). *Re-thinking learning and re-learning thinking.* Retrieved May 13, 2013, from www.youtube.com.

Newberg, A., & Waldman, M. (2010). *How God changes your brain.* New York, NY: Ballantine Books.

Ng, F., Pomerantz, E., & Lam, S. (2007). European American and Chinese Parents' responses to children's success and failure. *Developmental Psychology, 43*(5), 1239–1255.

Nixon, J. (1974). *The alligator under the bed.* New York, NY: G.P. Putnam & Sons.

Nobel Prize (2009). *The Nobel Prize in Physiology or Medicine 2009.* Retrieved from http://nobelprize.org/nobel_prizes/medicine/laureates/2009/

Novotney, A. (2009). Resilient kids learn better. *Monitor on Psychology, 40*(9), 32–33.

Obama, B. (2009, September 8). *Goals, work, and success.* Presentation to the students of Wakefield High School in Arlington, Virginia.

Ogden, C., Carroll, M., Kit, B., & Flegal, K. (2012). Prevalence of obesity and trends in body mass index among U.S. children and adolescents, 1999–2010. *Journal of the American Medical Association, 307*(5), 483–490.

Ophir, E., Nass, C., & Wagner, A. (2009, August 24). Cognitive control in media multitaskers. *Proceedings of the National Academy of Sciences, 106*(34), 15583–15587.

Orey, M., McClendon, V., & Branch, R. (Eds.). (2006). *Educational media and technology yearbook (Volume 31).* Englewood, CO: Libraries Unlimited.

Orpinas, P., & Horne, A. (2006). *Bullying prevention: Creating a positive school climate and developing social competence.* Washington, DC: American Psychological Association.

Owens, J., Belon, K., & Moss, P. (2010). Impact of delaying school start time on adolescent sleep, mood, and behavior. *Archives of Pediatrics and Adolescent Medicine, 164* (7), 608–614.

Paivio, A. (1990). *Mental representations: A dual coding approach* (2nd ed.). New York, NY: Oxford University Press.

Paley, R., Norwich, G., & Mar, J. (2010). *The body book for boys.* New York, NY: Scholastic Paperbacks.

Patrick, C. (1955). *What is creative thinking?* New York, NY: Philosophical Library.

Penrose, R. (2002). *The Emperor's new mind. Concerning computers, minds, and the laws of physics.* New York, NY: Oxford University Press.

Perez-Pena, R. (2013, February 1). Students disciplined in Harvard scandal. *The New York Times.* Retrieved from http://www.nytimes.com/

Perry, N. (Director). (2013). *Scarred* [Television series]. Retrieved from www.mtv.com/shows/scarred/series.jhtml New York, NY: MTV.

Peterson, P. (2010). *Saving schools: From Horace Mann to virtual learning.* Cambridge, MA: Harvard University Press.

Peterson, P., & Hess, F. (2008). Few states set world-class standards: In fact, most render the notion of proficiency meaningless. *Education Next, 8*(3), 70–73.

Pew Research Center (2010, July 9). *Will Millennials 'grow out' of sharing?* Washington, DC: Pew Research Center.

Piaget, J. (1954). *The construction of reality in the child.* New York, NY: Basic Books.

Piaget, J. (1963). *Origins of intelligence in children.* New York, NY: Norton.

Piaget, J. (1969). *Psychology of intelligence.* New York, NY: Littlefield, Adams.

Piaget, J. (1970). Piaget's theory. In P. Mussen (Ed.), *Carmichael's manual of child psychology* (Volume 1) (pp. 702–732). New York, NY: John Wiley.

Pincus, D. (2012). *Growing up brave.* New York, NY: Little, Brown, and Company.

Pink, D. (2009). *Drive: The surprising truth about what motivates us.* New York, NY: Penguin Group.

Plato, & Rowe, C. (Ed.) (2012). *The Republic.* New York, NY: Penguin. Original work written by Plato in 360 B.C.E.

Plucker, J., & Baer, J. (2008). *Essentials of creativity assessment.* New York, NY: Wiley.

Pompili, M. (2011). *Exploring the phenomenon of suicide.* Hauppauge, NY: Nova Science Publishers.

Posner, M. (2012). Attention in a social world. New York, NY: Oxford University Press.

Prensky, M. (2010). *Teaching digital natives.* Thousand Oaks, CA: Corwin Press.

Prinstein, M., & Dodge, K. (2010). *Understanding peer influence in children and adolescents.* New York, NY: Guilford Press.

Prior, J. (2007). *The American freshman: Forty year trends 1966–2006.* Los Angeles, CA: Higher Education Research Institute.

Project on Student Debt. (2012). *State by state data.* Retrieved from the Institute for College Access and Success: http://www.projectonstudentdebt.org

Raghuveer, G. (2010). Lifetime cardiovascular risk of childhood obesity. *American Journal of Clinical Nutrition, 91*(5), 1514S–1519S.

Rathvon, N. (2008). *Effective school interventions: Evidence based strategies for improving student outcomes.* New York, NY: Guilford Press.

Ravitch, D. (2010). *The death and life of the great American school system.* New York, NY: Perseus Books.

Redman, B. (Ed.). (1977). *The portable Voltaire.* New York, NY: Penguin.

Reyna, V., & Farley, F. (2006). Risk and rationality in adolescent decision making: Implications for theory, practice, and public policy. *Psychological Science in the Public Interest, 7*(1), 1–50.

Rideout, V., Foehr, U., & Roberts, D. (2010, January). *Generation M²: Media in the lives of 8-to-18-year-olds.* Menlo Park, CA: Kaiser Family Foundation.

Rideout, V., & Hamel, E. (2006). *The media family: Media in the lives of infants, toddlers, preschoolers and their parents.* Menlo, CA: Henry J. Kaiser Family Foundation.

Rimm, S. (2005). *Growing up too fast.* Emmaus, PA: Rodale Publications.

Ripkin, C., & Wolff, R. (2006). *Parenting young athletes.* New York, NY: Penguin Books.

Robinson, K. (2011). *Out of our minds: Learning to be creative.* West Sussex, England: Capstone.

Rogers, C. (1961). *On becoming a person.* Boston, MA: Houghton Mifflin.

Rosen, L. (2010). *Rewired: Understanding the iGeneration and the way they learn.* New York, NY: Palgrave Macmillan.

Rosen, M. (2007). *This is our house.* London, England: Walker Children's Paperbacks.

Roseth, C., Johnson, D., & Johnson, R. (2008, March). Promoting early adolescents' achievement and peer relationships: The effects of cooperative, competitive, and individualistic goal structures. *Psychological Bulletin, 134*(2), 223–246.

Rothstein, D., & Santana, L. (2011). *Make just one change: Teach students to ask their own questions.* Cambridge, MA: Harvard Education Press.

Rotter, J. (1972). *Applications of a social learning theory of personality.* New York, NY: Holt, Rinehart & Winston.

Rowling, J. K. (1999). *Harry Potter and the chamber of secrets.* New York, NY: Arthur A. Levine Publisher.

Rubenstein, S., & McCarthy, J. (2010). *Collaboration on school reform.* New Brunswick, NJ: Rutgers University School of Management and Labor Relations.

Rubin, K., Bukowski, W., & Larson, B. (2011). *Handbook of peer interactions, relationships and groups.* New York, NY: Guilford Press.

Rudman, L., & Glick, P. (2010). *The social psychology of gender.* New York, NY: Guilford.

Ruffman, T., Slade, L., Devitt, K., & Crowe, E. (2006). What mothers say and what they do: The relation between parenting, theory of mind, and conflict/cooperation. *British Journal of Development Psychology, 24,* 105–124.

Runco, M. (2006). *Creativity: Theories and themes: Research, development, and practice.* San Diego, CA: Academic Press.

Runco, M., & Albert, R. (2010). Creativity research: A historical view. In J. Kaufman, & R. Sternberg (Eds.), *The Cambridge handbook of creativity* (pp. 3–19). New York, NY: Cambridge University Press.

Ryan, A., & Ladd, G. (2012). *Peer relationships and adjustment at school.* Charlotte, NC: Information Age Publishing.

Sacks, O. (2011). *The mind's eye.* New York, NY: Vintage.

Sahlberg, P. (2011). *Finnish Lessons: What can the world learn from educational change in Finland?* New York, NY: Teachers College Press.

Salmivalli, C., Kaukiainen, A., & Voeten, M. (2005, September). Anti-bullying intervention: Implementation and outcome. *The British Journal of Educational Psychology, 75*(3), 465–487.

Santelli, J., & Crosby, R. (2009). *Adolescent health: Understanding and preventing risk behaviors.* San Francisco, CA: Jossey-Bass.

Savage, D., & Miller, T. (2012). *It gets better: Coming out, overcoming bullying, and creating a life worth living.* New York, NY: Plume Penguin.

Savage, J. (2008). *Teenage: The creation of youth culture.* New York, NY: Viking.

Savage, T., & Savage, M. (2009). *Successful classroom management and discipline: Teaching self-control* (3rd ed.). Thousand Oaks, CA: Sage.

Schulz, L., Bennett, P., Ravussin, E., Kidd, J., Kidd, K., Esparza, J., & Valencia, M. (2006). Effects of traditional and western environments on prevalence of type 2 diabetes in Pima Indians in Mexico and the United States. *Diabetes Care, 29,* 1866–1871.

Seligman, M. (2012). *Flourish: A visionary new understanding of happiness.* New York, NY: Free Press.

Selye, H. (1956). *The stress of life.* New York, NY: McGraw-Hill.

Shariff, S. (2008). *Cyber-bullying: Issues and solutions for the school, the classroom, and the home.* New York, NY: Routledge.

Shepard, R. (1967). Recognition memory for words, sentences, and pictures. *Journal of Verbal Learning and Verbal Behavior, 6,* 156–163.

Shepard, R. (1990). *Mind sights.* New York, NY: Freeman.

Shumow, L. (2009). *Promising practices for family and community involvement in high school.* Charlotte, NC: Information Age Publishing.

Siegel, D. (2006, January). The effects of physical activity on the health and well being of youths. *Journal of Physical Education, Recreation and Dance, 77*(1), 11.

Siegel, L., & Welsh, B. (2007). *Juvenile delinquency.* Belmont, CA: Wadsworth.

Singer, D., & Singer, J. (2007). *Imagination and play in the electronic age.* Cambridge, MA: Harvard University Press.

Singer, D., & Singer, J. (Eds.). (2011). *Handbook of children and the media.* Thousand Oaks, CA: Sage.

Smagorinsky, P. (2011). *Vygotsky and literacy.* Rotterdam, The Netherlands: Sense Publishers.

Small, G., & Vorgan, G. (2009). *iBrain: Surviving the technological alteration of the modern mind.* New York, NY: William Morrow.

Smink, F., van Hoeken, D., & Hoek, H. (2012). Epidemiology of eating disorders: Incidence, prevalence, and mortality rates. *Current Psychiatry Reports, 14*(4), 406–414.

Smith, K., Moriarty, S., Barbatsis, G., & Kenney, K. (Eds.). (2005). *Handbook of visual communication: Theory, methods, and media.* Mahwah, NJ: Erlbaum.

Southwick, S., & Charney, D. (2012). *Resilience: The science of mastering life's greatest challenges.* New York, NY: Cambridge University Press.

Sternberg, R., & Subotnik, R. (Eds.). (2006). *Optimizing student success in school with the other 3 Rs: Reasoning, resilience, and responsibility.* Charlotte, NC: Information Age.

Stevenson, R. L. (1886). *The strange case of Dr. Jekyll and Mr. Hyde.* New York, NY: Scribners.

Stone, J., & Lewis, M. (2012). *College and career ready in the 21st century: Making high school matter.* New York, NY: Teachers College, Columbia University.

Storey, J., & Graeme, S. (2005). *Managers of innovation: Insights into making innovation happen.* Malden, MA: Blackwell.

Strom, P., & Strom, R. (2008). Improving American schools. In D. McInerney & A. Liem (Eds.), *Teaching and learning: International best practice* (pp. 111–132). Charlotte, NC: Information Age.

Strom, P., & Strom, R. (2009). *Adolescents in the Internet age.* Charlotte, NC: Information Age Publishing.

Strom, P., & Strom, R. (2011a). Teamwork skills assessment for cooperative learning. *Educational Research and Evaluation, 17*(4), 233–251.

Strom, P., & Strom, R. (2011b). Cheating in middle school and high school. In K. Ryan & J. Cooper (Eds.), *Kaleidoscope: Contemporary and classic readings in education* (pp. 49–56). Belmont, CA: Wadsworth.

Strom, P., & Strom, R. (2011c). *Career exploration poll.* Retrieved from www.learningpolls.org.

Strom, P., Strom, R., Walker, J., Sindel-Arrington, P., & Beckert, T. (2011). Adolescent bullies on cyber island, *NASSP Bulletin, 95*(3), 195–211.

Strom, P., Strom, R., & Wing, C. (2008, December). Polling students about conditions of learning. *NASSP Bulletin, 92*(4), 292–304.

Strom, P., Strom, R., Wing, C., & Beckert, T. (2009). Adolescent learning and the Internet. *NASSP Bulletin, 93*(2), 111–121.

Strom, P., Strom, R., Wingate, J., Kraska, M., & Beckert, T. (2012, June). Cyberbullying: Assessment of student experience for continuous improvement planning. *NASSP Bulletin, 96*, 137–153.

Strom, R., Amukamara, H., Strom, P., Beckert, T., Strom, S., & Griswold, D. (2000). Parenting success of African American fathers. *Journal of Research and Development in Education, 33*(4), 257–267.

Strom, R., Beckert, T., Strom, P., Strom, S., & Griswold, D. (2002). Evaluating the success of Caucasian fathers in guiding adolescents. *Adolescence, 37*(145), 131–149.

Strom, R., Lee, T., Strom, P., Nakagawa, K., & Beckert, T. (2008). Taiwanese grandmothers: Strengths and learning needs as perceived by grandmothers, mothers, and granddaughters, *Educational Gerontology, 34*, 812–830.

Strom, R., & Strom, P. (2007). New directions for teaching, learning, and assessment. In R. Maclean (Ed.), *Learning and teaching for the twenty-first century* (pp. 115–134). New York, NY: Springer.

Strom, R., & Strom, P. (2010). *Parenting young children: Exploring the Internet, television, play, and reading*. Charlotte, NC: Information Age Publishing, Inc.

Strom, R., & Strom, P. (2011). A paradigm for intergenerational learning. In M. London (Ed.), *The Oxford handbook of lifelong learning* (pp. 133–146). New York, NY: Oxford University Press.

Strom, R., & Strom, P. (2012). *Learning throughout life: An intergenerational perspective*. Charlotte, NC: Information Age Publishing, Inc.

Strom, R., Strom, P., & Beckert, T. (2008). Comparing Black, Hispanic, and White mothers with a national standard of parenting. *Adolescence, 43*(171), 525–545.

Strom, R., Strom, S., Strom, P., Makino, K., & Morishima, Y. (2000). Perceived parenting success of mothers in Japan. *Journal of Family Studies, 6*(1), 25–45.

Strom, R., Strom, P., Strom, S., Shen, Y., & Beckert, T. (2004). Black, Hispanic, and White American mothers of adolescents: Construction of a national standard. *Adolescence, 39*(156), 669–686.

Subrahmanyam, K., Greenfield, P., & Tynes, B. (2004, November). Constructing sexuality and identity in an online teen chat room. *Journal of Applied Developmental Psychology, 25*(6), 651–666.

Tally, B., & Goldenberg, L. (2005). Fostering historical thinking with digitized primary sources. *Journal of Research on Technology in Education, 38*(1), 1–21.

Tapscott, D. (2009). *Grown up digital: How the net generational is changing your world*. New York, NY: McGraw-Hill.

Tapscott, D., & Williams, A. (2010a). *Macrowikinomics: Rebooting business and the world*. New York, NY: Portfolio Penguin.

Tapscott, D., & Williams, A. (2010b). *Wikinomic: How mass collaboration changes everything*. New York, NY: Portfolio Trade.

Taylor, M. (1999). *Imaginary companions and the children who create them*. New York, NY: Oxford University Press.

Temple, P. (2006). *Identity theory*. San Francisco, CA: MacAdam/Cage.

Thompson, C. (2008). *The best of technology writing 2008*. Ann Arbor, MI: University of Michigan Press.

Thorndike, R., & Thorndike-Christ, T. (2011). *Measurement and evaluation in psychology and education*. Upper Saddle River, NJ: Pearson.

Tienken, C., Goldberg, S., & DiRocco, D. (2009). Questioning the questions. *Kappa Delta Pi Record, 46*(1), 39–43.

Tizard, B., & Hughes, M. (2003). *Young children learning*. New York, NY: Wiley-Blackwell.

Toffler, A., & Toffler, H. (1970). *Future Shock*. New York, NY: Random House.

Toffler, A., & Toffler, H. (1980). *The Third Wave.* New York, NY: Bantam.

Toffler, A., & Toffler, H. (1990). *Powershift.* New York, NY: Bantam.

Toffler, A., & Toffler, H. (2007). *Revolutionary wealth.* New York, NY: Alfred Knopf.

Tominey, S., & McClelland, M. (2011). Red light, purple light: Findings from a randomized trial using circle time games to improve behavioral self-regulation in preschool. *Early Education and Development, 22*(3), 489–519.

Torrance, E. P. (1963). *Education and the creative potential.* Minneapolis, MN: University of Minnesota.

Torrance, E. P. (1965). *Rewarding creative behavior.* Englewood Cliffs, NJ: Prentice-Hall.

Torrance, E. P. (1995). *Why fly? A philosophy of creativity.* Norwood, NJ: Ablex.

Torrance, E. P. (2000). *On the edge and keeping on the edge.* Westport, CT: Greenwood.

Torrance, E. P. (2002). *Torrance Tests of Creative Thinking.* Bensenville, IL: Scholastic Testing Service.

Torrance, E. P., & Ziller, R. (1957). *Risk and life experience: Development of a scale for measuring risk-taking tendencies.* Lackland Air Force Base, San Antonio, TX: Research report AFPTRC-TN 57–23-ASTIA Document No. 09826.

Turkle, S. (2011). *Alone together: Why we expect more from technology and less from each other.* New York, NY: Basic Books.

Twenge, J. (2007). *Generation me: Why today's young Americans are more confident, assertive, entitled—and more miserable than ever before.* New York, NY: Free Press.

Twenge, J., & Campbell, W. (2010). *The narcissism epidemic: Living in the age of entitlement.* New York, NY: Free Press.

Twenge, J., Gentile, B., DeWall, C., Ma, D., Lacefield, K., & Schurtz, D. (2010). Birth cohort increases in psychopathology among young Americans, 1938–2007: A cross-temporal meta-analysis of the MMPI. *Clinical Psychology Review, 30*(2), 145–154.

Umberson, D. (2006). *Death of a parent.* New York, NY: Cambridge University Press.

Underwood, M., & Rosen, L. (2011). *Social development.* New York, NY: Guilford Press.

United States Bureau of Labor Statistics. (2013). *Occupational Outlook Handbook 2013–2014.* New York, NY: McGraw-Hill.

United States Department or Education. (2012, November 26). *States report new high school graduation rates using more accurate common measurements.* Washington, DC. Retrieved from www.eddataexpress.ed.gov

United States Department of Education, National Center for Education Statistics. (2013). *National Assessment of Educational Progress.* Washington, DC: United States Department of Education, National Center for Education Statistics.

United States Department of Justice Federal Bureau of Investigation. (2013). *A parent's guide to Internet safety.* Retrieved from www.fbi.gov/stats-services/publications/parent-guide/parent-guide

United States Office of Juvenile Justice and Delinquency Prevention. (2011). *Special report: Federal Agency Task Force of Missing and Exploited Children.* Seattle, WA: Amazon Digital Services.

United States Secret Service. (2012). National threat assessment center. Secret service safe school initiative. Retrieved April 22, 2013 from http://www.secretservice.gov

Vandal, B. (2010). *Getting past go: Rebuilding the remedial education bridge to college success.* Retrieved from Education Commission of the States, available at http://www.gettingpastgo.org

Vohs, K., & Baumeister, R. (2013). *Handbook of self-regulation* (2nd ed.). New York, NY: Guilford Press.

Vose, D. (2008). *Risk analysis: A quantitative guide.* New York, NY: John Wiley.

Vygotsky, L. (1978). *Mind in society.* Cambridge, MA: Harvard University Press.

Vygotsky, L. (1994). The development of thinking and concept formation in adolescence. In R. Van der Veer & J. Valsiner (Eds.), *The Vygotsky reader* (pp. 185–265). Cambridge, MA: Blackwell.

Vygotsky, L. (1998). The collected works of L. W. Vygotsky. In R. Rieber (Ed.), *Child Psychology.* New York, NY: Plenum.

Wagner, J. (2012). *The gamer generation: Reaping the benefits of video games.* Seattle, WA: Amazon Digital Services.

Wahlberg, M., & Mahr, J. (2011, August 28). State paid sex offenders as baby sitters. *Chicago Tribune.* Retrieved from http://articles.chicagotribune.com/2011-08-28

Wahlstrom, K. (2013). A long winter's nap. *Connect,* Winter, 18–19. Minneapolis, MN: University of Minnesota.

Wallace, M. (Ed.). (2008). *The way we will be 50 years from today: 60 of the world's greatest minds share their visions of the next half century.* Dallas, TX: Thomas Nelson.

Wallach, M., & Kogan, N. (1965). *Modes of thinking in young children of the creativity-intelligence distinction.* New York, NY: Wadsworth.

Wargo, E. (2009). Resisting temptation. *Observer,* 22(1), 10–17.

Warrell, M. (2008). *Find your courage.* New York, NY: McGraw-Hill.

Washington State Office of the Attorney General (2013). *Dating Rights and Responsibilities.* Retrieved from Washington State Office, April 20, 2013, http://www.atg.wa.gov/

Watters, A. (2011, November 3). *Plagiarism differences in high school and college students.* Retrieved http://www.mindshift.kqed.org

Weigel, D., Martin, S., & Bennett, K. (2005). Ecological influences of the home and the child-care center on preschool-age children's literacy development. *Reading Research Quarterly,* 40(2), 204–233.

Welch, J., & Welch, S. (2005). *Winning.* New York, NY: Harper Collins.

White, A., & Swartzwelder, S. (2013). *What are they thinking: The straight facts about the risk-taking, social networking, still developing teen brain.* New York, NY: W.W. Norton.

Whitley, B. E., Jr., & Keith-Spiegel, P. (2002). *Academic dishonesty: An educator's guide.* Mahwah, NJ: Erlbaum.

Whitten, L. (2011). *High school student opinion polling on career exploration.* (Doctoral dissertation), Auburn University, Auburn, Alabama.

Willard, N. (2007). *Cyber-safe kids, Cyber-savvy teens: Helping young people learn to use the Internet safely and responsibly.* San Francisco, CA: Jossey-Bass.

Williams, R., & Newton, J. (2006). *Visual communication.* Mahwah, NJ: Erlbaum.

Willingham, D. (2010). *Why don't students like school: A cognitive scientist answers questions about how the mind works and what it means.* San Francisco, CA: Jossey-Bass.

Wilson, G., Grilo, C., & Vitousek, K. (2007). Psychological treatment of eating disorders. *American Psychologist, 62*(3), 199–216.

Wolak, J., Mitchell, K., & Finkelhor, D. (2007). Does online harassment constitute bullying? An exploration of online harassment by known peers and online-only contacts. *Journal of Adolescent Health, 41*, S31–38

Wollack, J., & Fremer, J. (2013). *Handbook of test security.* New York, NY: Routledge.

Wolpe, D. (2009). *Why faith matters.* New York, NY: HarperOne.

Wong, G. (2005). *Skills for going to school.* Los Angeles, CA: Horizon Research Corporation.

Wormeli, R. (2006). Differentiating for tweens. *Educational Leadership, 63*(7), 14–19.

Ybarra, M., Diener-West, M., & Leaf, P. (2007). Examining the overlap in Internet harassment and school bullying: Implications for school intervention. *Journal of Adolescent Health, 41*, S42–50.

Yuill, N., & Ruffman, T. (2009). *The relation between parenting, children's social understanding, and language* (Grant # RES-000-23-0278). Brighton, England: Department of Psychology, University of Sussex.

Zeigarnik, A. (2007). Bluma Zeigarnik—A memoir. *Gestalt theory, 29*(3), 256–268.

Zelazo, P., Carlson, S., & Kesek, A. (2008). Development of executive function in childhood. In C. Nelson, & M. Luciana (Eds.), *Handbook of developmental cognitive neuroscience (2nd ed.)* (pp. 553–574). Cambridge, MA: MIT Press.

Zuckerberg, M. (2011, May 18). *Innovation and entrepreneurship: What it takes.* Retrieved from NewSchools Venture Fund, www.newschools.org. Presentation to NewSchools Summit 2011, NewSchools Venture Fund and the Aspen Institute, Burlingame, CA.

Zweig, J., & Dank, M. (2013, February). *Teen dating abuse and harassment in the digital world.* Washington, DC: Urban Institute.

CPSIA information can be obtained at www.ICGtesting.com
Printed in the USA
LVOW03s2002120115

422511LV00005B/205/P